Aksara Bhagavad Gita

Haribakth & Vaishnavi

wp **walnutpublication**.com

INDIA • UK • USA

Copyright © Haribakth & Vaishnavi, 2022

Hardcover ISBN: 978-1-957302-19-5

First Published in January 2022

Published by Walnut Publication (an imprint of Vyusta Ventures LLP)
www.walnutpublication.com

USA

6834 Cantrell Road #2096, Little Rock, AR 72207, USA

India

#625, Esplanade One, Rasulgarh, Bhubaneswar – 751010, India

#55 S/F, Panchkuian Marg, Connaught Place, New Delhi - 110001, India

UK

International House, 12 Constance Street, London E16 2DQ, United Kingdom

PRAYERS

||नाहम् कर्ता, हरि कर्ता||
||हरि कर्ता ही केवलम||

I do not do anything.
It is Only Hari who does it.
It is HIM only always.

My prayers and repeated obeisance to:

- Lord Ganesha, remover of all obstacles, who acted as scribe in penning Mahabharata, who understood the import of Gita before penning the same.
- The holy trinity and the sampradaya they have founded to disseminate this knowledge.
- Vyasa Maharishi who composed and dictated the (Gita) Mahabharata to Ganesha.
- Vivasvan, The Sun God who was privy to God's instructions eons ago.
- Arjuna the most fortunate who heard it first-hand.
- The originators of four sampradaya and their successors.
- Saraswathi Matha, the goddess of learning.
- Uddhava who had the fortune of hearing Uddhava Gita and to his successors to whom he passed on this wisdom.
- All those who study, pray, contemplate, worship Gita or Govinda.
- The almighty Lord Himself.

अध्येष्यते च य इमं धर्म्य संवादमावयो :|
ज्ञानयज्ञेन तेनाहमिष्ट :स्यामिति मे मति :|| 70||

adhyeṣhyate cha ya imaṁ dharmyaṁ saṁvādam āvayoḥ
jñāna-yajñena tenāham iṣhṭaḥ syām iti me matiḥ

He who studies this sacred dialogue of ours, by him I shall have been worshipped by the sacrifice of wisdom, such is My conviction.

This effort of mine is being offered as a sacrifice unto Him. This is done to give Him pleasure and to incur His pleasure. May He be pleased with this work! May He bless me that I please Him in perpetuity and that I will be dear to HIM (in perpetuity)!

DEDICATION

ACKNOWLEDGMENTS

My parents for their blessings.

My daughter for her encouragement and illustrations for this book.

My wife, for reposing faith in my abilities and being a source of encouragement.

My brother, who is the driving force behind this book.

My cousin, Sukumar Muthya, who suggested the format for cohesion and integration of chapters.

N Mahalingam, my friend, guide and philosopher, who acted as a conscience keeper of Gita and my conscience keeper as well.

My niece, Ms. Arpana, for overseeing the birth of the book.

Contents

BOOK - I

1. INAUGURATION & PRESS MEET

All leading media had their representatives covering the opening of the Parthasarathy Institute of Gita studies.

They had arrived well ahead of the designated time. Christina was hurrying to catch up with the Event Managers, where some last-minute instructions were to be conveyed. Journalists caught up with her and demanded an interview. She tried avoiding them when she saw Mr. Brookes, Coordinator making gestures pointing towards the audience. She swept her glance in the direction pointed out and saw her friend, Haripriya with another gentleman, waving at her in the form of greetings. She waved back and gestured indicating that she would join them once she becomes free. She told Brookes to attend to and minister to all their needs, to which Mr. Brookes nodded his head-indicating assent. Brooks went back and guided them from their place to VIP enclosure in the front, from where they could have a vantage view. The inauguration ceremony would start after the Press meet.

Somnath and Haripriya were witnessing the goings-on seated comfortably in the front row. The press persons were seated comfortably and Christina was facing them

J1   How are you feeling after selling more than a million copies of your book?

CH: Feels nice, more so as it is my first writing exercise, but I see myself more as a missionary than an author.

J2   But your happiness isn't reflected on your face.

CH: Because the book is a means and not an end. The launch of this institution is a testimony to the fact.

J1:   And the mission is to propagate the Values of Gita here?

CH: Partly correct, 'here 'part may be amended to here, there and everywhere.

J1:   Your take on Guru is unorthodox and controversial, isn't it?

CH: a Controversy is a literary tool employed by the author to build a theme, pouring life into it, make it interesting, and discover contrasting and divergent insights, hitherto undiscovered. It may be taken with a pinch of salt.

J3:   Aren't you being unfaithful to your religion?

CH: Why, Gita is not a religion nor restricted to any religion, race, or country. It is precisely for this reason that efforts on missionary scale are required. People do not know what they are missing. I will do my part as a part of Yajna unto the Lord, Krishna.

J2:   I have read your book and found it interesting, but I am unable to make out if it is fiction or non-fiction.

CH: Have you seen the movie, URI? Uri is a place in India. The same was captured in a dramatized form and a movie made with the same name. Whether it is a fact or fiction? It is a fact, captured in a movie in fiction form.

You may term it as creative non-fiction or pseudo-fiction. I have presented truth in a dialog form so as to make the narrative more interesting.

J2: What is the fiction part and what is the non-fiction part? You owe it to the readers to help them segregate the chaff from the grain.

CH: You are a true guardian of journalistic values. Well, it is like this.

This doubt would crop up in the minds of any reader. The title of the book would hardly help and the contents would further confuse them.

Is it necessary to know the same? Isn't it enough if the reading was interesting? – **NO**. Twenty-first-century netizens are already living and growing up with the belief in the canard that God and Gita is mythology. They are entitled to know the truth.

The book can be termed Non-Fictive. The characters and conversations, excepting ones found in the Gita, are all fictitious. The places are real. The core philosophy being expounded is NON-FICTION. Appropriate references as to the source are made. Whether it is acceptable or not, does not diminish the factive element of what is propounded. IT constitutes the core beliefs of the author.

Gita part, quotes on Gita, sloka number, etc. are all whole and unambiguous truth. The expositions therefrom are all truth. The places mentioned, pilgrimage centers are also factual. The subject matter of debate is the truth. The debate, various groups participating in the debate and the characters therein are all fiction. HP, Haribakth, and I myself are all aliases of the author lending voices to them.

The author is expressing his views through them. I myself am a creation of the author. TG and KA are modeled after the alter ego of the Author. Some of the dialogs have indeed taken place in a non-formal environment.

J2: Are you not misappropriating Krishna's' legacy?

CH: The Lord's legacy is not material wealth which is finite and exhausts on anybody appropriating it. It is an ocean and inexhaustible where anybody can draw upon to whatever extent she is capable.

J2: Is it Gita that is the subject matter or something else? It appeals to logic, it is also in tune with the observable reality, but I am not fully convinced as to how it is different and how the subject is Gita and not something else in the garb of Gita.

CH: God is infallible, as are His words. In the Gita, God has spoken 574 Slokas, due to which it is cloaked with infallibility, it being the words of whose it is. Our observation with existing reality appears at variance with what is spelled out in the Gita.

All the existing books and commentaries explain what is said but cannot validate with what exists or explains what is prevalent but cannot reconcile with what is said. At times other scriptures are relied upon which is okay but to the logician devotee, it invalidates the completeness and infallibility concept of what is said by God and hence unacceptable.

Thence began my quest at reconciliation, the base being God, His words and actions which are infallible, not subject to change and not negotiable. Any change should be in our thought process so as to be in tune with His words. A reconciliation of thought process from the existing/prevalent known as observable with what is said by the Lord. Thus was this book conceived and born.

J3:   You have invited seers/monks to inaugurate this function but you have castigated them in your book. Isn't your stand inconsistent?

CH: Creating controversy is a literary tool for developing a theme and to ferret out the truth. Nothing more or nothing less. I hold them in high esteem, but I hold Him in higher esteem, which you may observe if you read my book carefully.

J5:   Notwithstanding the commercial success of your book and the acquisition of a large fan following, your book is garbage because it is your words and not true to His words. The readers lack discrimination which has added to your success.

CH: Thank you for your honest opinion. I will not defend myself. I will pass on the question to God. God defends His devotees. This is His reply as stated in Uddhava Gita 23.21.

'Oh, Uddhava, whatever insignificant or useless activity performed even out of fear or such other emotions, if it is unselfishly meant for me, It tantamounts to the highest form of religion.'

J3:   I feel that you have made your words bigger than Gods' words. Your comments.

CH: Is it possible? Please understand my book in perspective.
- Gita is a noun a personal or proper noun.
- Gita is also a verb, as it shows an action or a state of being.
  - My book is an adjective, describing the proper Noun "Gita"
  - My book is also an adverb describing the verb "Gita" by answering, the how, why, where, when and what, etc. of the contents of the Gita.
- Gita exists and will continue to exist even during the cosmic dissolution, with or without my book.
- My book cannot exist without Gita.
- My book is co-extensive with Gita.
- Now, is it possible for an adverb to exist without the verb?
- Or can an adjective exist without the Noun which it describes?

Please stick to journalistic ethics and values for which I had complimented you just a few moments ago. Saying this, she turned towards Priya and gave her a wide grin and a thumbs-up sign, which Hari reciprocated. Christina had come of age.

The snub to J3 was captured by electronic media and flashed across all the TV channels live. Haripriya could not believe that her friend who would always remain in the background was capable of giving such a caustic but well deserving reply. She was gushing with pride.

J3:   I am sorry, I …..

CH: Yes, I suppose I judged you hastily, you please re-read my book, unlike in a perfunctory way which other fictions are read. You will find the truth about my answers. I also invite you and your group of colleagues here, to enroll for the online outreach program specially designed for busy professionals.

J4:   Have you covered the entire Gita in your book?

CH: No, some things are left out.

J4:   But Gita is complete and your book …..

CH: Yes, it is complete with the capacity to assimilate more to make it more complete i.e. infinitely complete.

CH: Please read the definition of complete for your answer. I acknowledge, I am not God and cannot replicate His feat.

J4:   Is another book in offing covering the missing parts?

CH: Possible. Or our students could continue where I left off. Our Institute will provide the missing links. Our students will pursue or research on those counts and could present a thesis.

With this, she excused herself and made her way to Haripriya. She greeted her with a warm hug. She greeted Somnath with a Namaste and made preliminary inquiries. She took them around the new building. She showed around the library, meditation hall and the prayer hall. She took them to the guesthouse, where visiting monks were put up. Both of them paid their homage to the monks and sought their blessings. They returned to the conference hall where the inauguration was to take place. The inauguration was done by the lighting of lamps by all the monks and by Haripriya and Christina. Christina welcomed them all. The monks made benedictory speeches and left after blessing the venture. Christina called out for Haripriya and introduced her as the feisty debate girl of the book. The recognition was instantaneous. There was all-round applause. Hari waved to them. She was asked to speak.

She greeted them with folded hands saying 'Namaste'. The memories of the past flooded her. Scenes of the debate, Christina's supportive role, the professors' benign encouragement, her fathers' unfulfilled deep-rooted desire, all flashed before her. She was in a state of euphoria. She was overcome by emotions of love and ecstasy. She commenced her speech with uttering 'Christina', **N K** and fell silent. Minutes ticked by and Hari couldn't speak. She was in raptures. She began to sob uncontrollably.

Christina understood her friend's feelings and her message to the audience. Hari wasn't in a normal state and couldn't speak. She made her sit down and offered her a glass of water She took it upon herself to explain Haripriya's message.

Friends, you have read the book. My pseudo name is N.K i.e. "Naham kartha, Hari Kartha"

My friend is overwhelmed by seeing her life dreams come true and her father's vision fructify. And she attributes it to me and hence uttered my name. The book and the institute is her brainchild. I am not the doer nor am I the cause. It was He always. By uttering my name, she is both thanking God and me and also reiterating that God is the doer and that she has no role whatsoever.

2. PARTHASARATHY'S LETTER TO HIS DAUGHTER

My dear Lavanya,

It has been more than three years since you migrated to Canada. I am missing you more than ever now. I wish you were here. I could have answered most of your queries, which I couldn't do earlier. As shared earlier, the debate has almost concluded. It appears God sent, to expand my consciousness and also a reply to all your doubts. Though cosmopolitan in outlook, I had a strong bias in favor of our Sri Vaishnava school of thought and this often reflected in my opinions, thoughts, and judgments. This prevented me from seeing the greater picture. I have already been updating you on the daily proceedings during our chat sessions. Now I will summarise the gist (which could have been my verdict if I had such a broad outlook as my students) for your benefit which is very specific to your queries. Whenever Hari spoke, I was always reminded of you. Of course, I don't have the right to sit in judgment and reduce the glory and grandeur of Gita, given my personal bias. I have convened a super grand jury to give their verdict.

The whole proceedings are an academic and research exercise, compatible with daily life observations. The same doesn't override the findings of the commentaries of the existing Acharyas. While the teachings of ancient seers are found pragmatic and put into practice by a very few persons, The observations put forth during the debate are in tune with reality and observation and pragmatic to the world at large.

When you read a book, you proceed with certain expectations and objects in mind. Gita reading is no exception. A reader could be just a curious, he could be seeking entertainment, he could be a critique, a seeker of knowledge, he could be reading for finding a solution to a problem, or exploring as a researcher or just wants to know other perspectives. With whatever object (in mind) you read your object gets fulfilled and with whatever question you approach, it will be answered. So, before reading the book, just make a note of your questions and objectives, and the end of reading compare it with what you noted.

There are many religions and sub religions. It is fairly consensual that God is one and omnipotent. Who is that God? And what do you call Him/ and how do you propitiate Him are the points of disagreement. Even within a religion, there are innumerable practices each contradicting and in conflict within the sub-sects and also other religions. Let us proceed from the point of common consensus.

It is a rule rather than an exception that people either tend to have a bias towards some religion, theirs or adopted or bias towards atheism or agnosticism. With inherent bias, it is very difficult to see the truth, howsoever in plain sight it is. When judging, it is necessary to overcome this bias. It is easier said than done. So, to make it easier, I suggest that wherever the scripture or Gita is mentioned, the same may be designated as a variable 'S' and wherever God or Krishna is referenced, it is denoted by the variable 'G'

They may offer their judgments forgetting that the subject is Krishna and the Gita. After delivering their verdicts, they may re-substitute the variables with their original values.

General observations about Gita.

Gita caters to all persons of any temperament nature/guna. It also guides people at any level or stage of their progress/journey/quest. Because each continues from that point forward wherein, he left his practice in his previous birth. This explains differences in understanding the same sloka by different persons. It is a scripture irrespective of your varna. It is sought by people seeking any of the purusharthas. God answers them in the way they approach Him. So, you can imagine the permutations and combination of different persons of different varnas and different combination of gunas and at a different level of evolution and different level of accumulated karma they are carrying, which all adds up to their understanding.

The Slokas in the Gita could be both standalone and/or also inter-se interrelated. Each sloka could fulfill the function of providing connectivity, refer to an earlier or later sloka or context, may qualify a sloka or may act as a disqualifying sloka. It could be repetition to give emphasis or to serve as a reminder.

Gods' words are unqualified with the only exception being it can be qualified by His own words. God's words make sense both when qualified and when standalone. When is it to be taken as qualified and when it is not qualified? When the single sloka alone by itself makes sense and is observed or found factual, it need not have a qualifier limiter. But it may not happen so as we may be at a lower stage of evolution, and hence a qualifier could be needed for us to understand the sloka and make sense. For example, God says "He who thinks of me while dying attains me". IF a person is advanced, He will get to remember God at the time of death. If he is in lower stages, he may not be able to remember. He shouldn't complain saying that God Himself says that He is the giver of memory and forgetfulness and did not give me memory. God has also said, always think of me. If we would have thought of Him at all times, we will definitely get to remember Him at our last moments.

The rule of the thumb is the more you are devoted and greater the Krishna consciousness the lesser are His words qualified to culminate in non-qualified single sloka. The extent of correctness or otherwise of an interpretation is person-time-place dependent.

Reading various commentaries and purports of different stalwarts and seers give you their perspective but can it be tested with your experience in your timeline and in your frame of things?

The method adopted in studying other subjects like Grammar, Law, Management, statistics, Logic, etc. using parsing, extrapolating, observation, case study etc. can be used to glean secrets hidden in the Gita.

The most common misconception is mistaking the practices, rituals, practices, and codes given by seers/sages to be God's words. Another misconception is ignoring the time, space and context of what has been told.

Gita could be used as a

- Reference Book.
- Knowledgebase
- Consulting Manual.
- Means to knowledge
- Guide to interpretation of
  - Bhagavad Gita
  - Of other scriptures.
  - THIS IS THE MAIN FOCUS OF THIS BOOK

Bhagavad Gita comprises of

- What God said.
- What God didn't say, meaning what he implied.
- What others said.

What God said could be:

- Statement of facts/events things or what is called a declarative statement. These end with a period(.) and in Sanskrit with a (|), Sanskrit equivalent of an English period, called purnaviram.
  - This could be a positive or affirmative sentence or a negative sentence.
  - Facts could be either acceptable or unacceptable.
    - If it is unacceptable, Is it verifiable or not? If it is verifiable and found verified, it becomes acceptable thereafter. If it is unverifiable, keep the conclusion in abeyance.
  - Non-verifiability is due to many causes including our low comprehension skills, our stage of evolution.

- o Another cause could be misinterpreting the passage in a literal sense where it was meant to be symbolic or allegorical. It could also be due to being behind or ahead of time.
- o As it is a statement of declaration, nothing is expected to be done. So, whether a fact is acceptable or not, conclusive or not doesn't matter.
- o An exception to this is it does matter wherein it is the very nature of the job of the person to come to a conclusion. For example, a historian has to decide whether a place of worship existed or not and make a report to the Government. A cosmologist, whose basic concern is the origin of the Universe etc. is another example. Hence, the objective of reading and the purpose is to be pre-stated.
- o It is a matter of consequence if it is acceptable only to the specialist whose object is reaching the conclusion of a matter of fact. For others, it is inconsequential, whether it is acceptable or not acceptable.
- o As no action is expected of these types of statements, mere belief or disbelief in them would cause neither gain or harm to anyone by sticking to such belief, whether it be factual or non-factual.
- o Gita 2.26 Explains very nicely of how to deal with declarative sentences. It says, even if you think that the soul dies, you must not grieve as it is inevitable.

  - ▪ Here, the fact is that the soul is immortal. You accept it and act based on that fact.
  - ▪ If you do not agree or accept the fact, even then you mustn't react (with grief), as the fact is a matter of truth and inevitable.
  - ▪ The sloka explains how to act when you do not accept the fact as fact or if you hold different opinion. Don't react or respond based on your perception of fact. Time will reveal the truth in true perspective.
  - ▪ **This sloka has wider ramifications and connotation as it applies to all declarative statements and is a parameter derived, inadvertently left out by Hari.**

- Next, it could be an interrogative statement. This ends with a question mark. When a question is asked, there could be any of the following five responses.
  - o Giving a detailed answer.
  - o God has answered many of Arjuna's questions.
  - o Answer in affirmative.
  - o Answer in negative.
  - o Answer by putting forth another question.
  - o God's such action not on record as it is a human trait.

- o Reserving the answer temporarily.
- o This is akin to reserving the judgment by courts only to be pronounced at a later date. This is a temporary deferment. God has adopted this technique, by answering Arjuna's question "*We do not* even *know* which result of this war whether we will conquer or be conquered" in BG: 2.6 by replying in BG: 11.34 as to who will win the war.
- o Ignoring the question by remaining silent.
- o This could be a diplomatic strategy to tell a person that he is wrong or when it is a stratagem to not side with conflicting sides.
- o Whether an answer satisfies the questioner or not? Arjuna was satisfied with all the answers. The answers could be to the questioner or addressed to all persons at large or it is addressed to the questioner for the benefit of mankind.
- o Misinterpreting and misunderstanding of questions (put forth by Arjuna) on our part is inconsequential. Misinterpreting and misunderstanding the answers (given by the Lord) are attended with negative consequences. Here the answers could be statement of facts or statements of consequences or opinion etc. Misinterpreting the questions of the Lord too has negative consequences. For example, God asks Arjuna if he has understood all that was taught to him. If we consider it to be addressed to Arjuna and not to us, we would be losers.

- The next type of God's utterances is imperative. It is a command and is to be executed. This is the most difficult area of interpretation because it is fraught with dangerous consequences by putting humanity at peril.
  - o When God gives a command, it is to be executed. God asked Arjuna to fight and he fought. If Arjuna wouldn't have executed the divine order, even then consequences at large would be the same that all the leading kings and soldiers in both camps barring a few exceptions will die. Krishna Himself has expressed this to Arjuna.
  - o In this type of statement, all the qualifiers in the Gita become active. For the sake of Correct interpretation, we have to question whether it is addressed to us? If it is addressed to us, should I understand it literally or allegorically? There could be a possibility that it should be understood literally but is addressed to Arjuna. If I understand literally, whether the call to action is applicable to me? Is there a state of war currently? Am I a Kshatriya for whom this clarion call is made? What are the consequences?
  - o The present state of violence all over the world due to terrorist activities can be attributed to the misinterpreting of scriptures.
  - o The call for jihad, crusade or Dharm Yudh, etc. was a call to take up arms when the situation so demanded. When the situation

changed, automatically the command to use arms is deemed withdrawn or void.

- o The best way to interpret this is would we appreciate or take it quiet if the opposite person decides to follow ancient commands to our detriment?

- Exclamatory sentences are those which express strong feelings. Arjuna is the author of many such exclamations. It doesn't make a difference to others if you rightly interpret or wrongly interpret any sloka with exclamatory sentences.

- The last type of utterances of God are benedictory in nature and express blessings and confer blessings besides the fulfillment of our desires or any boon gifted by God. Here too, interpretational errors are inconsequential vis-à-vis others.

The sum and substance of the analysis of the type of statements are that only commandments or imperative sentences are a call to action and required acted upon. Before acting upon it, it should be deliberated and properly interpreted. This is especially so when the consequences of our actions are borne by humanity at large. For interpretation, parameters may be used. The responses to each type of statement are different. A benedictory verse cannot be acted upon nor can an exclamatory sentence be answered.

The rules of interpretations are closely and intricately related to the
- Type of sentences.
- Identified parameters.
- Experiential and observable reality.
- Scientific observability /acceptance.

The rules etc. can be observed and highlighted and found acceptable in other branches of learning like Law, Grammar, Logic, Science, Management, Mathematics, etc.

How were the rules framed? They were framed based on the parameters. How was Parameter identified and on what authority? Parameters were identified based on the attributes of the Gita. The authority too is derived from God/Gita. Isn't the identification process obsolete and unscientific?

There isn't anything more scientific than the Gita. Just see the explosion of Artificial intelligence applications, be it Drones, Siri, Echo, or Robots. They are all non-human but endowed with intelligence. Intelligence in AI is represented by
- Objects.
- Events.
- Performance.
- Facts

- Knowledge Base or Library.

Knowledge comprises of
- Procedural knowledge. (Rules and procedures)
- Declarative knowledge (Objects and facts)
- Heuristic knowledge. (Rules of the thumb, Dynamic and situation-based)
- Meta Knowledge (Knowledge about knowledge)
- Structural knowledge (Relationship between objects and concept)

AI uses Frame representation structure in building intelligent non-beings. Frame representation is a structure consisting collection of attributes and its values to describe itself to itself and the world.

The Parameters identified in and from the Gita are all nothing but attributes that describe itself to the world (of readers). The science of AI is a recent phenomenon over the past decade. Gita has been in existence since time immemorial or at least 5200+ years back.

For anything to be acceptable for a rational being, it should be either experienceable, of Verifiable or his faith in the belief should be strong.

- All things aren't experienceable or verifiable. For example, certain events/phenomena occur very infrequently or rarely and you wouldn't be able to witness it unless you are at the right time and right place. Some examples are Total solar eclipse can be viewed from the same place only once in 45 years, or if you travel to some point once in 18 months. Haley's comet made an appearance in 1986 and the next appearance is not scheduled before 2061. Brahma Kamal is supposed to bloom once in 2 years. Blue moon can be seen only once in two years. Your non-witnessing the same doesn't alter the fact of the occurrence of the event.
- Futuristic events or antique pasts appear unbelievable and fictitious when first mooted or when read as history.
- Lack of requisite skill, be it technical, emotional, or spiritual hampers proper understanding.
- Our imperfect senses add to our woes. Dogs can hear sounds in frequency which we humans can't. An eagle's vision is far clear and distant than ours.
- Understanding is an effect. Every effect should have a cause. You have to discipline yourself, and practice to come to the level of understanding, as an Olympic athlete wins a medal.
- Lastly, there are five factors which bring about accomplishment of all action as is mentioned in BG: 18.13 & 18.14. If any factor is missing or substandard, the results accordingly suffer. If you want perfect understanding, your endeavors and dedication should also be perfect.

Finally, about the reconciliation between different versions of the Gita, which is right version, a doubt almost everyone entertains, or alternatively consider only the adherents of their school of thought is correct:

God spoke Gita to Arjuna. Although He addressed it to Arjuna, He meant it as a broadcast to the humanity at large.

This is made clear by God revealing that He wants to revive the lost knowledge and also by God's imparting knowledge of other Varnas and other Dharma and not restricting to Arjuna's Dharma. God also says that He is the giver of knowledge and ignorance. Among the literary devices as regards perspective, there are four namely,

- First person narrative, with use of I pronoun narrating the story.
- Second person narrative is telling the story with Your pronoun.
- Third person limited narrative is about He or she being told.
- Third person omniscient narrative is about he or she but narrator has full access to thoughts and experiences of all the characters in the narration.

God has used different perspectives within the narration. His status as a narrator and as a fact is omniscient. He knows about all the characters in the narration, and also the subject who is listening/reading the narration unlike in the case of mundane author/literature.

Accordingly, they have understood the narration as willed by the narrator. The narrator willed it so considering the ability, skills, credit of piety and other such variables. This is seen many times that the cosmic vision witnessed by different devotees at different points of time were different and their description/commentary would be different as intended to be perceived by them by the supreme Lord.

The same Gita is differently understood by different people depending on their stage of evolution and other variables, meaning, one book Gita acts as a guide to a beginner, novice, intermediate and advanced Sadhakas and also transcendental devotees. I have unshouldered a huge responsibility after the verdict. Do take care of yourself.

Your loving Dad.

3. JURY APPOINTMENT

<u>From the desk of Justice Parthasarathy (Retired)</u>
<u>And Professor, Sri Venkateshwara University</u>

Dear readers/Gita lovers/Spiritual enthusiasts,

Being a Gita lover/Spiritual enthusiast/Reader, you have been co-opted as an ex-officio member of the jury and called upon to decide whether the issues raised hereinafter in the proceedings is proved.

Firstly, the background, a verbal altercation took place between students, which turned into a spat. The subject was Bhagavad Gita. Both the parties were seekers of truth. One group consisted of a motley crowd of students who sided with the different denominations of interpretation of the Gita as propounded by their Guru's/Masters. The other side contained a lone girl with an unorthodox viewpoint, propounded by her for the first time. The established and well-trenched group claim that the new version is concoction and not as per the tenets of what God has said, nor does it come anywhere close by to the viewpoints of any of the existing Acharyas. They further charge her with blasphemy and belittling their Gurus and misrepresenting God's words. Each claimed that their version was true to the exclusion of others. The lone defendant, on the other hand, claims that Gita being infinite and God's words, can easily subsume her views also, even whilst agreeing with the existing philosophies, subscribed to by her opponents. She further claims that Gita is inclusive and all versions/denominations of Gita are but part of the Whole that is the Gita. Her apparently preposterous claim is that Gita is the source of scriptures of any religion/sect, hence it is non-sectarian. She buttresses her claim by showing that the Parameters enunciated in the Gita can be applied to any scripture of any religion to arrive at a correct and relevant conclusion. They have approached me to determine whether there was an occurrence of blasphemy and whether great spiritual leaders have been portrayed in a bad light. There ensued a debate on the lines of Court, with some pre-determined rules and regulations.

An opportunity was given to the defendant to put forth her case, wherein she defends herself against the charges and also puts across her unorthodox and uncharted views.

Considering the force of arguments which appear flawless, and the exalted subject matter, I felt that the onerous responsibility is shared and collective wisdom be crowd-sourced. Hence your co-option.

You will be privy to insider's view .... their background, their convictions, their idiosyncrasies, etc. That you have been co-opted for jury duty, is an affirmation that you are qualified for the same and sit in judgment. No legal knowledge or expertise is called for nor is any formal qualification required/expected. You may be wondering; how then can you sit on judgment? The answer is just as jurors do, though they do not have any formal qualifications.

It is my duty to advise you on the rules of law that you must use in deciding this case. These rules are contained in the chapter titled 'Rules for the impending war'. After I've completed this advisory, you may begin your deliberations alone, or in group/s.

- You must decide whether the Dharam Rakshak group has proved beyond a reasonable doubt that the Defendant is guilty of disrespecting Gurus and the scriptures which is venerable.
- You must also decide if the unorthodox issues presented by the defendant are proved or has the plaintiff been successful in countering the presentment of the defendant and thus her presentment is not proved or rendered invalid.
- You may choose to add other issues raised in the narrative, (informal discussions between students or students with their parents, etc.) though they may not be figuring in the courtroom altercations and hence not enumerated in the list of issues provided.
  o Your decision must not be influenced by external considerations.
  o Your judgment should not be clouded by your personal prejudices or bias or your faith.
  o You must also follow the rules of law explained by me even if you do not agree with me or the rule of the law being put forth.
  o A "reasonable doubt" is a real doubt, based upon your reason and common sense after you've carefully and impartially considered all the evidence in the case.
  o "Proof beyond a reasonable doubt", is proof so convincing that you would be willing to rely and act on it, without hesitation, in the most important of your own affairs. An issue is deemed proved if it is:
    ▪ Substantiated with acceptable evidence, real or circumstantial.
    ▪ Substantiated with facts or reality
    ▪ Substantiated with experienceable reality.
    ▪ Relevant to the present time and place.
  o Remember, not all that is spoken is evidence in the case and it isn't binding on you.
  o You may disregard anything spoken in a lighter vein, personal attacks, or any other matters not pertaining to the subject matter of discussion.
  o Unsubstantiated statements may be ignored or held to be not proven.
  o In considering the evidence, you may use reason and common sense to make deductions and to reach conclusions. You should not be concerned about whether the evidence is direct or circumstantial.

- o   You will find the list of issues involved on which you would be deliberating, along with the proceedings. You will decide, whether the issue is proven beyond a reasonable doubt.
- o   Each issue must be considered separately and the conclusion reached as to whether proved or not.

When deliberated in groups, your verdict or the verdict of other group members, whether proved or not proved need **NOT** be unanimous. All of you may be in agreement or in disagreement. What is being implied herein is that there could be multiple verdicts and each of them could be true/partly true.

Each of you must decide the case for yourself, but only after fully considering the evidence with the other jurors. While you are discussing the case, do not hesitate to reexamine your own opinions and change your mind if you become convinced that you were wrong. But do not give up your honest beliefs just because the others think differently. Remember that in a very real way you are judges – judges of the facts. Your only interest is to seek the truth from the evidence in this case.

A verdict form (List of issues involved with possible outcomes) is prepared and annexed along with the proceedings, for your convenience. You may give your own verdict ignoring the standard 'possible outcomes' given to you.

You may email your verdict to Justicesarathy@gmail.com

Jurors, I am thankful for your time and commitment to your sense of duty.

Regards

Justice Parthasarathy.

4. VERDICT FORM

Sl	Subject raised	Issues to be considered	Possible verdicts
1	Gita not subject to interpretation	1. Whether Defendant has interpreted Gita 2. Whether Other commentators have interpreted Gita	1. The defendant has been faithful to the letter and spirit of the Gita. 2. The defendant has taken liberties to interpret Gita. The defendant has interpreted Gita within the framework as mentioned in Gita itself.
2	Gita supports self-learning also.	1. Whether Gita requires crutch of preceptor 2. Gita can be self-learned	1. Gita supports self-learning along with traditional Gurukula type of learning. 2. Learning from the preceptor is the only valid form of learning as per Gita.
3	Gita can defend itself	Gita can defend itself without external reference	1. Gita doesn't require external defense as all Defence rests in itself. 2. Gita requires the help of other scriptures.

Sl	Subject raised	Issues to be considered	Possible verdicts
4	Gita is a study in concepts and conceptual analysis. This is implied in the BG: 2.42 wherein God warns Arjuna to be wary of flowery words/language of Vedas.	Gita should be studied conceptually along with semantic study.	1. The conceptual study is distortion and contaminating the pure original. 2. Gita is best studied as a concept in conjunction with the syntactic and semantic study, which has God's concurrence.
5	Gita has Parameters	Gita has parameters and our understanding should be confined within the framework of parameters	1. Gita doesn't have parameters. 2. There are Parameter like slokas but aren't identified as such. 3. Parameters in Gita a strong possibility.

Sl	Subject raised	Issues to be considered	Possible verdicts
6	Uses of Parameters	They serve as a benchmark, reference or as a decisive factor.	1. When there is no parameter, the question of use doesn't arise. 2 It has no utility. 3 They serve as a reference, benchmark, and guide.
7	Hari Chitta or Gods supreme will exists and prevails over all else	Whether it exists and if it overrides everything else.	1. Gita doesn't mention Hari Chitta. 2. God's supreme will prevails over everything else.
8	God's words take precedence over His actions.	Whether God's words take precedence over His actions?	1. There is no such mention in the Gita. 2. It is so implied in the Gita
9	Gita parameters could be in the form of words, for example, inference, or analogy.	What are the forms of parameters?	1. Parameters are only those that are expressed. 2. Parameters could be in any form.

Sl	Subject raised	Issues to be considered	Possible verdicts
10	Parameters could be existential, principal enunciating, guiding or derivative.	Types of Parameters	1. Gita doesn't support or mention parameters. 2. Parameters could be of any four types as mentioned 3. There could be more types not specified.
11	The parameters of Gita are defined by the glories of God called as Krishnaness/Gitaness	Whether glories of God serve as parameters	1. Glories of God aren't parameters 2. Glories of God serve as parameters
12	Gita is the study of all by way of generalizations.	Whether most of Gita is generalizations?	1. Gita is not generalizations, maybe partly, but not most of it. 2. Yes, Gita is a generalization of Knowledge.
13	Parameters throw light on intricacies, provide deep insights into other slokas and ancient histories like Mahabharata and Ramayana	What Parameter does?	1. There are no Parameters. 2. Parameters provide deep insights and give framework and benchmark of scriptures besides doing other things.

Sl	Subject raised	Issues to be considered	Possible verdicts
14	God is omniscient, omnipresent, and omnipotent with all 6 opulence in fullest measure. As a natural corollary, His words are supreme	Whether God and His words are supreme?	1. Neither God nor His words are supreme. 2. Only God is supreme. His words need not be supreme as words tend to be distended. 3. God and His words are supreme.
15	His words being supreme, His words cannot be qualified by words of any other, excepting His own words.	Can God words be subject to qualification by others' words?	1. Gods' words may be viewed in light of writings of great Acharyas and other scriptures. 2. Gods' words cannot be meddled or mixed with words of others.
16	Some parameter slokas permeate/pervade all other slokas	Do some slokas permeate all slokas?	1. Yes. 2. No. 3. Possibly.
17	Gita states that let scriptures be your authority. Naturally, Gita itself is scripture and greatest authority.	Whether Gita is scripture or not?	1. Gita is not a scripture. 2. Gita too is a scripture. 3. Gita is the final authority irrespective of it being a scripture or not

Sl	Subject raised	Issues to be considered	Possible verdicts
18	Gita is made up of variables and constants which are used to make generalizations.	Do generalizations in Gita comprise of variables and constants?	1. Neither generalizations nor variables and constants occur in the Gita 2. Yes. Constants and variables have been used to make generalizations effective.
19	Gita is made up of variables and constants which are used to make generalizations.	Do generalizations in Gita comprise of variables and constants?	1. Neither generalizations nor variables and constants occur in the Gita 2. Yes. Constants and variables have been used to make generalizations effective.
20	Gita has at least five types of sentences, The declarative, the interrogative, the imperative, the exclamatory, and the optative.	Does Gita have five types of sentences as claimed?	1. No. 2. Yes. There are five types of sentences in English grammar, and all those types occur in the Gita.
21	Instructions in Gita could be for All persons A particular person For a class of persons	Whether Gita is general, specific, or universal?	1. Gita has verses that are uniform. 2. Gita has verses that are general, specific, and universal.

Sl	Subject raised	Issues to be considered	Possible verdicts
22	Gita is context-based.	Whether the study of Gita should be context-based?	1. Gita should be studied as it is. 2. It should be understood based on context
23	Gita is infinite and complete knowledge.	Gita being complete whether the need for consulting other scriptures arise?	1. Gita cannot be both infinite and complete at the same time, both being opposite to each other. 2. Gita open-ended, hence infinite. 3. Being complete, consulting Other scriptures are redundant.

Sl	Subject raised	Issues to be considered	Possible verdicts
24	Earth is a prison full of miseries.	In view of it being a prison, our endeavor should be to get out of the same rather than strive to make our stay comfortable.	1. Earth is a joyful place. 2. Being a miserable place, we must put efforts to alleviate miseries. 3. Efforts should be to get out of prison which is the cause of miseries rather than alleviates miseries.
25	Attachments of senses to sense objects is the cause of joys and sorrows.	Whether the solution is distancing senses from sense objects or bearing stoically with resultant pleasure and pain?	1. Either method is suitable to overcome sorrows. 2. A combination of both would yield the best results.
26	That which is temporary is material and that which is Permanent is spiritual. That which accrues and exists even after death is permanent.	Difference between material and spiritual	1. The distinction made is incorrect. 2. The distinction made is correct. 3. There could be other distinctions besides these.

Sl	Subject raised	Issues to be considered	Possible verdicts
27	Crime is an act prohibited by the law of the land and sin is an act contrary to God's will. It is a transgression of divine law.	Difference between crime and sin	1. The difference is not correctly enunciated. 2. Distinction nicely spelt out on basis of Gita.
28	Spiritual credits can be used for material gains but not vice versa	Is there a difference between spiritual and material credits? How it is put to use?	1. There is no such thing. 2. There is a difference between both and cannot be used interchangeably. 3. Though there is a difference, they can be used interchangeably although not advisable.
29	Material pursuits and spiritual pursuits are mutually exclusively.	Can both be pursued simultaneously?	1. Yes. Both can be pursued together. 2. No. They cannot be pursued together at the same time, which delays our progress.

Sl	Subject raised	Issues to be considered	Possible verdicts
30	The threefold gunas are ubiquitous, changing and is different from the twofold nature of the soul	Whether twofold nature of the soul, the divine, and demoniac is different from gunas and whether gunas are changing and twofold nature is constant?	1. The difference doesn't exist, if it does exist, it is inconsequential. 2. There is a fundamental difference, one constant and the other changing.

Sl	Subject raised	Issues to be considered	Possible verdicts
31	The threefold gunas and also two-fold nature of the soul is not absolute. It is a concept measured with pre-defined individual lower and individual upper values within which it oscillates/stabilizes.	Whether the threefold gunas have individual limits of upper and lower values? Do these limits differ from individual to individual? Whether Gunas confine themselves within these values and the dominant guna being the identifying type of the being? Does it extend to other spheres like actions, behavior, results, thoughts, etc.?	1. The concept is imaginary and doesn't hold merit. 2. The concept is an extrapolation explaining varied behaviors of different persons under different time periods and different circumstances and can be applied to other spheres profitably.

Sl	Subject raised	Issues to be considered	Possible verdicts
32	There is a scale of measurement of Krishnaness/Gitaness.	Whether Krishnaness comprises of six opulence, qualities of blemishless ness, supremely independent, complete, causeless, and imperishable. Does such a scale of measurement exist? Wherein higher the Krishnaness, more proximate to truth and closer to absolute?	1. Imaginary and doesn't hold water. 2. The revolutionary concept attempts to answer many a paradox, worth exploration.

Sl	Subject raised	Issues to be considered	Possible verdicts
33	The three gunas bear similarity to Atoms.	Whether Sattva, Rajas, and Tamas are identical or similar to Proton, electron, and neutron?	1. A theory without evidence. 2. A probability worth exploring.
34	The three gunas represent the trinity of Brahma, Vishnu, and Maheshwara.	Are the trinity three deities presiding over the three gunas?	1. There is no such mention in the Gita. 2. A good lead to explore.
35	The demonic and divine could be matter and anti-matter	Is the distinction between spirit and matter the difference between demonic and divine?	1. Again, just a theory not backed with evidence. 2. There are both similarities and dissimilarities but cannot conclusively accept nor rejected without further research.
36	There are five causes of accomplishment of actions.	Whether Gunas are a performer of action, body/self is the medium through which action is performed and God is the impeller of action?	1. The body and person is the cause of action and its results. 2. The five causes of action and its' results are correct and are an observable phenomenon.

Sl	Subject raised	Issues to be considered	Possible verdicts
37	You can only act, the results thereof are not in your hands.	Is it a fact that you only initiate a process of an action? The actual act and its results aren't in your control	1. Man is his own maker of destiny. Any fruit obtained is the result of his acts. 2. It is an observable phenomenon that we initiate only the process. The actual act and the results thereof are not in our hands.
38	The cosmic form shown to God is real	Whether the universal form shown to Arjuna was illusory or real?	1. God doesn't have form. 2. The vision shown is illusory. 3. God has many forms and the cosmic form is one such real form.
39	All actions have taint excepting those of God.	Should we refrain from actions due to taint?	1. Don't perform tainted actions. 2. As taint is a part of any action like a thorn is a part of the rose, perform actions focusing on positives. See the positive part of other actions instead of criticizing them.

Sl	Subject raised	Issues to be considered	Possible verdicts
40	The results of any action are commensurate with effort, ability, capacity, and deservedness.	Are result, a function of all and not just one of these factors?	1. Not necessarily. We see anomalies in our daily life. 2. These factors explain the anomalies proving the contention to be correct.
41	The essence or heart of Gita or the prime sloka is Karmanye vadikarasya	Is the selected sloka heart of Gita as claimed?	1. Yes. Karma yoga is the essence of Gita which is defined by this sloka. 2. No. There are varying perspectives between views of a Bhakta yogi, Gyana yogi, Jnana yogi, and a Karma Yogi.
42	All actions and results comprise of the material and spiritual component in varying degrees.	Whether the claim is factual and observable?	1. It is just a theory not backed by the study. 2. It is a hypothesis with merit and needs to be researched.

Sl	Subject raised	Issues to be considered	Possible verdicts
43	What is the difference between the spiritual and the mundane?	The four distinguishing features of spirituality are 1) permanence 2) no loss of efforts 3) freedom from fear and 4) no adverse results.	1. The distinction made is not valid or proved. 2. The distinction made is valid and observable and backed by the words of the Lord in the Gita.
44	The word 'Time 'has many connotations and used in the Gita to connote different things.	Whether the word 'Time' acquires different meanings like God, an instant, an object, appropriateness, time-period-span, a unit of measurement, a harbinger of change, context, perspective, etc. as being claimed?	This is stretching the imagination too far, a case of extreme poetic/bigotic license Language/grammar supports all the said meanings, and the word has been used differently to mean what is claimed at different places. This interpretation makes sense of the slokas in tune with observable/verifiable facts.

Sl	Subject raised	Issues to be considered	Possible verdicts
45	Context is an all-pervasive auto-updater, usually implied in Gita and in all scriptures.	Does context pervade Gita and other scriptures? Does it auto-update contents with the passage of time making it current and relevant?	Claims made are possible though not proved. One of the best explanations which bring relevance to scriptures and shields it from obsolesce and makes it relevant at all times.
46	Context is made up of time and space.	Are time and space the main components of context?	1. No, not at least in the conventional sense. 2. Possibly, in addition to other components.
47	Time and space are also used as adjuncts.	Do they add to the meaning of the sentence which is already complete in and by itself?	1. Preposterous Claim. 2. Possible and plausible

Sl	Subject raised	Issues to be considered	Possible verdicts
48	Sacrifices listed by God are highest in the hierarchy of order of precedence followed sacrifices referred to by God in other scriptures like Vedas, etc.	God has listed sacrifices and also referred to sacrifices mentioned in other scriptures like Vedas. Do the mentions in Gita have precedence over others referred to?	1. Sacrifices all stand on par, and there is no distinction based on which scripture it is stated. 2. Sacrifices, like mind control, pranayama, etc. precedes those in other scriptures with further sub-hierarchy of Sattvic, Rajasic, and Tamasic inter-se amongst themselves.
49	Study of Gita is a spiritual practice and in itself is a sacrifice of the highest order	Is the Study of Gita a spiritual practice? Does it qualify to be termed sacrifice?	1. The study of Gita is a knowledge-seeking and intellect provoking exercise and nothing more. 2. The study of Gita is a sacrifice within the ambit of Gods' definition of sacrifice and a superlative one at that as it endears you to God like nothing else.

Verdict Form

Sl	Subject raised	Issues to be considered	Possible verdicts
50	Daily activities like yoga, pranayama, and mind, and sense control, the study of scriptures are all acts of sacrifice.	Do these activities constitute sacrifice as mooted in the Gita by the Lord?	1. They are just mundane activities and health exercises without any godly connotation. 2. They are sacrifices if they meet certain requirements depending on motivation and purpose behind those activities.
51	Faith in self, in our abilities and in God is an essential element for success in our endeavor.	Is faith mandatory?	1. Faith is a catalyst and hastens result, not mandatory. 2. Faith is an essential ingredient.
52	We are identified by our faith.	Are we identified by our faith?	1. Not necessarily. 2. Yes, identified by faith to which we belong or faith which we profess, or faith with which we believe and act.
53	Detailed knowledge at the quantum level may not always be necessary, except when so specializing.	Would general knowledge suffice without requiring specialized knowledge?	1. How can you perform your duty with general knowledge? 2. Truly said, and is an observable phenomenon.

Sl	Subject raised	Issues to be considered	Possible verdicts
54	Focus on the main purpose.	Don't get deviated from the main purpose by minor distractions.	1. It is a general statement, unconnected with Gita. 2. Gita related and verifiable in daily life.
55	Conduct yourself with others how you expect others to conduct with yourself.	Is it a determinant of segregating correct from incorrect action?	1. This statement is too general and theoretical. 2. Gitas' prescription to determine right from wrong at an individual level with personalization and customization.

Sl	Subject raised	Issues to be considered	Possible verdicts
56	God hasn't mandated/approved/upheld religious conversion, whatever be the means.	Has God decreed conversions or does it meet with His approval?	1. God has mandated devotees to convert others and is standard instructions on part of God whatever the religion be and is also approved by God in the Gita. 2. Religious conversion by moral suasion, inducement, or coercion doesn't yield spiritual results by itself nor does it endear you to your new god or disfavor you from your old god. Not found in any scriptures, and where present, is a manmade subsequent insertion without divine sanction.

Sl	Subject raised	Issues to be considered	Possible verdicts
57	On the spiritual plane, what is achieved by religious conversion?	Whether claims made by preachers are true? What spiritual benefits accrue to the converter and the converted?	1. The benefits of conversion are, as held out by the respective scriptures. 2. Change of religion changes only the externals, i.e. the rituals and customs and has no bearing on your spirituality or your relationship with God.
58	The mind is a good servant and a bad master.	Is controlling the mind prescribed in the Gita and is beneficial?	1. True from psychology point, but does not have Gita nuances. 2. Gita prescription and observable in daily life.
59	Knowledge of the purpose of the action is better than the action itself.	Is it required to know what and why of any action more than the action itself?	1. Action produces a result, not why and how we perform an action. 2. Of course, without knowing the purpose, our efforts would be directionless and this is what God says.

Sl	Subject raised	Issues to be considered	Possible verdicts
60	Any proposition or theory should be practical, relevant observable and appropriate.	Isn't it so?	1. It is possible that an intellectual theorizes and another executes. We can't say that theoretician is useless. 2. What practical utility does a theory have which is imaginary and cannot be translated into reality, other than serving purposes of entertainment?
61	Rituals by itself are not spiritual. The results thereof could be material, spiritual, or a combination of both. The resolve and motivation behind are more important than the ritual. The rituals may be dispensed with, without any spiritual loss.	Do rituals form a core part of spirituality and mandated by God? Does dispensing with it tantamount to disregarding god and turning away from spirituality?	1. Rituals are prescribed by great seers. It isn't for us to question but to follow. The performance of rituals is beneficial but doesn't form the core essence of God's teachings. There may not be any loss on the spiritual front due to the non-performance of rituals.

Sl	Subject raised	Issues to be considered	Possible verdicts
62	God is one.	Is there only one God? How do you reconcile with Gods projected by different religions?	1. Either there is no god or each religion has a god as per different claims, as all claims have some basis. 2. The Gods being propitiated by different religionists all have qualities of omniscience, omnipresence, omnipotence, and benevolence, mercifulness, etc. in abundance underscoring the fact that the Gods being referred by different religionists are same though being called/referred differently.

Sl	Subject raised	Issues to be considered	Possible verdicts
63	God responds to our prayers in the way we approach/seek/pray or desire.	Are God's answers to prayers customized or personalized?	1. There cannot be separate answers/rules for different persons. The law of equality applies. 2. God's answer is customized and personalized. This is not restricted to His answer as to the fulfillment of needs but extends to His response to our desire, visualization, our mode of worship, etc.
64	Cause and effect as a parameter help us analyze things in a more effective manner.	Does Gita mention cause and effect study and is it effective?	1. IT is a general truism without specific mention in the Gita. 2. The whole of Gita is a study of cause and effect by implication throughout Gita and is verifiable. A parameter because of its repeated occurrence and ubiquity.

Sl	Subject raised	Issues to be considered	Possible verdicts
65	Each cause and effect may comprise of both spiritual and material components.	Are there two elements in cause and effect?	1. This claim appears a bit farfetched and not tenable. 2. Absolutely, as Gods will is one of the five essentials of results of any action, besides, the motive and object determine the spirituality thereby underscoring the fact that though the act is material, the motive and object may be to please God, the best example being Arjuna fighting Kurukshetra War.
66	Cause and effect analysis establishes that God does exist by leading circumstantial evidence.	Does Cause and effect analysis establish the existence of God?	1. Circumstantial evidence being a secondary form of evidence should not be necessarily relied upon. 2. It leads us to an inescapable conclusion about Gods' existence.

Sl	Subject raised	Issues to be considered	Possible verdicts
67	IT is an existence that can be proved conclusively. Non-existence cannot be proved.	Can non-existence be proved?	1. It can be proved but not conclusively. 2. The essentials for proving non-existence don't exist and hence it cannot be proved.
68	All issues framed pertains to Gita by way of mention either therein or by way of derivation or implication.	Are the issues being deliberated herein sourced from Gita or is it irrelevant?	1. The issues raised are not relevant to Gita. 2. The issues framed pertains to the Gita either by way of mention, derivation, or implication. Many of them form the core essence of the Gita.

Sl	Subject raised	Issues to be considered	Possible verdicts
69	The parameters mentioned herein acts as a parameter for any religious scripture and can be used as an interpretive tool	Are the parameters mentioned general and universal so as to be useful as parameters for application in interpreting any religious scripture?	1. No concept called parameter in the Gita, even if present,is confined to Mahabharata of which Gita is a part or at best any Hindu scriptures. 2. From the arguments put forth, there can be no doubt about the general and universal application of Gita for interpreting the scripture of any religion.
70	The concept of Parameters put forth are fictional or mere creation and not in tune with reality.	Whether Gita supports Parameters? Whether the subjects put forth are truly representative to qualify as a Parameter?	1. The Concept of parameters in the Gita is a fictional creation and has no bearing on the real Gita. 2. Gita has mentions of parameters and actively supports the same. The subjects selected as parameters are chosen correctly.

Sl	Subject raised	Issues to be considered	Possible verdicts
71	The Author has taken literary license beyond scope reaching unacceptable levels	Whether Literary license is taken, and if yes, has it been grossly abused to unsustainable levels?	1. The literary license being prerogative of the author, but has taken it to another level making the non-fiction literature a fictional literary piece. 2. The license was taken only to provide clarity and make it more readable and intelligible without changing the material/spiritual nature of the script.

Sl	Subject raised	Issues to be considered	Possible verdicts
72	The word interpretation is interpreted and used correctly.	Whether the proper meanings from amongst the different available meanings of interpretation taken so as to arrive at a proper conclusion?	1. The basic rule that scriptures must be taken literally and not interpreted is violated, thus vitiating the entire proceedings. 2. The selection and interpretation are correct because, elucidation thereafter of passages becomes more relevant, meaningful and makes better sense.

Sl	Subject raised	Issues to be considered	Possible verdicts
73	Mostly, the proceedings conform to the juristic and scriptural standards.	Are the proceedings fair and equitable or is it just a kangaroo court enacting a farce?	1. The entire trial is a sham with basic scriptural literalism and juristic interpretation being compromised. 2. The entire proceedings are fair and true and the conclusions reached are tenable.
74	Gita has within itself rules of interpretation, codified so as to interpret, conclude, and crosscheck our conclusion.	Are these rules extrinsic to Gita as in case of other scriptures or is intrinsic and contained in Gita per se? Does it also provide across-check?	1. Claims made are imaginary. Gita hasn't spoken or stated any rules or benchmark. 2. Rules are set forth in Gita along with methods of the cross-check. It is for us to identify the rules and not deny the existence of the same merely because it is not bracketed under nomenclature 'RULES"

Sl	Subject raised	Issues to be considered	Possible verdicts
75	Gita has provided a missing link by setting forth rules of interpretation.	The rules of interpretation are missing links because a mortal cannot judge/evaluate the immortal.	1. Rules already existed under the branch Hermeneutics. Hence, the rules of interpretation cannot be attributed to the Gita. 2. It is definitely a missing link because it establishes the rules are of divine origin without the blight of human imperfections. This can be better appreciated by comparing other scriptures where rules of interpretation are distinct from what is being interpreted.

Sl	Subject raised	Issues to be considered	Possible verdicts
76	Rules of interpretation of scriptures are universal and not confined or restricted to the Gita.	The Existence of the study of hermeneutics as a separate branch of study is proof of the universality of application.	1. The rules of interpretation don't hold good, as Gita has not formulated any such rules. 2. The rules of interpretation pertain only to Bible or only to Gita depending on the faith of the person interpreting. 3. The rules of interpretation have universal application.
77	Can nonverbal cognitive skills be used to judge conclusions derived from verbal cognitive skills?	Our Paradigm being nonverbal, can we use this parameter to test the commentaries of great seers whose paradigm was syntactic and semantic?	1. Yes. Parameters should good for all and at all times as the very name parameter implies. 2. No. The units involved and the scale of measurement are different and hence not possible.

Sl	Subject raised	Issues to be considered	Possible verdicts
78	Gita is truly metacognitive.	Is Gita through Gita is metacognition? Does our paradigm underscore this?	1. Neither is Gita metacognitive nor is the paradigm presented illustrative of this property. 2. Gita through Gita is metacognition in action.
79	The paradigm presented is truly reflective of metacognition with practical application and emphasis on categorization and pattern identification.	Does the paradigm put forth support Categorization and pattern recognition? Is it theoretical or also has a practical application?	1. There is no categorization or pattern recognition in the presented paradigm. 2. Categorization as verbal and non-verbal done and identified patterns as defined in metacognition from text present in the Gita and harnessed/leveraged it thereby demonstrating the use and practicality.

Sl	Subject raised	Issues to be considered	Possible verdicts
80	Your overall judgment/verdict on the issues.	Are the arguments put forth by the defendant convincing, logical, and acceptable? Does the new perspective conform to the teachings of the Lord?	1. The defendant could not establish the innumerable claims made. Her motives may be above board and intention may not be to degrade other sects, but the claims thereof are preposterous and ought to be rejected. 2. The arguments put forth by the defendant are a fair attempt in presenting Gita in a new perspective which is by and large convincing, logical, acceptable and conforms to the teaching of the Lord, though not in the conventional sense.

Sl	Subject raised	Issues to be considered	Possible verdicts
81	Overall assessment of the views put forth	Some of it makes sense, some of it may be farfetched. Whether to be accepted or rejected? IF accepted is it final?	1. Not acceptable especially those that are held not proved. 2. Accepted. However, neither the acceptance nor rejection is final. The issues raised to serve as a building block for further exploration of alternative perspectives.

OTHER OBSERVATIONS   OR

NON-STANDARD VERDICT

Sl	Subject discussed	Reference verdict form or daily proceedings.	Possible verdicts

5. MAIL FROM THE PAST
THE YEAR 2019

It was a weekend evening. Haripriya and her husband Somnath were sipping Tea and discussing their future plans. Their son had just finished his schooling and was seeking advice as to his future. They heard the doorbell ring. Som got up to attend the door. He returned with a big packet received from the courier boy. It was addressed to Priya's Father and had postal marks of U S. Haripriya took the packet and opened it. There were two letters one addressed to her and another to her father. It was accompanied by a book. She opened the wrapper of the book and noticed "**Millionth Copy**" "**SIGNATURE Edition**" emblazoned on the cover page. It was from Christina, her friend with whom she had lost touch a long time ago. Her focus shifted to the letters. She slowly opened the letter addressed to her father.

It ran thus:

Dear Sir,

This is Christina, your daughters' friend. I had the opportunity to visit you and have a chat about your ideas. I do not suppose you remember me. I was at Priyas' place in Tirupati under an exchange program. I had come to study and research about Bhagavad Gita. After the conclusion of the program, I visited you and you gave me rare insights into the Gita. I have used the knowledge of my tenure here and submitted my dissertation, which was accepted back home. A debate took place, wherein your daughter defended your version of the Gita. This formed the basis of my dissertation and future research.

During our discussion, you have enlightened me about many other perspectives about the Gita hitherto unknown to me or any others.

I not only found it interesting but also found it path-breaking, promoting communal harmony and embracing the concept of Vasudaiva Kutumbam or the concept of the universal family. I also found it time-defying and relevant. It also subsumes the teachings of all other religions.

You were kind enough to hand over to me the manuscript wherein you had jotted your ideas. Your ideas were brilliantly put forth by your daughter in the debate. It was then that. I decided that I would pursue Gita with your line of thinking.

During the course of the research, I have transcribed the entire debate that took place back in college and added your insights. I have taken your ideas and given a story narrative to make it more interesting without compromising the core philosophy and got it published. The book received an overwhelming response. It has been translated into 12 languages so far. It is a prescribed book for Gita studies in four universities. At least 4 universities over here have prescribed this book as a standard reference book for Gita.

We have established an institute devoted exclusively to Gita research and studies. It is named "PARTHASARATHY INSTITUTE OF GITA STUDIES" Our Institute can boast of having the biggest collection of Gita's of almost all the commentators. We have also tied up with at least a dozen institutions that have offered accreditation. It has the following departments

- o Comparative Gita studies.
- o Comparative studies of Gita and other religious scriptures.
- o Interdisciplinary Gita and science research covering
- Gita and psychology.
- Gita & Mathematics.
- Gita and science.
- Gita and quantum physics.
- Gita and God particle, Boson's particle research.
- Gita and astronomy.
- Gita, Sanskrit, and Computers.

India Foundation, Vaishnava Forum, Sanatana Trust Inter-Religious harmony foundation, Modi Trust, and many other institutions have pledged support.

A function is scheduled on Gita Jayanti falling in the month of December **and I desire that you be the chief guest.**

Monks of at least 9 orders from across the globe would be adorning the dais **along with you** and honoring us during the opening ceremony. I request you to grace the occasion and confer your blessings. Separate formal VIP invitation, Flight tickets, etc. would be sent to you on your acceptance of the invitation. Please humor your protégé by attending the same. Looking forward to seeing you soon

Dandavat Pranaam

Christina

A small tear dropped from Priya's eyes. Her husband noticed this and slowly pulled the letter from her and started reading it.

Priya opened the second letter addressed to her. It read thus:

Dear Haripriya,

My letter must have come as a surprise to you. Once I returned to the USA, I got busy. I lost touch about your whereabouts, along with that of many other friends. Besides, I had a nagging doubt, can a 6-month acquaintance be termed friendship? Will Haripriya accept me as a friend after being silent for so long? Time was running out. It was now or never. I searched Google and Facebook. I found many Haripriyas.

I searched the photos and zeroed in on you once the photos identified you and scraped your contact details and am couriering this letter. I did not want to spoil your surprise by befriending you on facebook.

Many Gita lovers and I have joined together to establish a new institute entirely devoted to the study and research of Bhagavad Gita. The inauguration of the same is scheduled in the latter half of December this year so as to coincide with Gita Jayanti.

Do you remember asking me at Kurukshetra, What Sankalpa you are performing? You further teased me saying that my dissertation would be accepted and I need not invoke Gods for the same.

I had smiled and avoided replying. Well, I had prayed that I should start an institute exclusively to study and research Bhagavad Gita with your fathers' philosophy as the base. This has fructified and hence I am letting the cat out of the bag.

I extend you a warm invitation. Please join us with your father and family. You are a VIP speaker with a one-hour slot. Many of my students are looking forward to hearing the fireworks directly from you and I am in no doubt that you will not disappoint them.

You would have acquired many more missiles in your armory since you last debated with which we can further the cause of the Gita. Would you be interested in trans-locating to the US? We would love to have you as our faculty. You need to work for 18 hours a week at our institute. If you are wondering if it is an offer, yes, it is an invitation and an offer. We will catch up with each other and speak about old times when we meet.

Your Loving friend

Christina.

Priya was unable to contain her emotions. IT was a mix of ecstasy and sadness. Her father's stand was vindicated and Christina and she had been instrumental in it to a major extent. Dad would be ecstatic.

She emailed a reply to her friend. She informed that her parents had joined the order of monkhood and renounced the world. They refrain from active participation in any mundane activity. I will inform them and their standard response would be "God bless". Their oft-repeated quote "Parents live through their children and achieve their dreams through them" has proved correct.

Daddy had a premonition of you doing something big, because when you met him and spoke to him.

He saw the commitment and perseverance in your attitude, more so, because he used to read your name with "T" silent and knew that you would put his views across the globe. After your meeting him and briefing him about the debate prior to your departure to U S, He also wanted to hear my arguments in the debate verbatim. Unfortunately, I did not have a recording or a transcript.

My father asked me not to idolize him or take him to be an ideal person. He confessed that he was a human with frailties. All his shortcomings were overlooked by God and made him privy to esoteric revelations. He himself told that he wants to pay for his Karma and confessed that he was a hypocrite in that he wanted NAME and fame but always postured that his work was an act of sacrifice. But Christina, I adore him not for what he did but for what he was – A chosen one to broadcast HIS WORD.

I thank you for all that you have done, for upholding my fathers' ideals, for remembering your friend and of course for the invitation. It would be my pleasure to attend the function.

Your loving friend

Haripriya

6. DOWN THE MEMORY LANE

Haripriya picked up the book and started reading. It transported her back to the college days of the year 2014. She vividly remembered all the events that unfolded.

She was studying at **Shri Venkateshwara University (SVU)** for a postgraduate degree in Law. She was staying at Universitylady's hostel. As the day scholars were more in number than the outsiders all lady students irrespective of the faculty were allotted rooms in the same hostel building. This gave her an opportunity to interact with students of other faculties put up in the same hostel. Most of the students were from the faculty of management or law. Girl students from **Shri Venkateshwara Vedic University (SVVU)** who were pursuing PG in religious studies too were accommodated in the same building. Few of them were pursuing law. Professor Parthasarathy was head of the Department of Law. He was a retired Judge, who had given up his job and promotion to be in the close vicinity of Lord of seven hills. He had settled in the holy town of Tirupati permanently giving up all interest in his ancestral roots in Salem. He was also designated as rector of the said hostel. The students had various groups depending on their area of interest. Some of the popular groups were the Spiritual study group, Gita lovers' group, India First group, etc. Apart from meeting on the last Sunday of every month, they were in touch through WhatsApp groups. Haripriya was a dormant member without attending any meetings or contributing anything to WhatsApp. She was busy with her academics. Little did she suspect that all this would change and she would be pulled into the vortex of a historical debate? During her last semester, a batch of foreigners descended on the hostel. They were here on an exchange program. Two were pursuing religious studies and others were in different departments. One evening she was sitting in the lounge and hearing Bhagavad Gita sung by Vanraj Bhatia on her mobile.

The girl sitting on the opposite side approached her and sought permission to sit next to her.

She exclaimed Wow, Gita! For more than an hour, she sat there transfixed and in rapture. Thereafter she introduced herself as a student of the Hindu University of America, Florida. Her name was Christina She informed that she had come here under an exchange program for completing her project on "The Gita" They exchanged pleasantries and left.

Christina would make it a point to meet Haripriya daily. During their conversations, she would contrive to steer the topic to Gita and hear attentively what Haripriya had to say. One day she asked Haripriya if she was a member of the Gita lover group. Hari replied in affirmative. Christina confided in Haripriya, that she is a Gita lover and had traveled halfway across the globe to study Gita. She had chosen SVVU considering that Tirupati is the abode of Lord Vishnu. She further confided that she is in search of correct translation/interpretation of the Gita. All the persons she met and interacted had helped her out by adding to her confusion, instead of clarifying her doubts. Everybody claimed that THE denomination of sects which they follow is the correct one and the Gita commentary of the head of that sect was the correct one. She asked Haripriya if she could help her. Haripriya asked how Christina zeroed in on her when there were many other students in her department. Further, she questioned Christina as to what made her think that she has the correct answer.

Christina informed that it was her name and also the devotion with which she was listening to Gita when she first met her. Besides, she said that it was a gut feeling.

Haripriya replied that she was willing to help if she could but she herself was nagged by the very same doubts with which Christina was beset. She told her friend that she will speak to her father but the trouble was her father held radical views that were non-conformist in nature. He had quarantined himself from all the thinkers of the traditional and orthodox school.

His views were unacceptable to anyone and he kept his views to himself but did not budge from his views nor get intimidated by scholarly debates. Haripriya felt that her father could have an answer but whether it would satisfy Christina, where it was rejected by a multitude of people?

Christina informed that she would acquire her degree and get a nice percentage but would not have self-satisfaction if her questions are not answered. She requested Haripriya to meet her dad and broach the subject. Haripriya was to leave for Kolhapur coming Saturday to attend the Navaratri festival. She promised her friend that she would speak to her dad and bring her an answer when she returns after the festival. And so it was that Hari left for Kolhapur with more than meeting her parents, and seeing Mahalaxmi in mind.

7. BACK HOME @ KOLHAPUR

THE YEAR 2014

Haripriya was seated in the train which was her namesake (Haripriya Express). She was returning home after a gap of more than four months. She was missing her mom and her cooking. She was feeling guilty for not missing her dad and decided to lie about it when asked by her dad, but lying wasn't her nature and she would always blurt out the truth. She was also missing her weekly visits to Mahalaxmi Temple along with her mother. Her mother would always drag her to the temple. Her weekly visits would recharge her batteries and provide her serenity. Now with Navaratri around the corner, the whole temple would be very crowded and would delay their return home, not that they minded. Half the population the city of Kolhapur would be decked in their fineries. In fact, the lady citizens of Kolhapur would have shopped extensively for the occasion and would have nine different colored dresses for each of the nine days. The color was fixed by tradition, and the presiding deity, Mahalaxmi herself would be setting the trend wearing different colors on each of the nine days, emulated by her devotees. She got down from the train, to an emotional hug and warm welcome from her mom, who had come to the station to receive her and hadn't informed her so as to surprise her. Well, she was now back at Maike (Parents or Mothers place) for was not Kolhapur the residence of the Spouse of Lord of seven hills? She forgot everything and was very excited back at her house.

In the evening, her father returned from the office. He made preliminary inquiries as to her wellbeing and health and her journey and settled back on his lounge chair with his newspaper but not before enquiring from her whether she missed dad way back at Tirupati. She gave him an innocent smile and he took it to mean yes.

The next day she accosted her father and asked him about what her friend Christina had prompted her to ask, about Gita.

He said, satisfy your taste buds by visiting Rajabhau Bhelpuri, you complete all your outings settle at home becoming become a fully resident Kolhapur and then talk to me, you know I don't like interruptions or breaks when we are chatting. She said Okay and rushed off with her mother.

At night, she found her father free doing nothing. She sat down with him and began a conversation.

Haripriya (HP): Dad, tell me about Gita.

Dad (DD): You have attended so many spiritual retreats like some Samadhi yoga, the art of loving, and some Yajna. What did they teach you there?

HP: I will summarize all that I learned. The following were the topics of discussion.

- o Who am I?
  - I am the soul and not the body.
- o Why am I here?
  - I am evolved to this stage in the process of evolution.
- o What is my destination?
  - Gods' abode or Gods' state is my destination depending on which program attended.
- o How do I reach my destination?
  - By following the instructions given.
- o How do I not reach my destination?
  - By not following the instructions given.
- o What are my duties?
  - That which is prescribed.
- o What is prescribed by Krishna?
  - As mentioned in BG
- o How do I know what is prescribed for me?
  - By deciding on my nature and lookup for the duties ascribed in accordance with my nature
- o How do I know what is my nature?
  - By looking up as to what are the traits of different kinds of persons and identify yourself with the traits most prominent in you.

These topics were discussed. Besides, they convinced us of the truth of some of the statements by way of explanation, by actual experience and by way of assumption/presumption.

DD: Now tell me, how did they come up with the answers?

HP: Maybe it was told by their preceptors.

DD: Who told their preceptor?

HP: Yes, through a chain of preceptors, but where does the buck stop?

DD: Exactly, can you find the answers given in your retreats in the Gita?

HP: Theoretically yes, after a pause, My God, what you are hinting is right Dad!

Three days had passed. She had completed all her purchases and met all her friends. She visited Cotton King, at Rajarampuri and bought a tee for her father. She hid it so that her father would be surprised when she presented it to him. She started painting Krishna with Gita's background on the tee and planned to complete it in 3-4 days' time so as to present it to her father. Her activities became more fixed and routine. She and her mother had planned to visit the temple daily at 5-30 AM. She would laze about at noon and meet her friends and take a stroll around different places around the city in the evening. She decided to catch her father at nine that night. After dinner, she accosted her dad and again broached the subject. He said, okay, we will commence from tomorrow, which is auspicious being Navaratri and escaped himself.

8. NAVARATRI CONVERSATION

The year 2014

Haripriya (HP): Okay dad, shall we commence?

DD: What do you want to know?

HP: About Gita.

DD: Why the sudden interest?

HP: There is a debate scheduled in our college and I would be holding the center stage, and she told her dad all that transpired at her hostel prior to coming to Kolhapur.

DD: You already know many things. You have read many books but still …

HP: Yes, but each of them differs from one another and everyone claims that their version is the truth and correct and that other versions are concocted.

DD: Then, how did you venture into a debate?

HP: Dad, I had heard you many telling times that whatever God spoke is the truth, and whenever some utterance of God connotes many meanings, all of them are correct and Gods' words cannot be restricted to one narrow meaning.

DD: Read Gita, any version, shorn of all commentaries or purports. It answers all your questions including how to acquire knowledge (Of Gita). Whatever stated therein is true. Whatever therein is implied is true. Whatever that is in agreement with what is said or what is implied is true.The rest of the thing should be taken with a pinch of salt.

HP: You mean Gita through Gita.

DD: Exactly, you are getting the drift now.

HP: Dad, please elaborate.

DD: Okay, I will not teach you Gita but teach you how to learn/understand Gita. That would be more permanent in nature.

HP: Oh, something like providing fish versus how to fish so that …

DD: Read Sloka 2.39

HP: So far, I have explained the nature of the soul from Sankhya point of view now I will reveal the same from Karma-Yoga point of view.

DD: So far, you have read, heard and understood Gita from a semantic perspective. Now I will take you around Gita through a conceptual perspective.

Can you see the analogy? Gita is not one dimensional but multi-dimensional. During the coming days, we will be dwelling on this perspective.

HP: Daddy, you have just formed another sentence in a fashion similar to the sloka in Gita and call it an analogy. I am unable to understand.

DD: You will in course of time, and anyway before you depart for Tirupati.

HP: Continue Daddy.

DD took a long breath and spoke:

Around 5300 years ago, the lord of infinite universes (Ananta Koti Brahmanda Nayaka), meaning lord of infinite universes) visited our earth planet and stayed amongst us earthlings as a common man and performed unearthly feats to the delight of His devotees.

The ostensible reason for His descent to earth was

- o To punish the wicked.
    - Achieved by throwing them repeatedly in lower wombs. (Not by just killing them)
    - (BG-16-19&20)
    - Killing or death is not a punishment. Flinging into lower wombs with the very remote possibility of coming out of the birth-death cycle is punishment.
- o To establish righteousness.
    - (BG-2-47)
    - Achieved by enthroning righteous Pandavas.
- o To sustain righteousness.
    - By enthroning Pandavas
    - Perpetuated righteousness by expounding The Gita.

How He sustained righteousness even after His departure to His own abode, is the subject matter. God was aware that His visit would be an eon later and that time would destroy everything. So, he intended that His song of wisdom in the form of GITA take His place to guide the faithful. Why Gita? Because it comes the closest second to God Himself, it being Imperishable, infallible, etc. Isn't it a fabrication? – No, God's intent has been expressed to His friend and Cousin, Uddhava, just prior to His departure (UG: 26-43 & 44) & to Arjuna (BG-18-68 & 69)

Arjuna had only two choices, either to kill or be killed, yet he could not make a choice. How much more difficult it is for us who have a multitude of religions, a plethora of scriptures, umpteen number of commentaries, number of Gurus, etc. How to make a choice? Simple, do it as Arjuna did, Surrender and follow the complete person and his complete guide.

God Himself preached Gita, WHY? He could have entrusted it to somebody like He advised Bhishma to mentor Yudhistara. The stamp of authority would be missing if it weren't HE.

One Book many solutions, a marvel that is Gita was born. In a nutshell about Gita:

- He gave Knowledge by way of Gita
- He gave means/reference/guide to knowledge by way of Gita
- He gave His very self by way of Gita
- He Himself spoke the Gita.
    - To provide a stamp of authority.
        - Because He is the greatest (BG-11-43)
- He lived His words.
    - To give credibility.
- He made it imperishable. (BG 4.1, I taught this imperishable science to Vivasvan)
    - To breathe immortality into it.
- He filled it with generalizations.
    - To make it universal & to make it concise.
- He condensed each complete portion into small chapters (3 chapters for 3 Yoga's).
    - So that each of such chapter caters to devotees of different temperaments.
        - Karma Yoga for the hyperactive active.
        - Bhakti Yoga for the emotional and the sentimental.
        - Jnana yoga for the seeker or the inquisitive.
- He designed His teachings keeping in mind the four types of devotees, the distressed, knowledge seeker, wealth seeker, and the devotee. (BG-7-16)
    - To cater to different desires/needs of seekers of different results.
- He condensed the cream of His teaching into one verse. (Give up all religions and surrender unto me) (BG-18-66)
    - To uplift the most degraded, and least intelligent to reach Him with least effort and least knowledge, but with huge expectations.
- He gave a master key in the form of parameters,
    - To check and confirm end results and to reassure ourselves if we are right.

- He made it dynamic and obsolete proof and relevant to the times to come in future
  - By putting built-in auto-updater into His teachings by splitting his teachings into Constants, variables, and dependent constants.
    - (BG-15-16&17)
- He sent teachers.
  - For those that required.
    - In the form of Gurus of various parampara'

- He became a teacher.
  - For those that sought His tutelage.
    - TO Vivasvan, Arjuna & Uddhava.
- For those who don't put any effort into learning, but always immersed in loving Him,
  - He residing in their hearts lit the lamp of wisdom in their hearts.
    - All the Vrindavan residents, who were simple cowherds but got transcendental knowledge.
- He made His teachings rigid (I am the only unchanging amongst all changing)
  - So that it is not tampered with.
- He made it flexible.
  - So as to suit persons in different millennia under different circumstances and differently-abled.
- He made it a study of concepts
  - So that the scope is wide enough to grasp the infinite.
- He made it semantic
  - So that the word has the same importance as the spirit behind His words.
- He made Gita subserve the objectives with which spoken
  - By imparting knowledge for the sake of posterity.
  - By inducing a righteous war, and destroying the adharmic forces.
    - To set an example to achieve four-fold objectives & four purusharthas.
- He made Gita objective
  - So as to make devotees learn it in an objective manner, devoid of subjective bias.
- He made it subjective so that
  - Subjective opinions are based on objective learning.
  - He overruled His own words

- To show His supreme will, supreme authority, and supreme independence.

DD took a long breath, after the monologue and asked for a drink of water. After sipping water, he continued. How has God communicated (revealed his intentions) with many persons at different times and different places in different ways, would give us an idea of the art of making distinctions. Gita reveals how to distinguish between jest and serious, implicit, and explicit, the implication of silence, decoding of gestures.

It also reveals when and how far to submit to bonafide Guru, understanding that inner voice is actually God communicating from within, learning from Gods'and gurus' actions which serve as an example to be followed, when to follow Gods' words and when to follow His deeds, etc.

- Direct communication.
  - Like with Arjuna, look, behold the army yonder with whom you wish to confront.
    - Take it literally without interpretation.
- Communication in jest.
  - With his consort Rukmini Mata
    - I am a cowherd, I ran away from Battle, I have nothing of my own, etc.
      - Look behind the message. However, Rukmini Matha, herself has given super rejoinder to each of the Lord's words.
        - This proves that even words of jest by the Lord have the truth.
- Communication through gestures.
  - By pointing to his thighs when Bhīma was fighting with Duryodhana.
    - Take a cue from the gesture.
- Splitting blade of grass and throwing away in opposite directions.
  - When Bhīma was wrestling with Jarasandha.
  - Take a cue from the gesture.
- Through disciplic succession.
  - Gita discourse to Vivasvan, Sun God, who shared the knowledge and to Manu, Ikshvaku, etc.
    - Learn from those who have learned.
- Through his different incarnations.
  - Lord Ganesha writing Mahabharata at the dictation and behest of Veda Vyasa avatar.
  - Lord imparting knowledge to the first Manu in his Matsya avatar.
  - Lord imparting knowledge through Hamsa avatar.
- Through ocular experiences.

- o   Sanjaya through clairvoyance and telepathy, by the grace of Maharishi Veda Vyasa.
- o   Arjuna through the vision of the cosmic form of the Lord.
- Through Silence.
  - o   When Arjuna lamented about the sins accruing for non-performance of Shradh
  - o   When Balarama killed Rukmi and Krishna kept silent
  - o   When Tulasidevi petitioned Krishna about her innocence.
    - ▪   Decipher silence.
- Through inspiration.
  - o   By residing inside the body and lighting the lamp of wisdom and bestowing knowledge to attain to him.
    - ▪   Learn to distinguish between your inner voice, which is Gods' voice and your mundane voice.

- Through medium of musical instruments.
  - o   Brahma Deva seeking knowledge fulfilled by the Lord with imparting it with melodies from His flute.
- Krishna through his exemplary actions.
  - o   Opposing adharmic actions against the whole world.
  - o   Reprimanding demigods for giving boons indiscriminately.
  - o   By breaking his vow to uphold his devotees' vow.
  - o   By breaking his vow to teach others to uphold dharma even at the cost of breaking his vow.
  - o   By attending Gurukula.
  - o   By Krishna paying respects to his friend Sudama.
    - ▪   Imitate Krishna's actions if in tune with His words, else follow His words.
- Through apparent cowardice.
  - o   By running away from the battlefield when facing Kalyavan.
- By breaking His own vow.
  - o   When he took up his chakra to kill Bhishma.
- By seemingly abetting adharma.
  - o   By asking Yudhishtara to speak falsehood.
  - o   By asking Arjuna to kill unarmed Karna.
- By failing in His mission.
  - o   During peace parleys with Kauravas.

All of them convey one or more messages, and it is this message that we should seek rather than the going behind mere words.

DD: Read out BG-1-25

HP: Taking out the book reads----

DD: Supposing Krishna says in the presence of all military commanders like Bhishma, Drona and others "behold, all the Kurus assembled here. –BG 1-25" & Arjuna chooses to understand it figuratively and thinks Kurukshetra is the mind, Bhishma and Drona represents aberrations of the mind causing conflict, what would be the outcome?

Similarly, you understand that it is the Kurukshetra battlefield live, and see the battlefield as God instructed, what do you see?

HP: How can we see? We are in a different place and different time zone, but Arjuna was in the same place and time zone, He understood literally, which is correct, and we too should understand it literally but also keep in mind that the instruction was meant for Arjuna.

DD: Others who heard the discourse on the battlefield say Sanjaya or Hanuman or other demigods understood correctly but didn't act, because, for them, it was meant for information and for Arjuna, it was meant for action.

DD: Now read BG-11-34.

HP: Kill Drona, Bhishma, Jayadratha, Karna and others who are already slain by me

DD: Can Arjuna understand it figuratively or can you understand it literally?

HP: No.

DD: Now, suppose Arjuna took this figuratively and thought that Duryodhana and Bhishma represented the certain negative quality of mind, and tries to overcome the same? If we take it literally, who do we kill? The instructions are the same. Arjuna is supposed to understand literally and we are supposed to understand figuratively.

DD: From the above conversations, what can we deduce?
- Some instructions are for specific persons.
- Some instructions are for a specific class of persons, say Kshatriya, etc.
- Some instructions are universal, meaning it is for all persons.
- Some instructions could be literal for one and figurative for another and both literal and figurative simultaneously for a third person.
- A few instructions are meant for all but are to be understood and acted differently, i.e., literally or figuratively.
- What is said, what is meant, what is understood, and what is to be done are all to be in synchronization.
- A few instructions, though common to all, different persons are meant to understand differently i.e., either literal or figurative and act, or shouldn't act or meant just for information.

- Both instructions and understanding depend on time, place, and person.
- Instructions and understanding also depend upon temperament, i.e., Satvic, Rajasic, or Tamasic.
- It also depends upon Varna, i.e., whether Kshatriya, Vaisya, etc.
- It also depends upon the capability and capacity (Yogyate) of the person beholding to comprehend.
- As nature, i.e., sattva, raja, and tamas keeps changing, TIME also plays a role in understanding.
- Nonbelievers cannot understand because they do not have the capacity to surrender, for example, Duryodhana, even if he is instructed, will not understand, nor will follow.

To summarize,

- Meaning of Lords' words is person dependent.
- It is meant for all but in a different sense.
- Time, place, nature, capacity, faith, and belief, etc. all matters to arrive at correct understanding.

HP: So, there could be many meanings?

DD: Yes, but it is more appropriate to say that there are many understandings (Perceptions)

HP: Which is correct?

DD: This is a grey area. Nevertheless, any perception, which glorifies the Lord, which enhances the glory of the Lord, which doesn't belittle the lord or His teachings and which are observable or experienceable is correct to a great extent.

HP: Is it? I am a bit skeptical.

DD: God Himself and His devotees have vouchsafed as to His glories, words, & Pastimes. This is the path, knowledge, parameter, and benchmark to understand. Let me explain with a mundane example. The standard of purity of gold is 24K. We test the purity of gold with the quantum of gold vis-à-vis other metals. **24K gold** is purest but too soft to use, so it is mixed with other metals to strengthen it.

We may draw a close parallel (Actual parallel is not possible) as under:

The glories of God Himself, His words, his pastimes are Pure Gold. Carat is the media of our understanding. Higher the carat, greater is our understanding. The higher the carat, purer our understanding.

HP: You said that God incarnates to punish the wicked, but in the war, all the warriors on both sides were killed. There were righteous persons on both sides, but all got killed even though they were righteous. Why punishment meted out to innocents?

DD: Death is not a punishment; it may be so in the mundane sense only. Actual punishment is being repeatedly struck in the birth-death cycle with chances of getting out of the cycle getting remote. Recollect, Krishna, saying that I repeatedly throw them into lower wombs. (BG-16-19 to 16-20). Birth and death follow each other endlessly until liberated.

Remember Krishna saying Death is inevitable for one who is born and rebirth is certain for one who has died.

HP: How to come out of the endless cycle?

DD: Good question.
- Think of God whilst dying and you attain Him.
- Dying during the bright half-year or the path of light ensures freedom from the cycle.
- Be devoted to the Lord, because His devotees do not perish.

HP: How can you think of God when you die, you don't know when you will die?

DD: Think of Him at all times so that you have Him in mind during death, for has, not the Lord said that by constant practice and detachment, you can control the mind? (And think of Him) Neither do we have control or power to decide the time of our death so as to schedule it in sync with the Suns' journey to the northern hemisphere.

That is the privilege of great saints, yogis, and seers. You may practice exclusive devotion to God, so that He may pull you out of the endless cycle.

HP: God gave knowledge by way of Gita, but how did He give means to knowledge?

DD: God has asked to approach spiritual masters and perform service unto them, who would then impart knowledge. (BG-4-34)
   o God has informed that knowledge is described in Vedic texts and in Brahma Sutras. (BG-13.5)
   o God has asked us to consult scriptures as to activities to be done and those to abstain. (BG16.24)
   o Entire chapter 13 of BG tells what knowledge is and what is ignorance and the means to acquire them.

HP: You said that He gave His very self by way of Gita, I didn't understand.

DD: Gita is the soul of the Lord and Lord is the soul of Gita. Both are inseparable and hence non-different from each other. Arjuna is one of the fortunate few who got God in both the forms, i.e., in person and in the form of Gita sermon. God in persona form and in the form of Gita handed Himself over to Arjuna whilst handing over His army to Duryodhana. In the Non-Gita context, Krishna surrendered Himself to Radharani, to Kubja, the hunchbacked lady and to Sudama, but was prevented from doing so by His consort, Rukmini.

HP: Give examples of God living out His words.

DD: The list is endless. His entire life was spent in protecting Dharma.
- o By always engaging Himself in activities, though He has no duties to be performed. (BG-3.22)
- o By opposing Adharma and siding with Dharma. (BG.24)
- o By subjecting Himself to the law of Karma even though He is not bound by Karma. (Cause & Effect)
  - ▪ Accepted curse of Gandhari and seeing His entire clan perish before His very eyes.
    - ▪ Being shot by the arrow of Jara, the hunter and repaying the karma of having killed Vali from behind in His Ram avatar (Vali is believed to have been born as Jara)
- o By killing His maternal Uncle and cousins and other warlords, to uphold Dharma overlooking their familial relationship.

HP: Why is surrendering unto Krishna, (BG 18.66) the cream of all His teachings?

DD: There are chatur sloki Gita, Eka sloki Gita, etc, reciting only 4 slokas or just one sloka, confers the benefit of having read the entire eighteen chapters of the Gita. This is as per scriptures. But I believe that 18.66 is the cream of Krishna's teachings.

sarva-dharmān parityajya mām ekaṁ śharaṇaṁ vraja
ahaṁ tvāṁ sarva-pāpebhyo mokṣhayiṣhyāmi mā śhuchaḥ

TRANSLATION:

Abandon all types of dharma – come and surrender exclusively unto Me. Do not fear, for I will surely deliver you from all sinful reactions. There are many reasons.
- • Firstly, you give up all your dharma, mind you, it is very difficult to give up pre-existing beliefs and thoughts.
  - o This results in reducing your burden.
- • You have emptied space in mind by removing trash and made a place for Gods' teachings.
  - o This gives you clarity.
- • You are surrendering unto God, implying you have reposed faith in God.

71

- o NO one surrenders unto another unless He has faith in that another person.
- By this, you have shifted your burden from your shoulder to God's shoulder.
  - o You have given a mandate to God to do needful for your upliftment. God has given you the freedom and will not act on your behalf unless you have mandated it.
- You have a supreme guarantee from almighty Himself, (just like sovereign guarantee) of deliverance (from the cycle of birth and death) and a decree, not to fear or worry (as all is taken care of).

HP: What are the parameters and master keys, about which you spoke?

DD: A key that opens all doors is a master key. Gita opens all doors, mundane and spiritual implying access to all doors and what lies beneath. It is a master key because it has the key to all i.e.
  - Dharma
  - Artha
  - Kama
  - & Moksha.

There are four types of seekers seeking 4 types of things, namely
  - Relief from distress
  - Knowledge
  - Wealth and other material things like power, prestige, etc.
  - Liberation or salvation.

Within Gita, there are certain slokas which act as cornerstones for other verses and serves as a key to other scriptures and verses. They have been termed parameters in my opinion.

HP: Daddy, please give one example.

DD:
  - o Hear my Supreme word. BG: 10.1
  - o There is nobody equal or greater than you. BG 11.43

If Lord were not supreme, His words too would not be supreme. Then, no one will follow Him or His words. Next, there would be a vacant slot for the supreme word and supreme person, who yields authority, and whose writ runs supreme, so that His words can be followed.

So, each of the Sloka in Gita is dependent on the above two verses and derives authority from the above two verses and runs on that (premise) Fact, that God and His words are the greatest.

The moment this fact is ignored, the entire teachings lose its authority and weight.

It creates lots of doubts and results in chaos, when in fact Gita is meant for clearing the chaotic mind to clarity. These two slokas bind all other slokas. Also, other slokas make sense only after accepting this Sloka.

Also, when there is a multitude of opinions and divergent conclusions culled from different references, the one mentioned in Gita scores/prevails over others. Supposing there are divergent opinions with the same reference point, i.e. the Gita, Then?

HP: Then what?

DD: You tell me.

HP: All of them are right subject to it actually exists in the Gita and also experiential by us in our daily life.

DD: If you are unable to experience the truth of it?

HP: Either you have not understood it properly or you have not come up to that level to experience the truth, we should continue our spiritual pursuit (Sadhana) with greater effort.

DD: Atta my girl!

HP: What is an auto-updater?

DD: Supposing, you are asked to compute the area of a rectangle whose length is 4 cm and breadth is 5 cm, you say it is 20 sq. cm. You quote $4 \times 5 = 20$, which holds good only in the instant case. You may generalize it by saying the area of a rectangle is equal to length multiplied by its breadth and mathematically represented by the equation

L (length) X B (breadth) = x (Area) which holds good for all values of L & B. Now, this isn't a new phenomenon. God used this trick while communicating the Gita. He generalized entire knowledge into Gita by using constants, variables, and dependent constants.

So His teachings hold good FOREVER, millennium after millennium without facing obsolesce. This also explains how His teachings are flexible or rigid or both rigid and flexible.

Whenever a generalization is made, there could be a fixed part, a changing part and a part which is flexible but dependent on the changing part for its values.

$$4 \times 5 = 20 \quad \ldots\ldots\ldots\ldots\ldots \text{ is rigid.}$$

$$L \times B = x \quad \ldots\ldots\ldots\ldots\ldots \text{ is flexible}$$

$$\Pi = 22/7 \quad \ldots\ldots\ldots\ldots\ldots \text{ is absolute and rigid.}$$

In the context of Gita,

"I am supreme" is rigid and absolute with reference to God.

"People everywhere follow my path" is flexible.

DD: Gita is complete knowledge, meaning completely useful at all levels. Why do we turn to Gita? Because Gita is a base to understand:

❖ God
- His actions,
- His teachings

❖ Humans
- Themselves
- Their actions and motivation

❖ Ourselves
- And the changes we are undergoing within us.
- Effective monitoring of those changes in a positive direction
- And our problems and deal with it effectively

Listen, here I will tell you Gita fixes to our everyday personal problems.

SN	GODS' SAY	BG-	DERIVATION/ CONCLUSION	REMARKS
1	Controlling of mind is difficult but can be Done with constant practice.	6.35	What is difficult can be achieved by constant practice. The mind is controlled by constant practice. And by renunciation	Solution for overcoming difficulties & mind control and avoidance of after-effects of the uncontrolled mind.
2	We develop attachment on objects we muse upon, which begets desire, non-fulfillment of this desire gives rise to anger, which leads to loss of discrimination, which in turn leads us to ruin.	2.66	Rein in the mind from material objects Muse/ remember God	Remedy for Excessive attachment Anger Indiscriminate sense of faculties

SN	GODS' SAY	BG-	DERIVATION/ CONCLUSION	REMARKS
3	Those, whose mind is lured by the flowery language of Vedas, are ensnared by it and do not go beyond material pursuits.	2.42	Do not be baited nor get carried over with the flowery language of the Vedas. (or Other scriptures/Gurus)	Be wary of smooth and slick talkers who lure you away from your path.
4	Closing the mind to external senses, fixing the gaze between the eyebrows, controlling the incoming and outgoing breath, controlling the mind and senses and reason becomes free from fear desire and anger.	5.28	Remedy for overcoming desire, fear, and anger.	It is very difficult as vouchsafed by Arjuna himself in the Gita, so God gives him an easier alternative

SN	GODS' SAY	BG-	DERIVATION/ CONCLUSION	REMARKS
5	Contact of senses with sense objects produces pleasure or pain. They last as long as the contact with object exists. Remain unaffected. Pleasures derived from contact of senses bring miseries. They have a beginning and an end.	2.14 5.22	Sensory pleasures are superficial and temporary. They end when contact with objects of pleasure/pain is removed. Remain unaffected by such pleasure or pain which is temporary	Remove the object of misery to overcome misery, eschew object of pleasure to preclude discontinuance of pleasure.
6	Lust, anger, and greed are three gateways to hell.	16.22 16.23	Eschew lust, anger, and greed	
7	I am in a state of confusion. I have taken refuge of you, please tell me what is good for me.	2.7	When In the state of confusion, take refuge of God. God knows what is good for us.	Remedy for confusion and faint-heartedness and also to know what is good for us.

SN	GODS' SAY	BG-	DERIVATION/ CONCLUSION	REMARKS
8	Death is certain for one who is born and birth is certain for one who dies. Why lament over the inevitable?	2.27 2.28	Reconcile with or come to grip with the inevitable.	Shows how to deal with loss due to death or any other inevitable event.
9	Perform your duty as per your nature, even if imperfectly. All actions are tainted.	18.47 18.48	Boring job, too hard, results not guaranteed, others will do, etc. are unacceptable.	The performance of duty is mandatory.
10	Do not yield to unmanliness. It is unbecoming of you. Discard your fears and fight.	2.3	Everyone has some special qualities, going against them is unbecoming of that person or the position held or the expectations of persons from him.	Supposing you are honest, don't succumb to the temptation of falsehood, if you are learned, don't give up the pursuit of knowledge for lucre.

SN	GODS' SAY	BG-	DERIVATION/ CONCLUSION	REMARKS
11	Yoga is not for him who is intemperate if work, food, sleep, or recreation. Misery is destroyed for those who are moderate in work, food, sleep, and recreation.	6.16 6.17	Be moderate in all your activities. Avoid extremes.	The formula for overcoming misery, follow the middle path.
12	Desire and wrath are the most sinful and enemies. Control your senses and eschew sinful desires, which destroys knowledge and wisdom	3.37 3.41	Eschew sinful desires. Control wrath and lust.	Don't trade knowledge and wisdom for wrath and lust.

SN	GODS' SAY	BG-	DERIVATION/ CONCLUSION	REMARKS
13	Forgive me as a father his son, a husband his spouse	11.44	It is difficult to forgive others but comparatively easier to forgive those whom we consider our own, say like your son or beloved.	Accept the other person as your own relative, friend, son, or beloved. this makes it easier to forgive them
14	Withdraw senses from their objects. Wisdom is firmly established.	2.58		Method to overcome temptation. Also, a method to convert knowledge to wisdom.

All problems are a physical manifestation of mental worries/problems. BG 1.27 to 1.30 describes symptoms of Arjunas' maladies and Krishna's diagnosis. BG: 1.27 says Arjuna was overwhelmed with pity and stuck by despair. Slokas 28 to 30 describes symptoms of Arjuna as weakening of limbs, dry mouth, body quivering, hair standing and trembling of hands burning of skin inability to stand and clouding of thinking ability. BG: 2.1 attributes it to pity, confusion, and grief. God correctly gauged the mental affliction from physical symptoms and addressed them. God is addressing the problem at the quantum level or at symptomatic level rather than suggesting superficial remedies.

Scientists have come up with amazing discoveries about their field in the Gita, which just goes to show the infinite meanings and capabilities of the Gods' Words.

Scientific foreknowledge in sacred texts is the belief that certain sacred texts document awareness of the natural phenomena that were subsequently discovered/validated by technology and science. Skeptics dismiss these as confirmation bias. Scriptural literalism is the process of aligning scientific observation with scriptural reading, unlike reverse scriptural literalism wherein scriptural reading is aligned with scientific observation.

Hence, even though we take what is stated in Gita as a FACT, and inviolable, our subjective understanding may corrupt the meaning. Hence, as in science, the conclusion reached must be capable of being experienced or must conform to facts established or experienced. In the case of non-experience, it could mean either that the understanding is wrong, or it is waiting to be discovered/found in the future or that you are yet to evolve to a higher level of awareness/consciousness, and not that what is written therein is wrong.

What appears to be a fairy tale of a Pagan Religion, the Great Indian Epics of Vedic Gods and Demons are in fact the most Sublime Psychology of the Higher Self / Consciousness

HP: But what is said by other gods may not be acceptable to other religionists.

DD: Acceptance and applicability or different. Gita is applicable to all. But, it may be acceptable only in a few communities. There is no' my God, his god their god 'etc. All is one. Remove this misconception. God is one but referred by different names. Gita itself says so. Remember the constant and variable concept enunciated during the discussions.

HP: Yes, I recollect. Thanks, daddy. I couldn't correlate and hence the muddle.

DD: Tools for better comprehension of Gita found in Gita itself. Some of them being Juxtapositioning, parsing syllogism and analogous logic.

Everything is present in Gita, if you are serious and have a discerning eye, find them. Let us see what's parsing.
- In a literary sense, it means resolving a sentence into its component parts and describe their syntactic roles.
- Parsing means to make something understandable by splitting a sentence and analyzing its parts.
- **Parsing** is also known as **syntax analysis** and **syntactic analysis.**
- In cybernetics, it means to analyze a string of text into logical syntactic components.
- Parsing means to make something understandable by splitting a sentence and analyzing its parts.
- It is the process of analyzing a string of symbols, either in natural language, computer languages or data structures, conforming to the rules of formal grammar. Traditional sentence parsing is often performed as a method of understanding the exact meaning of a sentence or word or phrase.

You have studied parsing in grammar classes. You have also employed parsing to study the intricacies of the law. We will apply that knowledge in the realm of the Gita. Before that, we will see what Juxtapositioning is.

Juxtaposition is a **literary** technique in which two or more ideas or characters, and their actions are placed side by side for the purpose of developing comparisons and contrasts. **Juxtaposition** is a term for the placement of two things close together for simultaneous examination

Whilst, in literature, this technique is employed for deriving contrasting effect and rhetoric effect, In Gita, this would give a new standpoint and throw new light on our understanding.

A syllogism is a deductive scheme of a formal argument consisting of a major and a minor premise and a conclusion.

It is a subtle but effective form of reasoning. In the Gita, we will employ a syllogism technique to derive the truth by juxta positioning words, slokas, and ideas.

These three tools can be applied in tandem together or in isolation.

Let us take Sloka 18.66 for parsing.

Abandon all varieties of dharma and just surrender exclusively unto me. I shall liberate you from all sinful reactions. Shed your fears. BG: 18.66

Abandon: is pretty straightforward and doesn't require interpretation. Here, God is asking you to abandon all dharma, inconsistent with His words, herein. He is asking you to give up all your dharmic activities, to the exclusion of surrender. Needless to add that when dharmic activities are to be given up, naturally adharmic activities too should be given up.

Perhaps, it would be better to say that abandon all adharmic activities in favor of dharmic activities and all dharmic activities in favor of surrender, as it is a process of evolving.

All Varieties: The word 'varieties' means different hues, shades, and colors of Dharma. It also means multiple dharmas of an individual. To explain, varieties mean under different circumstances and different times. It could be good times, testing times, possible circumstances, impossible circumstances, etc. It could also mean, the same individual in different rights and capacities. Multiple dharmas mean, dharma/duties conflicting with one another to be followed by the same individual simultaneously. Let us take a few examples.

The case of Raja Harishchandra is a good example. He embraced vow of truthfulness and was true to his vow at all times and all circumstances, even in seemingly impossible situations. The Vow of celibacy and protection of the Crown of Hastinapur by Bhishma is another case. It was Bhishma's dharma to be true to his vow.

But he also had a duty of protecting higher dharma by subordinating his lower dharma of truthfulness and protect Draupadi from shameful transgressors.

An individual has many rights in different capacities, say as a son, a father, a King, a husband, a friend, etc. these could overlap or cloud a sense of justice.

Dharma: The word 'Dharma' needs to be understood. There is no single-word translation for dharma in English. The term dharma has a number of meanings.

Basically, it means "what is right".

- Dharma denotes acceptable behavior which is in agreement with duties, rights, laws, conduct, virtues, and "right way of living". It also means "in accordance with the cosmic scheme of things".
- Dharma means the eternal cosmic law of the cosmos, inherent in the very nature of things.
- Dharma differs from individual to individual depending on his Varna.
- Dharma can also mean the maximum good of the maximum people. This is my version and may be taken with a pinch of salt.

What is the right behavior, differs from person to person, time place, and circumstances? What may be considered right for Arjuna, may be considered wrong for Duryodhana.

Now, when God is asking you to abandon all varieties of dharma, He is asking you to give all the dharma as defined above, your version of right behavior, your rights, your concept of duties, conduct, etc. He is asking you to give up your interpretation and action of the right way and follow His say.

Surrender: Means subordinating your dharma and karma and very self to God's words. This is also called Sharanagati, or Atma-samarpan.

What constitutes surrender is explained in the previous verse, BG: 18.65

Always thinking of Him, devotion to Him, Worshipping Him, bowing down to Him constitutes surrender. It will take you to God. God gives His Supreme assurance. This is better understood by knowing who doesn't surrender to Him, namely the foolish, the evil-minded, the illusioned, and the demoniac. BG: 7.15. So, to surrender, it is a pre-requisite to be intelligent, noble-minded and divine in nature, not illusioned.

To me alone:Means, surrender unto Him exclusively. Why surrender only to Him? Isn't God demanding and egoistic? See it from a mundane angle. Can you serve two masters simultaneously? Suppose you surrender to two individuals; you are true to neither of them nor true to yourself nor to your interests. Again, Surrendering to Him confers the highest, i.e., freedom from death and birth cycle. So, when you have the superlative, why pursue second best? It also means surrender to the spirit alone, matter and spirit do not go hand in hand.

Liberate: Liberation is the highest ideal, the ultimate pursuit. It is being with God, in His abode, free from the cycle of birth and death, forever ......

From Sins: This is a pre-requisite to attain to God or His abode. God purges your sin and takes you into His realm.

Don't fear: Means, God holds out guarantee and asks you not to worry about your future outcomes. This is reiterated by God in verse no 9.31, wherein God

God on Memory

- o From Me comes memory as well as forgetfulness. BG: 15.15
- o Anger leads to loss of judgment, which in turn causes loss of memory. When the memory is lost intellect is destroyed and when the intellect is destroyed, one is ruined.BG: 2.63
- o By Your grace, I have regained my memory. BG: 18.73
- o Always remember Me and perform your duty by fighting in the war.BG: 8.7
    - ■ Both you and I have had many births, I remember them all but you have forgotten. BG: 4.5. From above, we can conclude that
    - • God is the source of memory and forgetfulness.
    - • Loss of memory leads to spiritual ruin.
    - • At all times, we should remember God.
    - • Arjuna himself underwent loss of memory and regained it.
    - • This was for the divine purpose of disseminating of Gita to the world at large.

HP: Daddy, one more example in juxtapositioning, please.

DD: Let us see the following slokas.

- • I am the beginning, middle, and end of all beings. BG: 10.20
- • I do not see in you any beginning, middle, or end.BG: 11.16
- • You are without beginning, middle, or end. BG: 11.19

The first sloka is uttered by God and the other two are observations of Arjuna. First, one is the perishable characteristic of all living beings under the superintendence of the Lord. The latter slokas are the characteristics of the Lord described by Arjuna as seen and experienced by him.

DD: Now, I will show you one example, where God directly and overtly contradicted/corrected Arjuna. This is very uncharacteristic of the Lord. He couches His words with euphemisms or remains silent except with non-devotees who do not understand subtleties, like His blunt talks with Duryodhana or Jarasandha.

- • Arjun says that Bhishma and Dronacharya are worthy of worship. BG 2.4.
- • God says you are mourning for them who are not worthy of grief. BG: 2.11
    - ■ What is being implied is that they are unworthy of Grief
    - ■ They may be worthy of worship
    - ■ Side with those who are siding you, they are more worthy.

DD: Let us understand God's advice on grief by juxtapositioning.

- o They are unworthy of grief. BG: 2.11
- o The body is latent, it manifests and again reverts to latency, why grieve? BG: 2.28
- o Birth-death-birth cycle is inevitable, why grieve? BG: 2.27

o   The eternal and imperishable dwells in all bodies, don't grieve. BG: 2.30

o   Great warriors will then think that you aren't fighting due to cowardice and speak ill of your valor. They will look down upon you and speak disparaging words about you. Being used to being respected, their words will bring you grief. BG: 2.34 to 2.36

What do you understand from these?

HP: What is said, namely?

- Don't grieve for unworthy.
- Don't grieve for the temporary or unreal.
- Don't grieve for the inevitable.
- Fight for your reputation

Why fight for your reputation? Because it is a worthy cause. It is permanent. It is real. The reputation does not perish with the body. Hypothetically speaking, during the war, anyone may die, be it Arjuna or Bhishma. Bodies of both are perishable, but their souls live on.

It is inevitable that all beings die. But it is the reputation which follows even after death.

DD: An analogy is a comparison between two objects or systems highlight things that are similar. Analogical reasoning is any type of thinking that relies upon an analogy. Arguments from precedent and analogy are two central forms of reasoning.

The argument from analogy is a special type of inductive reasoning whereby perceived similarities are used as a basis to infer some further similarity that has yet to be observed. Analogical reasoning is one of the most common methods by which human beings attempt to understand/appreciate the subtleties and abstracts of the unknown or unstated from the known and stated.

Analogical arguments have been in use since ancient times and forms part of scientific, philosophical, and legal reasoning. An analogical argument substitutes a complex abstract with a simple one simplifying the understanding. This results in complexities being made easy to grasp and remember.

HP: And Gita uses it?

DD: No. The simple part is present. It is for us to spot it, and apply it appropriately to the complex part. Some analogies are overt, meaning expressly stated by God. They are similes/metaphors. Most of them are covert. Spotting them is like decoding the key which demystifies God's words.

HP: Daddy, please demystify.

DD: Please refer BG: 5.24

asks Arjuna to state on oath that His devotees do not perish. This is also borne out by God's statement in 11.34, stating that He has already killed Bhishma, Drona, Karna, and others in the enemy camp. This is in response to Arjunas' dilemma over the outcome in war, which he expresses in verse 2.6. God is saying, just carry on with the motions of duty faithfully. I will ensure a favorable outcome, without you needing to fear the outcome.

See, we have used juxtapositioning and parsing together. We have put Sloka 18.66 ahead of sloka 18.65. Parsing isn't just breaking sentences.

HP: Daddy, please give another example of parsing.

DD: Okay here is another example of parsing in another sense, not word wise.

I am the ritual, I am the sacrifice, and I am the oblation, I am the medicinal herb, and I am the chant, I am the clarified butter, I am the fire and the act of offering. BG: 9.16
- o God is Mantra
  - Chanting/japa is a sacrifice.
- o God is a Noun.
  - God is an herb.
  - God is fire.
  - God is butter.
- o God is a verb.
  - God is a sacrifice.
  - God is an act of offering.
  - God is chant.

This verse indicates all-pervasiveness/omnipresence of the Lord in
- Living beings.
- Non-living beings
- Actions.

Now, let us take BG: 9.34

God says 'Keep your mind engaged in me, become my devotee, perform actions for my sake, Surrender unto Me. You will certainly come to Me.'

Controlling the mind and senses is a Sattvic act. Being devoted to God is a transcendental act. Performing action is a Rajasic act. Both Rajasic and Sattvic acts, when done in service of God, takes you to Him.

HP: What is cause and effect analysis?

DD: These verses are plain and straight, with no hidden meaning or derived meanings. Just parse and you come to your own conclusions.

You were to tell about Syllogism

DD: Yes, let us now see some examples of juxtapositioning. This automatically creates syllogistic expressions.

About sacrifices.

- Without performing sacrifices, one can never live happily in this life, what to speak of life hereinafter? BG: 4.31
- Among the Yajna (sacrifices), I am Japa sacrifice, the repeated chanting of holy names. BG: 10.25
- I am Gayatri among the Japa. BG: 10.35
    - Perform Japa, which is the best among sacrifices, preferably Gayatri Japa. You will get happiness herein and thereafter.
    - Meaning, don't pursue other sacrifices like animal sacrifices, or other elaborate rituals. Chanting itself will yield the desired results. This is also the prescription modern generation in this Kaliyuga.

Duties and Caste vis-à-vis God

- There is no duty prescribed for me in all the three worlds, nor do I have anything to gain or achieve. Yet, I am engaged in activities. BG:3.22
- The duties of the Brahmins, Kshatriyas, Vaishyas, and Sudras are prescribed according to their aptitude, in accord with their nature. (And not by birth).BG:18.41
- Deluded by gunas, people do not know me as beyond gunas. BG: 7.13
    - Duties are prescribed for all Varna.
    - No duties are prescribed for Krishna.
    - He prescribes duties.
    - Krishna does not belong to any caste or Varna.

Knowledge and Silence

- I shall impart that knowledge, knowing which nothing else remains to be known. BG: 7.2
- Amongst Knowledge, I am knowledge of self. BG: 10.38
- I am the source of Knowledge. BG: 10.4
- Among secrets, I am Silence. BG: 10.38
- I have shared the topmost secret with you BG: 15.20
- I have shared Secret more secret than the secret itself. BG:18.63 &18.64
    - God has imparted complete knowledge in His discourse.
    - Whatever is secret is unsaid (silence).
    - As God's different statements cannot be incompatible with each other, Knowledge which is secret or unsaid is shared by implication.

- One who finds happiness within, is active within, rejoices within, illumined within, and is in perfection. He is liberated attains the Supreme. BG: 5.24
  - This is the original sloka
  - What is meant is that, look inward. You will find all that you seek externally.
- One who finds happiness in Gita, within Gita, rejoices in teachings of Gita is in perfection and attains supreme.
  - This is the derived one.
  - Here, instead of 'within' I have substituted 'within Gita'
  - You needn't look externally for any other scripture. All your answers are found in Gita.

HP: The analogy is not convincing. Though they may be true, it appears contrived to the uninitiated.

DD: Well, how about this example?
- I am the eternal seed of all beings. BG: 7.10
  - By analogous reasoning, of Scriptures, Gita is the seed of all scriptures.
  - This holds good as both by way of analogous reasoning as well as, Gita being non-different from God.

  The seed has the ability to give birth to life. It has the ability to be in hibernation both in the manifest and unmanifest stage. When planted, it springs into life. Gita too sprung back to life after millions of years after grafted by the Lord in Arjunas' heart.

DD:One more example would make it clear.
- For those whose minds are attached to the unmanifest, is troublesome. Worship of the unmanifest is difficult for embodied beings. BG: 12.5
  - Here, humans are embodied beings (Possessing physical bodies), and they cannot visualize abstract unmanifest, due to the dissimilarity.
  - Hence, God asks them to pray to a personal Form. BG: 12.2
  - Dissimilarities make things difficult to grasp
  - Hence the study of the unknown from the known similarities.

Going a step ahead, the Study of Gita is advocated, seeing God in person requires evolving over umpteen number of birth-death cycle. God in Idol form is just visible and may or may not evoke that veneration, love, attachment, etc., because we tend to subconsciously think of it as an idol, except when in deep prayer for a split millisecond. Gita remedies this as it enables us to visualize Him in all His glory and splendor and diverts us from us hankering after His goodies to hankering after Him.

HP: You mean to say analogies are present in Gita and we must just apply to reason?

DD: Yes and No. Overt analogies are present like, say, "O tiger among men" or like "a lamp not flickering in wind" They are straightforward and don't require dwelling on them. The covert ones are difficult. There isn't an analogy, in this case. There are just statements, which we have to take as an analogy and apply in real-life contexts.

They are also applied to interpret or see things in a proper perspective while studying, say Mahabharata or Ramayana or any other Puranas.

HP: Gita is ubiquitous. It is also read by all. Although they all read the same scripture still, how they come to different and wrong conclusions?

DD: That is a risk which we have to be aware of when using   analogous reasoning. They should be appropriate and pragmatic. They may come to different conclusions but need not necessarily be the wrong conclusion unless it is a case of:

o   Mistaking temporary for permanent and vice versa.
  ▪   Money, wealth, fame, etc. pursued even though temporary.
  ▪   Spiritual pursuit relegated to the background, even though permanent.
o   Mistaking path for destination and vice versa.
  ▪   Reaching God is the destination.
  ▪   People mistake God as a means to fulfill desire rather than an end in itself.
  ▪   Mistaking performance of rituals, attiring as prescribed, and other externals as the destination.
  ▪   They are means or paths to God, not an end by itself.
  ▪   Your proficiency in rituals or other acts need not necessarily mean you are nearer to the destination or you are superior to others.
  ▪   Proficiency therein, need not necessarily mean higher plane of evolvement in spirituality.
o   Confusing the path to be the only Path.
  ▪   This thing is built into the psyche of most of the people of all religions.
  •   They believe only their God is ispo facto true and others are worshipping imaginary gods.
  •   Another misconception is that the methodology of worship and rituals performed by them is the only one that produces desired results and all other methods are wrong and does not meet with the approval of God.

- Mistaking knowledge for ignorance and vice versa.
  - The same adamancy in clinging to the view that only their god is God and their mode of worship is acceptable is ignorance. This is mistaken to be knowledge.
  - A person looking at all religions and practices equally is taken to be ignorant.
- Not translating theory into practice and faulting Gita for non-translation.
  - Not practicing what is said in Gita may not yield results. Their lack of application causes failure, which is shifted to Gita.
  - This is a generalization and holds equally good for any scripture.

- Taking literals to be symbolic and vice versa.
  - Assuming the Kurukshetra war to be symbolic of conflict between good and bad in the mind is an example.
  - Taking the commandment, kill your enemies literally, instead of symbolically understanding to mean overcoming enemies
- Assuming general instructions to be specific and specific ones to be general.
  - Assuming all instructions are applicable to all.
  - Reality is there are different instructions to Brahmins, Kshatriyas, Vaisyas, and Sudras, and some instructions for all.
- Mistaking the complete to be a part and part to be a complete whole.
- "Surrender unto me, I will deliver you" is complete by itself.
  - It is a mistake to assume it as just one verse, a part of Gita
- Mistaking Gita to be incomplete, as it is a part of Mahabharata.
- Gita is complete in itself.
- Superimposing our finiteness on Gods' words.
  - Self-evident.
- Pursuing Gita through means like Dwaita, Adwaita, VIsisht Dwaita, Dwaitadwaitaverse, etc. instead of by way of Jnana Yoga, Gyana Yoga, Karma Yoga or Bhakti Yoga.
  - People worship Me with many methods. Some see Me as is non-different from themselves, whilst others see Me as separate from them. Still, others worship Me in the different manifestations of My cosmic form. BG: 9.15
  - God does not endorse a single path. He shows paths and it is we who make a selection. Each path has its flavors and has its own pros and cons.
- Surrendering our thinking faculties to human interpreters, even in face of evident fallacies.
  - God has gifted humans with the ability to think and the ability to discriminate.

- We should put it to use, rather than accepting vested interpretations out forth by some.
- This blind acceptance in the face of contrary evidence is destroying the world.

Spiritual growth is not visible immediately as it is not tangible and extremely slow and may take many lifetimes of birth and death. People stop their practices, thinking that it is not working. It is the faith that prods on.

HP: Does God exist? If Yes, How and proof thereof. Gitas' views on the existence of a god or otherwise.

DD: There is no clear consensus on nature or even the existence of God. But both faith and facts are not a function of consensus and is independent of it.

Monotheists conceive God as the Supreme Being and the principal object of faith. Their concept of God, attributes of omniscience (all-knowing), omnipotence (unlimited power), omnipresence (present everywhere) and existing eternally. These attributes are used either by way of analogy or in a literal sense as distinct properties of God.

This idea is consistent with the teachings of Gita, wherein it is stated that God is Omniscient, omnipresent, omnipotent, and eternal. They believe that God is benevolent.

Some monotheists hold that there is only one God, and may claim that the one true god is worshiped in different religions under different names.

The view that all theists actually worship the same god, whether they know it or not, is especially emphasized in Hinduism and Sikhism. In Islam, God is beyond all comprehension or equal and does not resemble any of his creations in any way.

- Theism holds that God is the creator and sustainer of the universe. God has been conceived as either personal or impersonal. Theism holds that God exists in real sense objectively, and independent of human thought. It holds that God is omnipresent, omnipotent and omnipresent and of course benevolent
- In deism, God is the creator, but not the sustainer, of the universe. Deism holds that God is transcendent. God exists but does not intercede beyond necessity.
- In pantheism, God is the universe itself. It holds that God is the universe and the universe is God.
- In atheism, God is believed not to exist.
- In agnosticism, God is deemed unknown or unknowable.
- Henotheism is the belief and worship of a single god while accepting the possibility of the existence of other gods.

- Panentheism is the belief or doctrine that God is greater than the universe permeates through it.
- Dystheism is a belief, a form of theism which holds that God may not be good as generally perceived and has a streak of malevolence. This belief stems from a need to explain the prevalence of evil.

God has also been conceived as the source of everything and the greatest being conceivable. Many philosophers have come out with theories with arguments for and against the existence of God.

God has also been conceived as being a non-material personal being, the source of all, and the "greatest conceivable existing person".

Non-theist views about God also vary. Some non-theists avoid the concept of God.

Some opine those questions of the supernatural, such as those relating to the existence and nature of God, are non-empirical, and better left to theologians. Nature and physical/material phenomena fall in the domain of science and better left to those proficient in science.

It is argued that the doctrine of a Creator of the Universe is difficult to prove or disprove, within the realm of science, and without invoking any divine beings.

If God exists, how do you describe Him? There are two approaches adopted in Sanatana Dharma or Hinduism.

In Gita, God describes Himself of all His attributes. The entire chapters numbered nine and ten is devoted to His description. Whatever has described by the Lord and heard by Arjuna in those chapters is seen, felt, and experienced by Arjuna. God, Himself concedes that He cannot describe Himself in entirety, but would give principal features.

HP: What about another approach you mentioned?

DD: The approach of God is positive and is full of affirmative sentences like I am the strength of the strong, I am the sun, I am Knowledge, etc. The seers or Acharyas, have attempted to describe God with a non-positive approach (Not necessarily negative). They proceed with the method of elimination like not this, not that, etc.

This is famously called Neti, Neti and is a part of the Vedanta. This very approach is used in proving mathematical theorems. It starts with the supposition 'proposition that it is not true, say like, Suppose $X \neq Y$'.

HP: Why do people have diverse views? What are the reasons for holding that particular view?

DD: The world and its' inhabitants are heterogeneous. That is the way of God. Their beliefs are based and shaped by many things.

Gita has explained that the nature of a person can be either sattva or rajas or tamas and that they are perpetually changing seeking dominance over each other. There is another classification mentioned by God. The divine and the demoniac. These two factors play a dominant role in shaping beliefs and faith. The persons with a predominance of demoniac traits are atheists. The persons with the dominance of the divine are all theists. The divinity may have been manifested or could be latent (waiting to be manifested later).

This interregnum period is the evolution period from man to human to divine. We have seen different beliefs and their names as per the academe. Let us see the views of people around us in daily life.

God doesn't exist, claim the atheists. There are two kinds of Atheists. The atheists who are so by their intrinsic nature, their belief not stemming from any external factors but from their own innate nature.

These have been described by God in the Gita as demoniac nature. God does not manifest to them, who are foolish and unintelligent. Gods' Maya covers their intelligence resulting in their delusion. BG: 7.25.

Grossly foolish persons, lowest among mankind, who are under delusion atheistic nature of demons, do not surrender unto God. BG 7.15

The second category of Atheists bases their belief on not being able to see God because God is unmanifest to them, because of lack of faith or due to association with atheistic persons, or due to holding the belief of their being intellectual or scientific. Their faith in their supposed knowledge/understanding of science or their faith in their alleged intellect, which they consider superior to God science prevents them from surrendering to the superior force and becoming theists. They could have been believers but changed belief after some bad experiences, for which they hold God responsible.

But is God really responsible? Both Yes and No. Gods' puissance works at the quantum level and God works at a universal or encyclopedic level. Cosmic cause and effect are at play at all times. God has enumerated five causes of action and result. They are the Body, the performer, the various senses, the different kinds of endeavor, and the Almighty. BG 18.14. The last-mentioned cause, God is the effect or result of earlier four causes. Thus, God is more of an effect than the cause of our actions.

While this category of atheists may transform to divine by removing the causes of demonic effects, the former category is doomed to depravation with a very remote chance of redemption. God, Himself has said that those persons would be hurtled repeatedly into demoniac wombs in the cycle of death and rebirth, thus failing to reach Him, resulting in their sinking to the abominable type of existence. BG 16.20.

HP: You have explained from the viewpoint of academia. I request you to explain in a practical day-to-day understandable manner.

DD: There have been debates on the subject from time immemorial. Convincing arguments have been advanced for both views. The fact that God exists has been proved conclusively just as it is proved that God doesn't exist.

The proof and the level of proof for concluding the debate offered by one side is not acceptable to the other side and vice versa. There has been subtle atheism without acknowledging that theirs' is atheist philosophy.

HP: What is subtle Atheism?

DD: Hiranyakashipu considered himself God. On the face of it, it appears straight or innocent, but on reading between the lines, you can understand that equating yourself to God is Atheism and this phenomenon existed even during Krita Yuga or Satya Yuga. In Dwapara Yuga, we see that Paundarika Vasudeva, claiming himself to be God.

In the present Kali Yuga, we see hundreds of people claiming themselves to be God and establishing Ashrams, etc.

Then, we have a class of people who believe that all are God in waiting but waiting to discover themselves self which is covered by ignorance. On losing their ignorance, they become full-fledged God.

HP: Are they wrong?

DD: Gita does not term them wrongful. They are at a different level of evolution. **After many births, they will realize** that Vasudeva is all, and worship Him with full fervor. God has Himself said the Bhagavad-gītā (7.19). Vāsudevaḥ sarvam iti, meaning, everything is Vasudeva only. God has not said that you, (meaning Haripriya or me is all), but said that He, Vasudeva is all. **They are yet to undergo many births to realize it but will manage it.**

Gita recognizes that they are different from the demoniac who is always caught in the birth-death cycle being demoted to lower and lower wombs in successive birth, without the possibility of them ever reaching God.

HP: How do you say that they are not wrong even if their views are incorrect?

DD: Hari, they are not incorrect. Because God Himself has informed different perceptions of Him that are held. He has upheld their perceptions at that level.

Otherwise, this passage would not have found its way into Gita. And, when it is said by God in Gita, He has said it. No second opinion, PERIOD.

It is not God in waiting. It is wisdom or knowledge in waiting ……. for the seeker. Rather a wise person, covered by ignorance on the path of wisdom, losing the sheath of ignorance.

Then, why is it not correct (at a higher level)? Because it does not fulfill or adhere to stipulated conditions like
- Concepts of Omniscience
- Concept of Omnipresent
- Concept of Omnipotent.
- Concept of God as a person without any blemish.

God, being who He is, i.e., God & time Himself, cannot have a period of time or place wherein those qualities are in abeyance and require efforts/action for Him to get revived into that state. This is substantiated by Gods' sayings:
o I have no work to perform nor anything to achieve.
  ▪ Meaning, He need not work to remove his covering of ignorance
o I am the strength.
  ▪ Meaning, He is already strong, needs no exercises, etc.
o I am knowledge.
  ▪ Nothing else is remained to be known by Him for which effort is required.
o I am time.
  ▪ He is omniscient, omnipotent, and omnipresent at all times …. At no point in time was He lacking or unaware of Himself.
o I am the giver of knowledge and ignorance.
  ▪ Self-explanatory
o I am the memory… giver of both memory and ignorance and its withdrawal thereof.
  ▪ Meaning He has not forgotten His Omni-qualities, requiring realization or effort
Many other questions would remain unanswered, like
o There would be many Gods.
o Who is superior to whom? Are equal? (God has said that there is none equal or superior to Him)

History has proved the existence of God. Not just in Hinduism but every religion says that God exists.

God has been seen by His messengers, or by prophets, seers, or His devotees and their experiences and descriptions have shared by them.

It is fanciful and pseudo-intellectual to accept that God existed or was recognized based on the history of just 2000+ years ago and onwards but not backward, ignoring earlier history.

God has been appearing on earth since Satya Yuga, under various guises beginning Matsya Avatara to Buddha Avatara.

As per other religionists too, God has appeared before His devotees and left a treasure mine of information.

Some of the widely held beliefs presently prevalent are
- o God doesn't exist.
- o God is Zero.
- o God is Nature.
- o God is some unseen supernatural power.
- o We are all God-in- waiting.
- o God is a chastiser.
- o God is our wish order-fulfilling person.

We have seen about atheists. Now we will examine shunya-vaada or God is Zero Philosophy.

We all know that "Shunya" means zero. Why do people think God is "Shunya"?

The possible reasons could be:
- God is so described in Vishnu Sahasra Nama in Verse 79.
- Mathematics sees it as a 'zero' or "nothingness". Physics views it as a vacuum or perfect absence of matter, meaning non-material i.e., spiritual. This description fits the description of God.
- Ultimately, everything reduces to zero —but God alone remains constant.
- God has no bad qualities; hence he may be addressed as Shunya or bereft of all blemishes.
- Zero acts as a catalyst. The value of any numeral in conjunction with zero increases in value, without Zero itself changing its value. This is akin to changes in our value when associated with God but without God Himself changing His value.
- Before the creation of this Universe, there was nothing…only darkness, no earth, or sky and only God existed. This existence of God in His primal state is called by some as Shunya state.
- Yoga has described Shunya as a state devoid of worldly miseries and God is in a constant state of Yoga Nidra. Yoga Nidra is among the deepest possible states of relaxation while still maintaining full consciousness
- Shunya separates Purusha from Prakriti, where Purusha is Consciousness and Prakriti is matter.
- Buddhists call Shunya a 'fullness' which is empty of the 'self'.

All the descriptions contain an element of truth and the arguments hold merit. But they are part truth. What God Himself has said about Shunya in the Gita? It is a matter to explore and ponder.

God as Nature:
People believe Nature is God. Why so? Probably because Nature provides us with all our basic needs, food, clothing, shelter, recreation, health. It is a natural response that man acknowledges the same. God reiterates His forms as nature in innumerable verses. Without knowing the intricacies behind, we were termed pagans, heathens, idolaters, etc.

Lord Krishna says:

This entire universe is pervaded through My unmanifest form, all beings abide in Me but I do not abide in them. BG 9.4

The Lord says that He is of two kinds of nature viz. Lower nature (*Apara Prakriti*) and Higher Nature (Para Prakriti). BG: 7.5

The lower nature is divided eightfold. They are 1. earth 2. water 3. fire 4.air 5. space 6. mined 7. intellect and 8. egoism. BG: 7.4

So, Is God nature? Yes, but God is not restricted to nature. Is nature God? Well, nature is a partial manifestation of God as it performs some of the functions of God, viz. creation, sustenance, and destruction.

HP: How do you manage to justify everything!?

DD: All justification is already there. I am only drawing from that infinite source of wisdom.

DD: The soul is very subtle and cannot be seen. When the soul acquires a body, it becomes manifest and when the body is lost it is unmanifest. Gita has given the analogy of clothes for the body and drawn a comparison of life and death with changing of clothes. Now, we are at liberty to change, as per our will and wish but changing the body isn't possible independently. We have to get into the body presented by God. But God has freedom of choice of body, whether to change or not to change, etc. Gods' body and soul are the same and non-different. When He is manifest to us, He has form, when He is unmanifest to us He still has form but it isn't visible. God can communicate in both manifest state and unmanifest state. Those who have seen or heard or experienced of His power in His Unmanifest state but not His manifestation, presume that He is a superpower without a body.

See, God Himself has described Himself/soul as immeasurable, inconceivable, subtle, incomprehensible, deluded by Maya, not manifest, beyond material conception, etc. How can atheists know God?

HP: So far, I have understood your explanation partly because of the faith factor. But as a student of law, how do I prove the existence of God beyond a reasonable doubt, when faith factor is lacking?

DD: The believers have a number of arguments in support of the existence of God. Some of them are
- Life comes from life.
  - The test tube baby argument is put forth.
  - They have ignored life is latent in the sperm and egg and manifests after combining.
- Every creation must have a creator.
- Each of the creations is sustained and there must be a sustainer.
- Each creation has a designer.
- Creation and sustenance aren't random and require intelligence. And intelligence presupposes the existence of an intelligent being.
- Each creation has a beginning, middle, and end.
- Nothing can come into existence without a cause.
  - Conveniently ignored by atheists.
- Universe operates on some laws of nature which are constant and unchanging.
- How can laws exist without a lawgiver?
  - Why Nature obeys those laws if lawgiver didn't have authority?

Just as believers have a number of arguments, nonbelievers too have many counter-arguments, some of them being:
- Seeing is believing, Show me God.
- Prove the existence of God in a lab-like environment.
- If God is all omnipotent and compassionate, why suffering? Either He is not all-powerful or He is not compassionate.
- Your worship/prayers haven't yielded any results. Or the results yielded are not due to God but due to human efforts.

One of the obstacles in acceptance of the existence of God is that He isn't seen or visible.

This appears logical but isn't, because there are persons who have seen God, in the ancient past as well and as recently as 1630 AD. Shivaji the Maratha King was presented with the sword by Goddess Tuljabhavani. Tukaram left for higher worlds in spacecraft sent by God.

I will reproduce another argument put forth favoring God's existence. Everybody believes in something invisible. Emotions and thoughts are invisible. Numbers and physical laws are invisible. Borders and constitutional laws are invisible. Love is invisible.

All of us have a rudimentary knowledge of mathematics, basic counting skills. Counting presupposes the existence of numbers. No one has ever seen or experienced a number because numbers are imaginary. We may show two pencils or three books and explain the numbers. Numbers are at best symbols or notation explaining a unit of measurement. Doesn't 1 or 2 exist? Symbols become real when it has utility.

Science *cannot prove the nonexistence* of God, just like the believer may not be able to prove the existence of God. A believer may prove the existence of God by overwhelming circumstantial evidence, but the same is unacceptable to atheistic minded scientists.

A believer makes certain assumptions whilst proceeding to prove God which atheists reject conveniently forgetting that they (Scientists) too, make certain assumptions whilst proving their theories.

Non-existence cannot be proven. Existence can only be proven through direct scientific measurement which must be consistently reproducible by experiment. Meaning after the experiment, we must be able to perceive it through our senses. But non-existence cannot be perceived by senses, nor measurable nor reproducible and hence cannot be proven.

Therefore, ***there is no proof that God doesn't exist*** or for that matter, any other being doesn't exist. This logic or debate could be extended to life after death, reincarnation, life in other planets, etc. If there were proof, the debate would be over.

A notable exception is the proof of impossibility. If the impossibility of the existence of God were proved, then it would be proof of non-existence. Two preconditions must be fulfilled to be held as proved. 1) There shouldn't be any unknowns and 2) A confined system. These exist in mathematics and are simulated by scientists and engineers. In all-natural circumstances, there are always unknowns, and systems are never confined.

People don't accept things blindly. In an age of science, people want empirical proof of everything. Empiricism can prove only material things because empirical proofs are perceived by senses, which are ultimately material. The study of science gives insights into the physical world and answers questions concerning the matter or the physical world. This is the limitation of science, restricted to study of matter, and cannot extend to non-matter or the spirit. God is not physical, but metaphysical, or spiritual. To know Him, you require metaphysical tools.

HP: Your strategy is very good. IT puts them on the back foot.

DD: Which one?

HP: Asking them to prove non-existence.

DD: It isn't a strategy, it is another way of research, or mode of study to get at the truth.

DD: Gita is not subject to interpretation. It should be taken as it is. This is what all Acharyas, seers, etc. do. But the paradox is still they come out with diametrically opposite meanings. For the purposes of explaining we will use the phrase "understanding Gita & studying Gita" to mean interpretation and use the same interchangeably just for this session.

Gita itself has enumerated various ways of studying, which we have seen very briefly earlier.

All the commentators have based their commentaries and purport on semantics or the word of God. They have come out with wonderful insights and great truths. But the absolute truth is all the truths plus something else (Truths+), meaning it is not complete knowledge, only what God has said is complete. This is one of the many differences between God and humans and Gods' works and humans' works. This difference should always exist. So, if God's works are to be interpreted or studied, how do you proceed?

HP: How?

DD: Recollect your high school days when your English teacher would give you sentences and ask you to parse it.

HP: I vaguely remember parsing, but do not remember what exactly we were doing.

DD: Parsing is resolving a sentence into parts and describe their syntactic role. In law school also, we are taught how to parse definitions. Here, each word in a sentence and each phrase in a sentence is examined. Syntactic relates to the rules of language. An example of something **syntactic** is a sentence that uses the correct form of a verb.

Semantics deal with the meaning assigned to the symbols, characters, and words. **Semantics** is the study of meaning in language. It can be applied to entire texts or to single words. For **example**, "complete" and "finish" technically mean the same thing, but students of **semantics** analyze their subtle shades of meaning.

In legalese, a definition is parsed word by word and phrase by phrase, and each element therein is an essential ingredient for that definition to hold true. For example,

The word "Offer" is defined in the Indian contract act, 1872 vide [section 2(a)]: - as under:

When one person signifies to another his willingness to do or to abstain from doing anything, with a view to obtaining the assent of that other person either to such act or to abstinence, he is said to make a proposal.

- When interpreting "Offer" we will parse the definition by splitting the definition as under:
  - When one person signifies to another
    - (It involves 2 persons) A person cannot make an offer unto himself, nor can an offer be made by non-person), communication by way of significance is another requirement.
- his willingness to do or to abstain from doing anything:
  - His willingness to act or abstain from an act is to be signified or communicated. General social communication won't do.
- a view to obtaining the assent of that other person either to such act or to abstinence:
  - The object is to obtain the consent of another person, mere communicating in jest without an object is unacceptable.
- he is said to make a proposal:
  - Such communication or significance is termed a proposal.

The above are the ingredients of an Offer in a legal context.

Now, the legal fraternity would apply both the syntactic and semantic rules in interpreting the definition. In the syntactic sense, the rules of grammar are analyzed and in a semantic sense, the meanings are analyzed.

Similarly, a grammarian and a linguist would analyze the sentence as regards to the meaning of words, within the context of rules of grammar followed, and the subtle differences arising out of use of specific words, or punctuation or form of words used, etc.

Now, this throws up endless possibilities. The same has occurred in the realm of the scriptures, especially in the Gita.

The Acharya, Pandita, saint, seers, etc., all interpret/study Gita on those lines and have offered their commentaries.

The commoners, have accepted the commentaries depending on their affiliation and understood them, according to their individual temperaments and treated their understanding as absolutes.

Now, what is preventing anybody from studying the Gita, independently and arriving at his or her own conclusions within the previously mentioned broad frameworks of parsing, semantics, and syntax? Of course, without disparaging the existing interpretations.

Is Gita to be confined to interpretations of a few individuals? Is Gita so finite so as to be confined to one particular mold? Is Gita stagnant? If yes, why is it described otherwise in Gita itself?

Within the syntactic and semantic model, there could be an "n" number of interpretations. If you explore the conceptual model, it throws up endless and overwhelming possibilities, the way Infinite really exists.

The best interpretation is to interpret literally. There is something called scriptural literalism which means the process of aligning scientific observation with scriptural reading.

The reverse process is to align scriptures with scientific observations. We should use both techniques. Changes cannot be made into what God has said, because it is unchanging and inviolable, so alternative methods of interpretation should be taken until reconciliation is affected.

Before proceeding further, the level of comprehension of the readers to be considered. What is this level of comprehension? Why take it into account? Why not take it as it is?

Because each individual's capability and capacity vary as does the level of comprehension. Gitas' teachings are interpreted at different levels of comprehension by each reader/sadhaka/devotee. Academia has broadly identified five levels of comprehension. They are

- Lexical comprehension.
- Literal comprehension.
- Interpretive /Inferential comprehension.
- Applied comprehension.
- Affective comprehension.

When comprehension levels are different, interpretations too would be different and varied. They may be correct at that particular level only. For example, the response of a primary school student and a college student for the same query would be different. What is 3-7 (three minus seven) elicits 'Not possible' response of a primary student and an advanced student would reply -4(Minus four). Both are correct at their level.

Now, to be able to understand in a more comprehensive manner, we should also be aware of, if not full knowledge of literary devices used in the Gita and its' effects.

When interpretation is being undertaken, we must be careful to identify the literary devices used in the context. Literary students identify devices, and understand the passage and the context and also analyze the devices employed and its fallout thereof.

This simple technique is not used in the realm of scriptures, except by seers and commentators, resulting in chaos to the extent of doubting the scriptures itself.

A student of the Gita should be able to identify the nuances of the language and the literary devices employed. And interpret it accordingly such that it makes sense and relevant in the prevalent times and context. And in line with acceptance by the scientific community. It should not contradict the scientific view and largely able to perceive/experience what has been interpreted.

- Syllogism: is a form of logical reasoning that joins two or more statements are made and a logical conclusion is derived. It is a form of deductive reasoning.
  - Gita is replete with derivative logic. In the Gita, two or more premises may or may not occur together or in proximity. It is left to the ingenuity of the reader to bring them together so as to derive a conclusion.
  - Examples of syllogism in the Gita.
    - I shall impart to you this confidential knowledge, knowing which you shall be relieved from material miseries. BG: 9.1
    - God, why is one impelled to sinful acts forcefully, even when unwilling BG:3.36
    - INFERENCE: Mere acquisition of knowledge won't liberate you and take you to your destination. You have to practice and implement what you have learned.
  - Self-control, austerity, purity, tolerance, honesty, wisdom, knowledge, and religiousness-these are duties of Brahmanas as per their nature. BG: 18.42
  - Heroism, power, determination, resourcefulness, courage in battle, generosity, and leadership are the duties of Kshatriyas born of their nature. BG: 18.43
  - Farming, cattle raising, and business are duties of vaishyas, and labor and service to others are the duties of sudras, born of their nature. BG: 18.44
  - There is no duty, prescribed for Me within all the three planetary systems, yet I am engaged in work. BG:3.22
  - INFERENCE:God has no caste and beyond designations of caste.
- Amongst the gunas, sometimes sattva dominates rajas and tamas, sometimes tamas dominates rajas and sattva and other times rajas dominates sattva and tamas. BG: 14.10
- The three gunas, Sattva, rajas, or tamas are manifested by my energy. They are in me, but I am beyond them. BG: 7.12
- INFERENCE: God is unchangeable, unlike the gunas.
  - Among the secrets, I am silence BG: 10.38
  - I shall tell you this knowing which nothing else remains to be known. BG: 2.7
  - When adharma becomes rampant, women of the family become corrupt and manes will be deprived of offerings of rice balls. BG: 1.40
  - I have heard that those who destroy family traditions dwell always in hell. BG: 1.43
    - INFERENCE: Krishna has answered Arjuna with pregnant silence. He hasn't answered it subsequently, unlike other queries of Arjuna which were answered subsequently, in any of the 700

verses. Offering of rice balls to manes, and rotting in hell as a consequence of non-offering of rice balls is untenable.

- Syntax: In grammar, the arrangement of words as elements in a sentence to show their relationship.
- Understatement: Is a way of speaking which minimizes the significance of something. When using an understatement, a speaker or writer often employs restraint in describing the situation at hand.
  - Entire Gita is a statement neither hyperbole nor understated, but the beauty is it is undervalued by half the populace being unaware of its significance.
- SILENCE AS A LITERARY DEVICE: Sometimes moments of silence become more significant and express much more than what is spelled out.
- Strategically placed silences and omissions is an effective literary device 'In every story there is a silence, some word unspoken. Until we have understood the unspoken, we cannot claim to have understood the heart of the story'. Silence is also used as total communication, in reference to nonverbal communication and spiritual connection.
  - Has not God said, "Among the secrets, I am silence" BG: 10.38?

Hari, that is a brief overview of the syllogism as a literary device. We have to identify what device employed and interpret it in light of the device employed.

The reader need not analyze afresh. A note of caution. These are literary standards in the English language and not Sanskrit. Many more secrets are hidden but poor me must pay a price for not learning the language.

HP: Many things stated by you earlier hasn't been clarified by you.

DD: Such as?

HP: Speaking in silence or speaking through silence etc.

DD: Gita is communication. Language is only one of the many means of communication. Gita has many non-language communications.

There are three basic **types of communication.**
- Verbal **communication**, in which you listen to a person to understand their meaning.
- Written **communication**, in which you read their meaning.
- Nonverbal **communication**, in which you observe a person and deduce the meaning.

Gita too has nonverbal communication as has Mahabharata. How Mahabharata is relevant?

Well, Gita is a part of Mahabharata is an oft-quoted answer. In Mahabharata, when fighting with Jarasandha, Krishna runs away from the battlefield. A novice would see it as an act of cowardice.

Gita tells us how to interpret Gods' actions, words, pastimes, etc. We can interpret Gods running away correctly in the light of the Gita.

HP: What about non-verbal communication in the Gita?

DD: Read Chapter 1.28 to 1.30.

HP: She reads out to herself ....

DD: Isn't Arjunas' body language communicating something?

HP: Yes, it communicates confusion and compassion.

DD: Parsing a literary work wrongly of say, Shakespeare, will harm you a little, but parsing Gita wrongly would give wrong conclusions and create havoc with unforeseen consequences.

DD: There is no religion called Hinduism, only a way of life (Sanatana Dharma) being followed by people of Bharata Varsha (India). People are heterogeneous and our land always enjoyed the freedom to pursue or follow whatever pleases them. Thus, we have three types of people
   o Monotheism, who believes in one God, who is supreme. Others are demigods or administrators of various departments or regions under the control of the Supreme God. Other religionists follow only one God without belief in any administrators etc.
   o Polytheists believe in many gods.
   o Atheists who do not believe in any God.
   o Advaitins who believe that they themselves evolve from human to GOD.

All these find mention in the Gita, though indirectly.

God preaching Gita is the greatest Yajna.

HP: How is it the greatest Yajna?

DD: God has no duties to perform, nor has He anything to be accomplished which He has already not accomplished.

 He wasn't happy or unhappy to be on earth nor was He unhappy in His original abode, Golok Dham. Yet He came here and enacted His pastimes with the welfare of us mortals in mind. If these two acts aren't Yajna, what else is Yajna?

HP: What is time as per Gita? God says He is the time in the form of death.

DD: That is just one facet of time. There are many more dimensions to time.

HP: What are they?

DD: In Gita, the word 'time' has been used at different places to mean different things. The sum of all those plus something else is time. Simply put, Time means the perspective in context. Everything should be viewed from the perspective of context. The major ingredients of context are time, space or place, and of course, other existing circumstances then prevalent.

HP: I couldn't understand, please explain daddy.

DD: Let us understand it from a mundane perspective, and apply it to the realm of Gita.

HP: Sure, starts coughing. This is accompanied by hiccups.

Mom shouts, go drink water.

DD: Gets up and rushes back with a cup of water and gives it to HP. She drinks it and after a few minutes, is relieved of the irritation in the throat.

HP: Tell me about the mundane viewpoint.

DD: Just now, mom advised to drink water and you drank. What do you learn from it?

HP: If you have hiccups or cough, drink water.

DD: Laughs, and if you feel thirsty?

HP: I will drink water.

DD: That analysis is superficial, in the present context. Let us dissect it to get at the truth.

- Mom asked you to drink water.
  o You obeyed her. You drank water.
- You stopped drinking water.
  o You didn't wait for the mother to ask you to stop drinking water.
- It relieved you of cough and hiccups.

When you were asked to drink water, it is implied that you drink it till such time you are quenched of your thirst or satisfied. When you are asked to sleep, it doesn't mean you keep sleeping until you are asked to wake up. Subsequent actions to be performed are implied. Here, the context is your getting a cough.

The call to action is not limited to drinking water, but stop drinking after the need is satisfied. When you are asked to do something, it holds good only till such time it is accomplished or as long as it is accomplishable, and is to be understood as such. In the present instant, that advice was directed to you only, not to me. But it is a useful remedy to whosoever gets hiccups. All these together form the circumstances. Your perspective is determined by circumstances and context. It is something like in economics, we have a Latin maxim 'Ceteris paribus' meaning, other things being constant.

Now, applying it to Gita, or to any other scriptures, people should not ignore the underlying circumstances or the context. Absolute surrender unto Him or His Words is laudable and difficult for an undisciplined and persons without faith. Factoring circumstances and context should not be taken as disloyalty or unfaithful. Nor should ignoring of the same be taken to be a sign of Devout or Faithful and beloved of God. Both the mistakes tantamounts to ignoring or superseding His words and has undesirable consequences.

HP: Oh, I see it now. Why can't we see God? I want a convincing reply. Everybody just says that we are not qualified and draw a comparison of attempting to meet High dignitaries like Prime Minister etc.

DD: They are right, but let us see Gods' perspective on the question as mentioned in the Gita.

- God is an Omniscient, ancient person, the Controller, subtler than the subtlest, of an inconceivable divine form. He is beyond all darkness of ignorance. BG 8.9
  o Controller implies under His control, whether He chooses to allow us to see Him or not.
  o Being subtle, He cannot be seen as we are not equipped to see subtle things. Subtle mundane things may be felt or may be seen with proper implements, but to see subtle God requires special spiritual merit.
  o His form, being divine is inconceivable.
- When not conceivable, how can you see unless specially qualified?
- The ignorant do not perceive the soul as it resides in the body, and as it enjoys sense objects. BG: 15.10
  o When our own soul is not being perceived by the majority, how can the super soul be seen or perceived without requisite spiritual merit?

HP: Yes, this appears more convincing. I recollect you saying that Gita is non-different from God. Is it? If so, how?

DD: It is like this. Gita is a personification of God. God is an incarnation of the Gita. They are inseparable. Hence, it is said that Gita is not different from God. Hence the words God, Git, and Krishna are used interchangeably.

HP: God says everything exists because I exist. If I don't exist, nothing can exist. BG: 10.39. How is it so?

DD: God says that all living beings are My eternal fragmental parts. So, all souls are a part of His whole.

You will understand this better with an analogy. Recall your grammar classes of school days. There are two types of alphabets, vowels, and consonants.

Most of the language has vowels and consonants. Vowels and consonants are defined variedly. But the crux of determining if a letter is a consonant or a vowel is a basic speech sound that can independently form a syllable. A consonant is a basic speech sound that can be combined with a vowel to form a sound syllable. See, the vowel has an independent existence, whereas a consonant cannot form a sound syllable without a vowel. Each consonant has a vowel component within itself. You test it.

HP mentally recalls a few letters and observes within herself that B, C, and D have E ending within itself F has A as the beginning. G has E ending and so on.

HP: Yes, daddy, you are right. Vowels can exist independently unlike consonants, just like the super soul exists independently unlike an individual soul. Isn't it another analogous reasoning?

DD: My daughter is catching on fast.

HP: But what is Brahma Gyan or Brahma Vidya? I have heard that it is the highest knowledge, but never come across any book titled Brahma Gyan.

DD: Gita itself is Brahma Gyan.

HP: Any reference?

DD: Lawyer daughter! You read Bhagwad Gita of Gita press. At the end of each chapter, they have the following sloka

ॐ तत्सदिति श्रीमद्भगवद्गीतासूपनिषत्सु ब्रह्मविद्यायां योगशास्त्रे श्रीकृष्णार्जुनसंवादेऽर्जुनविषादयोगो नाम प्रथमोऽध्याय: ॥ १ ॥

Thus, in the Upaniṣad sung by the Lord, the Science of Brahma, the scripture of Yoga, the dialogue between Śrī Kṛṣṇa and Arjuna, ends the first chapter entitled "The Yoga of Dejection of Arjuna."

This is also stated in The Gita of Swami Sivananda also.

Note the word Brahma Vidya, and in translation, the "Science of Brahma"

HP: I see.

DD: Shall we break for now?

HP: Of course, it was tiring, I understand.

They dispersed. The next day, the phone rang and Priya picked up her phone. IT was from her friend Christina.

Christina: Good morning, how is everything?

HP: Fine, she briefly told her about the discussion with her father.

She also told her about her visit to the temple. Christina asked for a description.

HP replied:

Navaratri is the festival of Goddess Durga, the celebration of Good over Evil. During Navaratri Goddess is worshipped in her nine forms.

The women across the country celebrate the nine forms of Durga, wearing different colors of dresses representing the different qualities of the Goddess. The Dress color codes for each day during the Navaratri, a trend set by Goddess Mahalaxmi Herself.

HP: What did you do?

Christina: Nothing special. I visited the professor.

HP: What transpired there?

CH: He was interested in knowing my background, and how I came to be interested in Gita.

HP: Please tell in detail.

CH: Here we go. I visited the professor in his office.

SUMMARY OF MEETING WITH THE PROFESSOR

CH: Good morning, sir.

Prof: Good morning, Christina, make yourself at home. How do you find the environment here?

CH: Warm and friendly atmosphere.

Prof: I see that you have joined the Gita group. Also, your entire semester under the exchange program is devoted to Gita.

CH: Yes sir.

Prof: What has drawn you to Gita to the extent of majoring in Gita and visiting the land of the Gita?

CH: Sir, I don't know. I was irresistibly drawn to it. Maybe, it was love at first sight.

Prof: What do your parents do?

CH: Father is a pastor at the local church and mother runs a home for destitute children.

Prof: Oh, I get it. For one who has strived in the path of Yoga, but couldn't complete it due to death, is reborn in a pious family, where he practices the same with greater determination and faith from the point where it was discontinued.

CH: Sir that is form BG 6.41. Am I correct?

Prof: Very nice. I appreciate your dedication and perseverance.

CH: Sir, how can a Christian pastor's daughter be involved in the yoga of Gita?

Prof: Why do you entertain doubts? It is not said in Gita that you would be born in a Hindu family, besides being pious or God loving is not the prerogative of a Hindu or a Jew or a Jain. God cannot be appropriated by any single person or religion. These are human misconceptions and act as obstacles to God-realization.

CH: Sir, you are Catholic in outlook.

Prof: Look, you got it. I am described by you as a Catholic in outlook, the descriptions fit though I am not a Catholic, but a Hindu. Do you see the universality of God in action?

CH: You put things nicely.

Prof: By the way, what was the purpose of your visit?

CH: There are many variants of Gita. I would like to know about the different flavors and the one which is authentic. I am studying Gita, not for academic accomplishments but for inner fulfillment.

Prof: It is like this.

SAMPRADAYA	BRAHMA SAMPRADAYA	LAKSHMI SAMPRADAYA	SIVA SAMPRADAYA	KUMARA SAMPRADAYA
ALSO CALLED	Madhva Sampradaya	Ramanuja Sampradaya Sri Sampradaya Srivaisnava Sampradaya	Rudra Sampradaya Visnuswami Sampradaya Vallabha Sampradaya	(From Sanaka Kumara) Nimbarka Sampradaya Nimbaditya Sampradaya Sanakadi Sampradaya
ACARYAS	Madhvacarya, Lord Caitanya	Ramanujacarya	Visnusvami, Vallabhacarya	Nimbarka
COMMENTARIES ON VEDANTA	Purnaprajna-bhasya	Sri-bhasya	Sarvajna-bhasya	Parijata-saurabha-bhasya
TATTVA	Madhvacarya: suddha-dvaita-vada (purified dualism) Lord Caitanya: Acintya-bhedabheda-tattva (inconceivable oneness and difference)	Visistadvaita-vada (specific monism)	Suddhadvaita-vada (purified monism)	Dvaitadvaita-vada (Monism and dualism)

1. Dwaita means Your Soul is different from God's Soul, God has created a totally different you, propounded by Madhvacharya.
2. Adwaita that is opposite of Dwaita
3. Only God soul exists all other things are Illusion. There is only one entity and hence called monism. Propounded by Shankaracharya.
4. Dwait0adwaita means "Dwaita+ Adwaita" God has transformed himself in your soul he is no more The God. Adwaita says you are illusion god only truth. In a way, there is one entity but two in existence. Propounded by Nimbarkacharya.
5. Visishtadwaita it is Vishishta+Adwaita supports qualified monism, Adwaita says God is only truth Visishtadwaita says we are a part of supreme soul, so conditional Adwaita. Propounded by Ramanujacharya.
6. Shuddhadwaita it is shuddha+Adwaita means pure monism. Here the world is not an illusion (as per Adwaita world is an illusion) God is the creator he has created all of us, he has created truth, "You are the God". Propounded by Vallabhacharya.
    *   Dwaita: You and God always separate
    *   Visishtadwaita: You are part of God
    *   Adwaita: You are God.

Each sampradaya has its own distinct commentaries on Vedanta. Sri Madhvacharya propagates suddha-dvaita or pure dualism. Madhvacharya and all other authorities accept them as the authoritative histories of the world. The Puranas are not in chronological order. The incidents mentioned in the Puranas are actual histories of bygone ages. Srimad-Bhagavatam being the essence of all Puranas is the Maha Purana.

"Madhvacharya Dwaita philosophy.

It establishes the status of Vishnu as Supreme Being. It emphasizes that there are two categories of realities, The Independent, and the dependent. According to Dwaita tenets, the aim of philosophy is to realize the difference between the Independent Reality (GOD) and the dependent realities (Jiva's & matter).

*   Jiva-Eshvara bheda
    o   The difference between the Supreme Being and the Individual Soul {God and Living things}
*   Jada-Eshvara bheda
*   The difference between the Supreme Being and the Non-Living Matter {God and Things}
*   Jiva-Jiva bheda
    o   The difference between the two individual Souls. Within the category of trees, there are apple trees and there are lemon trees. If this has been misinterpreted for division in caste then it is NOT the mistake of the Acharya. It may be the difference

between two individuals of the same family like two brothers exhibiting different characters even though born from the same parents, for example, Ravana & Vibhishana.

- Jada-Jiva-bheda

The difference between Individual Soul and Non-Living Matter There is the category of trees and there is the category of hills. Trees and Hills belong to different categories.

- Jada- Jada-bheda
  - o The difference between Non-Living Matter. Within the category of books, there are religious books and there are fiction books on a shelf.

This scheme of pancabheda is not illusory - as it is cognized, maintained and controlled by the Supreme Lord, for there can be no illusions for God.

Visishtadwaita: The Philosophy of Sri Vaishnavism

Visishtadwaita proposes that ultimate Reality, although one, is not absolute, without any differentiation. They admit the reality of the world and the plurality of souls within this world. The world appears real because it is real and not due to some form of illusion or Maya.

Visishtadwaita teaches three fundamental categories of Reality namely God, Soul, and Matter. Though there is an absolute difference between God and the other two categories of Reality, and for that matter between soul and matter, ultimate Reality is considered one because the soul is a part of God.

"Nimbarka's philosophical position is known as 'Dwaita-Adwaita' or 'Bheda-bheda'. The categories of existence, according to him, are three, i.e., 'chit', 'achit', and 'Eshwara'.

Chit and achit are different from Eshwara, in the sense that they have attributes and capacities, which are different from those of Eshwara. Eshwara is independent and exists by Himself, while chit and achit have existence dependent upon Him. At the same time, chit and achit are not different from Eshwara, because they cannot exist independently of Him. The difference means a kind of existence that is separate but dependent, while non-difference means the impossibility of independent existence. Thus, Nimbarka equally emphasizes both difference and non-difference, as against Ramanuja, who makes difference subordinate to non-difference.

For Nimbarka the highest object of worship is Krishna and his consort Radha, attended by thousands of Gopis, or cowherds of the celestial Vrindavan. Devotion according to Nimbarka consists of 'Prapatti', or self-surrender.

Shankaracharya's Advaita:

The Advaita Vedanta focuses on the following basic concepts:

Brahman, atman, Vidya (knowledge), Avidya (ignorance), Maya, Karma, and moksha.

- Brahman is the Ultimate, Supreme Reality. Brahman is eternal. It is indefinable. Brahman can be considered as Pure Consciousness.
- Atman is the inmost Self or Spirit of man. Both Brahman and Atman are not different realities. They are identical. For practical purposes, they are referred to separately, which they are not.
- They are two different 'labels' for one and the same reality behind all matter and all beings of the universe.
- Avidya (ignorance) means not only an absence of knowledge but also erroneous knowledge. A man trapped in Avidya does not know what is real and thinks that the appearances are real. He equates his existence with the physical body. Under the influence of Maya and Avidya, he dissociates himself from the Ultimate Reality.
- When the man acquires knowledge, he realizes that he is one with supreme or Brahman.
- Moksha is freedom from the bondage of ignorance, passions, karma, and avidya. This is Moksha (kaivalya) or liberation. Moksha is to be attained here and now during this life span only.

Rudra Sampradaya:

Origin of Rudra Sampradaya is traced to the Hindu deity Shiva, known as Rudra, who passed on the knowledge imparted to him by Lord Vishnu to mankind. Vaishnavism considers Lord Shiva as the first and foremost of Vaishnavas or follower of Lord Vishnu.

Rudra sampradaya is divided into two main types: Vishnuswamis, or followers of Vishnuswami and the Vallabhas founded by Vallabha. This sect follows the philosophy of Shuddhadwaita or pure monism to Krishna. The youthful Krishna is worshipped alone or with his consort Radha. The infant Krishna is worshipped by the sampradaya.

Shri Vishnuswami is the founder-Acharya of the Rudra Sampradaya. Vallabhacharya is another famous Acharya of Rudra sampradaya, albeit with differences from teachings of Vishnuswami.

Vallabhacharya accepts four works as authority:
1) The Vedas.
2) Bhagavad- Gita.
3) Vedanta-sutra.
4) Srimad-Bhagavatam.

The order of these works is based on the fact that the doubts in each preceding work are removed by the succeeding one. The doubts in the Vedas are to be removed by the light of the Gita; those in the Gita in the light of the Vedanta-sutra; those in the Vedanta-sutra in the Srimad-Bhagavatam.

- The Lord was alone, without a second, at the beginning of a cycle. He desired to be many for the sake of pleasure and as he desired millions of souls came instantaneously out of Akṣhara Brahman like sparks from a fire. The soul is an amsha or part of Brahman and is eternal.

- With a view to enjoying Lila, the Lord suppressed the element Ananda in the soul, who consequently became subject to bondage and wrong knowledge. The Lord, in order to bring about variety which is essential for the sake of pleasure, makes the soul varied in nature.

c) The Lord has created the universe out of His own self for the sake of Lila without suffering any change whatsoever and is related to it as the spider is to its web. For the sake of diversity, the Lord makes the souls subject to His power of avidya which is the root cause of the ideas of "I" and "mine".

d) Samsara, which is solely made up of ahamkara (I-ness or egoism) and Mamata (my-ness or the idea of pleasure), has to be destroyed by means of knowledge, devotion, etc.

These are the beliefs of different schools of thought. There are many other different philosophies but are only a variant of these four.

Prof: Many terms may appear confusing, more so because the same words are used to mean different things at different times and places and persons and also by the same persons in different contexts. You may take Brahman to mean soul, super soul, God or Paramatma or even Brahman. You may understand Jiva as a living entity and Moksha as Brahman, the abode of God, or a liberated state of mind. Jada means non-living things. Eshwara means controller, i.e., the God. Bheda means differences. Samsara means the birth-death cycle. This is the gist. Some of it may remain unintelligible to you now. You will understand the same on your own at the appropriate time.

CH: Sir, you have told me about their philosophy, but not their views on Gita.

Prof: Each of the school of thought interprets Gita in a manner to be in tune with their tenets and supports their philosophy.

End of meeting with Professor *******************

HP: Nice. I will be leaving by noon and be back by tomorrow. See you tomorrow.

CH: Looking forward to being with you. Bye.

Hari completed her lunch and packed her things. She bid goodbye to her dad and Mom.

DD: Anything more?

HP: Visit me at Tirupati.

Her father just smiled in response. He was feeling sad that they had to part ways.

Her father hugged her and placed an envelope in her hand. It contained five "Two-thousand-rupee notes". He excused himself saying that he has preoccupations in office and cannot come to the station to see her off the next day.She ran into her room and presented her dad with a packet, which contained the tee she had painted. Her dad opened it and was overwhelmed. It was just what he wanted but couldn't find it anywhere.

He thanked Hari and placed another packet in her hand. Hari opened and saw a Gift Card. It was charged with fifty-five thousand five hundred fifty-five rupees. Hari was taken aback. Her father told her that it would finance their proposed trip to Dwarka and Kurukshetra. Hari gave him a peck on his cheek and walked towards the waiting cab. They both made her promise to call them once she reached her campus. Hari sat back in the train looking forward to meeting her friend in Tirupati.

BOOK - II

vadah pravadatam aham

वाद : प्रवदतामहम् || *BG: 10.32*

Among debate, I am the right type of reasoning

9. HOW IT ALL BEGAN

The year 2014

The meeting of the Gita group was scheduled at 18-00 that evening. Christina dragged along Haripriya to the venue saying that if she wasn't interested in participating, at least be a passive spectator. Haripriya reluctantly joined her friend. The discussion had just started.

The discussion was going along the following lines.

Someone was quoting

तद्विद्धि प्रणिपातेन परिप्रश्नेन सेवया ।

उपदेक्ष्यन्ति ते ज्ञानं ज्ञानिनस्तत्त्वदर्शिनः ॥ 4.34॥

तद् viddhi praṇipātena
paripraśnena sevayā
upadekṣyanti te jñānam
jñāninas tattva-darśinaḥ

Learn the truth by approaching a spiritual master inquiring from him submissively and by rendering service unto him. They will impart knowledge to you. BG-4-34

"When in doubt, ask Guru, render service unto him. He will teach you."

Yes, I always ask my Guru, he cleared my doubts. He belongs to the X parampara. We follow that parampara.

- o My Guru is the best, we follow Y parampara.
- o I follow Z parampara in accordance with the advice of our Guru.
- o I like Swami Vivekananda's, Bhagavad Gita. That is the truth.
- o Why not Mahatma Gandhi's Gita, It is so simple.
- o No, your choice is wrong. Only what my Guru spoke is correct.
- o All of you are wrong.
- o How can you claim supremacy of your Guru?
- o Has not My Guru defeated your Guru by refuting the claims of your Guru?The priests from my parampara can be found in all temples across the country, which proves that we are right and hence

o the divine task is assigned to our folks. You can check in any temple for yourself and find that our priests are in charge.

o Don't brag. Your Guru ran away in mortal fear and yet you follow him.

o Your Guru was sent to prison for embezzlement, what have you to say about the same?

o Wasn't your Guru excommunicated? Still, you find fault with us.

o Don't think we don't know about the sexcapades of your Guru.

o My Guru was most ancient, first to write a commentary, hence treated as original and correct.

o My Guru appeared subsequently and corrected the errors in the works of your Guru. Hence his version is to be preferred.

Such discussions were in progress. The decibel levels also had reached a crescendo. As Christina was considered impartial, she is an American without any stakes in their arguments, they asked her to determine as to who is correct. Christina was at a loss as to what to do. She nodded at Haripriya, indicating that she takes it upon herself to reply, to which she agreed.

Haripriya asked them to discuss Gita rather than the merits of the Guru and their leanings. But they said that that was what they were doing when some persons claimed that their viewpoint is the only truth and all other teachings contrary to their view is an untruth.

The same claim was made by everybody. Haripriya suggested that they turn to Gita and rely more on Gita than on the words/teachings of their respective Guru's. They claimed that Gita is very complicated and not intelligible to ordinary mortals and that they must approach a bonafide Guru, but everyone was claiming that their master was the only bonafide Guru. Further, they said that they were discussing Gita 4-34 as suggested by Haripriya but unable to arrive at a consensus. Haripriya asked them that if they read Vedas, which was the repository of all knowledge and all of them were followers of Vedic dharma? They replied that Veda is very complicated and the present Yuga was damned with people full of ignorance, weak, ill-health and quarrelsome. Maharishi Vedavyasa, having foreseen the inability of future inhabitants to understand Vedas, He out of immense compassion, wrote the Puranas and to further make it easy, for the most degraded persons in Kali Yuga, who would not even comprehend Puranas, wrote Mahabharata and Ramayana, wherein all the essence of the Vedas are found and which is easily intelligible to them. Hence, they have not ventured to study Vedas. Haripriya reasoned that as Gita is a part of Mahabharata and they should be able to understand the same. Similarly, as Bhagavata was a Purana and Uddhava Gita was a part of it, they should be able to understand the same without any difficulty.

The students countered that they had understood it correctly all right, but their co-students did not understand it and were persuading others to follow their incorrect beliefs without substantiating or establishing the correctness of their beliefs.

Haripriya reiterated that to resolve the issue and proceed further in the quest of knowledge, they may either go to the next verse or accept Gita, a personification of the Lord Himself as Guru and give primacy to the words of Gita rather than their personal Guru. What your Guru teaches, Gita too can teach but not vice versa.

In the Mundane world too, haven't we seen that what a subordinate staff can do, his supervisor can do and what the supervisor can do his manager can do and what the manager can do, his boss can do but the reverse is not the case. TO buttress her claim, she quoted

Krishnam Vande Jagadguru, (Krishna is the one and only Guru of all Guru).

All the fellow students were undecided. She also said that only the childish say that my path is different from yours and, only mine is correct and the other path is incorrect, because, the fruits of all paths of God are the same. Hasn't God Himself said in BG: 5.4 that as far as the fruits are concerned, both Sankhya yoga and Karma yoga are the same? They were in a state of anger and unable to see the via media offered to overcome the impasse. The leader among them was fuming and shouted.

Haripriya, you don't know Sanskrit. You are not competent to comment on Gita. You have not come through the tutelage of any Guru. You don't belong to any parampara or the authorized disciplic succession either by birth or by discipleship. Your comments are not authorized/bonafide and cannot be accepted as correct.

Her other friend shouted you are like a blind person who not only falls in a ditch but misguide along others to doom by taking them on your path. Your say is just ranting and speculative and does not hold water. There were murmurs all around.

Most of the students assembled seem to agree with the leader though not with her comments or the way it was put across. Hadn't Haripriya contradicted and belittled their spiritual masters? If they do not defend their spiritual beliefs, who will do so was the psyche in their minds. A few were making conciliatory gestures and asking Haripriya to see the truth in what was told. Both Haripriya and Christina were surprised at the sudden turn of events.

All persons who were so divided just a few moments ago and held contrary opinions had united to fight against Haripriya.

Haripriya was shocked and hurt that her friends had turned against her. Tears welled up in her. Her own friends against her, and that too the ones whom she had tried to help and unite. She couldn't take it and said, I will not respond and sat down.

Christina asked the dejected Haripriya not to give up. She further told her that she would ensure that Haripriya had a level playing field and that she should proceed. She rose and called for the attention of all. She could understand that an opinion given by anybody should have the force of authority. She asked them if they were interested in sorting the matter out. They replied in affirmative and asked her to decide. How about organizing a moot court with all the trappings of a real court wherein all can present their views just like in a debate but with the semi-formal atmosphere of a court, she said. She further suggested that they could request Professor Parthasarathy to adjudicate. Some persons objected, saying that they did not have a legal background or knowledge. Christina replied: Even I don't have a legal background and I am from the department of religious studies, unlike many of you who are students of law. The moot court is only a forum or platform for debate. The form would be of moot court and actual proceedings would be informal or more of a debate. Moot court is mooted so that there is an authority to have controlled and guided discussions. It would be more of an exercise in exploration of truth than fixing the guilt or damning an opinion, what do all of you say?

Everyone accepted the proposal. Was not Professor Parthasarathy more learned and experienced than Haripriya, a chit of a girl? The professors' knowledge of Gita was legendary. He had studied in depth the commentaries of different Acharyas in original in their own language, be it Sanskrit, Hindi, Tamil or any of the Indian languages. Besides, he was known for his sense of fair play and always genuinely concerned about the student's growth, be it academic or spiritual. So it was decided that they hold a moot court to debate about Gita. The next evening, all the students along with Christina approached Prof Parthasarathy and appraised him of the happenings of the previous evening.

They requested that He adjudicate the proceedings of the Moot Court. At first, the professor was reluctant, but after their repeated pleas, he thought he saw a spark of spiritual fervor in many of his students. He accepted. He also reiterated what Christina said: That it was more of a debate in quest of truth and the form of the court is given for the purposes of steering the debate in the right direction and also to avoid acrimony and from deviation towards personalities rather than the subject.

10. RULES FOR THE DEBATE

The students had formed groups of their own ilk based on their beliefs. The names of the group reflected their ethos. Their nicknames too reflected their strong ideology and the direction of their bias.

Some of the nicknames were assigned by the friends in the rival group taking into account the personae of the person which was resented at first but subsequently accepted sportively. A few had more than one nickname, one given by friends of the same group and another by a rival group.

The following students formed Dharam Rakshak Group (DR).

Sudipta	Trikala Gyani (TG) for rival group and Pandita by close friends.
Shubha	Shunya Aryabhata(SA)
Veena	Proud Hindu(PH)
Sandhya	Sadhguru ki Jai(SJ)
Pushpa	Aham Brahmasmi(BA)
Tulasi	Hare Shyam(HS)
Anushka	Know All(KA) by a rival group and walking encyclopedia by her close friends.
Srilata	Taraka Shastri(TS)
Maheshwari	Prakriti Daivam(PD)
Suhasini	Shaktih daivam(SD)

The God is great (GG) group comprised of

Saira	Insha Allah (IA)
Gurpreet Kaur	Sat Shri Akal(SSA)
Mary	Hail Mary(HM)
Sarita	Jai Jinendra(JJ)
Gautami	Buddham sharanam gachammi(BG)
Harshitha	Jesus saves. (JS)

The disbeliever's group (DB) had the following members.

Vinodini	Indian Comrade(IC)
Sanjeevini	Indian first (IF)
Dhanu	Salman my hero (SMH)
Pavitra	Peacenik (PK)
Aparajita	Atheist by belief (AB)
Vijaya	Carnivore (CR)

The following students did not wear any affiliation and were fun-loving, friendly and social and participated in all the activities of all groups. For clarification, grouped under Non-Aligned—(NA)

Suma	Ask Google (AG)
Trupti	Only Veg (OV)

Archana	Yahoo answers (YA)
Padma,	I love Amit (ILA)
Bhanu	Silent Observer (SO)
Christina	Naham Karta Hari Karta (NK)
Devaseni	Bahubali (BB)
Sheela	Quora clarifies (QC)
Pooja	Salman my hero (SMH)
Bharathi,	I love India (ILA)
Virati	Only Veg (OV)

Just like before the Mahabharata war, both the warring parties met and formulated rules to be followed during the course of the war, the students met and discussed the rules of the debate and arrived at the following consensus.

1. Truth is that which is in accord with facts or reality. It also refers to authenticity.
2. The criterion for determining truth is
    a. What God has stated in the Gita
    b. What others have said in Gita and in line with Gods say
    c. It is found in Gita by implication
    d. is derived from what is said in Gita or implied in Gita
    e. It is experiential, pragmatic, and relevant.
    f. What is experienced by one may not be the same as others' experiences, likewise, relevance is also person dependent, as is pragmatism?
    g. To elaborate
        i. Any external statement made is deemed proved if stated in the Gita or implied by what is said in the Gita.
        ii. Any statement/quote made from Gita is deemed proved if it is relevant, practical, or experiential.
3. Gita being the highest truth, does not require proof. But acceptability thereof is subject to (2) above.
4. External statements, facts, incidents references, etc. must necessarily be in line with Gita for acceptability/proof.
5. For the purposes of debate, all versions of the Gita are equal and acceptable.
6. The Actual utterances in Gita have primacy over all commentaries or purports.
7. The words uttered by God Almighty in the Gita has precedence over the words uttered by others.
8. Other scriptures may be referred but would rank second in the hierarchy to what is stated in the Gita.
9. Krishna's handling of any matter during his sojourn on the earth would serve as precedents.
10. Throughout the proceedings, the students would be referred by their nicknames so as to cause the least pain to those vanquished and to better

convey the personality of the student and also to make it more impersonal so as to keep them in the spirit of involved–disinterestedness.

11. Professor Parthasarathy would be the final adjudicator and his verdict would be final and accepted by all without any reservations. The subject matter being Gita which is deemed work of God, Non-believers precluded from participation. May only act as observers. Participation in voting and debate is not allowed.

12. Matter other than Gita, including Hindu practices, other scriptures Hindu or otherwise Dharma Shastras, etc. is out of bounds, except for the purposes of reference meaning they may be quoted in support of arguments for additional weight, but Gita would be the clincher.

13. The residual matters of both the participating groups and observers can be discussed separately as a truth exploration mission without the trappings of a debate.

14. It may be undertaken in a separate forum of discussion.

15. Only theists/believers are allowed to participate in the proceedings to the extent they are affected.

The following considerations were taken into account in formulating the rules.

- o Gita only is the subject matter.
- o Other scriptures not universally accepted even amongst the Hindus.
- o Hindu practices are not universal nor do all the practices have the sanction of scriptures or even if sanctioned, the sanction is not universal.
- o Gita being the voice of God, including non-believers does not serve any purpose.
- o Believers of other religions and communities are included as God is one and they address Krishna with their own names as per their conditioning and environment.

11. K – 1, GITA V/S GURU

Prof Parthasarathy was seated on the dais. All the students were assembled. Professor banged his gavel and asked if everyone was ready. The students indicated readiness.

The Professor asked who would be presenting the case on behalf of the Dharam Rakshak group (DR) and God is a great group (GG) and Disbelievers (DB) group? All the group members discussed amongst themselves and suggested that TG present the case on behalf of all the three groups. TG, however, insisted that this does not prejudice the right of any member of another group to put forth their case apart from TG. She was asked to put up a list of documents she would be relying upon. TG informed that she would rely on Bhagavad Gita as followed byDualists' followers. This was found unacceptable by members of other groups each claiming that their book be taken on record. Finally, it was decided by consensus that the Gita of ISKCON and the Gita of Swami Chinmayananda would be taken for the purposes of debate. The consensus was arrived at by divergent groups after noting that all the versions of Gita are unanimous on the issue of approaching Guru for obtaining knowledge and the said editions were currently most widely accepted. TG however again insisted that this does not preclude her group or other groups from producing an additional version of Gita at a future date if found necessary. She further informed that they may rely on all the Upanishads, Vedas and Puranas if need be. There was no objection as expected by her and she already congratulated herself on the expected victory.

Prof: TG, please make your opening statement and begin your presentation.

TG: Gita is absolute. It is the voice of God. Many Acharyas have offered commentaries on the Gita to bring out the true meaning of the Gita, to us lesser mortals.

By ourselves, we may not grasp the true meaning. Knowing this, God has advised us, mortals, to approach the Guru and obtain Knowledge. In support of my claim is the following quote:

TG: Quoted verse no 34 from Chapter 4 of Bhagavad Gita and also translated it for the benefit of all as under:

तद्विद्धि प्रणिपातेन परिप्रश्नेन सेवया |
उपदेक्ष्यन्ति ते ज्ञानं ज्ञानिनस्तत्त्वदर्शिन: ||4-34||

tad viddhi praṇipātena paripraśhnena sevayā
upadekṣhyanti te jñānaṁ jñāninas tattva-darśhinaḥ

Learn the Truth by prostrating before a spiritual master. Inquire from him with reverence and render service unto him. He will impart knowledge because he has seen the truth.

Next, she claimed that Gita is supreme and must be followed in Toto and that it is not subject to interpretation.

Further, she briefly mentioned the disagreement all of them had with Haripriya, the sum, and substance of which was

1. Everything HP says goes against what is said by all the Acharyas.
2. Her version does not conform to any of the existing versions.
3. Her say is not mentioned in any scriptures.
4. It does not have any Guru nor has any followers.

She mentioned that she was ready to be examined by her and when her turn to present the case comes, she would unmask Haripriya for the fraud that she was in front of all.

Prof: Is that all?

TG: No sir, as far as the dispute about Guru is concerned, this is it.

Professor asked if anybody had any objections.

The objections of disbelievers (DB) who had joined with DR group was

- There is no God. Krishna is fictitious and hence Gita is fictitious
- Constitution of India is the ultimate and not Gita

The objections of believers (GG) were

- Gita is restricted to one community that is the Hindu community and that too believed only amongst the Brahmins and more so Vaishnavas and not others.

The Professor designated the Group "Disbelievers" as observers and forbade them from participating in the debate save as observers. On their questioning the judgment, he informed that debate is arranged to examine the veracity of different versions of the Gita. He advised them that they may have another debate about the existence or otherwise of God. In the interest of fair play, and not to deprive them of opportunity, they may participate as observers. They may not raise objections nor can they vote in the proceedings ruled Professor. Further, he designated the GG group as disinterested stakeholders and restricted/confined their participation to areas wherein they had a stake. Other individuals too were designated observers and could participate or vote only as far as it infringed on their rights or they had something in stake in the proceedings.

Prof: Hari, Your witness.

HP: You mentioned that Gita is supreme & must be followed in Toto?

TG: Yes.

HP: Gita is not subject to interpretation?

TG: Yes, I have already told so.

HP: Does that non-interpretation clause apply to only this verse or the entire Gita?

TG: With a smirk, why to entire Gita of course.

HP: About following in Toto, I suppose that it extends to the whole of Gita?

TG: Yes, undoubtedly.

HP: What happens when we query spiritual master?

TG: He imparts knowledge/truth as he has seen them.

HP: Is this the only way?

TG: There may be many ways, but Gita says so, & Gita is absolute and benchmark for us believers.

HP: How did Vivasvan acquire knowledge?

TG: Directly from Krishna.

HP: How about Uddhava?

TG: Directly from Krishna.

HP: How about Sanjaya?

TG: Through optical and ocular reception from Krishna directly through Lord Vyasa's' grace.

HP: How about Manu & Ikshvaku?

TG: Through their Guru by way of disciplic succession.

HP: Didn't Sanjaya, Uddhava, Arjuna, etc. not learn through Guru?

TG: Krishna himself officiated as their Guru.

HP: Which is better, learning directly or through the medium of a Guru?

TG: How can everybody learn from Krishna?

HP: You have not answered me.

TG: Learning directly of course.

HP: Does not Gita represent Krishna?

TG: Yes.

HP: Does not Krishna represent Gita?

TG: Yes.

HP: Why cannot we learn from Gita?

TG: Yes, we too learn from Gita through the medium of Guru.

HP: What does Chapter 4-2 say?

TG: Refers to the book and replies: This knowledge is lost due to the passage of time. I myself taught this Yoga to Vivasvan, who taught it to Manu who in turn passed it on to Manu.

HP: What is the effect of time on knowledge?

TG: It gets lost.

HP: Effect of communication passing through many persons?

TG: Original message gets lost/distorted.

HP: Doesn't it mean original learning is better than through many mediums?

TG: That is modern management perception.

HP: Is it perception or fact?

TG: It is fact.

HP: Then, Gita too is subject to distortion when passes through many hands?

SILENCE.

HP: Waiting for your answer?

TG: All management prodigies read standard books and not necessarily learn directly from the author.

HP: Exactly, because, they read firsthand what the author has written and understood it without many filtrations enroute.

TG: Curses herself for not anticipating the question.

HP: Does reading the authors' works directly reduce the utility than when hearing from the author?

TG: Yes.

HP: By how much?

TG: To an extent but not to a substantial extent.

HP: Please read out BG-10-11.

TG: Out of compassion for them, I, dwelling in their hearts, illumine their hearts with knowledge.

HP: So, we may learn by god's illumination directly?

TG: Yes, but you must be qualified.

HP: Are we discussing qualifications?

TG SILENCE

HP: In the hierarchy of precedence, whose words have higher precedence, Guru or God?

TG: God of course.

HP: Do you believe in the maxim "Krishnam Vande Jagat Gurum"

TG: Yes, it means that I bow down to the Universal Guru.

HP: Is it Your say?

TG: No, it is also mentioned in Gita 11-43 & 11-44 that Krishna is the greatest Guru.

HP: So, should we prefer the greatest or the second greatest?

TG: The greatest is not available to us commoners & hence......

HP: Isn't Krishna available to us in the form of Gita?

TG: They both are not the same.

HP: Can we not become uncommon from common?

TG: We can through a Guru.

HP: How did Ekalavya become a great archer?

TG: Through his Guru, Dronacharya.

HP: Didn't he accept a statue of Dronacharya as GURU?

TG: Dronacharya was his guru and the statue was only symbolic.

HP: Okay, let me put it this way, did Dronacharya teach Ekalavya or not?

TG: No

HP: How did Ekalavya learn and get expertise?

TG: He learned himself.

HP: So we can learn by ourselves?

TG: No, He learned by his prayers to Guru (in form of a statue)

HP: Okay, Suppose, I accept Gita as my Guru, and worship it, Can I learn or not?

TG: It is useless to argue with you. You tell me how he learned?

HP: He learned through God.

TG: What nonsense are you blabbering?

HP: I seated in the heart of all, light the lamp of knowledge said Krishna (BG-10-11)

TG: Flights of fanciful imagination on your part.

HP: Who is the giver of fruits of Karma?

TG: Krishna.

HP: So, when Ekalavya, practiced archery (Karma) who gave results?

SILENCE

HP: I am seated in everyone's heart, and from Me comes memory, **knowledge,** and forgetfulness

BG-15-15. So where from Ekalavya got knowledge?

SILENCE.

HP: Endowed with faith, seekers worship and seeks favors from others (demigods/Gurus/Parents), etc.) And obtains his desires. But in actuality, these benefits are bestowed by Me alone. (BG-7-22) Who bestowed knowledge on Ekalavya?

SILENCE.

HP: Then, does reading Gita and following the same constitute obedience to Gita or only following Gurus' instructions constitute adherence to Gita?

TG: We are liable to misunderstand when we read on our own.

HP: Please answer to the point. Your opinions are not the subject matter.

TG: Yes. Reading Gita and practicing its tenets also constitutes adherence.

HP: Those who worship the demigods go to the planets of the demigods, but My devotees ultimately reach Me. (BG-7-23) So where do worshippers of Guru go?

TG: Neither Krishna nor Gita has specified where worshippers of Guru go.

HP: Isn't there a planet called/dedicated to Guru?

TG: Yes.

HP: If you have a choice between Guru and God, whose words do you select?

TG: Both their words are always in concurrence, if it is not so, it is our misunderstanding.

HP: When the demon king, Bali was confronted by both his guru, Shukracharya, and God in his Vamana Avatara, whose words did Bali respect?

TG: Lords' words, but he was shorn of his kingdom and pushed deep into nether worlds

HP: And then, what did he get in return?

TG: The lord as his security guard in the nether world plus an assurance that in next manavantara, he would be ruling the heavens as Indra.

HP: In the final battle between Duryodhana and Bhima, what was the result?

TG: Duryodhana was given a mortal blow resulting in his death.

HP: Whom did Duryodhana follow and whose advice did Bhima follow?

TG: Bhima followed the advice of God ignoring the advice of his Guru and Duryodhana followed the advice of his Guru, Balrama and fought as per the rules of warfare even though he saw Krishna gesturing to Bhima to aim the blow on his thigh.

HP: So, what does it mean?

TG: You are twisting the truth.

HP: I am not twisting the truth. I am highlighting things so as to put the same in a proper perspective.

HP: Hasn't God asked to give up all dharma and surrender unto Him?

TG: Yes, in BG-18-66.

HP: Then, doesn't it supersede earlier instructions to seek Guru?

TG: No, they run concurrently.

HP: How do you execute it, I mean concurrently?

TG: I will follow Guru & I will surrender to GOD.

HP: Both instructions are mutually exclusively. If you follow Guru, you are compromising on that part of Gods' instruction wherein He asks to abandon religion.

TG: But all people do so.

HP: Does it make it correct? Does the majority determine what is correct or incorrect?

SILENCE

HP: I will quote Krishna -----You alone know yourself by your own self oh God of all, God of gods, O Supreme Person, Lord of the universe! (BG-10-15), who knows Krishna?

TG: Krishna ALONE KNOWS Himself by Himself.

HP: Then, should we learn from one who knows fully or from one who knows lesser?

TG: Shouting, are you implying that our Guru is ignorant, how dare you?

Prof: Banging gavel, silence please, I don't find anything objectionable in HP's question.

HP: What I am asking is who between the two, God and Guru knows more?

TG: God of course. But Guru's learned from God.

HP: Should we learn from Giver or seeker?

TG: You don't learn from Guru, who is compelling you to? Go seek from God Himself. You fancy yourself to be Arjuna or Uddhava.

Prof: Please follow discipline. TG, such things are not expected from students at this level and neither from lovers and adherents of Gita.

HP: We will see the same from a mundane day-to-day perspective. You seek knowledge from childhood to completion of education.

After completion of education, you are on your own, with Job responsibilities, etc. You won't be attending University lifelong. Likewise, Shishya's move out of Gurukula. But God accepts you any time.

HP: Is Guru a path or destination?

TG: Guru is a path.

HP: And is God is a path or destination?

TG: God is both a path and destination.

HP: Then, which do you prefer?

TG: I prefer Guru.

HP: And not God?

TG: Yes God

HP: God or Guru?

SILENCE

HP: What, won't you take a direct flight to Delhi, if you have a choice rather than take a detour?

SILENCE

HP: Is Guru a cause or effect?

TG: Guru is the cause.

HP: And God?

TG: He is both cause and effect.

HP: Then, which should we choose?

TG: Both cause and effect, I mean both Guru and God.

HP: How?

TG: The effect of my Gurus teaching determined my personality. Isn't Guru an effect also?

HP: Are the effect of God and the effect of Guru the same?

TG: You draw your own inferences and follow your own path to hell.

HP: DoesBhagavata Purana say anything about Gurus?

TG: Yes, In the Uddhava Gita section.

HP: Who is the Guru mentioned there?

TG: Not one but 24 Gurus are mentioned.

HP: Please name some of them.

TG: Earth, Air, Sky, Water, Moon, Sun, Pigeon fish, etc. ....

HP: When inanimate is acceptable as Guru, is it wrong to accept My Lords' Gita as Guru?

TG: Okay, proclaim your guru serpent or fish as your Guru and fool yourself and others.

HP: This is the limit, Sir...............

Professor sternly, TG, no personal overtones.

TG: It is not so mentioned by my Guru hence ...

HP: For your information, the discourse of Lord Vishnu in Matsya avatar to Manu, is Matsya Puran and

TG: Sir we will have a break. I need to consult my other partners. (Everybody was thus far spellbound but now realized that they indeed needed a break)

Prof:Agreed. We will break for 15 minutes and assemble here thereafter.

TG along with all his supporters huddled in a corner and asked why everybody left her in lurch instead of supporting her. They told her that she was representing them all. She reminded that she had already claimed that her presenting the case would not prejudice the rights of other members and they also can open up when she was cornered. Everybody promised that they would also take an active role in articulating their views.

All the participants reassembled again.

The professor gestured that the debate could begin.

HP: Thank you, sir.

HP: Have I ever contradicted or criticized Gita of the versions in which you believe?

TG: No.

HP: Than how do you say that what I said goes against all Acharyas?

TG: Your say is not reflected in what great seers and philosophers say.

GG: Yes, it goes contrary to what the Acharyas of any or all of the parampara says.

HP: Which is the correct version

GG: Each one of them put forth that their version is correct and that the version put forth by others is wrong.

HP: Who is the best judge of any work?

TG: The author of the work himself.

SA: Whatever God said.

HS: Whatever Krishna said.

HM: Whatever Christ said.

HP: Isn't Gita and Krishna infinite?

GG: Yes.

HP: Than aren't you limiting your understanding?

    NO REPLY

HP: Aren't you demoting Gita from Infinite to finite?

    NO REPLY

TG: But their version is as incorrect as yours is.

HP: How?

TG: Our preceptor has defeated scholars of all other denominations and established that we are correct.

HP: Haven't you admitted just now that the best judge of any work is the author himself?

TG: I will correct my answer. Our preceptor is the best judge.

GG: Chorus by the entire group-- No, what our preceptor said is correct.

HP: How can all of you be correct?

GG: Chorus by the entire group --Our preceptor has understood Gita correctly.

HP: What about other preceptors?

GG: Chorus by the entire group --They are wrong.

HP: How?

GG They are interpreting Gita, but our preceptor just repeats what God said.

HP: How can you say so?

GG: Chorus--That is what God meant.

HP: How can you determine what God meant? He could have meant what any one of you say, or what a group of you say or what all of the group say or He may not have meant anything of what any of you say?

GG: Our preceptor's commentary states that ....

HP: Due to lack of consensus, wasn't it decided that only actual verses/translations will be taken and not commentary?

SILENCE

HP: Do preceptors say have greater value than what God says?

SILENCE

HP: Does Gods Gita require the crutch of what preceptors say?

SILENCE

HP: Gita is complete, isn't it?

SILENCE

HP: Answers, please?

DR: Please provide a reference that Gita is complete.

HP: Krishna tells Arjuna, that after knowing this nothing else remains to be known. Gita-7-1 & 7-2. Is this correct as per all the versions of the Gita DR group follows?

DR: Yes but ....

TG & JG: Acharya did not say so

HP: Aren't we discussing Gita, or is it the Acharya we are discussing?

TG & JG: Gita also did not say so

HP: Please recite Chapter 7 Verse 2

TG: Goes through the verse and says that it is not what God said.

HP: You have seen it in the book yourself.

TG: This is an English translation, not translated properly

HP: Please bring your own translation in consonance with the ideas of your preceptor.

TG: My preceptor has spoken in Sanskrit just as Parmatma has spoken in Sanskrit.

HP: Please provide a translation of what has been said.

TG: As both have spoken in Sanskrit, I do not have the translation.

HP: Shall we presume that what is commonly accepted translation is good enough here?

TG: You don't know Sanskrit; how can you speak about Gita?

HP: Is Gita restricted to Sanskrit knowledge holders?

TG: Yes.

HP: Then isn't it limiting the grandeur, opulence, and magnanimity of the Lord and Gita?

TG: Not only have you misunderstood but also misleading others with your fabrications. It is not you who is speaking but your arrogance.

HP: Are we discussing my merits, competencies, and shortcomings or Gita?

PROF: I think it is time I interfered in the proceedings. TG, you have flouted all the rules which were agreed upon. You are not putting forth your say nor are you accepting what told. Your criticism is ill-founded and not healthy or constructive. Please contribute positively and if you cannot, please restrain from making personal attacks and refrain from negative tactics. Be graceful when outmaneuvered, do your homework well, and then participate here or in any other fora.

TG: I disagree but withdraw my personal comments without apologies. I express my dissent.

PROF: It is better. Exercise your choice.

TG & JG: You have said that you haven't disagreed with what our Acharyas say but now ....

HP: I am defendant and you may cross-examine me, when I present something new, not when I am defending myself. Still, in pursuance of truth, I reply, I didn't disagree but neither did I agree.

GG: How do you disagree with us without agreeing either? Please explain.

HP: I agree that the versions of all preceptors could be correct but the say of their followers that only their say is correct is disagreed by me.

GG: Even if the preceptors say that only their version is correct?

HP: The preceptors would have told correctly but being misinterpreted by the followers, and even if it has been told, it would have reference to some context and the followers taking it out of context. If it isn't the case, the preceptor is not genuine.

TG & Others:You have shown our belief and faith in poor light. Okay, we are wrong. Present your so-called correct version.

PROF: Please, no personal attacks. Henceforth rephrase your query so as not to hurt anybody. Remember the creed of lawyers towards opposing parties and counsel.

"We offer fairness, integrity, and civility. We shall attempt to resolve differences and, if we fail, we shall strive to make our dispute a dignified one." **Is it understood?**

PROF: HP, you have so far defended yourself successfully against the allegations made by all groups, but what exactly is your perspective has so far been confined to your hostel room discussions. TG and group have a valid point. Tomorrow, present your side or version about the Gita. Otherwise, it is unfair. You only criticize/disagree/agree ambiguously but do not put yourself in the line of fire, by facing cross-examination. I won't allow shoot and scoot in my court.

HP: Yes, Sir.

HP: Now to defend myself against the charges leveled against me: I have followed the words of Gita and also quoted the verse and reference. Does following God constitute rebelling against Acharya?

TG: You are not following Gita but your imaginary version of what you suppose is said in Gita.

HP: Is conformance to the existing version essential to be innocent and does nonconformance constitutes guilt?

TG: Isn't nonconformance to law treated as guilt?

HP: Isn't what is said in Gita treated as what is said in scriptures, i.e., isn't Gita a scripture?

TG: Gita has asked us to follow scriptures as a guide, it hasn't said that it is scriptures itself.

HP: TO have credibility is a guru and a follower necessary?

TG: You are a one-man Guru and Shishya and follow yourself.

HP: Sir, A small request

Prof: Yes, what is it?

HP: I will not defend Gita

Murmurs in the group. Many in the DR group opined that HP had lost her nerve and hence her battle. They further assumed that she is withdrawing as a measure of redeeming grace.

Prof: Do you want to withdraw?

HP: No Sir, Gita will defend itself. I request that the case be made against Gita. In other words, I request you confer the status of a living person on the Gita.

DR: We object. She will be defeated but Gita will be considered defeated.

DB: She is scared of defeat. God cannot defend himself, hence not to be allowed.

HP: Gita knows no defeat. They are legal precedents like
      i.The idols in Ayodhya were conferred with living status.
      ii.So too the river Ganga.
      iii.Besides, I will be quoting Gita and not my words.
      iv.In Gita itself, it is stated that where there are Krishna and Arjuna there is no defeat.
      v.In Gita God says I am not the doer. (BG18-16 & 3-27)

Prof: I see the logic in the argument of HP both in the legal sense and in Gita-sense.

I am unable to ascertain the need for the same or her motives. Nevertheless, as she will quote God with references in Gita, her plea is allowed.

ALL ARGUMENTS PUT FORTH BY HP IN COURSE OF THE DEBATE, WITH APPROPRIATE QUOTES FROM GITA & IN COURSE OF DEFENDING GITA WILL BE DEEMED TO BE MADE BY SRIMAD BHAGAVAD GITA (SBG) AND RECORDED ACCORDINGLY. **This privilege is not available when she is defending herself instead of Gita.**

Prof: Okay, HP, proceed.

HP: Sir, my examination is complete.

Professor: TG, you may cross-examine HP now.

TG: Do you have any GURU?

HP: Yes.

TG: Then, why do you spit venom on GURUs?

HP: That is your understanding. I follow the hierarchy of precedence and hence God supersedes GURU. I suppose, your faith also has the concept of a hierarchy of precedence. Besides, if you go through the transcript of the day's proceedings, it will become clear as to who is spitting venom.

TG: Do you respect him?

HP: I don't just respect him. I treat him as next to God & incidentally, I respect all preceptors irrespective of affiliation or religion.

TG: To which parampara does he belong?

HP: Same as to the faith which you profess.

TG: Isn't it hypocrisy?

HP looks at the professor for support who is engrossed in making notes and couldn't make eye contact.

TG seizing an advantage, Abandon Guru and all other religious practices and go to GOD as per His instructions.

Prof: Sarcastically, TG you abandon all debate and proceed with your witch-hunt.

TG: Sorry, sir.

TG: Who is Sandipani?

HP: He is the Guru of Lord Krishna.

TG: Who is Vasishta & Vishwamitra?

HP: They are the Guru of Lord Shri Ramachandra, former is Kula-Guru, and the latter is Shiksha Guru.

TG: So, you are greater than Shri Ramachandra or Lord Krishna that you don't require a Guru?

HP: The lord was setting an example for us. Regarding who is greater, I didn't make any such claim.

TG: Then, why are you following fabricated philosophy instead of following His example?

HP: God has offered us many choices, and the freedom to opt for any choice and I have opted for a choice that suits me.

TG: But not what lord did?

HP: What God said has primacy over what God did.

TG: So, God's actions are subordinate to His words. He says something and practices something else, is it?

HP: Sorry, I put it wrongly. God is blemishless. His words, actions, etc. too are all blemishless and beyond mundane

TG: Then?

HP: The rule enunciated is for us to follow and not a commentary on God, His actions or words. They are all par excellence. It is safe and rule of thumb to adhere to His words where His actions apparently differ from His words.

HP: Will you accept alterations and interpretations of what your Guru has said?

TG: No, it tantamounts to blasphemy.

HP: Then, why I can't adhere to my Gods' words with the same unflinching faith?

TG: Because they are not Gods' words but your words, hence I don't accept.

HP: Please quote my words and Gods' words and segregate where my words are superimposed on Gods' words.

LONG SILENCE, after a long pause,

TG: Okay, you mean to say we may learn by our efforts without help from preceptors, is it?

HP: Yes, it is possible.

TG: You attended a swimming coaching camp recently?

HP: Yes.

TG: You also enrolled for the motor driving course?

HP: Yes, what are you driving at?

TG: Why did you approach an institution? You could have learned it on your own or better still, you could have opted for a correspondence course?

HP: It can be done, but for practical sessions, we must approach the teacher.

TG: See, that is the importance of a Guru, especially for practical purposes.

HP: Nicely put, but there can be exceptions. How did the first swimmer or the first person to drive vehicle learn? She didn't have a guru, isn't it? Again, there Archana and Suma have learned swimming on their own. It made things difficult, but it can be done.

TG: I am speaking generally and not about the exceptions. Even in the realm of spirituality, Guru is necessary and the ill consequences of not having a Guru are highlighted many times. The pursuit of spirituality is not mere theory and is more practical than is car driving or swimming and necessarily require training.

HP: Please tell me the instances of ill consequences of not having a Guru.

TG: Indra lost his kingdom due to the absence of advice from Guru. Demons didn't allow their Guru Shukracharya to leave them even at the cost of the princess being made handmaid of Shukracharya's daughter because they knew the value of the preceptor. Even Asuras know the value of Guru, leave alone Suras, yet you pose as an intellectual and belittle Guru. Besides, assuming you become a scholar without Guru, and by your own self-efforts, self-destruction too cannot be far off like in the case of sage Yavakrida.

SILENCE.

TG: Am I correct? Have I given appropriate instances?

HP: You didn't get the title Trikala Gyani or Panditji simply, you earned it.

TG: Thank you HP, Sir that is all from my end.

Prof: HP, do you have anything to say?

HP: I will quote BG: 4.39 "Those who have deep faith and have controlled their mind and senses attain divine knowledge". See, another form of obtaining knowledge. Here too there is no mention of Guru.

SILENCE

Prof: TG, any rejoinder?

TG: No sir.

Prof: Christina, for the purposes of this debate, you are assigned the role of a Registrar. Christina, you are nonaligned and hence more acceptable to all sections. Prepare a report of proceedings on a daily basis and submit it to me a week after the conclusion of the last day proceedings. I will require a week to study the same from all angles & perspectives before giving the verdict.

We will break for today and meet again at 18-00 Hours tomorrow. Thank you all of you.

POST-DAY END –1 DISCUSSION

All the students rushed to their rooms but not before agreeing to meet in TG's room to discuss and to plan strategies for the next day, just like in the Mahabharata war.

Christina was worried. She did not know how to prepare a daily report. She was afraid because she did not have a legal background. She made her way to HP's room to consult her. Haripriya received her warmly and allayed her fears. She suggested to Christina that she could use a template which she (HP) would devise. Thereafter, Christina would only have to fill in the core details of what transpired in the debate. Christina heaved a sigh of relief and hugged her friend in a genuine burst of love. She promised to collect the template from her around 11-PM.

The Template

DAY-1/2/3....

- Issue involved:
- Issues cropped up/raised in course of discussions.

It is proved through ---

- Quotes in Gita.
- Implied in the sayings of Gita.
- Implied by sequences/ juxtapositioning of verses of Gita.
- Implied by way of quoted precedents.
- Implied as the sole/primary conclusion after the presentation of arguments.
- Implied by personal experience.

All the groups met in the lounge. Their reactions were mixed. They liked the method of bringing the truth to fore.

DB group and GG group opined that it was a legal method adopted in court, wherein there were many more rules and restrictions and in a formal atmosphere.

DR group opined that it was the ancient custom of Santana dharma technique which is modeled in question-and-answer format. IN fact, there is an Upanishad titled Prashnopanishad wherein questions are put by a disciple and the Master answers. Here, the disciple may make queries but not in a challenging manner but in a submissive manner like a supplicant. Cross-examination isn't allowed here volunteered someone else.

Some compared the method to the Socratic Method. Each of them espoused their own method as best but agreed that in the end, it is the truth that matters and not the methods adopted for arriving at the same.

The Dharam Rakshak (DR) group again assembled in the room of HS. Their discussion was on the following lines.

TG: It is easy to criticize but difficult to espouse a cause in a foolproof way countering all possible lines of criticism and to make it unassailable.

BG: Exactly, did you think of that when HP was putting forth a new paradigm? You had the strength and logic of all those who tread the path and their works to fall back upon. You tried to silence her who did not have anything except her belief, persistence, and faith.

TG: Whose side are you on, HP or mine? If you want, you may join her.

KA: Don't quarrel. Tomorrow we will use the same technique she used and pick loopholes in her theory.

TG: How?

BG: We will object to each thing she says.

KA: Every time she says something, we will demand that she show reference in Gita.

KA: You are lucky.

TG: Why?

KA: She could have asked about distance learning option now widely available, and outreach programs now in currency. She could have questioned if present-day learning through apps and online courses are trash in the absence of a teacher.

TG: Maybe, it didn't occur to her.

KA: Don't underestimate your opponent. It does not stop me from admiring that girl for her originality, analysis, fighting spirit and stand-alone for what she believes is right.

TG: Go defect to her side, we are friends from childhood and you forsake me for this new kid and go running behind her.

KA: Don't be a grouch. I will stand by you.

PH: All are missing moments when TG cornered HP.

TG: When?

PH: When you asked her to learn swimming and driving through a correspondence course.

AB: There is one more instance when she overpowered her.

PH: When?

AB: When she quoted the instance of Yavakrida, Brihaspati, etc. She had no answer.

PH: Maybe, she is not aware of the story of Yavakrida.

KA: Don't become complacent. There isn't much that misses her eye. She may not have a response, but that doesn't mean she is unaware of history/Puranas. This is evident from her complimenting you admiringly and without grudge.

TG: I am reminded of the poem, sweet are the uses of adversity. We get to know our true friends. All along, PH and AB were silent but are sympathetic to my viewpoint.

KA: Get over it. We are all with you. Now let us disperse.

With this, they made a beeline to their rooms.

Christina visited Haripriya to collect the template. She asked if it was okay if she asked some questions to clear her doubts. Of course, responded Haripriya.

Should we really not follow Guru asked Christina? Haripriya clarified:

God has given innumerable choices, including the choice of seeking a Guru. Guru too can bestow knowledge. In the case of Genuine Guru, they can also bestow salvation, but the actual bestowing is done by God by empowering Guru. God doesn't allow his devotees to fall and Gurus are the greatest devotees of God, at least most of them.

There is a popular belief that IF God rejects you, Guru can accept you and plead with God, who will not refuse the Guru, but If Guru rejects you even God does not help you. But if you make God Himself Guru, well ....

There is another famous song, extolling God that He is the mother, Father, Relative, and friend. What I meant was Guru have their own place in the hierarchy and play their role as teacher, not play the role of God, they may play the role of the path to God. Many followers of Guru misappropriate the legacy of Guru and make them bigger than God, to serve their interests.

How nice it would be if all accepted Gods' words as it is in Toto with the same faith and dedication as they accept Gurus' words.

Christina countered that they may claim that you are misappropriating the legacy of God, what then? But suddenly checked herself as she muttered, they cannot make God bigger than God, and even if they did so, it hardly matters, yes, I understand.

Truth is one but multi-dimensional. Belief is essential but cannot be a substitute for truth. But just that it appears implausible need not necessarily mean it is Untruth offered HP.

Christina asked if she still cannot comprehend it completely and requested that she answer with reference to slokas from the Gita.

Hari read out from her copy of the Gita:
- Always think of Me, be devoted to Me, worship Me, and offer obeisance to Me. Having dedicated your mind and body to Me, you will certainly come to Me. BG 9.34
- Always think of Me, be devoted to me, worship me, and offer obeisance to me. Doing so, you will certainly come to me. This is my pledge to you, for you are very dear to me. BG 18.65

- o See, God has not told, fix your mind on Guru, be devoted to Guru, sacrifice to Guru, have Guru as the supreme goal. What he has asked us is to respect guru, serve him and make inquiries submissively, who will, in turn, give you knowledge.
- o The existing practices are over-reach on the part of over enthusiasts. If you sacrifice to Guru, It goes to Krishna, He is the only recipient of all sacrifices or charities. If you pray to Guru, you will attain Guru. If you pray to Krishna, you are also praying to Guru, for Isn't Krishna Himself both Brihaspati and Shukracharya? BG: 10.2. Among priests, I am Brihaspati & BG: 10.37... I am Shukracharya among the thinkers.

Christina asked HP about Yavakrida and the episode of Guru leaving Indra. HP told her the story associated therewith. Yavakrida was the son of the sage Bhardwaj, a learned Brahmin. He wanted to acquire mastery of Vedas without studying under a Guru.

He performed penance and Lord Indra dissuaded him from attempts to use penance for acquiring knowledge, twice on two different occasions. Yavakrida was adamant and continued with his efforts against the sane counsel of Indra. Indra appeared before him and blessed him "Go and study the Vedas, you will become learned." Yavakrida studied and became a scholar but without the rigors and discipline of study under Guru's tutelage. He once misbehaved with the daughter in law of another sage, Raibhya. Enraged, the sage created a demon and an ogress by his mystic power who killed Yavakrida. Yavakrida couldn't escape with all his knowledge of Vedas, as his access to water to purify himself was cut off by the demon. A study under preceptors would confer blessings along with inculcation of humility and patience apart from regular knowledge.

Yavakrida had knowledge but not what accompanies knowledge that is acquired by association and rendering of service to Guru, which brought about his downfall.

Once, Indra under the influence of pride and egoism and failed to pay respects to Brihaspati, his Guru, in the royal assembly. Brihaspati left silently and made himself invisible. With no one to guide, Indra lost his kingship.

Shukracharya was the preceptor of demons. Once, due to the high handedness of the princess in dealing with Shukracharya's daughter, he threatened to leave them. The king of demons appeased him by offering his daughter, the princess as a maid to serve Shukracharya's daughter Devayani. See the price they paid to retain the Guru and you can judge the importance they attached to Guru in those days.

In conclusion, we may learn without the preceptor, which may be attended with ill consequences which can be warded off by learning under a Guru as in

Yavakrida case. Also, we would be missing the inculcation and discipline part, the grace, the blessings, and a person to look upon when in trouble.

Christina expressed her puzzlement over her respect to preceptors but at the same time taking a stance against them. Hari replied that there is no contradiction in her stand. She respects them and loves them but loves and respects Him more.

Christina referred to the actual fight wherein Gurus were subjected to mudslinging which necessitated the debate and asked if it was a fact and hence recommending bypassing Guru. Hari replied that such black sheep exist in all religions and communities, who bring disrepute to the institutions they represent. Christina mentally recollected all the not so holy escapades of different religious heads of different religions and different denominations which had kept the media busy for over the past decade even in her country.

Hari continued saying that the institutions and their philosophy are different from the persons representing them. All these are a recent phenomenon, a characteristic of Kali Yuga.

Gurus, especially those prior to two generations before us always commanded a place second only to God. Also, The Original Guru and most of the successors were spotless without any blemish. You may gauge their spiritual power obtained by askesis by the fact that they could award benedictions or curses, create their own planet, show path to God, etc.

They had that much Tapo- Shakti. She asked HP, to elaborate her views on the Sanskrit language. HP replied that it was preferable to have knowledge of Sanskrit but it is not mandatory. It is the language of gods, meaning the choice language of superhuman species.

This is borne out by the fact that studies say that it is most suitable for computer coding as it is most unambiguous and pithy. This is human perception. God, Himself discriminate based on language, caste, creed, race, species, etc. He has devotees from animal species like, Gajendra an elephant, who didn't call out in the Sanskrit language to God to rescue him but called him in animal language. The monkeys playing with Krishna, the cows and calves all weren't proficient in Sanskrit. Christina said that the faithful in Christianity prefer prayers in Latin. HP responded saying that it is okay as long as they understand the prayers or the meaning or spirit behind it. Christina was partly satisfied but was too tired and sleepy to continue her interrogation. The bell struck 11-00 and all of them decided to stop for the day.

12. K - 2   SEMANTICS V/S CONCEPTS

Prof Parthasarathy arrived 10 minutes before the scheduled time. He arranged his scribbling pad and looked around. All the students had arrived.

Prof: Good Evening! Shall we start he asked?

Chorus Good evening, yes sir.

Prof: HP are you ready to present your case?

HP: Yes sir.

Prof: HP Proceed, present your case. I suppose you will commence with chapter 1 and proceed in chronological order?

HP: No Sir,

Prof: Okay, start with any chapter as you like.

HP: Sir, my presentation is not chapter- wise at all sir.

Prof: Oh, you want to present it in a summarized fashion covering all the chapters!

HP: Not summary sir.

Prof: Perplexed and curious, then what and how do you propose to present?

HP: I want to present a paradigm suggesting an alternate approach to Gita.

Prof: What does the model do?

HP: The Paradigm is
- Study of Gita as a subject matter.
- Study Gita a manual for everyday living.
- Study Gita as a reference book
- Study of slokas as generalizations
- Use Gita as a benchmark to evaluate
  - Our understanding of Gita
  - Our understanding of other scriptures
  - Our understanding of divine actions stated in scriptures
  - Our understanding of our actions/responses and other's actions in light of wisdom contained in the Gita.

It is about how to understand Gita as Gita is not open to interpretation.

TG: Sniggering, Oh! A great Pandita has come and will teach all of us how to understand Gita.

BG: Brihaspati himself has descended to impart knowledge.

KA: A true scholar eh! Dandavat pranaam Acharya mahoday!

Prof: Need I remind all of you, as to the rules of the game and personal conduct?

TG, BG & KA: Sorry sir.

HP: Yesterday, we had a lengthy discussion wherein I espoused the concept of Gita through Gita which is the primary concept. We have also discussed the supremacy of Gita over Guru. Today we will see how Gita is a concept thence needing to be studied conceptually. How Gita is objective and what are the objectives of Gita. How the concept-based approach scores over a semantic-based approach were also another query.

The issues dealt with yesterday when we discussed Gita through Gita, all find mention in the Gita.

HP continues ... I had before me two options, the first one being to take the version of any Acharya, and analyze it through the pre-defined parameters. That would not serve the objective.

It would only create a greater divide and would be construed as impertinence/criticism by the adherents and blasphemy by diehard adherents. So, I chose to proceed as per the second option though it is more difficult than the first option. I chose to present first my Paradigm of the Gita.

After the conclusion of the entire presentation, we may test to analyze any one version of the Gita if all are agreeable. Originally, God scripted Gita to subserve certain objectives.

TG: What are the predefined parameters? Who has defined them? We are interested more in Gita than your paradigms.

BG: What are the objectives of Gita? Is it your creation or is it authenticated and documented?

HP: My entire paradigm is about a conceptual study of the Gita. God meant it to be a conceptual study.

He meant it to be objective. The study thereof too is to be objective. Gita is parameterized in the sense, it envisages knowing from the Gita, learning from Gita and application of our learning to cross-check the correctness or otherwise of our learning. I will present each of the parameters in the course of the proceedings. The pre-defined parameters are taken from the Gita itself. So, the question any mortal defining the parameters, myself included does not arise. The objectives of the Gita too are defined in the Gita itself. We will use the objective model to define our objectives and study Gita objectively. We will see how Gita is a conceptual study. We will use the parameters to test the correctness of our application of the semantics of the Gita. The Objectives of Gita were
At a lower level:
*   To persuade Arjuna to discharge his duties by fighting in the war.

At a higher level:
1. To destroy the wicked.
2. To deliver the Pious.
3. To Re-establish Dharma
4. To revive ancient knowledge for fulfilling the (3) above
5. Fulfill the desires of the devotee seekers
   a. Of Wealth
   b. Of knowledge
   c. Freedom from misery
   d. Moksha/Gods abode

The objectives stated from 1-3 is mentioned in Gita 4-8

The objectives stated in 4 above are stated in Gita 4-2. (It is derived or implied)

The objectives stated in 5 above is stated in Gita 7-16

In view of the same, the suggested paradigm too is objective, both as regards to achieving objects or the object-oriented approach and as an objective approach devoid of personal bias, for hasn't the Lord Himself been objective both in approach and in conclusion?

All the Acharyas have a semantic approach towards the Gita. Their purports and commentaries were semantic-based.

TG: Quote reference for object-oriented approach.

HP: Objects of Gita can be inferred from the following slokas.

- Always think of Me and become My devotee. Worship Me and offer your homage unto Me. Thus, you will come to Me without fail. I promise you this because you are My very dear friend. BG: 18.65
- Abandon all varieties of religion and just surrender unto Me. I shall deliver you from all sinful reactions. Do not fear. BG: 18.66
- For one who explains the supreme secret to the devotees, devotional service is guaranteed, and at the end, he will come back to Me. BG: 18.68

Outcomes mentioned therein are the objects of Gita, i.e. you will reach the abode of God or attain moksha, thus freeing yourself from the repeated cycle of birth and death, reactions of sin is taken care of by God, Devotion to God which is on a higher plane than Moksha is guaranteed. This apart, four purusharthas can be achieved.

In the said verses, objects are expressly stated. There are many instances wherein it has to be inferred. Hence, even our understanding and perspectives have to be object-oriented.

TG: Where is it implied? Give an example with a quote.

HP: Okay, here we go.

    a) Both of them are ignorant, the one who thinks the soul can kill and the one who thinks the soul is killed. The soul doesn't kill nor can it be killed. BG: 2.19(It only occupies another body)

    b) If you think that the soul is subject to constant birth and death, even then you should not grieve like this.

    c) Death is certain for one who has been born, and rebirth is certain for one who has died. Therefore, you should not lament over the inevitable. BG: 2.26 & BG 2.27.

        a) It is a fact.

        b) It is a wrong perception not based on facts as happens in real life many times.

- A minor derivative is don't grieve over the inevitable.
- Major derivative, which is implied is
  - Your actions should not be based on thoughts or perceptions of facts. Base your action on your objectives. In this case, Arjuna is grief-struck and this grief is hindering the performance of his duty, and an obstacle to his objective, which is killing his enemies or victory in the battle.
  - Krishna advises him to come out of grief. Certain outcomes are inevitable, hence de-focus from by-product called grief and bypassing the question of correctness or otherwise of perception, focus on the objective called duty/War.

Krishna Himself focused on the objective of re-establishing Dharma. Another example is of Krishna not fighting so as to attend Rukmini Swayamvara.

TG: Should it not be semantic-based?

HP: It should be panoramic, with emphasis on all its elements like concept, semantics, objectives, etc.

TG: Supposing you go by only semantics?

HP: You would be guilty of limiting God's words to mere words. There is a possibility of being stuck in a time warp. You may be out of touch with reality, be judged obsolete, and termed irrelevant. But Gods' words cannot be any of those. Hence, syntax and semantics should be viewed in light of concepts and not in isolation. Likewise, concepts too should be viewed in conjunction with semantics.

TG: Can you give an example?

HP: Sure.

- People will speak of you as a coward. For a Kshatriya who is used to respect, infamy is worse than death. BG: 2.34

- Enemies will think that you fled from the battlefield out of fear, and will disrespect you. BG: 2.35

These are the words of the Lord to Arjuna as well as us to go by the words, literally i.e., semantic way. When Ashwattama was bound and arrested, Bhima and Krishna tell Arjuna to kill him and not show mercy. Draupadi, being a noble lady with a feminine heart, asks Arjuna not to kill him. Krishna asks Arjuna to act in such a manner that pleases/satisfies all.

Arjuna, understanding the intentions of the Lord, Shaves the head of Ashwattama, and removes the gem inbuilt in Ashwattama's forehead and drives him away. This act makes him lose his lustre and humiliated which is considered equivalent to death.

See, Krishna asks Arjuna in the former incident to act literally and in the latter instance to understand symbolically.

This has another connotation. God upholds law/dharma. The Lord is always within the confines of Law/Dharma. He is independent. Whenever He flouts His own law, He is exhibiting His supreme independence. At all times, He follows His law.

Sometimes He adopts stratagem to be within the confines of law although it appears to be incorrect, like in the above instance. Another key takeaway is the primacy of concept over the Word, though this may not always be the case. This is of course with a divine greater purpose. The Killing of demon Hiranyakashipu within the confines of boon is another example.

TG: Is semantic-based learning wrong?

HP: No. In fact, in the proposed paradigm, the principles enunciated are semantically based. We have all heard of the **Veda Vakhya** or the principle of unquestioning acceptance of the words in the Vedas.

In a similar vein, the words of God stand at a much higher level than Veda Vakhya. **Bhagavad Vakhya supersedes Veda Vakhya.** & I implicitly and unquestionably believe **Bhagavad Vakhya as** stated in the Gita.

TG: Isn't God's words (Bhagavad Vakhya) semantic?

HP: Isn't God's words Concept-based also? Should we limit God's preaching to word-based understanding, ignoring the concept? Doesn't Hari Chitta (Pandurangacha Marji) override Hari Vakhya?

TG: (Stumped, as Hari quoting her belief, but quickly regaining composure, Meaning? Would you please elaborate?

Prof: HP, please tell us what is Hari Chitta for the benefit of the audience who may not be familiar with local lingua.

HP: Gods' supreme will is called Hari Chitta.

Prof: That is good, carry on.

TG: Where is Hari Chitta mentioned in the Gita?

HP: BG 10.8 says, everything moves from Me, meaning if He wills it otherwise, so it will be.

HP: Vakhya is a medium to express a concept. The goal envisaged by the concept must not be derailed by words.

TG: I am not clear, please give an example.

HP: It can be seen in the following instances; the supreme will of God prevails over the will of individual will. God achieves His purposes irrespective of individual Arjuna toeing the line or not.

> Arjunas' will be superseded by Gods' will

- God asks Arjuna a Kshatriya, to shoot an unarmed, helpless Karna, which is against Dharma as taught by the Lord himself. Herein, Hari Chitta scores over Hari Vakhya.
- Even without your fighting, not all of them in the enemy camp and most of your soldiers will survive.
- Deluded, you say you will not fight, but forced by nature you will fight.
- Karna is a great warrior. He is noble and son of Lord Surya, who learned Gita from Lord Himself. He is the half-brother of Yama, God of death himself. Yet God willed that he should die, and neither his father nor his brother Yama could help him because God had willed it that way.

TG:If it shouldn't be semantic-based, on what should it be based? Sanskrit words which are beginningless have natural contact with objects. This is called Padashakthi. This the intrinsic power of the word to disclose their meaning by themselves is called Arthashakti. This intrinsic power of words is found in other languages also but to a limited extent, unlike Sanskrit, wherein it is found infinitely. How then do you say that a semantic-based approach is wrong?

HP: I didn't say that it shouldn't be semantic-based. I only proposed an alternate basis.

TG: Meaning semantic approach is wrong?

HP: Truth is multi-dimensional. What can bear truth-values? The following qualify to hold truth-values:

- Statements
- Sentences
- Propositions
- Theories
- Facts

- Assertions
- Beliefs
- Opinions
- Doctrines.

Truth is not limited to the above, nor are all the above truth. Torah has 70 facets, meaning single Torah text can be legitimately understood in a variety of ways at a multiplicity of levels all of which have a degree of truth. All the above has an element of relativity and subjectivity.

Back home, Mahabharata itself has at least three different meanings. Gita which is a part of Mahabharata also should have at least three meanings. Three levels of language are used in Mahabharata.

Samadhi bhasha conveys the glory of the Lord and must be accepted as it is.

Darshana bhasha is of two types:

i) Whatever conflicts with what are stated before and after is Darshana bhasha. This naturally has to be interpreted in tune with what is stated before and after or else it has to be rejected.

ii) Whatever is merely a restatement of some other Darshana quoted for refutation or to show the non-tenability of Darshana.

iii) Guhya bhasha is that which is different from Samadhi and Darshana bhasha. In the case of the Guhya bhasha, its deeper meaning has to be taken, rejecting the apparent meaning.

Each Sloka in Vishnusahasra Nama has 100 meanings. It cannot be said that only one meaning is correct and the other 99 meanings are wrong.

Again, Mahabharata has three layers of meaning namely:

- Astika.
- Manvadi.
- Auparichara.
   o The story of the Mahabharata, centering around the personalities of Sri Krishna, the Pandavas, etc., is the Astikadi layer of the meaning. This layer is designated as Astika because the Pandavas whose story is narrated have been great Astika, that is to say, they had great faith in Sri Krishna.
   o The Manvadi layer of the meaning is that meaning which conveys the virtues represented by Yudhishthira, Bhima, etc. Yudhishthira represents dharma, Bhima Sena represents bhakti, Jnana, Prajna, Medha, etc.

o The third layer of meaning viz., auparichara is the meaning that brings out Narayana as the meaning of each word of the Mahabharata.

Coming back to the present day, when finite humans' works have multiple connotations and hailed as a scholar/philosopher, why can't infinite Gods 'works be confined to semantics only devoid of concepts?

This being the case, how are you rejecting the meaning of other Acharyas and say that only your meaning is correct?

TG: Than what should it be based?

HP: I propose a concept-based study and understanding with an objective view/approach in conjunction with semantics.

TG: Meaning semantics is also co-opted?

HP: Gita itself is more of a concept-based philosophy than a semantic-based philosophy, besides we will be trapped in the web of semantics and can't proceed forward.

TG: Is it your view or can you quote authority?

HP: If Gita were to be entirely semantic-based then there wouldn't be Uddhava Gita. Bhagavad Gita itself would have been repeated verbatim to Uddhava by the Lord using the very self-same words. But God chose to speak Uddhava Gita. Now the underlying messages in both the Gitas' are completely the same.

There are many other scriptures both in Hindu and Non-Hindu literature wherein the sum and substance are the same but the words are varied due to place, time, level of consciousness of the target group, etc.

Uddhava Gita and Bhagavad Gita were uttered by the same Lord in the same avatar in the same eon around the same period of time to equally high souled devotees, Arjuna and Uddhava. So, there is no change at all due to the time place or the level of consciousness. Hence it is more concept-based and a little of semantic-based.

God hints as much in BG-2-42 & 2-43, wherein He cautions Arjuna to be wary of the flowery language of the Vedas, emphasizing the secondary status of the language of words or semantics/syntax over the concept.

TG: At the outset, it was decided that Bhagavad Gita would form the base and you wouldn't rely on other scriptures. Remember you yourself had proposed the inclusion of the rule. Now you are quoting/referring to Uddhava Gita.

HP: Yes. I am not putting forth what is not found in the Bhagavad Gita found in other scripture, in this case, Uddhava Gita. I am giving this example to show that Bhagavad Gita is more concept-oriented.

TG: I object. Reference to Uddhava Gita should be disallowed.

HP: Sir, I ....

Prof: TG, hear the given explanation carefully and the circumstances under which it is being given. Do not argue for the sake of argument or to score brownie points. HP, please proceed.

TG: Sir, it is unfair. My objections are reasonable and as per pre-agreed terms.

Prof: I extend the benefit of the doubt and assume that your objection is genuine and bonafide. I presume that you have not understood the point of law correctly, which I will spell out for your benefit. HP is not taking anything afresh, that is not stated in Bhagavad Gita, but taken from an external source and ascribing it to Gita to prove her point.

She is only making external references to matter already found in the Gita and comparing it so as to find out if the approach is semantic or concept based. If you are convinced, It is good, if not, I suggest you go back to first-year law school and return after brushing up your basics. HP, please continue.

Professor became all ears and eyes. For the first time in his legal career, he could not anticipate what was coming next. He looked forward to an interesting session ahead. Based on the countenance of HP and her unorthodox views and flair for putting across her views, he was also anticipating twists and suspense's to come up in the coming days.

HP: Thank you, sir. Such circumstances may recur in the future which may unnecessarily consume the time of all students as well as the professor. I request you to also take on record "Uddhava Gita" and accord it the same status and privileges as being accorded to the Bhagavad Gita.

Prof: Accepted. Registrar,

Christina: Yes sir

Prof: Christina, please make note of the acceptance and amend records at all suitable places.

TG: What are concepts and what is semantics and how a concept is superior to semantics?

Prof: TG, it is outside the purview of discussion. Do not deviate from the subject on hand, the Gita.

TG: Sir, how ....

Prof: I will rephrase your question, just confirm if that is what you had in mind. What are the concepts propagated in the Gita? Wherein in Gita, does concept score over semantics? Does the semantic approach also produce a result or is it redundant in favor of concept?

TG: Yes sir, thank you. That is correct and exactly what I had in mind. Inwardly, TG thanked the professor for having given her an escape route.

HP: Concept-based approach scores over semantic-based approach as:
- Follows the spirit behind the words.
- Infinite possibilities as defined by the mind.
  - Not to be misinterpreted as the mind is wild and uncontrollable
    - Because "of the senses, I am the mind" (BG-10.22)
    - Concept, as defined by the Word is the conclusion.
    - The concept being mind-driven, and mind always oscillating between sattva, rajas, and tamas, Infinite possibilities open up with different combinations.
    - The concept approach is more futuristic and malleable and adaptable. Many a time, concepts can be validated only in the future.

Semantic approach scores over a concept-based approach
- Follows the letter, useful where exactitude is required.
- Infinite possibilities as defined by the word.
- Word is the decider/clincher.

Semantics are not to be ignored or discarded as they are very important as without that, the concept cannot be expressed. The conceptual approach does not make semantic redundant. The Seers have experienced the truth in semantics. Suppose an idea is being explained, and the same is disseminated across the community by different community leaders, their words could be different, but the idea they are putting forth is the same. Same too is the case with Gita. But Words should not be relegated to secondary status, especially because they are the words of the Lord Himself.

Sanskrit is called the language of the gods. This is not said in lighter vein because not only is Sanskrit the mother of all languages but all Sanskrit words has what is called Artha Shakti, inherent in them. It means that those words by itself express meaning.

We have to question ourselves, can Gods' omnipotence be restricted/confined to the words of a particular Acharya or their sect?

TG: Can Gods' ideas be confined to concepts of an individual rookie?

HP: It is not of an individual but a Super Individual, whether it is restricted or unbounded, and who is fettering the words or concepts will become clear after the conclusion of the debate.

TG: You mean to say that great seers don't know about non-verbal communication and concept-based learning and you are greater than they are and discovered something new unbeknownst to them?

HP: I have not made any such claims nor implied any such thing. The seers have used those concepts in their commentaries/explanations, but have not stated or mentioned them, probably because it was very obvious and the general populace aware of the same unlike the accursed present generation people of Kaliyuga, who are characterized by limited intellect, shorter life span, quarrelsome by nature and mired in miseries.

TG: You have sidestepped two points.

HP: Which points?

TG: Your pre-determined parameters and paradigm.

HP: Not mine, I am parroting what is said in Gita. About the paradigm, I have already told that it is

- Concept-based without discarding semantic approach
- Objective in approach and conclusion
- Panoramic (360°)
- Inclusive and not divisive, i.e., acceptance of interpretation of all Acharyas.
- Non-reliance on external scriptures, for
  o How to learn.
  o Actual learning.
  o Cross verifying the correctness or otherwise of our learning.

A diagrammatic representation would make it clearer. She goes to the board and draws.

Sl	Approach/study type	Remarks	
1	Literal	1 & 2 Interdependent	Panoramic or holistic
2	Figurative	Same as above	
3	Random		
4	Chronological		
5	Non-Chronological		
6	Individual Sloka	Complete by itself	

7	Chapter-wise	Some chapter complete in itself	
8	Other communication channels		
9	Broad & narrow sense		
10	Others Unknown or unspecified		

About the predefined parameters, the entire Gita and our discussions rest on those parameters.

TG: Okay, tell us.

HP: I wish to make an opening statement and thereafter, each of the issue what I raise may be cross-examined.

TG: I have no objection if the group is okay with it.

Chorus—we don't mind.

Prof: Smiling in jest let the court bend to the wishes of her Highness, make it a statement, not opening statement. They would, however, be subject to examination by the other group. TG, note down all your queries and put forth after completion of the delivery of the statement.

HP: Thank you, sir, agreed.

HP: continues taking a deep breath, everybody accepts that God is the greatest and also His words are the greatest. There is near unanimity as to the supremacy of the Gita, but nonetheless, there have been constant conflicts amongst votaries of the Gita, claiming the legacy of the Lord and the supremacy of their say to the negation of the say of others. This set me thinking- Who is correct and why that someone is correct and some other one is wrong? If someone is wrong, why do people still flock to the person propagating wrong ideas? In most of the cases, the possibility that they being wrong was remote and is to be ruled out, because, they had experienced the truth first hand after intense meditation for a long period of time and also had a vision of God. In many cases, they appeared on the earth at Gods' behest and were associates of God in His original planet.

It is also popularly believed that they are Avesha Avatara of God or His associates or implements/tools etc. Everybody claimed that Gita has all answers and I took it literally and began my exploration of the Song of God. The answers were staring at me but I was blind not to see or grasp the truth. But how can you be in dark, with the light of Gita in hand and His grace? My approach was wrong. I was looking for answers to Gita outside Gita.

It was like a person searching her lost wallet in a place other than where it was lost because the place where he had lost did not have light.

"Gita answers all "is a concept with many other sub-concepts, Gita is non-different from God is another concept, and these unshackled my mind from words to concept.   By this, all the divisions disappeared and all the interpretations of great seers found their rightful place with each occupying their own space. It was also observed that all the great seers had kept silent on some verses or certain aspects of a few verses. Those verses are important on which I built my base. The reasons for its importance are:

- They provide the base.
- They explain certain core principles of the Gita.
- They highlight some very important properties/characteristics of Gita either through words or through implication.
- Not only the slokas, but their position of placement in Gita also conveys certain things.
- Other slokas/verses rest on the essence of these slokas. Hidden mysteries & Incidents in Bhagavata or Mahabharata get unraveled through these slokas.
- We may enunciate certain principles and sub-principles, to navigate into the ocean of Gita based on the above.
- By previously mentioned ways, we may determine the correctness or otherwise of our comprehension.

They formed the edifice of the Gita, the very soul of the Gita, on which most of the verses of Gita rest. Without these, the **Krishnaness** or the **Gitaness** of the Gita would be incomplete. It would have felt like fire without heat and light or water without liquid and thirst-quenching properties. I chose those verses for building my model.

In view of the same, these slokas and their derivatives are taken as parameters.

These parameters may be classified as

- Existential parameters
  - Because other verses can't exist or derive meaning without these slokas.
- Principle enunciating Parameters.
- Guiding parameters
  - Because these verses act as guides to understanding the intricacies of Gita
- Implication parameters
  - Because they imply some meaning which is not apparent or gauged prima facie

> Two new words, Krishnaness and Gitaness is introduced into the vocabulary, as there is no better way to express Infinity.

What is Krishnaness? What is Gitaness?

o The unique characteristics found in Krishna is termed Krishnaness. Similarly, the characteristics found in Gita may be termed Gitaness.

• What are these characteristics? Those characteristics which God has described Himself in Gita... Chapter 7.

• ….. As I am the strength of the strong, I am the taste in water, etc…

 ▪ The six opulence's like, most knowledgeable, most handsome, etc.

 ▪ Other Unique qualities like completely independent Blemish-less etc.

 ▪ Omniscience, omnipresence and His omnipotence.

• What is the use of this Krishnaness?

 o This helps in a proper understanding of the GitaIt helps in understanding the scriptures like Puranas, Mahabharata, and Ramayan, etc.

 o Acts as a benchmark

 o Resolve conflicts and confusion in daily life in light of God's teachings.

HP: I have completed my statement.

TG: The word parameter is not mentioned anywhere in the Gita. It is my friend's invention. Nor has it been used as such by any commentator so far.

HP: Entire Gita comprises of 700 verses. The commentaries of all commentators are more than thrice or four times the content of the Gita. Some of them run into volumes. There could be many words/slokas in the commentaries not found in the Gita but are widely accepted, because of the concept value attached therein.

TG: Why have they been taken as parameters? Why not other verses? Are other verses inferior? Isn't each word of God equal?

HP: They are identified as parameter slokas as

 • State certain facts, which act as support/base to all other slokas.
 • Imply certain facts.
 • Derive certain facts.

These facts, derivatives, and implications throw light on intricacies, provide deep insights of other slokas vis-à-vis other slokas or incidents in Mahabharata/Bhagavata. Our understanding, logic, or conclusion of any slokas or incidents in Bhagavata or Mahabharata must adhere to the above. Since it determines the correctness or otherwise, it is categorized as parameters. There could be other slokas also. I could gather this much with my limited knowledge.

An easier mundane explanation, Pure water has the characteristics/properties of being liquid, thirst-quenching, transparent and refreshing. We drink it only if the above characteristics are found.

All words are equally important and have their own role. Other verses may serve other purposes. The characteristics of these verses must be fulfilled while studying other verses or studying Mahabharata or Bhagavata. If fulfilled, our conclusion may be termed correct.

An example would clear the confusion. The first parameter is God is supreme.

Supposing, you are reading Bhagavata and conclude that Krishna is a coward as He ran away from a battle with Kalyavan, or when battling Jarasandha, you are ignoring the first Principle that Hari is supreme.

TG: The next question was how could opposite views and conflicting claims be correct?

HP: This was answered by the very proponents of each school of thought, with each explaining why their say is correct, validated by Gita itself which recognizes different approaches.

TG: But how opposing views of different Acharyas can be correct?

HP: The Lord exists both internally and externally, in the moving and nonmoving. He is both far and near. He appears divided though he is undivided. BG-13-16 & 13-17.

- Just as God comprises of opposite things in Him and outside Him, similarly His work Gita supports opposing truths /views which are reflected in conflicting views held by the Acharyas...
- Each Acharya has had the vision of God, which God chose to show that particular Acharya.
- The Cosmic vision shown to Arjuna was different from the one seen by Bhishma, Yashoda-Maiyya, Sage Uttanaka, or Markandeya. It was also a different form of the Lord which was displayed in Kauravas Sabha, wherein it was ordered that Krishna be arrested.
- Similarly, the Acharyas too had different visions, the experiences of which they shared with their contemporaries and disciples.
- From the mundane perspective, The Acharyas were having a semantic-based outlook with each advocating a particular meaning attributed to a word or phrase.
- In BG 2-24 to 2-26, God has told that if you think of the soul as subject to birth and death, then you have no cause for lamentation for the inevitable, similarly, if you hold that the soul is immortal, then too, you should not

lament as it is only the body that perishes. See, both are opposing views and God is substantiating how each of them is correct.

- Here it should be noted that the subject is not whether to lament or not to lament, but perform a duty or abandon duty, but we ignoramus personae shift focus from significant to insignificant. Similarly, while reading any of the Sloka, our focus should not be lost in arguing who or what is right or wrong, but de-focus from the insignificant path to the significant goal.

- One more example, In BG 9-4 & 9-5, God says that He is in all beings, all beings are in Him, but He is not in them. God is substantiating His three opposing views within Himself.

TG: What is a significant goal?

HP: We had discussed yesterday, what is our objective? There could be two types of objectives, mundane, and Spiritual.

On the mundane plane, you might have the objective of Acquiring wealth and another material objective, Freedom from distress, Seeking Knowledge On the spiritual front, you may want to escape from the cycle of birth and death by attaining God.

TG: Is Arjuna Ignorant?

HP: Can a close associate of Almighty be ignorant? God has publicly declared on many occasions that Arjuna is His bosom friend since time immemorial: BG: 4.5. Both have endured the bonds of friendship from eons at a stretch under different incarnations.

TG: Then, Arjuna is shirking from duty? ....

HP: Remember, God is the giver of knowledge and memory—BG: 15.15. God has temporarily withdrawn the knowledge and memory from Arjuna for a greater cause.

TG: You said that God and Gita are non-different, how?

HP: Isn't Gita, the Soul of Krishna?

TG: Yes.

HP: Isn't Krishna, the Soul of Gita?

TG: Yes.

HP: Do you still harbor doubts that Gita is non-different from Krishna?

TG: No, but ....

Prof: HP, remember that there are others too who may have doubts but not expressing it. It is in the fitness of things that you elaborate on how Gita is non-different from Krishna for the benefit of others.

HP: Okay sir. Most of you would have heard of the story of a poor Brahmin who worshipped Gita and recited Gita and implicitly believed in the Gita verbatim. How he scored off the verse, and God corrected his understanding is well known. Do you still don't subscribe that both are non-different?

TG: I recollect you saying that the slokas of Gita are generalizations, isn't it?

HP: Of course, I stand by my words.

TG: Please elaborate.

HP: Gita is a generalization of knowledge, in segments. Hence, it is more concept-based than word-based. If it is word-based, the concept of generalization cannot be applied to most of the slokas.

TG: Why so?

HP: The concept of completeness of Gita would suffer from infirmities.

There would be derogation/degradation of Gita from infinite to finite.

TG: Please explain.

HP: It is like using numerals instead of symbols variables and constants. Each statement would hold good only by itself and only in itself, without any practical value.

TG: I didn't get you.

HP: Gita would be static, and not evolving dynamically with changing times, and tends to get redundant.

TG: Redundancy is dependent on adherents and not on the scripture.

HP: That is more dangerous. People tend to adhere to the word rather than the spirit. It would not be pragmatic nor realistic but have only the backing of the vested orthodoxy, or the ignorant blind followers. The following is more emotion-based than on reality. The world would be put into peril. The 26/11 act of terror is a case on point.

TG: I request HP to provide the sloka numbers she would be relying upon or slokas which she will be taking up tomorrow. That way, we will be fully prepared and be having a more meaningful discussion.

Prof: Hari, it would be in the fitness of things that you provide the information sought.

HP: Sure, I propose to select a few slokas from amongst the following as parameters. Not all slokas may be used or there could be a stray addition or two.

HP: The slokas with their derivatives selected for discussion:

1. **Lord Hari is supreme,**
   a. Vouchsafed by undermentioned slokas,
      i. BG: 11-41 &
      ii. BG: 11-42
2. I am in the entire universe & the entire universe is in me, but I am not in them. BG: 9-4 & 5. Highlights Omnipresence of God and oneness of Gita and God.
3. Krishna is the supreme Teacher. BG: 11-43 & 11-44 (Others are secondary)
4. Only God can know God by Himself. BG 10-15 & 10-16 (Others are second best)
5. I taught this to Vivasvan in an earlier eon, for reviving this, I am revealing it to you. BG: 4-1 to 4-3. (Unchanged/imperishable for millions of years)
6. Gita is complete knowledge, knowing which nothing else needs to be known. BG: 7-1 & 7-2(Completeness of Gita due to which external reference to other scriptures is redundant or not required)
7. Do not work with an eye on the fruits of action. BG: 2-47
   a. There are five causes of action and results. BG 18-16 & 18-14
      i. Results are not caused just by your actions but the other four factors.
8. I am beyond both perishable and imperishable. BG: 15-16 & 15-17
   a. Beyond variables, constants, temporary and permanent.
9. In whatever form they pray to Me I answer them in that way. BG: 4-11
   a. Customized answers
10. I reincarnate in each eon to subdue adharma and establish dharma.BG: 4-7(Objectives)
11. My devotees don't perish, state this on oath oh Arjuna. --BG: 9-31
    a. Gods guarantee like a sovereign guarantee of Government
12. I am the custodian of secret in the form of silence.   BG: 10-38
    a. I have told you the most confidential knowledge, and nothing else is hidden from you. BG: 7-2
13. What use is all the details of this knowledge, Arjuna Suffice to know that I support the whole universe with a fragment of myself? BG: 10-42
    a. Some things are not necessary
14. The soul is unborn and eternal. If you suppose that the soul is subject to death, then also you mustn't grieve for the inevitable.BG: 2-46
15. Thus has this wisdom which is more secret than secrecy been imparted to you, ponder on it and act as you deem fit. BG: 18-63
    a. Choice of decision left to you.
16. I have told you the most confidential knowledge, and nothing else is hidden from you.BG: 7.2
17. Vedas emanate from God. --BG: 3.14 & 3.15
18. I envy no one and am partial to none.BG: 9.29

19. Any sacrifice, charity austerities, etc. done without faith does not yield results.BG: 17.28
    a.   Faith an all-important pre-requisite for any endeavor.
20. My illusion has disappeared, I have regained my memory by Your grace.BG: 18.73
    a.   And not by my effort
21. I know the past, the present, and all things that are yet to come. I also know all living entities, but no one knows me. BG: 7.26
    a.   Brings out the omniscient characteristic of the Lord.
22. I exist in the hearts of all beings O Arjuna, It is because of Myself that a being's memory and wisdom exists- 15-15
23. You cannot see me with your eyes, I bless you with celestial vision. BG: 11-8
    a.   The individual effort is not sufficient, Gods' grace required. Even though Arjuna was a great devotee, He could not see or behold the cosmic vision of the Lord.
24. I have regained my memory not by my efforts but by your grace. BG: 18-73
    a.   God is a giver and withdrawer of all qualities.

25. That knowledge which sees all as undivided amongst divided is in nature of Sattva, which sees being a separate entity is Rajasic and one who is obstinate that only he is correct BG: 18-20 to 18-22.
    a.   It offers a tool to test your understanding.
26. All actions have some taint. BG 18.48
    a.   So, don't give up the performance of duties.
27. Fix your mind on me, if you cannot do it, seek me through the yoga of practice.BG: 12-8 to 12-11. (Alternative choices offered)
28. If you are slain in battle, you will attain heaven, if you are victorious, you enjoy the kingdom. BG: 2-37. (Example of the 'If' analysis in the Gita)
29. Everything which is glorious, brilliant and powerful, know it as a spark of my splendor. Bg: 10-41 & 10-42
30. A true yogi observes Me in all beings, and also sees every being in Me. BG:6.30

Treats all equally on this analogy.

Prof: Good, TG, does it satisfy you?

TG: Yes sir.

Prof: I think we will continue tomorrow. It is getting late.

Everybody breathed a sigh of relief. Some were tired, others were hungry, and some others needed a break. Everyone started leaving the hall towards the Mess.

Post-Day End –2 Discussions

After dinner, TG and her gang huddled in their room. The discussion went on thus.

KA: You have pulled a coup.

TG: How?

KA: By asking prior information on future discussions. We will be forearmed and better prepared.

TG: HP fell for it and the professor too didn't suspect our motivation.

KA: She was stupid enough to give the rationale behind the sloka even when we asked only for the sloka.

PH: There is logic in her say. It wasn't an argument for the sake of argument.

TG: Okay, then we will discontinue the debate and accept her superiority.

Everybody … Be a sport TG. Don't go off handle when genuine compliments are given to the deserving.

KA: Still, It will be an uphill task for HP. She has committed to around 30-40 slokas on her own foolishly and we can trap her at least in 10-15 slokas if we make a thorough study. We already know the slokas and we have commentaries of 5-6 different Acharyas.

TG: Study the slokas listed and mark the soft spots. I will concentrate on the forgotten links reminded by the professor. All of you study the list and inform KA, or me we can trap/corner her.

TG: Our cross-examination would be thorough. You may pass on your ideas written on a slip of paper when I am at crossroads.

Thus ended their discussion before retiring for the day.

Christina and HP met at Christina's room.

They both settled comfortably on the sofa. Christina asked if the concept is superior to word and more important than word.

HP: It is not a concept versus semantics as has evolved from the debate. Both are complementary and supplement each other. Does semantics come from concept or vice versa? From God's perspective, the concept comes first and then His words.

In fact, words aren't necessary at all, but for the unintelligent humans. He can just execute by so willing.

From the human perspective, concepts could be derived from words and words could be derived from concepts. When concepts are within the framework of

His words, it is factual. When concepts are outside the framework of His words, it is fiction/fantasy, just as when our words are out of the framework of His words/concepts.

Concepts provide continuity, by rekindling and reawakening the self. It is always dynamic and provides fodder for thought. Concepts are usually unmanifest and accepted or recognized after manifestation. Some concepts are always abstract. There always exists an element of uncertainty in concepts which is overcome by faith.

If only word is considered, ignoring concepts, God, the world, actions and results and all possibilities are reduced to Finite. If only concept is taken into account, the fear of it being fact or fiction arises. This also hinders communication as a major part of the communication is always verbal and semantic oriented at least among human beings.

Christina asked HP to elaborate her stand with an actual case study by taking up a sloka and dissecting the same. This, she argued would give more clarity and help understand better. HP agreed and proceeded.

Verse 7.21 to 7.23 is a classic verse for the undertaking case study because it is both concept-oriented and also semantic oriented. It is also a good verse for study by parsing.

- Whatever celestial form a devotee seeks to worship with faith, I steady the faith of such a devotee in that form. BG 7.21:
  o Semantic understanding.
    ▪ God has a form.
    ▪ Faith in particular form enhanced as per the desire of the devotee.
    ▪ Being a devotee is a pre-requisite
    ▪ Faith is an essential ingredient.
    ▪ Worship/sacrifice or some form of action is required.
  o Conceptual understanding.
    ▪ Devotees desire to worship a particular form of God.
    ▪ Actually, the devotee has some desires due to which he propitiates a particular form or particular god.
    ▪ This inherent desire of a devotee is recognized by God. (See next sloka)
    ▪ To obtain the desired object, a form of God is worshipped.
    ▪ In a broad sense/mundane sense, the primary cause of worship is the desire and not desire for any form.
    ▪ The ever-compassionate Lord answers their prayers by fulfilling their desires in whatever way (includes even seemingly impossible things, as nothing is impossible for God)

   they have sought directly or through gods depending on whom the prayers are offered to.

   • Manifesting from a pillar as half man, half Lion is the best example of seemingly impossible boons conferred.

o Here, in the conceptual study, we are using analogous logic by identifying a similar pattern and replacing the "whatever form" with "whatever sought" or "whatever prayed for"

o This is also in tune with the Variable/constant construct.

   • Endowed with faith, the devotee worships a particular celestial god and obtains the objects of desire. But in reality, God alone bestows these benefits. BG 7.22:

o Fulfillment of our desire is the primary motive of God, more than our primary purpose of worshipping God. To that end, a form of God is worshipped. God sees through our desires and fulfills it. Here, God recognizes the primacy of our desire over the primacy of form, for isn't He called Bhaktavatsala?

But the fruit gained by these people of small understanding is perishable. Those who worship the celestial gods go to the celestial abodes, while my devotees come to me. BG 7.23:

- This is again reiterated in sloka 9.25, wherein God says that His devotees come to Him and worshippers of manes, etc. go to manes and so on.
- Semantic Understanding.
- God is different from the gods (demigods).
- Krishna emphasizes that He is different from gods.
- Small understanding... .... > Finite pursuits...> finite results.
- Correct understanding.... Worship God, Permanent results.
- Mundane desires ...> mundane efforts...> mundane results.
- Spiritual desires....> Spiritual approach...> spiritual results.
- Conceptual understanding.
- Needless to add that He is different from us human beings or other Jivas (living beings).

Christina asked what are the main concepts dealt with in the Gita. Hari replied that there are many concepts, some of them having been explored, established, and stabilized, many yet to be discovered.

The main concepts and sub-concepts in the Gita are

- The supremacy of Krishna, God.
- The distinctions between perishable and imperishable, body and soul, soul and super soul, absolute and relative, knowledge and ignorance, the changing and unchanging, the mundane and the spiritual.
- Study of Gita through Gita.

- The futility of searching for permanent happiness on temporary earth.
- Study of cause and effects, actions and results.
- Concepts of duty and sacrifice.
- Time, space, and faith as a qualifier of all slokas.
- The effects and ill effects of workings of the mind.
- Bridging differences between scriptures and existing reality.
- The concept of completeness and conclusiveness.
- Determination of ultimate achievement.
- Salvation or Moksha
- Types of nature or gunas
- Body, soul, and super soul

Christina queried how is it that there are many things which remain yet to be discovered?

Hari replied that Gita being infinite, 'everything is already discovered' cannot hold true. Besides, all the explorations thus far have been from the angle of semantics and syntax. Concept-oriented exploration is uncharted territory. Christina asked a brief about parameters.

HP: I list some slokas or its derivatives which may be categorized as parameters with the function it performs for your benefit. I will be taking up most of these for discussion whilst defending myself in the forthcoming sessions.

CH: Please tell me the story of how Gita and God are non-different.

HP: Okay.

HP: There was a devotee Brahmin couple, who would seek alms in just three houses and be content with it. They led an austere and contented life centering around Krishna and the Gita. The husband, Arjunacharya would study Gita minutely and write a commentary.

Once he became so engrossed in studying that he forgot to seek alms and had to return empty-handed. When he sat to read Gita, he read verse 9.22 wherein God had stated: "I provide what they lack and preserve what they already possess". Somehow, this didn't strike a chord, especially as he had just returned empty-handed and was still hungry. He reasoned, that God didn't mean, Himself personally, but through some other media. He scratched the line. When he went out, Krishna and Balarama, in the guise of two boy disciples, visited the house and dumped it with groceries, fruits, and vegetables and left.

The boys had injuries on their bodies and on being enquired, informed that their Guru had punished them. The wife was feeling sorry for the boys. Her request for them to stay until their Guru came was not heeded. THE Brahmin returned and was surprised and told his wife that he had no disciples.

It then dawned on him that it was the divine Lord Himself who visited his place with all his needs. His defacing of Gita had found its' mark on God's body.

CH: Very nice. I haven't come across the story.

Christina showed her the summary prepared by her of previous day proceedings. HP enquired as to what it was and on being informed of its contents, refused to go through it or suggest changes. She informed that the Professor would be the best judge, and she will not be a judge in her own cause nor suggest changes as it would tend to be biased in the promotion of her own cause. Thus ended the second day of debate.

13. K-3   GOD IS SUPREME

Everybody had arrived and already seated in their designated places. Christina greeted TG with a "Good evening which was acknowledged with a nod and her" best of luck "didn't elicit any response from TG. The Professor arrived and occupied his seat.

Prof: Good evening, friends, Let the show begin.

TG: HP, you blew the bugle, please follow up.

HP: Good evening, friends, consults her notes and proceeds to make a statement as under.

Lord Hari is supreme. This is vouchsafed by the following slokas.

- There is nothing higher than I am like pearls strung on a thread.   BG: 7.7
- I am the supreme Akṣhara   BG: 8.3
- Persons knowing Me as Supreme Lord of the universe, free from illusion and released from all evils.   BG: 10.3
- The ignorant don't know My supreme eternal nature.   BG: 9.11
- I see you of infinite prowess.   BG: 11.19
- God is addressed as **God of gods** by Arjuna.   BG: 11.45
- God is omnipotent:
  - OH, greatest of all.   BG: 11.19
  - You are of infinite process.   BG: 11.40
  - Oh God of gods   BG: 11.45
- God is Omnipresent:
  - The entire universe is in Gods' body.   BG: 11.13
  - Space between heaven and earth is covered by God.   BG: 12.20
  - The entire world is pervaded by Me.   BG: 9.4
- God is omniscient:
  - I know all, the past, present, and future.   BG: 7.26
  - I am intelligence & knowledge.   BG : 10.4 & 4.5
  - You are the knowable and the known.   BG: 11.38
  - I am kshetrajna in all the bodies and knowing this is true knowledge.
                                                                                    BG: 13.3 and 6.29

TG:It is already known. You are just quoting sloka reference. How and why, He is great and why it is a parameter are the questions you need to address.

HP:There are six kinds of identified opulence. Having even one of them to a minuscule extent would be considered a great achievement, even though it may not be permanent. Lord has all the six opulence's to an immeasurable extent and always and at all times. They are

- Infinitely beautiful.
    - "All that is beautiful, glorious, or powerful are my creations reflecting but a spark of my splendor." BG 10.41.
    - When His creations are so, how beautiful could He have been?
- Infinite knowledge.
    - From Me originate knowledge and intellect. BG: 10.4 and 10.5
- Infinite strength.
    - Same like said in BG: 10.41
- Infinite wealth.
    - Four kinds of persons pray to Me, the distressed, the seekers of knowledge, the seekers of wealth or worldly possessions, and those who are situated in wisdom and seek Me.BG: 7.16
    - God is infinitely wealthy is implied herein, when all seek wealth from God, it means He has wealth to bestow upon His devotees.
- Infinite fame.
    - BG: 10.34, among feminine, I am fame.
- Infinite renunciation.
    - Actions cannot bind Me. I remain detached and indifferent as a neutral observer. BG: 9.9
- Besides, He has the following **unique** qualities at all times and places, again to an immeasurable extent, namely:
- Supremely independent.
    - I am the original seed of all existences. BG: 7.10, original meaning independent and causeless.
- Free from flaws/blemishes at all times.
    - BG: 11.42… Oh Achyuta, (Infallible one).
- Infinite attributes and qualities.
    - Tell me your divine glories and qualities. BG: 10.18
    - I will tell you of glorious qualities in brief for they are limitless. BG: 10.19
- Completeness.
- Eternal/imperishable.
    - BG: 11.42… Oh Achyuta,(Imperishable one)
- Uncontrolled by any but controller of all.
    - BG: 10.15. Oh, ruler of all, lord of the universe
    - BG: 9.11. They don't know Me, as supreme Lord of all beings.
- Non-difference between qualities and possessor of the qualities.
    - I am the Vedic ritual, I am the sacrifice, and I am the oblation offered to the ancestors. I am the medicinal herb, and I am the Vedic mantra. I am the clarified butter; I am the fire and the act of offering. BG: 9.16

    o   I am the only enjoyer and master of all sacrifices. Therefore, those who do not recognize My true transcendental nature fall down.BG: 9.24

Please note that these characteristics are peculiar in that it is uniqueness restricted to GOD. Others do not have these attributes.

Because of these, He is supreme and so are His actions and deeds.

HP: These are the most important Slokas. The Entire Gita rests on it. Hence, the slokas, 7.7, & 8.3 are designated as one of the Parameter Sloka.

TG: I acknowledge that Hari is great and so stated in not only Gita but in all other scriptures, but disagree about the parameter part. Who decided it is a parameter? I suppose that it is you, who are you to decide that it is a parameter?

HP: It is just a nomenclature or classification for better comprehension. It is a spontaneous identification of a natural homogeneity amongst designated parameter slokas. You may reject the classification after hearing out my say after completion of the entire debate.

TG: Okay, so it is just a classification and Hari are great, so? Much ado about one thing?

HP: This sloka is very important, as all other slokas have the quintessence of this sloka in them.

TG: How can it be? She reads out sloka randomly selecting BG- 1.15, "Lord Krishna blew His conch shell Panchanjanya", shows how the essence of Lord is supreme is present in this sloka?

HP: Read sloka 1.19, it says the heart of Kauravas shattered. Because Krishna was present and He blew the bugle.

  You may argue that it is said that their hearts were shattered because of the collective sounding of instruments and it is so stated, but notice that there wasn't any effect on Pandavas when Kauravas blew their war instruments.

TG: Krishna was present, not Gita.

HP: Gita and Krishna are non-different. If Gita was not present in Kurukshetra, where is it present? I request you to allow me to present my views. You may make a note and put forth your objections after completion of my say.

TG: Please show how they are non-different.

HP: Yes, in due course. Just like consciousness is present all through the living being, likewise, this sloka permeates all other slokas in Gita and provides life force.

TG: Consciousness is a scientific/medical term having no relation to Gita. You make a good storyteller with imaginary takes about God's words. Besides, this also goes against your stated "Gita through Gita paradigm". You propose to show something and show something else. Your references are outside the Gita and beyond the terms of reference for the debate.

HP:
- BG 10.16   How do you pervade all universe?
- BG 9.4   By Me is entire universe pervaded.
- BG 11.40   You pervade the entire universe.

Thus, it is said in the Gita.

Just as it is said above in the Gita, Just as God pervades the entire universe, all beings and non-beings, moving and non-moving, similarly too does the previously mentioned sloka permeates all other slokas in the Gita.

Also, anything to be acceptable should be experiential vis-à-vis our day-to-day practical life. It was in that context that the consciousness was explained in a mundane manner.
- Hear My Supreme word. BG: 10.1
- There is nobody equal to or greater than you are. BG 11.43
- The Supreme Truth exists both internally and externally, in the moving and nonmoving **BG** 13.16
  - God is asking Arjuna to listen to His supreme word, meaning His word is supreme.
  - God states that there is no truth greater than He is, hence don't go in search of something that doesn't exist.
  - Now, the entire Gita is His words, so listen to Gita.
  - Further, He states that He exists internally and externally in moving and non- moving objects.
  - If Lord were not supreme, His words too would not be supreme. People would look up to the non-exist supreme person (other than the lord) they would follow the one wielding authority, not necessarily scriptural authority.

So, each of the Sloka in Gita is dependent on the above two verses, 11.41 & 11.42 and derives authority from the above two verses and runs on that (premise) Fact, that God and His words are the greatest. The moment this fact is ignored, the entire teachings lose its authority and weight creates lots of doubts and results in chaos, when in fact Gita is meant for clearing the chaotic mind to clarity. These two slokas bind all other slokas. Also, other slokas make sense only after accepting this Sloka.

Similarly, God says that "All that is beautiful, glorious, or powerful are my creations reflecting but a spark of my splendor." BG 10.41.

This sloka too permeates all the slokas in the Gita and hence classified as a parameter.

Another effect of the above slokas is when there is a multitude of opinions and divergent conclusions based on different sources, the one mentioned in Gita scores/prevails over others.

TG: Suppose, the source is Gita itself but opinions differ, like in our case. This debate itself was convened because of conflict of opinion from the same source.

HP: You are partly right. This debate was convened for resolving our difference of opinion. The source was not the same, but different. The source of each participant is the ideology of her Guru/parampara, and not what is propagated in the Gita. All of you were debating the denomination of Gita as understood by you according to the tenets of your GURU.

The real source is GITA. I attempted to shift your focus from your existing beliefs to the one mentioned in the Gita.

This gathering was convened so as to reconcile differences between various groups and arrive at the truth. We have already seen earlier that the teachings of Guru are not wrong and how conflicting multiple viewpoints can all be correct simultaneously. It will also be shown how to crosscheck the correctness or otherwise of our understanding with the help of parameter slokas.

TG: And only your source is Gita, eh?

Prof: TG, please …………

HP: From the statement "Hari is supreme", we can derive as under:

Gods' words cannot be qualified by other words. Only His words can qualify His words.

TG: It is well known that we have to take God's words literally. Nowhere is it said that you derive something, and misconstrue derivation as Truth and pass it on as Gods' words in the Gita.

HP: Supposing, what I say weren't literally true, IT faces the situation and circumstances like the classic literary piece, "The Animal Farm" by George Orwell.

In it "All are equal" is modified and replaced with "All are equal but some are more equal".

The consequences would include
- Sanctity is lost.
- It is ridiculous.
- The distinction between original and fake is blurred.

- o It is something akin to modifying Picasso's painting or Michael Angelo's sculpture.

God is Supreme. His words are supreme. Other words are lesser in supremacy and secondary to God's words. Modifications to God's words are not acceptable, nor are His words allowed to be qualified with words of others. God's words are independent of others' words. ONLY HE CAN QUALIFY HIS WORDS.

TG: Debates are won by logical points, precedents, and expert opinions, not your opinions.

HP: What I have said is very logical and proceeds naturally as a corollary or a derivative to the first statement. It is also experiential. The extrapolation technique is extensively used in Analytics, Data Science, Management, Research, etc.

TG: When Gods' words cannot be qualified by others' words, how can God's words qualify His own words? Isn't it implying that God has made a mistake and is correcting it by qualifying words? You are linking one verse with another unconnected verse and calling it qualifying verse.

HP: God can condense these seven hundred verses also into a single sloka with qualifications contained in that very one sloka, but can lesser mortals like you and I understand what is stated in one sloka when we cannot clearly comprehend what is expanded into seven hundred slokas?

HP: Gita is the briefest version of complete knowledge, comprising of just 700 verses, which itself has hundreds of commentaries to help understand them. Imagine Gita with a single verse and the amount of confusion it could cause.

TG: Still, it is not stated in the Gita and you are manufacturing a parameter from sloka and claiming Gods' sanction for the same.

HP: TG, I have not stated lightly that "Gita is all and all is contained in Gita". It is my core belief and faith. I am aware that you and your gang have devised a strategy more to corner me rather than to get the truth, hence you are demanding reference in Gita even though you have no other objection to my response. So be it. Please read BG 13.20.

TG: Reads out as under:

Kaarya-kaaran-kartritvehetuh-prskritir-uchyate
purushah sukhduhkhaanaam bhoktritve hetur-uchyate. BG: 13.20

Next, reading the translation as under:

Prakriti is said to be responsible for bringing forth the evolutes and the instruments, while the individual soul is declared to be the cause of the experience of joys and sorrows.

TG: Puzzled, but how is this verse connected in any way?

HP: Just as the Prakriti is responsible for bringing forth evolutes, similarly the statements that "God is supreme & God's words are supreme bring forth many evolutes, of which I have quoted just one.

Again, as mentioned in BG 13.21, the three gunas are evolved from Prakriti, just as if many things have evolved from 'God is great' & 'Gods words are supreme'

TG is stumped. There is a round of applause from all and the professor suddenly realizes that he too is clapping. The professor calls for order.

The professor was enjoying the debate and marveling at the skill of his students. TG for his comprehension of legal niceties and raising objections and HP for her ingenuity and logic in the application of appropriate principle of the Gita to counter TG's objection.

As a teacher, he was proud of his protégé, though he loathed TG's intolerance and dogmatic stance.

TG: Okay, assuming that the said sloka pervades all other slokas, please give examples of your derivation of the non-qualification clause.

HP: Okay, for purposes of example let us take: God has told

Fix your mind on Me, be devoted to Me, sacrifice unto Me, bow down to Me, by doing so, you will surely attain me. BG: 9.34.

Now, someone tells you what to wear, and asks you to kill Goat / chicken or any other animal as a sacrifice, seeks hefty fee and tells that this is what God has told and quoted scriptures, this shouldn't be acceptable. They are superimposing words from some other scriptures over God's words. Other words cannot qualify God's words.

God's words only can qualify God's words. For example, in the above, if a person is bowing down before the deity, he is praying loudly, and performing worship, but **lacks faith**, his activities are of no avail.

TG: Faith is important, but I wonder where it is mentioned in the Gita.

HP: It has been mentioned in at least 9 to 10 places. For the present context, any sacrifice, charity, austerities, etc. done **without faith** does not yield any results. BG: 17.28. See, here, Gods' words uttered in BG 9.34 is qualified by what is said by God in BG 17.28. Any activity done without faith is not fruitful.

Here, both the utterances were made by God Himself, in the same avatar in the same eon to the same Arjuna in that very Gita. So, it is unambiguous and we can safely assume that the latter sloka qualifies the former sloka.

TG: Can what God said in a different eon or in different scriptures be taken to qualify what is said in the Gita?

HP: Yes, IT cannot qualify Gita, as the context changes. What is said in Uddhava Gita may be taken to qualify what is said in the Gita and vice versa?

Here, the Avatar is the same and the eon is the same although the subject-candidate is different because the object was the same, that of disseminating true knowledge to establish Dharma.

Prof: Wanting to test HP's depth of study of Gita, can you give a few more examples of qualification and non-qualification of God's words by words of others?

HP: Let scriptures be your authority to guide as to what is to be done and what is not to be done. BG: 16.24. Some scriptures enjoin animal sacrifice. So, is it to be done? God also mentions the animal sacrifice part, how to reconcile with Gita? Here it is understood that what is said in scriptures is qualified by what is said by God in the Gita. Gods' words overrule scriptures if Gita is taken not to be scripture.

The above verse, 16.24 is qualified by verses

Abandon all varieties of religion and take refuge of me alone BG: 18.66

- A true yogi observes Me in all beings, and also sees every being in me. BG: 6.29
- A Yogi sees the same super soul (God) all living beings. BG: 5.7
- A perfect yogi sees all living beings equally and responds to their joys and sorrows as if it were his own. BG: 6.32
- The yogis, see with equal eye, all living beings in God and God in all living beings. BG 6.29

The sum and substance of these qualifying slokas are:

- See all creatures as God's creation similar to yourself.
- See God and godliness in all creatures.
- Do to others, only those acts which you feel good if done to you by others.
- Such an attitude in a person is dear to God.

If you perform animal sacrifices, you are violating the instructions in BG 18.66 and ignoring BG 6.29, wherein you are advised to abandon animal sacrifice, and also put yourself in the place of the animal about to be slaughtered.

Prof: That is about the qualification of words by God in other scriptures. What about the words of other than God?

HP: The words of seers and great devotees are always in tune with Gods' words. Wherever there appears to be deviation, IT would be due to our misunderstanding. It could also be due to the prevalence of a different set of circumstances than when it was said. In such instances, we may be guided by Gita, or more specifically the parameters are given in the Gita.

TG: There could be more than one sloka each of which holds contradicting views. That is why we have to refer to seers.

HP: Each of the persons will understand the sloka as per their innate capacity and knowledge which would be true and applicable to that particular person. What it means is that the same sloka may mean different things to different people at different times and different places. Differing slokas and differing meanings for the same sloka are a choice of menu offered by God, and each accepts that interpretation which suits his innate nature and ability. This is the beauty and versatility of His words. This further underscore the supremacy of GOD.

TG: Supposing it is not understanding but misunderstanding as per their innate capacity, then?

HP: It is possible and happens oftentimes. This is the drawback of that person. That is why the parameters are given by God to cross-check our understanding.

TG: You mean you wash off your responsibility and let them fend for themselves?

HP: There could be a hundred ways and two hundred cross-checks but if somebody chooses to go the 101st way where there is no path, she has to pay with consequences.

TG: Ultimately, you are not standing by your philosophy.

HP: Show me any scripture, law, principle, or software logic which holds good at all times for all persons, even when you do not adhere to the guidelines of dos and don'ts or do not follow the prescriptions. Is it the fault of the creator or author or is it the fault of the end-user?

TG: We are discussing your scripture, or your principle, the onus lies on you.

HP: I have fulfilled my onus; it is for you to show that it is otherwise. Okay, you tell how God is not great?

TG: I didn't say so.

HP: But nevertheless, you oppose me. Presuming I am wrong, please put forth the correct perspective.

SILENCE

PROF: HP, is your presentation over, TG, do you have anything to say or any counters to her presentation?

Both of them replied in negative. The professor adjourned the proceedings for the day.

HP and Christina walked slowly towards their hostel. Christina had doubts about professors' competency/integrity. She ventured to ask HP about it.

HP: Why do you have such doubts?

CH: You put forth your say. TG could not counter you by logic, nor would she present her counter perspective. The professor was more eloquent in silence. Hence, I got a doubt.

HP: I am in the dock. My principles are on trial, not hers'. It is for me to prove my point. She just has to UN-prove my stand.

The professor plays by rules. If he noticed something unjust, he will definitely remedy the same.

They had then reached their hostel and bid each other good-bye and parted. The next day, Christina took her summarization to the professor and handed it over to him.

He beckoned her to sit and started reading the same.

SUMMARISATION BY CHRISTINA

Summary report of daily proceedings—Day 1

The debate commenced with the filing of charges against Haripriya by a motley crowd of groups who were represented by Trikala Gyani.
The following charges were imputed against Haripriya.

- She contradicts the sayings of all established Acharyas.
- Her say is not in conformance with any of the existing versions.
- Her version does not find any mention in any of the scriptures.
- There is neither any Guru nor any follower believing or practicing her version.

Issues involved vis-à-vis charges against Haripriya-

- Does the non-conformance of existing scriptures constitute guilt?
- Is it necessary to agree with all pre-existing scriptures?
- Does the version of Haripriya has the backing of scriptures or is it mere shooting in the air and a figment of her imaginative mind?
- Is Guru-Shishya or Teacher-Pupil relationship necessary for learning?
- Isn't self-learning without Guru possible?
- Can Gita officiate as Guru?

A consensus has been arrived by all the groups as regards the following:

- Gita is absolute.
- Gita is not subject to interpretations or modifications.

    o   As such, Gita would be the final determinant as to who or what is correct.

TG has quoted from BG-4-34, "learn the truth by prostrating before the spiritual masters and they will impart knowledge.

HP has in course of her arguments, did not disagree with the contentions of TG and her group, but contends that there are alternate methods of learning or obtaining knowledge. This has been borne by experience and also mentioned in Gita. She has also averred those alternative methods are more result-oriented and substantiated this with quotes from Gita.

- Time distorts knowledge, hence learning directly from the source is preferred.
- There are earlier precedents for learning directly.
- God is more knowledgeable than Guru is and hence prefers learning directly from God, giving primacy to Gods' words followed by Gurus' words.
- Precedents have been offered as to the consequences of giving primacy to Gurus' words over Gods' words with disastrous consequences.
- Do as Krishna say rather than what He does. Precedents have been quoted showing that God imparted knowledge in His form as Paramatma residing inside us. This was also validated with a quote from Gita.
- At some point, many of us would have experienced our inner voice guiding us.
- Krishna is the giver of fruits of Karma, so it is He who gives us knowledge- this too is validated through Gita's quote.
- It is implied that worshippers of Guru may go to Guru instead of going back to Godhead and this is implicitly validated by Gita's quote.
- God has asked us to give up reliance on all Dharma and surrender unto Him.
- Surrendering unto Guru constitutes disobedience of Gods' instructions and is validated with Gita Quote.

- God is giver and Guru is seeker, seeking from guru tantamounts seeking from another seeker making it secondary to directly seeking from the giver (the God). Validated through Gita's quote.
- God is both a path and destination, but Guru is just a path. If Guru is a destination, it is the second-best destination. Validated with Gita's quote.
- Learning from inanimate things and lower species of living beings is approved by God in Uddhava Gita, implying that Gita can officiate as Guru.

- It is also logically implied that limiting Gods' words to a single meaning is an injustice towards the infinite God and His infinite words.

COMMENTS/OBSERVATIONS

TG has quoted one verse of Gita and shown one precedent of Gita wherein Krishna Himself had a guru.

- HP has given relied on nine references from Gita and one from Uddhava Gita and offered six precedents countering the lone reference and lone precedent offered by TG.
- HP has given four instances wherein the conclusion is implied and logically expounded and also experiential.
- TG could not anywhere counter present arguments to the satisfaction upholding his say over that of Haripriya, nor could she defend her presentation.

In light of the above, it may be concluded as under:

- All the issues raised about Gita and Guru are correct and true.
- The lone issue of approaching the Guru, put forth by **TG too is not INCORRECT** and this is accepted even by HP.

As regards the imputations against HP, TG could not offer convincing arguments, as to how HP can be held guilty.

Some issues are kept in abeyance pending discussions.

The professor nodded appreciatively. He said it was good, but he prefers a transcript of actual proceedings. This he said would ensure his independence and non-bias. Also, it would help overcome misquoting or misreading of original proceedings. He asked her to transcribe the actual proceedings and give it to him after the conclusion of the entire debate. Christina thanked the professor and took leave of him.

14. K 4 IMPERISHABLE AND PERISHABLE

All the students were sitting and ready. The professor was also ready. He asked them to start. HP: I will continue by presenting my next parameter.

- There are two kinds of entities, the perishable (Kshara) and the imperishable (Akshara) imperishable. The material entities are all perishable and the spiritual beings imperishable. BG: 15.16
- Besides these two, the Lord Himself has entered into these entities and provides support. BG: 15.17
- Because He is transcendental and beyond both the matter and the spirit, and because He is the greatest, He is referred to as Purushottama in the Vedas and people. BG: 15.18.

TG: Slokas are accepted, but about parameters, we are skeptical.

HP: This is one of the most important slokas and hence designated as a parameter.

TG: Pray, tell us how it is important other than it being uttered by the Lord.

HP: Is Gita spiritual or material?

TG: It is spiritual.

HP: So, it is imperishable?

TG: Yes, it is imperishable.

HP: Meaning it is unchanging?

TG: Yes, it is unchanging, we understand perishable as changing and imperishable as unchanging for the purposes of this debate.

HP: Then why there are so many flavors of the Gita? Each of them differs from another?

TG: Each of them has evolved with time.

HP: Then it has changed, so it is not spiritual? Again, it means that the last evolved one is the best and others are second best, but it cannot be so for the simple reason that Gita is unchanging and it is not evolved. It is the same ... that was taught to Vivasvan-the Sun god and that which was taught to Arjuna five thousand years ago.

TG: You speak both ways, something like hunting with the hounds and running with the hares. Tell us definitely, what is correct.

HP: Both are correct.

TG: How can both be correct when they are completely poles apart?

HP: God has said that there is a perishable entity, a non-perishable entity and He is beyond both.

These could be individuals or a collection of individuals or other matter forming a universe.

Meaning there are at least four entities, one which is constant, the other one which varies and another which varies with changes of another external variable and lastly the Lord Almighty who is beyond all these. How God is beyond perishable and imperishable?

- o In bodily concept, God doesn't have a physical body, His soul and body are non-different. It is made up of Bliss and knowledge.
- o The soul never dies, but His body too never dies, as is body and soul are the same.
- o Then, what happened to the body, when Jara, the hunter shot at the Lord?
- o God has answered this as under:
  - Although I, the Lord of all living entities am unborn and imperishable, yet I appear in this world by virtue of *Yogmaya*, my divine power BG: 4.6.
  - Fools deride Me when I descend in the human form. BG: 9.11
    - Meaning, God's appearance, and disappearance are different from our birth and death.
    They are His pastimes. He has assumed human form and would play the role of a human being to the hilt. It is akin to a drama wherein an illusion is created that the actor would lose his head in a battle, but in reality, His head is in place.
- o In the non-bodily concept,
  - God is beyond changing, unchanging and both
  - God has said that He is time and time always changes
  - Thus, He is beyond both.

Extending the same analogy to Gita also, Gita has parts that change, some parts which remain constant or fixed and some parts changing depending on its controller or the dependent variable.

Gita also qualifies to be an imperishable being or an entity, this qualification being derived from Gita being non-different from GOD. This imperishable being is beyond both perishable and non-perishable simultaneously just like God.

The constant, it is unchanging. An independent variable keeps changing. A dependent variable changes depending on the values of an independent variable. An entity that is beyond change and dependence and independent always is constant.

TG: Don't talk in circles and ambiguously, when you can't explain properly.

HP: Let us visit mathematics for an answer. The clue lies there.

TG: Objections, out of bounds as out of scope and irrelevant.

HP: Please allow me, if after you hear me out, if you find it irrelevant you may expunge my statements off record. Also, it was agreed prior to the commencement of the debate that to prove the veracity of a statement it must be experiential. You may correlate the mathematical part with what is stated in the Gita.

TG: Looks at her friends, and on their nodding, asks HP to go ahead.

HP: Thank you, my friend. Let us go back to our school days and recollect Algebra. We had arithmetic expressions and equations. Equations being identified by "=" symbol and expressions without those symbols.

Algebra is defined as understanding patterns, relations, and functions representing and analyzing mathematical situations and structures using algebraic symbols, using mathematical models to represent and understand quantitative relationships and analyzing the change in various contexts.

Algebra is used to create mathematical models of real-world situations and to handle problems. Rather than using words, algebra uses symbols to make statements. Algebra often uses letters to represent numbers.

Algebraic reasoning is a process in which mathematical ideas are generalized from a set of particular instances, establish those generalizations, and express them in a concise and pithy manner.

Algebraic thinking is about generalizing arithmetic operations and operating on unknown quantities. It involves recognizing and analyzing patterns and developing generalizations about these patterns. In algebra, symbols may be used to represent generalizations.

In algebraic expressions, letters represent variables. These letters are actually numbers in disguise. In this expression, the variables are X and Y. We call these letters **"var**iables" because the numbers they represent can vary—that is, we can substitute one or more numbers for the letters in the expression.

Typically, numbers toward the end of the alphabet are designated as variables and those toward the beginning of the alphabet are designated as constants.

To evaluate an expression means to find its value. If there are variables in the expression, you will be asked to evaluate the expression for a specified value for the variable.

Since the variables are allowed to vary, there are times when you want to evaluate the same expression for different values for the variable.

The first step in evaluating an expression is to substitute the given value of a variable into the expression. Then you can finish evaluating the expression using arithmetic.

In advanced mathematics, a *variable* is a symbol that denotes a mathematical object, which could be a number or a collection of numbers (a matrix or a vector or a function or a set)

An algebraic identity is an equality that holds for any values of its variables.

For example, $(x+y)^2 = x^2+y^2+2xy$, the identity holds for all values of x and y

Then there is this definition of constraints, which are nothing but defining the lower and upper range of values which a variable can assume. This is to ensure meaningful results. Supposing attendance of students is to be consolidated, the no of days in a month cannot exceed 31 and Sundays cannot exceed five a month. So the variable "days" "d" should be between 1 and 31. It cannot be a negative figure, a fraction or above 31.

Constraints exist in real life and hence need to be accounted for in the Algebraic model.

Now, this nomenclature of constants and variables applies to Gita also and mentioned in Gita itself as perishables and imperishable. Why and how? Because, a thing is said to have perished when it has lost its form or varied its form and imperishable means remaining constant, retaining original form. Entire Gita comprises Dependent variables, independent variables, dependent constants, and constants. Individual souls are constants and The Lord Almighty is the sole perpetual beyond any of the nomenclature of constants or variables.

TG: Is this algebra class or a debate?

Prof: Isn't it pretty obvious? Still, Hari please elaborate for the ilk of TG and others.

HP: Just like in Algebra, Gita too is about understanding patterns, relations, and functions and understanding relationships and analyze the change in various contexts. Applications of both are used in the real-life world, but in the case of Gita, it addresses real-world after-life part also.

Whilst algebra uses letters to represent numbers, Gita uses words, slokas or silence to represent classes, individuals, expected response, values ethics, etc. Both Algebraic reasoning and Gita reasoning refers to the process of generalizing ideas from instances and establish generalizations therefrom. Both Gita's thinking and algebraic thinking are about generalizing known quantities for the future evaluation/resolution of the unknown. In algebra, letters are numbers in disguise, whereas, in the Gita, words/slokas represent underlying principles that need to be evaluated like an algebraic expression. In both cases, the same expression may need to be evaluated with different varying values. In both Algebra and in the Gita, constraints need to be identified and defined and results are to be considered only thereafter, otherwise, you may arrive at absurd and inconsistent values, something like GIGO, garbage in and garbage out 'principle' in computer jargon.

In a further simplification, you may substitute Gita for algebra and slokas/words for letters in my earlier statements, just prior to this elaboration without affecting the meaning to a very great extent.

Let us do so as to understand the true import of the Gita. In a simple way.

Gita is defined as understanding patterns, relations, and functions representing and analyzing Real life and historical situations including Gita situations and structures using Slokas, words phrases, etc. using Conceptual Gita models to represent and understand quantitative relationships and analyzing the change in various contexts.

Gita is used to create models of real-world situations and to handle problems. Gita uses words, phrases silence, etc. to make statements.

Gita's reasoning is a process in which Gods' ideas are generalized from a set of particular instances, establish those generalizations, and express them in a concise and in a pithy manner.

Gita's thinking is about generalizing thinking operations and operating on unknown quantities. It involves recognizing and analyzing patterns and developing generalizations about these patterns.

In Gita expressions, the words, phrases, statements may represent variables or constants depending on the context. To evaluate an expression means to find its value. If there are variables in the expression, you will be asked to evaluate the expression for a specified value for the variable.

Like algebraic thinking, Gita thinking requires skillsets of recognizing patterns and developing generalizations but this is for us humans, for God already has that knowledge of all, past present and future, He has given us Gita by incorporating all His patterns in the form of generalizations. We, mortals, need not think, suffice it to identify the patterns and generalizations and act accordingly.

Like Algebraic reasoning, God has already reasoned out problems and solutions and generalized them and put it in the Gita.

God has already seen all the patterns, relations, and functions and structures in our day-to-day life. He has created the Gita Model on the lines of Algebra (Actually it is vice versa) to handle real-life situations. This model is only a template, which could have many sub-models within it.

Just like in Algebra, in Gita too, the variables are allowed to vary, when you want to evaluate the same expression for different values for the variable when your object is comparing differing meanings or you are researching. Further, in the

Gita, there could be occasions, when the variable itself is changed/varied instead of the value of the variable. Simply stated, either the value of the variable is varied or the value of the variable could itself be another variable.

The first step in evaluating an expression is to identify variables and constants and substitute the given value of a variable into the expression., keeping in mind the constraints. Then you proceed with the evaluation of the expression.

Gita evaluation is a bit difficult. One of the reasons being there is no distinct symbols to represent any type of variable or constants, unlike in algebra, wherein variables are always represented by letters and numerals represent constant and dependent constants are represented by letters.

The arrived results too could be words, phrases, or statements unlike in Algebra, wherein it is always numerical.

In advanced mathematics, a variable is a symbol that denotes a mathematical object, which could be a number or a collection of numbers (a matrix or a vector or a function). In Gita, too a variable can be an individual, or a collection of individuals, a defined set of characteristics or properties in isolation or in collection or sub-collection.

A Gita identity is an equality that holds for any values of its variables.

For example, $(x+y)^2 = x^2+y^2+2xy$, the identity holds for all values of x and y, similarly in the Gita

Anything addressed to Arjuna, we can safely substitute Arjuna with ourselves/or any other seeker within constraints and context.

Then there is this definition of constraints, which are nothing but defining the lower and upper range of values which a variable can assume. This is to ensure meaningful results. In Gita, constraints, GOD-Almighty is always a constant, meaning you cannot substitute yourself or others in God's place. Further, the limitations of ability, nature, God's grace, etc. form the constraints on your evaluation.

Constraints exist in real life and hence need to be accounted for, but unlike in algebra, constraints itself keep changing.

These thinking, reasoning, patterns generalizations, models, etc. are for us mortals, a gift from God, the source of all knowledge, meaning algebra and all science have their origin in God and can be plainly seen in the Gita. Mathematicians have incorporated a small portion of this knowledge in the sphere of mathematics with applications in some spheres. For the skeptical,

Gita has evolved earlier (5300+ years ago in recent times and millions of years ago in ancient times) than algebra, and all that is found in algebra is already present in the Gita.

TG: What is said or being implied is not in consonance with facts. Perishable and non-perishable refer to the body and soul.

It does not say that it refers to the slokas in Gita also. Besides leading seers have interpreted this sloka in different ways, not in the way being claimed by HP.

Prof:Say, it is not in consonance with your belief and not in consonance with what is said by different seers, don't say not in consonance with facts, and else prove facts. Gita is so infinite, so sublime, there could be many more facets which still has to see the light of the day.

While following the trodden path is foolproof and easier, Body, mind, society, and horizons should not be allowed to stagnate by restricting them to a single way of thought. Hari is proposing a new outlook, give it a hearing before junking it. If it is incompatible with facts, junk it, not otherwise.

The professor was feeling proud of his student for her forceful and near-flawless submission, nevertheless asked her to give suitable examples, with the intention to gauge the depth of her understanding and also for making comprehension easier to other students in the audience who were half at sea. Hari, please enlighten the class with appropriate examples.

HP:For example, solving simultaneous equation uses the substitution method:

The substitution method is most useful for systems of multiple equations in multiple unknowns. The main idea here is that we solve one of the equations for one of the unknowns, and then substitute the result into the other equation.

The substitution method can be applied in four steps.
1. Solve one of the equations for either $x =$ or $y =$.
2. Substitute the solution from step 1 into the other equation.
3. Solve this new equation.
4. Solve for the second variable.

Now in Gita context
- Those who seek My refuge, even though they are of lower birth-women, vaishyas sudras attain to my abode. BG: 9.32
- According to the three modes of material nature and their aptitude of work ascribed to them, the four divisions of human society were created by Me BG: 4.13
- Farming, cattle raising, and business are the qualities of work for the vaishyas, and for the sudras, there is labor and service to others. BG: 18.44
- From the above slokas, we may derive as:
  - Classification is according to aptitude and nature
  - Menial service providers, cattle rearing community traders, etc. to attain to Me if they seek my refuge.

This removes the misconception that category is birth based. Again, the main determinants are the performance of prescribed duties and seeking refuge, not birth.

Prof: Good, provide a more revealing example to remove any ambiguities in understanding. Remember you are addressing your friends and not just me.

HP: It is very simple, everybody read/study/research Gita, why don't they say it is instructions for Arjuna and not for them? It is because they unconsciously put themselves in place of Arjuna i.e., they substitute themselves instead of Arjuna. We are only pointing out or documenting what has been in vogue for more than 5000 plus years. Now, Arjuna was asked to shoot and kill his adversaries, Bhishma, Drona, Karna, etc.

We don't have those persons to kill, nor are we supposed to kill our adversaries. Then how are we to understand Gita? IT should be noted that there are five types of sentences in the English language as is in the Gita.

Sentences have different purposes:
- A declarative sentence tells something. (There is no one superior to Me.)
- An interrogative sentence, or question, asks something. (Have you understood what I said?)
- An exclamatory sentence, or exclamation, says something out of the ordinary. (Oh King, God has revealed his cosmic vision!)
- An imperative sentence, or command, tells someone to do something. (Listen to my supreme instructions.)
- An optative sentence contains optative subjunctive, used to express a wish like "May you live long" "peace be upon him" etc.

Not all sentences are instructions nor all instructions are for all persons. Some sentences, just state facts. Some statements exclaim and others question as yet others confer blessings. There are instructions for a class of person say, Kshatriyas, another set for Brahmins, etc. Okay, supposing TG is a Kshatriya, should she kill me as I am her adversary now? Here the concept of context comes into the picture. This raises the question, what is a context?

Context is the background, environment, setting, framework, or surroundings of events or occurrences. Simply stated, context means circumstances forming a background of an event, idea, or statement. The most important influence on what is appropriate and how messages are interpreted is called context. There are six kinds of context. All six kinds of context are present for every act of communication; but in different settings, one or another may become more important.
- Physical Context: It includes the material objects surrounding the communication event and any other features of the natural world that

- influence communication. (E.g., Kurukshetra battlefield, how it is arranged, Reasons for the battle, etc.)
- Inner Context: This includes all feelings, thoughts, sensations, and emotions going on inside of the source or receiver which may influence how they act or interpret events. (E.g., Confused, Fear, pity, and sympathy, Anger, etc.)
- Symbolic Context: This implies all messages exchanged that occurred before or after a communication, event and which influence source or receiver in their actions or understandings of the event. (E.g., previous discussions prior to the run-up of the battle influence how you understand).
- Relational Context: The relationship between the sender and the receiver(s) of a message. (E.g., father-son, God-devotee, Guru-Shishya, expert-layman, friend-friend, etc.)
- Situational Context: What the people who are communicating think of as (label) the event they are involved in, what we call the act we are engaged in. (e.g., being in class, being on Warfield, discoursing, etc.)

- Cultural Context: The rules and patterns of communication that are given by (learned from) our culture and which differ from other cultures. (E.g., Vedic culture, Brahmanic culture, South Indian culture, etc.)

While studying Gita, the above has to be taken into account. Is the context mentioned in the Gita? It is implied in the Gita. Where is it mentioned/implied in the Gita?

Gita Context:

Apart from the above-mentioned types of contexts in the material world, another type of context as recognized by Gita which is

Time, Nature (Sattva, Rajas, and Tamas), the five causes of action and result as mentioned in **18**-16 & 18-14, the place of action, the performer, the senses, the endeavor, and ultimately the Super soul.
- In Gita, Krishna asks Arjuna to fight.
- Just prior to the battle, the very same Krishna asks Duryodhana and Kauravas to shun war and effect compromise with the Pandavas.
- Krishna Himself vows not to fight but just play the role of a charioteer.
- Krishna had earlier run away from the battlefield against Jarasandha.

See, the different connotations about fighting depending on the context.

Context is the most important variable and of numerous occurrences making it most difficult to identify and apply properly. Context is only implied and not codified which makes many stumbles.

Context is best understood ideally by recreating or simulating all the variable ingredients therein, but that is next to impossible, the next best alternative is to make suitable allowances for the same.

Prof: Can you give some examples?

HP: Surrender all your duties and seek only my refuge. 18.66

Here contexts could vary depending on the person, meaning each is advised to give up his duty and surrender, and the duties vary according to the person. IN this context, what is asked to be given up varies upon the caste of a person. A Brahmin refusing to fight cannot be said to be giving up his duty, in case of Brahmin, God is asking him to give up ritualistic practice and surrender unto Him.

This is exemplified in the Kurukshetra war, when God asks Arjuna to kill Bhishma from behind Shikandin, or when God asks Arjuna to shoot Unarmed Karna, which is against the very core of Dharma preached by God Himself.

Prof: Hari, May I simplify what you want to say? Many of your friends are still at sea and wondering what you are saying.

HP: Sir, it would be my privilege and you would be honoring me if you do so.

Prof: Mahabharata (History), our daily life, etc. are the fields. Incidents therein both in history and our present daily life have problems which need to be unraveled. These problems have certain patterns, which can be generalized. These patterns have been incorporated in the Gita. A skillful solution provider should be able to spot the patterns and generalizations made therein and apply it in his evaluation of expression of life or history. Whilst working on the same, the constraints affecting the results should not be lost sight. The biggest variable in the Gita is the context. This is very difficult to recreate hence allowance is to be made for contexts. Hari, have I summed up correctly?

HP: Blushing, yes, of course, sir, I couldn't have put it in a nicer manner.

Prof: Dear students, see it like this.

God formulated His Gita, a book/guide which subsumes all knowledge. He did this by generalizing all knowledge with help of variables and constants and putting it across like formulae in maths or Sutras for Sanskrit lovers. Many Acharyas have come and left their indelible mark by offering their insights by way of purports or commentaries. Each of them viewed in a different way. Because each has evaluated the expression with different values for variables and came up with different values for answers because the answer is a dependent constant. But we lesser mortals quarrel stating that our Guru is correct or sect is correct or religion is correct etc. Hari, am I correct?

HP: Thank you, sir, it is exactly what was in my mind but was unable to communicate.

Prof: In our day-to-day life, we can see that some things changes and some remain unchanged. Place, time, persons, and circumstances change. That which is said to a person in one place under particular circumstances may not hold good to another person or at another place or under different circumstances.

TG: Sir, you have clarified on her behalf and partial.

Prof: So be it. If Lord Himself was found to be partial to Arjuna, I too emulate my lord by being partial to Hari.

This snub was too much for TG to take. She excused herself for a few minutes and walked out of the hall. Some of her friends accompanied her. She drank lots of water but was unable to digest the snub. Her friends consoled her but were outshouted by TG. Her friends pointed out her fault, that of casting aspersions on the professor that too on his person, who was known for his impartial and ethical values. In spite of cajoling a lot, she refused to attend the remaining part of the session. Know All (KA) asked if any other person is interested in fulfilling TG's role temporarily for the day. Srilata (Taraka Shastri) was willing but needed persuasion. Everybody requested her to don the mantle which she agreed. They entered the conference hall.

Prof: Where is TG? Shall we continue in her absence or shall we break for the day?

Chorus, we will continue.

Prof: Who would represent the DR group?

TS: Sir, I will hold the fort for the day. TG will take over from tomorrow.

Prof: Is it okay, Hari?

HP: If all are agreeable, I am okay. TG is a variable and not indispensable and can be substituted just like any other person, including me.

Prof: Okay, proceed. TS, do you have any objections or questions or can Hari proceed?

TS: Let Hari proceed.

HP: Let us see the effects of employing variables in the Gita.

Effects of variables in Gita:
God has used the Constant and variable tool to achieve:
- Generalize patterns.
- Identify generalizations and patterns.
- To easily commit to memory and recall when needed.
- For deciphering and application.
- Insurance against obsolesce.
- Evaluate same expression for different values.
- To put to multifarious uses.

Deciphering Gita, we may say as under:

- What is said by God is: Contextual constant.
- What is said by others: Variables, a better word is perishable.
- What is understood by all: Variable and perishable?
- What is meant: that which is spoken by God, (Contextual Constant.

TS: You had earlier said that variable and perishable are synonymous and used interchangeably, now you are saying is it different?

HP: It was TG who said so, but I agreed with her. Nevertheless, the usage of the word is contextual. In the two instances, perishable fits the bill better.

TS: After identifying variables and constants, what next?

HP: Just as if you evaluate the expression, you evaluate the verse. Before that, you have to identify the pattern which suits the context, substitute the variables, and check the outcomes.

TS: With what do you check the outcomes?

HP: Check them with the parameters.

TS: Check them with parameters for what?

HP: For being in accord with our day-to-day experience or with well-established facts.

TS: Why should it be in line with experience or established facts?

HP: Otherwise, it would be considered the mere theory, impracticable, unbelievable and fit to be discarded rather than act as a guide and a book to be revered.

TS: What parameters and where is it found? Is it mentioned in the Gita?

Whole class bursts into laughter. Before the professor rebukes TS, HP takes over.

HP: That is what is being discussed and would require many more sessions to conclude. I have chosen them from the Gita itself and given a reference. They are found in Gita, and we are in the process of identifying those parameters.

Prof: Cite some instances in Gita, where a verse/phrase or sloka takes different values and yet satisfies the verse (like equation) meaningfully.

HP: Herein is the list of variables in the Gita, which can be generalized. The list is illustrative only and not exhaustive.

Sl	Ref	Variable	Possible values
1	1-25	War	Duty
2	1-25	Armies Pandavas Kauravas	Team favorable to us (PRO) Team opposing us (Con)
3	1-27	Fathers,Sons, Grandfathers, Friends relatives, etc.	Persons favoring our Righteous objective & Persons opposing us
4	1-33	Victory,Kingdom, Pleasures	Favorable results consequent to our acts
5	1-36	Kill them	Overcome opponents
6	1-47	Bow and arrow	Implements or tools of the trade
7	2-12	For those who should not be grieved for	Anyone opposing just causes be it our own kin (Variable and could take many values)
8	2-18	Therefore, fight.	Therefore, perform your duty. (Variable in a variable, could take many values)
9	2-30	Oh, descendant of Bharata (Arjuna).	Any person with faith in Krishna & His words
10	2-31	Great opportunity for Kshatriya	Kshatriya by nature, need not necessarily be Kshatriya by birth
11	2-33	Righteous battle	Any Righteous cause
12	2-42	The Vedas	Any of the 4 Vedas individually or collectively or a combination of both. At a higher level, It could be any scripture
13	2-61	Meditate on me	God by whatever name He is called
14	3-21	Whatever a great man does	Substitute any great person

Sl	Ref	Variable	Possible values
15	3-35	Better is one's own duty	One's may be substituted with either Brahmana, Kshatriya, Vaisya or Sudra
16	4-11	Whatever way they worship me	Worship includes prayer, propitiation, sacrifice, etc.
17	4-32	Various sacrifices prescribed in Vedas	Sacrifices are a class. It could be Knowledge sacrifice, Material sacrifice, etc. as prescribed in Gita apart from what is prescribed in Vedas
18	6-35	The mind is hard to control	Mind includes senses, thoughts, words deeds action, etc.
19	16-4	That enemy has been slain by me	Enemy= Adversary Slain=overcome

TS: You mean evaluating the unknown factors in an expression like in Algebra?

HP: Yes, but only partly.

TS: Why partly?

HP: We cannot limit the scope of Gita just to words or expressions and evaluation of them to arrive at the unknown.

TS: How else do you broaden the scope?

HP: This classification of perishable/imperishable, Temporary/permanent, spiritual/material, divine/demoniac is not restricted to human beings or just living entities.

Professor too craned his neck, eager not to miss out expounding of something new. There was no reaction or counter from TS, necessitating him to ask HP to elucidate.

HP: It extends to beings/bodies, actions, thoughts, results of actions/thoughts, products/by-products.

TS: How?

HP: Supposing, you stood first in the inter-collegiate debate and received a citation and a prize.

The prize and citation may remain or not, the feeling and the history in records remain. Another example is if an online transaction made, it carries the date, time-stamp with other info and logs which is of use to cyber forensic auditors/analysts. In the Kurukshetra war, those killed lost their bodies but existed in another sphere. The act was over but not it's after-effects like guilt syndrome, altered course of perception, and changed the course of future action. Like living beings, actions and its results too have a perishable and non-perishable component.

TS: Be more unambiguous.

HP: Every action has a result, Yes, or no?

TS: Yes.

HP: The result could be positive or negative.

TS: yes.

HP You either accrue piety or incur sin agreed?

TS: Yes.

HP: This accrual or incurring has to be experienced?

TS: Yes.

HP: So, the action may be temporary, but the effects are imperishable or permanent.

TS: Yes.

Prof: Not necessarily. IF you have used up the merits then it becomes temporary.

HP: Sir, if the merit accrued is insufficient?

Prof: It could be either way.

HP: Let me put it this way. There are two outcomes, material and spiritual.

Material outcomes get exhausted by experiencing enjoyments or by experiencing sorrow, but spiritual merit stands to our credit, which would take us a step forward, wherefrom, our future spiritual endeavors commence in the next birth.

Prof: I concede, your logic makes sense. Glancing at the clock, shall we conclude?

Everybody said yes, and the session concluded.

Christina and Hari walked together into Christina's room. Christina was all praise for her presentation. She confessed that she herself always confined the explanation of perishable and imperishable to mere physical bodies. Hari clarified; it is not restricted to beings. It extends to all actions, words, products,by-products, and results of all actions. Each of these would have two components, meaning, the results, the products, etc. One is perishable and another is imperishable. People fall into the trap of words and restrict themselves to a strict interpretation of words, thus finitizing the infinite. Hari continued …

Variables are used extensively in mathematics and algebra. In mathematics, a defining variable is a symbol, such as X, used to describe any number. When a variable is used in a function, we know that it is not just one constant number, but could represent many numbers.

Contrasting this with Gita, no symbol is used. Words or phrases are identified either as variable or constant and dealt with accordingly.

USES OF VARIABLES.
o   They help to generalize things or phenomena.
o   They help to condense voluminous data.
o   They help in remembering things.
o   It helps in limiting the quantity without truncating quantity or compromising quality.
o   They drive the research process

      ▪   In the realm of mathematics/science or in the context of Gita these are observable.

Types of variables:

•   There are three main types of variables, namely independent variables, which can be controlled or manipulated, dependent variables, which are affected by our changes to the independent variables, and control variables, which must be held constant.

•   The variable that the scientist changes during the experiment are the independent variable. Think of the experiment as a "cause and effect" exercise. The independent variable is the "cause" factor. The dependent variable is what is measured or observed. It is the "effect" in the cause-and-effect relationship.

•   In order for the results to be accurate and meaningful, other factors that could affect the outcome of the experiment should be kept the same, or controlled. These other factors are called controlled variables or "constant variables". This would generally be context.

The examples of each type of variable and an example of a function are seen in the table of possible values above. God is always constant. Taking God as a variable has disastrous consequences. Christina appeared satisfied with the answer. They dispersed.

15. K-5 GITA IS COMPLETE KNOWLEDGE

By now, interest had been developed in all the students. Some were interested in the subject matter, others in the sparks that flew, and some were there for entertainment value. The professor entered at 6 PM. He responded with a gesture to be seated in response to the students greeting him with a warm good evening.

Prof: TG, are you ready or would TS continue on your behalf?

TG: No sir, I will be doing the job. TS has made a mess of yesterday's proceedings.

Prof: It is a part of the game, it wasn't intentional, HP just came up with good responses, and that is it. Okay, Hari, please proceed.

HP: God has told Arjuna, "I shall now impart this knowledge and wisdom, (both theory and practical aspect) (phenomenal and noumenal) both as the world sees it and as it really is by itself, after knowing this, nothing further remains to be known. "BG: 7.2

Noumenal is a thing or event that is known about, even though it cannot be detected by any of the five human senses. This is the opposite of the ordinary world of appearances or of phenomena.

- This means Gita is complete. A natural corollary therefrom is

- There is no need to consult any other book or source for original knowledge.

  o Both may be treated as a parameter.

TG: Substantiate your tall claims. How can Gita, a Poetry consisting of just 700 verses be complete knowledge?

HP: It was agreed that Gita is the base and whatever is said therein is undisputable and to be accepted. Hasn't God said so?

TG: God has said so but that is not what is meant.

HP: You mean God said something and meant something else?

TG: Don't twist my words. Then why other books are available? What about mundane knowledge? Shouldn't it be pursued? Various preceptors have put forth purports and commentary differently, the words jnanam and vijnanam as theoretical and practical, mundane and transcendental, general and the esoteric, etc. Nowhere has the corollary been stated.

HP: Complete implies a conclusion, objective or a destination or parts. Other literature may be referred or pursued to get clarity etc. not as an original source of knowledge. For example, we refer a guide or a reference book but we do not dispense the main textbook. Some do not refer to guide, yet others refer only the guide and not textbook.

TG: It was also agreed that apart from being found in Gita or being implied by Gita, it should be experiential. Please base your argument on the day-to-day experiential level. Does Gita include Python coding, or say tax-saving lessons or Android operating system?

HP: Okay, what does the word 'complete' mean? How is it defined? The word takes many meanings. Some of the popular meanings are:
- Having all the necessary parts, elements, or steps and not lacking in anything.
- Brought to an end or the conclusion, end of a journey or reaching the destination.
- Highly proficient.
- Not limited in any way.

So, from the above, we may see that completeness presupposes existence of

Parts and whole, parts combining to become whole or whole by itself.
- Start or commencement of anything, the path traversed or the journey and the reaching of the destination.
- Limitations and proceeding and reaching a state of non-limitation.

Incomplete means
- Not having all parts.
- Unfinished
- Some things missing.

Whether Gita is complete or not should be ~~judged~~ viewed from the above perspective, at the experiential level.

Purpose/ object/destination too should be pre-defined. This way, you may check whether completed, reached, limited, or otherwise. When you say, pre-defined, who defines? You should define it. More precisely, God has defined and offered multiple choices, you opt from one of the pre-defined choices.

We will see some examples of the multiple choices offered in the Gita by God.
- To Arjuna
  - To kill or not to kill.
  - To surrender unto Gods' will or to stick to his own whims and fancies.
- To Us.
  - Perform your duties as per prescription and reap pleasant consequences or do what you please and reap unpleasant consequences.
  - Control the mind or let the mind control you.
  - Pursue your efforts or surrender unto Him.

- Pursue knowledge as differentiated from ignorance in the Gita, or remain ignorant by considering ignorance as knowledge.

Coming to' how it is possible', There are 118 elements of which 94 occur naturally. An element is a basic substance from which other things are composed. Each individual element is made up of invisible particles called atoms. The atom is the smallest complete unit of an element. A compound is the product of two or more elements being combined. These are fixed. All matters are a combination of these elements. These are the basic building blocks for any matter. Each matter cannot be listed individually.

There could be much matter still to be discovered. Gita is like a complete listing of all Atoms. Like all Atoms are identified and listed, so too all basics or fundamentals are listed in Gita which serves as a building block.

The numbers 118 and 94 may be erroneous or subject to change, the concept therein holds good. Identifying and knowledge about elements tantamounts to the knowledge of all matter and can be said to be complete.

Likewise, a numeral system is a method of expressing numbers. It is a mathematical notation for representing numbers of a given set, using digits or other symbols in a consistent manner. The numerals from zero to nine can express any number to represent any quantity. Here the base is taken as decimal or ten.

The same can be to base two, termed binary, comprising of just zeroes and ones. Any quantity can be expressed with just a few numerals and some small finite number of symbols.

In the realm of language, English has just 26 alphabets, a combination of which yields vocabulary and conveys and communicates everything.

Sanskrit is the original language, mother of all languages and termed language of gods. This has also been recognized as the language of exactitude and most suitable for computational purposes and compatible with computers and artificial intelligence.

As said earlier, the words in Sanskrit are formed/ based on the characteristics or properties of subject/objects expressed through words and have an inherent capacity to convey meaning with the finite number of alphabets. New words can be formed using just prefix or suffix to existing words.

TG: You mean to say if you know alphabets from A to Z and numerals from zero to nine, you are a scholar and know everything.

Prof: TG, avoid using you, your, etc. in your arguments.

HP: There is something called the level of understanding and levels of consciousness. Let us say, a second standard student knows all the numerals and alphabets as per his curriculum, his knowledge is complete.

Languages and mathematics are also studied even at the college level and at the research level. There the expected level of knowledge comprises elements and the manipulation of elements. The alphabets, punctuation, etc. and numerals and a finite number of operators are basic building blocks. Skill sets in using them determine who is knowledgeable or otherwise.

For sake of argument, let us consider TGs' proposition, supposing Gita is not complete...

TG: No, I agree Gita is complete, it is said by God Almighty Himself. I don't agree with the part 'Consulting other sources or scriptures is not necessary'

HP: Tell me, have you experienced Gita is complete? How do you justify it without experiencing it?

TG: I haven't experienced it, but great seers and preceptors from my parampara have experienced it.

HP: Then you are relying on their experience and not your own?

TG: It was agreed upon, prior to the debate that it should be experiential hence ......

Prof: Hari, you put forth the proposition and you are presenting the case, yet you are cross-examining the opposition, it isn't allowed, even though TG hasn't objected.

HP: Sir, I was replying to her in her own coin, I will not do it. See, it is like this—Arjuna not only heard what God said but also saw it and experienced what was said by God.

HP: Now, about the consulting other book's part, suppose you have a logarithmic table, the book will you consult any other book, for solving logarithmic equations? A medical student having 'Gray's Anatomy',

An English grammar student having Grammar by Wren & Martin would surely not consider consulting another book on that subject.

TG: I have seen many persons consulting other books. Even Gita enthusiasts consult many books.

HP: It isn't necessary. Gita books may have been consulted for knowing others' points of view or to have different flavors on the same subject. It could also be to do a review of others' works or know other's perspectives. The subject matter too could have been presented in a more interesting manner or put across after simplification, which attracts readers to read them.

What others do, read/consult other scriptures apart from the Gita doesn't alter the fact that Gita is complete.

TG: Gita is a part of the epic, Mahabharata, then how can it be complete?

HP: Just now, you agreed that Gita is complete ....

Prof: It is of academic interest and also for the benefit of a heterogeneous audience. Please answer Hari.

HP: It is said that what is found in Mahabharata is found everywhere, but what is not found therein cannot be found anywhere. This establishes the completeness of the Mahabharata. In Isha Upanishad, we find the invocatory sloka

(Om poornam-adah poornam-idah poorna-aat poornam-udachyate)
(Om poorna-asya poornam-aadaaya poornam-evaa vashishyate)
Om, that is complete, this is complete, From the completeness comes the completeness If completeness is taken away from completeness, only completeness remains. Here God is referred to like that, and the individual soul is referred to as this.

So, Gita with Mahabharata is complete and Gita taken away from Mahabharata is also complete.

Even in Gita, The slokas

- Give up all religions and surrender unto Me. BG: 18.66

- To those whose minds are always absorbed in Me, I provide what they lack and preserve what they already have. BG: 9.22

Are complete in itself.

Each of the chapter of Yoga, namely

Bhakti Yoga, Jnana Yoga, Dhyana Yoga, and Karma Yoga are complete in itself and can stand-alone.

TG: Grudgingly, nicely explained, please inform from Gita's perspective also. But, prior to that, I have an objection, you are straying away from Gita, and quoting Upanishad. You are deviating from the agreed set of rules.

Prof: TG, it was answered for the benefit of others and as a matter of academic interest. If you insist, we may expunge the same from records, however, this part will not be considered for arriving at conclusion or judgment.

HP: God has been described in the Gita as Saguna Brahma, (BG: 6.47 & 4.7) meaning full of qualities, i.e., the entire gamut of qualities in existence and Nirguna Brahma, (BG: 14. 27) or having no qualities, meaning the qualities are latent and not manifest. When God is full of qualities including completeness, similarly Gita too is full of all qualities in full, including those yet to manifest. Gita is complete both in parts and complete in whole also. How does Gita achieve completeness? As discussed, the very first day, Gita is objective and object-oriented. Gita achieves completeness by

Stating objectives namely.
- o Artha
- o Dharma
- o Kama
- o & Moksha.
- Actions delineating how to achieve those objectives by
  - o Kshatriya
  - o Brahmanas
  - o Vaisyas
  - o Sudras
  - o Bhakta's
- How to understand/interpret them
- Cross-checking our understanding with the benchmark mentioned in the Gita, herein called parameters
- Consequences of those actions
- Application of the previously mentioned knowledge.
- Being open-ended.

At another level, Gita is complete because,
- o It is generalized so as to fit into any scheme of things any time anywhere.
- o It speaks about manifest, unmanifest and beyond them both.
- o It is about the past, present, and future.
- o It deals with real, and unreal.
- o It covers all three types of nature, i.e., Sattva, rajas, and tamas.

Gita is self- contained as it acts as a base to
- ▪ Understand God and Gods actions
- ▪ God's teachings in the Gita.
- ▪ Human Actions
- ▪ Ourselves and resolutions of our problems
- ▪ Crosschecking our understanding with the benchmark provided in the Gita.

Now, let us see how a single word AUM represented by the symbol ॐ represents everything. Vedic texts equate Aum with Bhur-bhuvah-Svah. It symbolizes "the whole Veda". They offer various shades of meaning to Aum, such as it is "the universe beyond the sun", or that which is "mysterious and inexhaustible", or "the infinite language, the infinite knowledge", or "essence of breath, life, everything that exists", or that "with which one is liberated". Hindus consider Aum to be the universal name of the Lord and that it surrounds all of creation.

TG: How can Om be complete? Any proof?

HP: I am the syllable ૐ in the Vedic mantras. BG: 7.8. When God says that He is the syllable ૐ, it is complete, just like He Himself is.

In Upanishads, there is a story, the underlying wisdom of which is:

Just by knowing a lump of clay, everything that is made of clay can be known. In the same way, by knowing a piece of gold, all that is made of gold can be known, since any differences are only words, and the reality is only gold.

A big banyan tree grows from seed so small that you cannot see it. The banyan fruit contains many seeds that contain the potential to bring forth many more giant banyan trees. Gita is both the seed, fruit and that banyan tree.

TG: HP is deviating from Gita and seeking inputs from Vedas and Upanishads, repeatedly.

HP: I have already told you about Gita. As it is not intelligible, I am taking parts from Upanishads and Vedas. It is like explaining the unknown (Gita) with the help of Known (Upanishads/Vedas).

TG: How dare you call me unintelligent? You are not the only one who knows Gita. Don't be under such delusions. I will clip you of your spiritual/scriptural arrogance now, once and for all.

HP: First, clip your tongue, (suddenly feeling guilty), I am sorry, I repeat TG, and all my friends out there, I am sorry for my outburst.

TG, how do you explain anything, we have to proceed from what is known to the subject and relating to what is not known. I didn't introduce anything new or unsaid in the Gita afresh.

The professor was livid with rage. He had seen many acrimonious court battles and the low-level filth bandied around, but his sense of righteousness was outraged. Especially because he construed it as a disrespect to his revered Gita.

Prof: HP, you too, I expected better from you, you have tendered an apology, good, I warn you against such transgressions, TG, be conscious of the gravity of subject matter under discussion, and behave in an appropriate manner. You are censured.

TG: Sir, I am sorry, but the punishment is harsh and not commensurate with my crime.

Prof: You are under-punished. You were awarded the lightest of the punishment. Are you aware of the gravity of your misdemeanor? Contempt of court is a small offense, not contempt of cosmic court.

The court is adjourned for fifteen minutes, ruled the professor. He needed to be alone with himself in privacy to mask his anger and get over it. He walked out of the room into his chambers.

All the students were stunned by such an outcome. This wasn't the professor they had known. HP was still trying to get over her guilt complex. TG was feeling less guilty but more scared of the verdict in view of his transgressions. She justified her aggressiveness with thoughts that all is fair in love and war. Also, wasn't it important to win at all costs, if she loses now in student days, how will she win for big clients in her future career? ..... so ran her thoughts. They just sat huddled. The room was silent with the usual buzz missing.

Twenty minutes later, the professor returned and sat in his chair. He did not acknowledge any greetings and gestured that the debate could start.

TG: I am censured. I fear your honors' wrath, I cannot proceed with the debate.

Professor, being kind natured could not hold on to his anger for long, least of all with his pupils. He asked TG to treat his rebuke as a lesson, and move forward, without fear.

TG: I am called unintelligent; I demand an apology.

HP: Unintelligible means impossible to understand and unintelligent means afflicted with a lower level of intellect.

The professor was aware and also convinced of HP's version, but keep in mind, the principle, Justice should not only be done but also appear to have been done, called for a dictionary and confirmed the correctness of HPs' say.

TG: A few issues arise. How can this be a parameter? The corollary is also not acceptable, they are not God's words but HP's flights of imagination.

Prof: I have been noticing that there are objections about the parameter and many questions based on parameters. I also observe that the entire debate and the presentation of HP hinge on the parameter. I advise HP to explain at length the parameter concept she has introduced in the Gita, on the penultimate day of the debate. She should tell why they are designated as parameters, how they are different from other slokas and the necessity of having parameters, and how it helps in understanding the Gita.

About corollary, they are natural by-products of any statement. This is used in all fields of study. I suppose HP has quoted Gita in support of corollary, yesterday.

The point put by TG is noted, but the corollary is accepted but would remain secondary to Gods' direct statements. Registrar, please make note of the ruling. Hari, please proceed.

HP: It is complete knowledge. What are the implications of it being complete knowledge? Isn't knowledge infinite, how can it be complete? Similar questions arose about pure mathematics. Bertrand Russell, the famous philosopher put across his Defence as:

- All Mathematics is Symbolic Logic and when this fact has been established, the remainder of the principles of mathematics consists of the analysis of Symbolic Logic itself.
- Mathematics is a summarized summary of generalized observations.
- Entire mathematics can be covered within a few statements.
- Any proposition can be reduced to a mathematical equation and can be proved by mathematics.

The observations of the renowned philosopher-mathematician-logician Bertrand Russell can be usefully employed in the field of Gita instead of mathematics and this would custom-fit Gita.

- By the same analogy, Gita too is a summarized summary of the entire gamut of principles of knowledge.
- Knowledge is infinite, but when the giver is infinite, the given object too becomes infinite.
- It is because of the infinite property of Gita that there are as many versions and commentaries on Gita.
- This is vouchsafed in Gita itself, 'Knowing this nothing else needs to be known (BG-7.2)'.
- The implication of it being complete knowledge is that we need not turn to any other scripture. This Gita is self-sufficient, complete, and illuminating.

TG: Except Gita, all other subjects are being put forward under the guise of Gita.

HP: Analogy is being given. Even God has given many analogies. This is to help understand the unknown from the unknown, as already stated earlier. Should artificial barriers be erected hindering learning?

TG: Something is agreed upon and some other thing is being passed on.

HP: Firstly, I have quoted Gita. It was agreed that what is stated therein constitutes proof. If mere quoting Gita were sufficient, this debate wouldn't have taken place. It would be a mere Gita recitation contest. Mere stating Gita verbatim or putting it, in other words, won't suffice nor serve the purpose. I am supporting my contention with other matters.

TG: Isn't quoting Gita sufficient?

HP: You say both things. Well, for the purposes of this debate only, when the matter referred or the disputed subject is something other than Gita quote, Reference of Gita would suffice. If the subject being discussed itself is a Gita quote, shouldn't I be allowed to put forth extraneous relevant matter in support?

TG: You have claimed that Gita is complete knowledge and also claimed that it is infinite?

HP: Yes, undoubtedly.

TG: Complete and infinite are descriptions opposing each other. How can Gita have both opposing characteristics simultaneously?

HP: Please, I couldn't understand your query. It is incomprehensible.

TG: Infinite means never-ending. It can accommodate more and more without saying" sorry, no space" Complete means, there is an end.

HP: It is a characteristic of God, beginning-less, middle-less and endless, similarly too it is with Gita.

TG: Is it in agreement with facts? Is it experienceable?

HP: That there are more than 4000 commentaries on the Gita is a testimony to the infinite character of the Gita. The commentaries are but another facet of the Gita, complete. Being infinite, it can accommodate any number of many complete ideas and yet have space for more ....

Any version or commentary that cannot accommodate newer concepts/ideas are static and becomes obsolete and redundant, but God's say is dynamic, self-regenerating, and endless, although complete. When one idea dies or becomes irrelevant, a more plausible concept is regenerated and becomes relevant.

TG: You haven't still answered me. Both the ideas/concepts are opposed to each other and cannot co-exist simultaneously.

HP: It can and exists, because otherwise, Gods' words become finite, which isn't the case. Neither can God works be incomplete.

TG: You are just beating around the bush.

HP: Ah, I get it. Let us use the word open-ended, which subsumes both 'infinite' characteristics and the 'complete' characteristics of the Gita.

TG: Gita is complete knowledge, HP, why are you pursuing your legal studies when you have complete knowledge?

HP: Please recall our earlier discussions wherein ....

Professor looked at the clock and asked if they could stop for the day? Most of them were hungry and chorused a big Yes with relief writ large on their face.

HP was relaxing in her room when Christina dropped in after dinner. After exchanging pleasantries, Christina said that there is one more view to buttress the argument that Gita is complete. HP was all-curious and asked her to share her viewpoint.

CH: I have read somewhere in Wiki, that Krishna is Purna Purusha, meaning complete Purusha.

In the general sense, Infinity means
- o   Time or space that has no end.
- o   A number that is greater than any assignable quantity or uncountable number.
- o   Anything endless
- o   Anything limitless

But according to the Indian concept, completion is represented not as ∞ (infinity) but as a circle (O). The circle shows completion and reflects its repetitive nature. This is in conformity with and about Gita. Because, the duration of time is measured as manavantara and Yugas, which is so mind-boggling. There is a repetition of yugas after each cycle. There is no end. There doesn't appear to be any limit either. It can be seen that opposites taken together form a complete whole. So the creation and destruction together make it a whole or complete. Happiness and sadness make a whole. The un-manifestation (dissolution) and manifestation form completeness.

HP: Very nice. I am impressed. But why did you not share your contribution during the discussion?

CH: It was between you and TG; besides, I wasn't sure of the relevance and appropriateness.

HP: I have a line of advice for you from Krishna Himself. For a doubting person, there is happiness neither in this life nor in the next. BG: 4.40. I don't doubt your ability, you too don't entertain self-doubts. Everybody gets to share new perspectives. I wish to add another point to what you have contributed. Purusha means the knower. Purna Purusha means the knower of the complete and the complete knower, which is Krishna Himself or Gita.

CH: Complete knowledge means spiritual knowledge, isn't it?

HP: Gita is a study of concepts, and not a manual of micro-level activities. At Gita level, God has said that "I am the beginning, middle, and end of all that exists. (Including Gita)

At an intellectual level, Gita deals at the cosmos level, not micro-level or macro level. It focuses on cosmos management and not macro or micro-management. It deals with spiritual pursuits and maybe unconcerned with material hankerings or mundane pursuits, although material benefits may accrue incidentally.

Somebody was ridiculing Gita, by asking if it teaches Java or Python. You can't look for geographic details in a book about statistics. God is not a Microsoft or Google Trainer. A CEO won't entertain/focus on day-to-day mundane matters.

From the legal perspective, Law doesn't deal with the frivolous. In fact, it punishes bringing vexatious and frivolous cases to courts. There are other religions and other scriptures dealing with mundane and daily pursuits and also includes what to wear, what not to wear, what to eat, how to beat your wife etc. Gita deals with objectives as stated in Gita itself. Four paths of Yoga for four types of devotee seekers.

CH: You have an uncanny knack of putting things in perspective.

HP: Yours faithfully unto her master's voice.

They took leave of each other on this note and bade goodnight to each other.

16. K -6 – EARTH DUKHALAYA WHY MEN COMMIT SINS

The Professor was already seated on his chair. Some of the students were seated at their designated places. Some were just outside the hall and engaged in frivolous discussions. He turned his attention to the students and inquired if they may commence the debate. A few students rushed outside to usher in others who were outside.

HP: Earth is the residence of miseries (Prison). The residents of earth's planet are always afflicted by miserable conditions. Hence, the prime endeavor of any intelligent person should be to get out of prison. I put forth this as a parameter. However, in reality, people tend to make efforts to make their stay on earth comfortable, not realizing that it is futile. Closely related to this parameter is the committing of sin. Persons are born to earth the consequences of their actions, both good and bad. So, the committing of sin, the why, how, etc. of the same is taken as another parameter.

TG: Why is it futile?

HP: Because the earth is a temporary place. The very nature of the earth is to give misery. The efforts made to make our life comfortable is temporary and dependent on the contact of senses with sense objects.

TG: But we do enjoy ourselves. We have our highs and lows.

HP: Yes, but they are born of contact of sense with their respective objects and ends when the contact ends.

TG: Is there mention of miseries in the Gita?

HP: Yes, not once but at least five times, of course in different contexts.

- Having attained Me, the great souls are no more subject to rebirth in this world, which is transient and full of misery, because they have attained the highest perfection. BG: 8.15
  - o Here, God is highlighting the misery-giving characteristic of the earth.
- Because you are not envious of Me, I shall now impart to you this very confidential knowledge and wisdom, upon knowing which you will be released from the miseries of material existence. BG: 9.1
  - o Here, God is telling a pre-requisite for getting knowledge for combating Miseries, i.e., non-enviousness.
- People who have no faith in this dharma are unable to attain Me, O conqueror of enemies. They repeatedly come back to this world in the cycle of birth and death. BG: 9.3
  - o Here, God is showing the temporary welcome extended by the landlady called earth and subsequent evacuation from the

earth. He also highlights another pre-requisite, Faith in Dharma.

- What then to speak about kings and sages with meritorious deeds? Therefore, having come to this transient and joyless world, engage in devotion unto Me. BG: 9.33
    - Here, again God underscores the transient and joyless nature of the earth, and also informs that even kings and great sages are not exempt, who having realized it has opted to take refuge in the Lord.
    - The solution to avoid rebirth by taking to devotional refuge in the Lord is put forth.
- Having gained that state, one does not consider any attainment to be greater. Being thus established, one is not shaken even in the midst of the greatest of miseries. BG: 6.23
    - Here, God shows that attaining Him is the pinnacle of achievement and even the greatest of miseries cannot affect such persons.
- One whose mind remains undisturbed amidst misery, who does not crave for pleasure, and who is free from attachment, fear, and anger, is called a sage of steady wisdom. BG 2.56
    - Here, God hints that this equanimity is cultivated and self-acquired by practice, due to which miseries do not affect the practitioner here on earth and also serve as a credit of piety which enables him to Gods' abode.
- By divine grace comes the peace in which all sorrows end and the intellect of such a person of tranquil mind soon becomes firmly established in God. BG 2.65
    - Peace is a pre-requisite for overcoming miseries and achieving happiness, which can be had by divine grace.
- But an undisciplined person, who has not controlled the mind and senses, can have neither a resolute intellect nor steady contemplation on God. For one who never unites the mind with God there is no peace; and how can one who lacks peace be happy? BG: 2.66
    - Disciplining of mind and senses required for contemplation on God which is in turn required for peace, which itself is a pre-requisite for happiness.
- Seeing all his relatives present there, Arjuna was overwhelmed with compassion and deep sorrow. BG: 1.27
    - Attachment to kinsmen is both an example of sorrow and one of the causes of sorrow.
- Your enemies defaming and humiliating you would be very sorrowful. BG: 2.36
    - Defamation and humiliation are also one of the causes of sorrow.
- Source of sorrow need not be you but could originate from others.

- Contact between the senses and the sense objects gives rise to fleeting perceptions of happiness and distress. These are non-permanent, and come and go like the winter and summer seasons. Bear with them without getting disturbed. BG: 2.14
    - o Contact between senses and sense objects generates perceptions happiness or unhappiness. They are impermanent. Sorrow and happiness are only perceptions.
  - Hence, humiliation, etc. need not be taken to heart.
    - o Detach the sense organ called the mind from the sense object of prestige, humiliation and your perception would disappear.
  - The unsaid: Don't allow sense organs to come into contact with senses.
  - The said: Endure them as they are temporary
- Perform duty, treating alike happiness and distress, loss and gain, victory and defeat. Fulfilling your responsibility in this way, you will never incur sin. BG: 2.38
    - o Sorrow or happiness is only mental perception. Treating them alike would absolve you of any sin.
- Persons endowed with equanimity of intellect, abandon attachment to the fruits of actions, which bind them to the cycle of life and death.

By this, they attain the state beyond all suffering. BG: 2.51
    - o Abandonment of attachment to fruits of action releases us from the bondage of the birth-death cycle, thus transcending suffering.
- Those who rise above the dualities of cold and heat, joy and sorrow, honor and dishonor, attain peace and are persistent in their devotion to God. BG: 6.7
    - o Added bonanza is devotion to God.
- Being temperate in eating and recreation, balanced in work, and regulated in sleep mitigates all sorrows BG:6.17
    - o Moderation in all activities is key to overcome sorrow.
- Having gained that state, one does not consider any attainment to be greater. Being thus established, one is not shaken even in the midst of the greatest calamity. BG: 6.22
    - o The pinnacle of attainment is that state when even the greatest calamity doesn't ruffle the person.

It can be seen that each action of God is complete. He isn't just telling that earth is an abode of miseries. He tells characteristics of miseries and earth, pre-requisites for overcoming the same, how to overcome the same and also provides divine intervention (by way of divine grace BG: 2.65), where our efforts are sincere but fall short.

TG: But God hasn't said the 'Why' part of it.

HP: Of course, He has mentioned it.

   Because it is transient or perishable.

- o   In all the worlds of this material creation, up to the highest abode of Brahma, you will be subject to rebirth BG: 8.16.

- The inmates too are subject to birth and death. (Inevitable)
  - o   For one who has taken his birth, death is certain; and for one who is dead, birth is certain. BG: 2.27
- The joy or sorrow ends when the sense organ loses contact with sense object.
  - o   The pleasures that arise from contact with the sense objects, though appearing as enjoyable is a source of misery BG: 5.22
- The different gunas perform impel different action which produces different results.
  - o   The fruit of actions performed in the mode of goodness bestows pure results. Actions are done in the mode of passion result in pain, while those performed in the mode of ignorance result in darkness. BG: 14.16
- The sins or piety accrued has to be exhausted by enjoyment or miseries which is generally done in the laboratory called Earth.
  - o   Having exhausted their merits by enjoying the vast pleasures of heaven they return to the earth. Thus, those who practice rituals, desiring objects of enjoyment, repeatedly come and go in this world. BG: 9.21
- Identification with the body or matter is another cause of misery.
  - o   The soul neither is born nor dies. The soul is without birth, eternal, immortal, and ageless. It does not perish when the body perishes. BG: 2.20

TG: You have said that joy and sorrow are temporary. What is temporary and what is permanent?

HP: Joy and sorrow in the mundane world are temporary. They have an end. The joy in the spiritual world is permanent. How to differentiate between spiritual and mundane? The key herein is temporary and the permanent. That which is permanent is spiritual and which is not is mundane.

TG: But how do you define spiritual and mundane? You have only given the key.

HP: That which accrues and exists even after death is spiritual.

TG: What is it that accrues? Even sins accrue, which is surely not spiritual.

HP: Thank you, TG, I stand corrected. A nice observation that I overlooked inadvertently. That merit due to practices which point wherefrom, we continue our spiritual pursuit in the succeeding birth either in the family of pious or the wealthy is spiritual. Similarly, that merit after exhausting which we fall down from the heavens or heavenly planets is mundane or material. Here merits include demerits also.

TG: Supposing, there is no succeeding birth, Moksha is attained, then?

HP: Thanks again, I have to rephrase my answer as That merit due to practices which point wherefrom, we continue our spiritual pursuit in the succeeding birth either in the family of pious or the wealthy is spiritual.

TG: Isn't it fanciful straying of mind?

HP: No. It is stated fact that good deeds direct men to heaven. Their stay therein is determined by the quantum of credit accrued.

- Having enjoyed the vast pleasures of heaven until the stock of their merits is exhausted, they return to earth. BG: 9.21
    - o   Here, we see that the residence at heaven is of finite duration, i.e., until the exhaustion of credit of merits.
    - o   It is also known that God and His abode is spiritual.
    - o   Further God and His abode are eternal and infinite.
- Hence, from the demarcation between spiritual and material, as stated, the conclusive inference is "That which accrues and exists even after death is spiritual".

TG: So, people are born on earth to undergo punishments or enjoy due to their sins or pious activities?

HP: Not exactly, they aren't undergoing punishment, but reaping the consequences of their actions.

TG: But the government or state punishes the culprit in case of crime.

HP: Maybe or may not be. Crime and sin or not synonyms. There could be an escape from Government laws or injustice, but not so in the divine law.

TG: What is the difference between crime and sin? How can a person be punished twice by the Government and God for one crime? What is divine law?

HP: Crime is an action or omission punishable by law. Sin is a transgression of divine law. Crime is relative and not absolute. That which is a crime for one person or a particular country may not be so to another person or country. The concept of crime too changes with times.

That which was termed crime one hundred years ago need not necessarily be so now. Sin is disobedience of divine law.

It is beyond the purview of human laws. Criminal law doesn't pursue a criminal after death, whereas sin haunts a person until such time there is reconciliation.

Sin is that negative credit which accrues due to performing prohibited actions, or non-performing of our prescribed duties. This accrued credit has to be exhausted by invariably experiencing unpleasant consequences.

There is no escape. Similarly, piety or Punya is the credit accrued due to our actions or inactions due to which we have to have pleasant experiences until such time the accrued merit is exhausted. These experiences may take many lifetimes. As each action generates positive or negative consequences, more of sins and piety is accumulated. The more the accumulation, the more we are caught in the web cycle of birth-death.

TG: Where has it been mentioned in the Gita? Though it appears logical, there should be some acceptable evidence, isn't it?

HP: Having exhausted their stock of merits by enjoying the vast pleasures of heaven, they return to the earth. BG: 9.21

TG: You mean, heaven too is a material world and activities therein too are material?

HP: Of course, you apply the test and arrive at your own conclusion.

TG: I am skeptical.

HP: Why?

TG: Because Indra and other gods too are in materialistic mode.

HP: Yes, to a very limited extent. They are thereby virtue of their virtuous deeds.

TG: I am not convinced.

HP: In all the worlds of this material creation, up to the highest abode of Brahma, you will be subject to rebirth.

On attaining My Abode, there is no further rebirth.BG: 8.16. So, when the creator Brahma and his world itself is material creation and subject to death, Indra and other gods are no exception. Are you convinced?

TG: Grudgingly, 'Yes'

TG: Doesn't the concept of sin too vary from person, place time, etc.? How to get rid of accumulation?

HP: Yes. It varies. The use of force in pursuance of duties is recommended for Kshatriya, but the same is not permitted for other classes. We may see it in the mundane world too. A judge may order execution to further the cause of justice in course of duties, but an ordinary man would be held guilty of abetment to murder if he orders a hit job. Regarding your latter query, God has given two options, either offer your actions to the Lord or perform actions in the spirit of duty treating alike the opposites that accrue. You would be absolved of sins.

- Dedicate all your works to Me. By doing so, you will be freed from the bondage of good and bad results. You will be liberated and will reach Me.BG: 9.28
- Fight in course of duty, treating alike happiness and distress, loss and gain, victory and defeat. By discharging your duties/responsibilities, you will never incur sin. BG: 2.38
- Those who eat the remains of Yajna/ sacrifice are freed from all sins.BG: 3.13
  o Here, eating should be taken in the broadest sense of "enjoy the results of" and not necessarily just eating. Here, Yajna or sacrifice means working for public welfare.

TG: But what about piety, or merits accrued?

HP: The same principle applies to piety also. Offer the results to God, or perform actions in a spirit of disinterested abandon in the outcomes. It is like general usage in languages, he includes she, man includes women, etc.

TG: Embellish your answer with an example.

HP: The Famous confrontation between Sage Vishwamitra and Sage Vasishta makes a good subject for a case study.

Sage Vishwamitra was a Kshatriya king and he unsuccessfully used force against Vasishta, the Brahmin hermit to usurp the divine cow, Kamadhenu, belonging to the latter. The results humbled Vishwamitra, but not his resolve.

He came with a bigger army and had to eat dust. He realized the superiority of spiritual strength over material strength and commenced his efforts to acquire spiritual strength. He acquired the same and lost it multiple times by utilizing his spiritual power for mundane purposes.

Once by dallying with the heavenly nymph, Menaka, and another time by creating his own universe or planet for Trishanku, a king of those times and another time by uttering curse in anger. At last, he realized the greatness of spiritual merit and achieved the exalted position of Brahma Rishi or the saint amongst Brahmins and had it acknowledged it from none other than his arch-rival, Sage Vasishta.

The above episode throws light on some intricacies of spiritual endeavors and mundane endeavors and spiritual outcomes and mundane outcomes.

- Whether the merit of Vishwamitra is material or spiritual? If spiritual, it shouldn't be exhausted. How did he lose it when he dallied with the celestial nymph, Menaka?
  o Sage Vishwamitra's earlier pursuits progressively changed from grossly materialistic to a tinge of materialism to spiritual. His final

and successful pursuit was spiritual. The sage's materialistic credit was exhausted. His final spiritual merit wasn't exhausted. Sage Vasishta's merit was spiritual.

- Whether material credits can be redeemed for spiritual goals? Can spiritual currency be redeemed for material goals?

  - Spiritual currency can be used for material redemption, but it is a bad bargain. This is realized by the sage Vishwamitra after multiple bad bargains. Material credits can be redeemed for spiritual benefits, but the swap rate or exchange rate is steep and is ill affordable. It is like trying to buy an expensive item which you can ill afford and therefore buy it an installment basis.

  - Any endeavor, with spiritual motives, yields result that are partly material and partly spiritual the spiritual result is accumulated, whereas the material result is exhausted by experiencing the joys. This accumulation goes on with each birth, you commencing on a spiritual pursuit from that point forward, where the earlier practice had stopped, until such time you reach God's abode.

- Spiritual endeavors and mundane pursuits are mutually exclusive. They don't go hand in hand. You can't pursue spiritual goals and material goals simultaneously. History is replete with kings and sages giving up their kingdom and riches to pursue the spirit.

  - This exclusive property is well known and is exploited by Indra, the king of gods who distracts practitioners from the spiritual path by offering material allurements.

  - This is why Brahmin's approach Kshatriyas for help when they themselves can curse the tormentor and destroy them.

TG: But the observable reality is something different. We cannot lead a completely spiritual life in mundane earth, nor have I come across anyone doing so. Is the entire population astray?

HP: I reiterate that both paths cannot be traversed simultaneously. The best compromise is that you be moderate in your material endeavors whilst pursuing a spiritual path.

God, Himself has advocated a median path with an optimum mix of spirituality and materialistic pursuits, which count as a spiritual way, or the yogic way.

Those who eat too much or eat too little, sleep excessively or sleep too less, cannot attain success in Yoga. But those who are temperate in eating and recreation, balanced in work, and regulated in sleep, can mitigate all sorrows by the practice of Yoga. BG: 6.16 & BG: 6.17

God has asked to fix the mind on Him alone and not to think of anything else. BG: 6.25

It is also observable that we cannot pursue two goals, and if we persist, we may not succeed in either of them. The idiom "don't ride two horses at once" would help you understand better.

TG: Nice case study so far. Please also give case law.

HP: Okay,

- o With little practice of this Yoga, there is no loss or adverse result, and even a little effort saves one from great danger BG: 2.40
- o When Arjuna questions the Lord, "Doesn't a person who deviates from Yoga get deprived of both material and spiritual success, like a broken cloud with no position in either world? BG: 6.38
  - ▪ This delineates the mutually exclusive property of spirituality vis-à-vis matter.
- o Completely renouncing desires arising from the mundane, one should restrain the senses and mind. BG: 6.24
  - ▪ Only spiritual, without mundane distractions advocated.
- o Fix your mind on Me alone. BG: 12.8
  - ▪ Advocates single-pointedness.
- o Regard Me as your supreme goal. BG: 12.6
  - ▪ Only goal.
- o Have Me alone as the final goal. BG: 6.14
  - ▪ These slokas seek singular focus on a spiritual pursuit.
- • The intellect of those who are on this path is resolute, and their aim is one-pointed. But the intellect of those who are irresolute is many-branched.BG: 2.41
  - o This sloka shows that multiple pursuits are irresolute.
- • The Lord replied: One who engages in the spiritual path does not meet with destruction either in this world or in the next. One who strives for God-realization is never overcome by evil. BG: 6.40
  - o Here, the permanent nature of spiritual merit is expressed.
- • On taking such a birth, their spiritual thirst is reawakened by the strength of the practice of their previous lives, and strive even harder toward perfection. They feel drawn toward God, even against their will, on the strength of their past discipline. With the accumulated merits of many past births, these yogis strive harder and attain the ultimate. BG: 6.43 to BG: 6.45.
  - o Here, how that credit of merit is used is shown.

TG: Case law for mundane merits?

HP: Am repeating what I said, having enjoyed the pleasures of heaven they return to the earth on finishing their accrued merit. They repeatedly come and go in this world. BG: 9.21

HP: The fall of Nahusha, the great king and his subsequent redemption is also another case on point. Now, we will discuss the subject matter of Sin, which we take as a parameter.

TG: How is it related to the earlier parameter, "Earth is Dukhalaya "?

HP: People are born on earth to bear the consequences of their sins or merit. Hence, there is an interrelation between the two parameters.

TG: Did God descend on earth to reap the consequences of sins or His merits?

HP: Why do you always take exceptions as a rule? God and His representatives come to earth for the upliftment of the populace here. The subject of sin has been dealt with in Gita in a number of slokas.

TG: Which slokas?

HP:
- Though they may be aggressors, we will incur sin by killing them. BG: 1.36 & 37
  - The consequence of killing is a sin.
- Although these men see no fault in killing one's family or perfidiousness in killing friends, why should we commit that sin knowingly? BG: 1.38
  - Sin may be committed in ignorance or knowingly.
- If, however, you refuse to fight this righteous war, abandoning your social duty and reputation, you will certainly incur sin. BG: 2.33
  - Non-performance of duties cause accrual of sin.
- Fight for the sake of duty, treating alike happiness and distress, loss and gain, victory and defeat. Fulfilling your responsibility in this way, you will never incur sin. BG: 2.38
  - Performance of duty without personal overtones --- is not a sin.
- Nice differentiation between crime and sin.
  - A war criminal may be tried and convicted as is seen in trials of post-world war II. Here, the defense of obedience to superior is not a valid defense.
  - Not so in the case of divine law. Acts performed in the course of duty doesn't attract sin.
- Those spiritual persons who eat the remnants of food that are offered in sacrifice are released from all kinds of sin. Others, who cook food for their own enjoyment, verily eat only sin. BG: 3.13
  - This must be taken in a very broad sense, not just food, but any other acquisitions like food, clothing, shelter, cattle, knowledge, joys, etc.
- Why does a person sin unwillingly, as if by force? Asks Arjuna? BG: 3.36

- o The Lord replies that it is due to lust born of contact with the mode of passion, which is a great enemy. BG: 3.37
  - Sin is committed because of a lack of discipline and restraint in cultivating and practicing dispassion
- Even if you are considered to be the most sinful of all sinners, when you are situated in the boat of transcendental knowledge, you will be able to cross over the ocean of miseries. BG: 4.36
  - o Spiritual knowledge takes you across the ocean of miseries safely, notwithstanding you being a great sinner.
- Some curtail their food intake and offer the breath into the life-energy as a sacrifice. All these knowers of sacrifice are purged of their sins as a result of such sacrifices. BG: 4.30
  - o Sacrifices cleanse us of sins.
- Those who are absorbed in God, with firm faith in Him as the supreme goal, such persons quickly reach the state from which there is no return, their sins having been destroyed by the light of knowledge.BG: 5.17
  - o Being sinless is a pre-requisite for residing in Gods' abode.
  - o Absorption in God with faith cleanses us of sin and also awards us His coveted abode.
- Having exhausted their merits by enjoying the vast pleasures of heaven they return to the earth. Thus, those who practice rituals, desiring objects of enjoyment, repeatedly come and go in this world. BG: 9.21

  - o Just like in case of merits, exhaustion after which you fall back to earth, In case of sins also, you are reinstated after having undergone the punishments/consequences of sin in the purgatory.
  - o The case of king Nahusha, an ancestor of Pandavas is a case in point. Yudhishthira' having to see hell for a few moments is another example.

As already said, a single sinful act may make us revolve in the birth-death cycle for umpteen number of times. Hence, it is advised to be wary of sin.

Prof: TG, do you have anything to add or put forth?

TG: No, sir.

Prof: let us break for the day.

Hari and Christina huddled together on a bench and were exchanging notes. Christina informed Hari that she was unclear on some issues even though they were discussed. She sought to know from Hari how both the parameters are related and why it is so important that they are taken as a parameter.

Hari replied that all the slokas referred to in the discussion collectively answer many questions like what is a sin? What are the properties of sin? How to identify sin? What are the consequences of committing sin? How to avoid sin? How to destroy accumulated sin etc. Regarding earth as a prison, she clarified that earth is a karma bhumi, a place where we perform activities that offer results, be it good or bad, unlike heaven or hell, wherein they go to reap the consequences of their actions.

The earth, a place of miseries, and sin are closely interrelated. Collectively, the slokas referred therein diagnoses cause of suffering and how to get rid of the same. Hence, it is taken as a parameter.

All beings in all the worlds commit sins, both knowingly and inadvertently. Nature or Gunas are the cause of committing sin. The causes of committing sin by different persons differ depending on the predominance of particular guna at that point in time.

Sattvic persons sin due to temporary loss of memory. It could also be due to knowledge temporarily overcome by desire. Here, the word memory is not used in the conventional sense.

It is meant as per usage used by God Himself. Memory herein means the memory of God and His writ. It also means non-performance of one's prescribed duties. A Rajasic person commits sin due to the predominance of passion and anger. A sin committed by a Tamasic person is generally due to ignorance. These are covered by the Lord in BG: 3.36 to BG: 3.38

They took leave of each other and left for their rooms.

17. K-7 GUNAS-SATTVA RAJAS AND TAMAS

The professor hurriedly walked in and sat down. He was following the proceedings very keenly. His curiosity was aroused. He couldn't anticipate what would come next. Hence, he made it a point not to miss even a word of the discussion. He signaled for the proceedings to begin.

HP:Today, I intend taking up the three gunas, i.e. Sattva, Rajas, and Tamas as parameters. In support thereof, I present the Slokas numbered BG: 18.40, 7.14, 7.15, 14.5, 3.5, and 3.33.

- No being herein or in any of the universes or among demigods are free from the three modes born of material nature. BG 18.40
- Divine Maya comprises of gunas. BG: 7.14
    o Meaning the three gunas collectively is called Maya and is under the control of God.
- Everyone is compelled to act helplessly according to instincts born of the modes of material nature. BG: 3.5
- Even a wise man acts as per his own nature, for everyone follows his nature. What is the use of repression of modes of nature? BG: 3.33
- Sattva, Rajas, Tamas, are gunas born of nature and bind the imperishable body dweller to the body. BG:14.5

These are very important slokas and hence being taken as a parameter. It is important both as a sloka and as a parameter. Hence, it spans four chapters, viz. chapters three, fourteen, seventeen, and eighteen. It has around 79 slokas that are dedicated to explaining this.

TG: Why are they important as Slokas?

HP: It is pretty obvious, isn't it?

TG: Don't escape answering by saying it is obvious. It may be for you and me, but not for others.

HP: Everyone is under the clutches of modes of material nature and it is inescapable.

Their actions too are dictated by their mode of nature. Repression of nature is not the solution. Each of the modes binds the body dweller to the body. As this is universal and helps us understand our nature and ourselves and regulate ourselves accordingly, it is important.

TG: Why are they important as parameters?

HP: They are so because:
- The slokas of threefold gunas, pervade all the slokas, making it universal.

- These slokas explain many phenomena and untie many knots of understandings, or shall we say misunderstandings.
- Most of the slokas are inter-related and acts as a qualifier inter-se between themselves.
- The phenomena explained covers a wide gamut of human understanding, encompassing all behavior patterns.
- These values hold good for all times and for all persons and at all places, meaning, explanations are practical, experiential and obsolesce proof.

TG: What phenomena are explained? Pertains to human understanding of what?

HP: Phenomenon of human behavior is explained. Human behavior is dictated by gunas or the modes of nature. There are many ways to look at Gunas and its results.

TG: When do they come to fore?

HP: When the body comes into contact with material nature. God says that men act helplessly according to the modes of their nature. Even wise men act helplessly and repression can't help. BG: 3.5 & 3.33

TG: Then, what is the use of battling something which cannot be controlled?

HP: It can be controlled.

TG: How?

HP: By taking refuge of God. As mentioned in BG: 18.61.

TG: Why should we take refuge?

HP: There are many reasons. The principal reasons are
  - Because Lord has told so.
  - Results accrue as per actions.
    - Action in Sattvic mode yields Sattvic results. BG: 14.15
    - Action in Rajasic mode yields Rajasic results. BG: 14.16
    - Action in Tamasic mode yields Tamasic results. BG: 14.17
    - Action in transcendental mode yields transcendental results.

To get good results, it is necessary to take refuge. BG: 18.59 & 18.61.

TG: We have heard of Sattvic, Rajasic and Tamasic modes. What is transcendental mode?

HP: That which is beyond any of the three gunas is transcendental mode.

TG: Any example of transcendental mode?

HP: Arjuna is a Kshatriya by birth and nature. The most dominant guna in kshatriya is Rajas, meaning, Arjuna should have fought in the battlefield with enthusiasm, which he didn't do. He was overcome by sattva guna at the time of the battle. He was advised to go into transcendental mode beyond all the three gunas and fight.

In our daily life, we come across people who are timid and peace-loving but showing exemplary courage (against their nature) in times of adversity for a larger cause. We have Karna, who is Rajasic by nature, sparing the lives of Pandava brothers in the battlefield in deference to the vow made to Kunti Devi, thus displaying transcendental mode of nature.

TG: Why is it necessary to be in transcendental mode?

HP: As seen earlier, Man is helplessly always in action in different modes of nature. Acting in material modes of nature causes bondage. To overcome bondage, we have to act in transcendental nature. To facilitate action in the transcendental mode of nature, we have to take refuge of the Lord.

TG: Actions cause bondage to what?

HP: Gunas cause bondage and yield results.

- Action in Sattvic mode binds the performer to happiness. The results of action in Sattvic mode are purifying, illuminating and gives knowledge besides freeing them from sins. BG: 14.6 & 14.16

- Action in Rajasic mode binds the performer to ceaseless activity and the result of such actions is anguish. BG: 14.7 & 14.16.

- Action in Tamasic mode binds the performer to lethargy, delusion, and sleep. The results of action in Tamasic mode is ignorance and delusion. BG: 14.8 & 14.16

TG: Gunas cause bondage. No one is free from modes of guna, meaning everyone is in bondage perpetually. Your words are fatalistic. Are God and Gita a problem creator or solution provider?

HP: You may get out of bondage by transcending the gunas as per Gods' advice BG: 18.59, you may also take refuge of Him as mentioned in BG: 18.62.

TG: The three modes of nature are very good in theory, but reality differs from what you are theorizing.

HP: I am not theorizing, just quoting Almighty, where does theory differ from reality, please be more specific rather than hurling general charge.

TG: Each person behaves differently to the same set of a given situation. Even the same person behaves differently at different places and at different times and circumstances. The same person may behave differently to the same stimuli at different times. The classification is an oversimplification of human behavior.

HP: The dominating gunas keep changing in any person. Each Guna attempts to suppress the other and play a dominant role. The behavior of a person changes depending on the guna dominant at that point in time. This is reflected in the actions of the man. Gunas are temporary, meaning they keep changing. SO, when a person is acting full of passion, we may take it that Rajas is dominant. Similarly, when a person is happy and full of knowledge, we may assume that Sattva is dominant. This explains the different behaviors of different persons or the same person in different circumstances. In fact, this so-called theory best explains the changing behavior of a person.

TG: Is your answer 'reality-check' answer or is it backed by Gods' words?

HP: It is both. Please refer BG: 14.10, wherein it is said that sometimes goodness (sattva) prevails over passion (rajas) and ignorance (tamas), sometimes passion (rajas) dominates goodness (sattva) and ignorance (tamas), and at other times, ignorance (tamas) suppresses goodness (sattva) and passion (rajas).

TG: What about those times when a person is not under the clutches of any guna or is normal?

HP: No person is free from the clutches of gunas. Gunas would be playing their role, at times, a person may act transcending the gunas, but it is an exception or a rarity.

TG: But this does not explain the difference in the behavior of two Satvic persons or two Tamasic persons. Besides, human behavior is far more complex than just pigeonholing into three categories.

If it weren't so, there wouldn't be a branch of study called psychology, with numerous specializations in that one subject like child psychology, industrial psychology, clinical psychology, etc.

HP: TG, my friend, you are arguing for the sake of argument and score brownie points. You yourself agreed that Gods 'words are supreme and not to be challenged. I have also clarified on a reality check, Okay, so be it. I presume you have a genuine doubt or argument. You believe in the dictum 'All is fair in love & war' to which I don't subscribe, but nevertheless needs to be countered.

God has told us that each guna is always competing with others for dominance. Each of them has a dominant position at some point of time or the other. When one guna is dominant, other gunas are not destroyed but are latent or in hibernation. Even amongst two persons with the same guna, we see different behavior to the same stimuli.

This is because of inherent differences in the innate capacity of the individuals. Let us suppose for the purposes of understanding, that gunas are measurable in units, and the maximum amount of gunas in a person is one hundred units.

This is divided amongst three gunas in different proportion and in different combinations. The possible number of permutations and combinations is the number of possibilities of human behavior.

Add to this the variables like capacity, ability, availability of resources, and God's will. The possibilities are infinite. Mind you, this is based on the assumption that the total Gunas has a cap of one hundred. IF the assumption is removed, the possibilities are just overwhelming. Yet you have the gall to say that Gods' words are theory and theorizing has no practical significance and is far removed from reality.

This is best explained diagrammatically. The total units of Guna are 100. Presently Sattva is dominating. Gunas are changing, hence the percentages of each guna keep changing. The constant predominance of a particular guna determines the personality of a person.

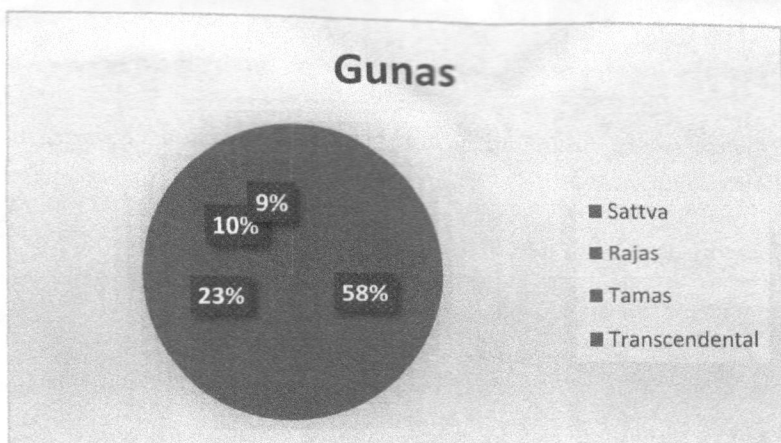

Gunas keep changing. We should strive to evolve to sattva guna and thereafter to transcendence. SO, it is basically a process of evolution of pre-dominance from tamas to sattva and thereafter to transcendence. There is an interplay of characteristics of gunas inter-se.

TG: Why confine the total to a hundred only? Why not ninety or one hundred ten?

HP: The supposition is made for purposes of better understanding. The upper limit of one hundred is indicatory.

The maximum is defined by the innate ability (Yogyate, meaning to the extent deserving, competent or qualified) this also includes the ability to accept and sustain. The number one hundred is just a numerical notation. It is used to quantify, and better appreciate the fact.

TG: What is the interplay of characteristics of gunas?

HP: It is best explained through examples. Gunas are always fighting over each other for dominance. There will always be a winner, a runner up and a loser. The gap between them determines the dominant personality of the individual. This is about the gunas. But the interplay of characteristics of gunas throws up more possibilities.

For example, a person may eat Sattvic food, have Rajasic firmness and Tamasic prayers. It can be many other possible combinations.

TG: Then how do you reconcile with them or account for the behavior?

HP: The characteristics are an indicator or an identifier that helps determine a type of personality. They are not personality itself, meaning, Gunas is the personality or more correctly speaking, shaper of the personality.

TG: Why or how is it so?

HP: Gunas shape characteristics, preferences personality, etc., and not vice versa.

Those may have other roots other than the gunas, say, for example, peer pressure affecting behavior, environment determining eating habits, etc.

TG: You yourself have said that going against nature is fruitless, as all are condemned to act as per their nature helplessly. How can there be evolution? How can the direction of change be evolution? It could be changing in the opposite direction from the dominance of sattva to tamas also.

HP: God has said that the mind is both a friend and an enemy. TO the one who controls it, it is a friend and to the one who is controlled by it, it is an enemy. BG: 6.5 to 6.8.

Further, when Arjuna expressed his difficulty in controlling the mind, God replied that although the mind is difficult to control, the same can be achieved by means of detachment and constant practice. BG: 6.35. For one who exercises control over the mind, there is evolution, and for the one where mind controls him, there is degradation.

TG: Don't give irrelevant replies. I asked about the evolution of gunas, not the mind. You are following the dictum "if you cannot convince, then confuse".

HP: Sense organs, mind, and intelligence are the seat of desire. BG: 3.40 in the next verse, God asks Arjuna to control the mind and sense organs. You may also experience that no action can be done without the use of mind. This is also reiterated by God in BG: 18.13 & 18.14. It is referred herein as senses, but it should be borne in mind that mind is also one of the senses and no action can be accomplished without the use of mind.

HP: As already said, there is no being anywhere in the three worlds who are free from the three gunas born of nature. BG: 18.40. As Gita is non-different from God, Gita too has all the gunas.

TG: Jumping with excitement, then Gita is subject to gunas and Tamas or rajas may have dominance over sattva.

HP: I am beyond the three modes of gunas. BG: 7.13. Hence, Gita is beyond gunas.

TG: Then, how are gunas present in Gita?

HP: The three states of material existence—goodness, passion, and ignorance, are in Me, but I am beyond them. BG: 7.12. God has given an analogy, which answers your question. God, being imperishable and gunas being perishable, they are in Him. He is in them, but he isn't in them. BG: 9.4 & 9.5.

TG: Just quoting verbatim without understanding, repeat, confusing instead of convincing, in which art you are a past master.

HP: Okay, tell me are you angry?

TG: No, frustrated by your roundabout answers maybe, but not angry.

HP: So, you don't have anger?

TG: I didn't say so. I do get angry at times.

HP: How can you get angry if you don't have anger?

TG: I have anger but it comes to fore only sometimes.

HP: By the same analogy, God has all gunas, but they manifest themselves only when needed.

Unlike in our cases, they come to fore without our control. This is just an analogy. I cannot give a better analogy at present. Besides, it is said that God is beyond Gunas, not God is devoid of Gunas. It further means that He has all gunas but not under its' clutches.

TG: Why? Your analogy fits the argument.

HP: Because God has no blemishes and anger is a blemish.

TG: But there are instances when God was angry, say when Prahalad was tortured by his father, etc.

HP: God wasn't angry, but displayed anger. He summoned the emotion called anger to come to the fore so as to better play His role as a protector and to better play His role as a half-beast, half-man, whose intrinsic characteristic is anger.

TG: Have you completed the entire wide gamut about which you spoke?

HP: Each of the gunas distinguishes itself from other gunas with respect to ......

Performer of Action. BG: 18.26 to 18.28
- Action
  - Action. BG: 18.23 to 18.25
  - Duties. BG: 18.42 to 18.45
  - Fruits of action. BG: 14.16
- Sacrifices
  - Charity. BG: 17.20 to 17.22.
  - Renunciation. BG: 18.7 to 18.9
  - Sacrifice. BG: 17.11 to 17.13
  - Austerity & penance. BG: 17.14 to 17.19
- Identifiers
  - Food habits. BG: 17.8 to 17.10
  - Faith or mode of worship. BG: 17.3 to 17.4
  - Symptoms. BG: 14.11 to 14.13
- Effect of death during the dominance of a particular guna. BG: 14.14 to 14.15
- Knowledge
  - Understanding. BG: 18.30 to 18.32
  - Firmness. BG: 18.33 to 18.35
  - Knowledge BG: 18.20 to 18.22
- Happiness. BG: 18.36 to 18.39
- Transcendence. BG: 14.20 to 14.26

TG: What are the types of performers and their distinguishing characteristics?

HP: Performer of action could be acting in any of the three modes, meaning, there could be a Sattvic performer, a Rajasic performer, or a Tamasic performer.
- A person performing his duty resolutely and with enthusiasm without being affected by success or failure is said to be working in Sattvic or goodness mode. BG 18.26

- A person is said to be in Tamasic mode when he works with an eye on fruits of action, is greedy, violent, impure and affected by the outcome of work with joy or sorrow. BG: 18.27

- A person is said to be working in Tamasic mode or in the mode of ignorance who is against scriptures, materialistic, stubborn, deceitful, and dilatory. BG: 18.28

TG: Talk about the action or the act itself?

HP: Just like performer, performance too has three-fold classification.
- That action which is in consonance with the scriptures, without attachment or aversion, and which is done without craving for the results thereof in the mode of Sattva. BG: 18.23
- That action which is done with great efforts to gratify senses and prompted by selfishness and pride is said to be action in the mode of Rajas. BG: 18.24
- That action performed in ignorance without considering one's own ability and consequences, which is injurious to others and impractical is said to be action in Tamasic mode. BG: 18.25

TG: Tell us about the classification of duties. Wait, Isn't duty too an action?

HP: We have the same threefold classifications for duties also. All duties are actions but not all actions need to be duties.

TG: What are the prescribed duties?

HP: The duties prescribed by God are
- The pursuit of Peacefulness, exercising self-control, austerity, purity, tolerance, honesty, wisdom, knowledge, and dharma are the natural qualities of Brahmanas, which duties they should perform.BG 18.42
- Heroism, power, determination, resourcefulness, courage in battle, generosity, and leadership are the natural duties to be performed by Kshatriyas. BG 18.43
- Farming, cattle rearing, and business are the natural qualities of Vaishyas and hence prescribed as their duties, labor and service to others are the natural duties of Sudras. BG: 18.44

TG: In earlier arguments, you have taken dictionary meaning in some cases and now you are taking the meaning as ascribed or defined in the Gita. You are inconsistent. The duties defined are different in both places. How do you propose to reconcile the same?

HP: Are you asking the difference between duties in our mundane life and the duties prescribed in the Gita? And how they are in conflict with each other?

TG: Partly yes. Should we be pragmatic and perform mundane duties expected of us or should we abandon our duty and follow Gita?

HP: All duties should be performed and none of the duties should be avoided. In fact, if you read carefully, you may observe that there is no conflict at all.

Gita says which duties are to be taken up by whom based on their aptitude. In this iron age of Kali, the 21st century, we have very little choice in the selection of our profession.

The duties mentioned in the Gita are more of an attitude with which to pursue duty rather than the performance of duty per-se. ideally, perform your duties in the innate spirit of your gunas or nature.

TG: Please explain with an example. Suppose a Brahmin is employed in the military, what should be his attitude in work? He cannot be peaceful or in self-control or pure or tolerant. In fact, he has to violate every principle of duty prescribed in the Gita, yet you say there is no conflict. You are living in a utopia of 2330 BC, in the age of Krishna.

HP: How I wish I were present at that age of Krishna! Supposing a Brahmin is employed in the military, He has to act as per the dictates of his undertaken profession but with the spirit of a Brahmin as mentioned in the Gita.

There is a precedent in Mahabharata which answers your query. In the great Kurukshetra war, there were three Brahmins, who fought the war. Their contribution too was immense. Dronacharya, his son, Ashwattama, and his brother-in-law, Kripacharya were all Brahmins and fought the war. They were Brahmins not only by birth but by nature also. It answers how a person who is in another profession other than his innate nature can perform his duties.

The duties of Brahmins based on their gunas reconciled with their military profession is:

o   The pursuit of Peacefulness.
  ▪   Peacefulness means inner peace or absence of mental conflict.
  ▪   The best example is Arjuna who was overcome with inner conflict.
o   Self-control.
  ▪   Means, control over all senses and mind besides control over gunas.
  ▪   By exercising such control, there is increased productivity (or destruction in this case)
  ▪   Drona could master Brahma Astra because of his purity and control of senses.
o   Austerity.
  ▪   Austerity means austerity of body, mind, and speech as defined in BG: 17.14 to 17.17
o   Purity.
  ▪   Purity means purity in thoughts; words deeds and in the body.

o   Tolerance.
  ▪   Tolerance includes tolerance of all adverse conditions and circumstances which a soldier may have to face.
o   Honesty.

- Honesty includes honest dedication (Your 100% or the best in yourself) to the profession.
- Dronacharya was honest in his loyalty to Duryodhana, even against his own conscience.

o Wisdom.
- Includes, when to act, when to retreat, when to accept the inevitable etc.

o Knowledge.
- Includes knowledge of self, abilities, and weakness as also knowledge about the capabilities of enemies.

o Dharma.
- Means what is right, be it thoughts, action, etc. vis-à-vis your station in life and circumstances

So, there could be Brahmin soldier doing duties of Brahmin, along with the mundane duty of soldiering or doing soldiering with the attitude of a Brahmin. Likewise, we may have a Vaisya soldier, Sudra teacher and so on.

Narrow or parochial interpretation by self-styled intelligentsia is the scourge who tries to bring disrepute to god's words.

God is infinite, His words are infinite, and accordingly, our understanding should conform and be in line with Infinite. Infinite understanding means it should be able to accommodate endless or 'n' number of ideas or views without conflict.

TG: You are not the custodian of intelligence or of the Gita. You mean Sudras should only engage in labor and menial service for the fault of being born in sudras womb for no fault of theirs?

HP: The duties of the Brahmins, Kshatriyas, Vaishyas, and Sudras—are determined/distinguished by their aptitude and attitude keeping in line with their gunas or nature. BG 18.41: TG, please note that God hasn't said that birth determines the duties, but the nature of the person determines duties.

A Brahmana achieves his objectives through self-control and knowledge. A Kshatriya achieves the same by controlling the body and others by the use of heroics.

A Vaisya achieves his objectives by increased productivity or returns to society by controlling resources and a Sudra achieves the same by controlling services, i.e., rendering service to the society. This is an observable phenomenon.

This holds good irrespective of the profession a person may be, whereas the same doesn't hold good in case of distinction by birth.

If you analyze carefully, you will observe that Brahmin's happiness is intrinsic and independent of others, A Kshatriya's happiness is derived from subjugating others, A Vaisyas' happiness is dependent on natural resources, and the Sudras' welfare and happiness are derived from the happiness and welfare of others.

TG: Does the fruit of action also have a three-fold classification?

HP: Of course. The same classification of Sattva, Rajas, and Tamas holds good here also.

The fruit of Sattvic action is good and pure, Rajasic actions bring pain and Tamasic actions yield ignorance: BG 14.16

TG: The observable phenomenon is different. Bad things happen to good people. Bad people are enjoying. Not all actions may culminate in desired results. A hard-working student may fail and an easygoing student may pass out in flying colors.

HP: As already said, it is the attitude with which action is performed, more than the act itself which confers result. There are other factors that determine the type of result. As that too is the subject matter of parameter, we will discuss them in a future session.

Prof: Registrar & TG, please make a note so that the question is not overlooked.

Both Christina and TG made notes in their dairy.

TG: You have classified charity, renunciation, austerity, and penance under sacrifice?

HP: Yes. Isn't it logical?

TG: It appears so. What are the three types of charity?

HP: It is same, Sattva, Rajas, and Tamas.

- Charity given to a deserving person, without expectation of anything in return, at the proper place and time is a charity in Sattvic mode. BG 17.20
- Charity given grudgingly, with the expectation of some reward or with a desire for results, is said to be in Rajasic mode.BG 17.21
- Any charity given at the wrong place, wrong time or to undeserving persons with contempt and in a disrespectful manner is said to be in Tamasic mode. BG 17.22

TG: How can charity, a good act be classified as bad?

HP: As already said earlier, an act by itself does not determine goodness or badness nor does it affect the results. Supposing you give food to an already well-fed man, he will throw it away, wasting your food, time, and effort and also depriving someone who is more needy or deserving. Similarly, you give money to a drunkard or gambler, when it is time for their fix, they will fritter it away gambling or drinking. God has clearly said that the fruits of Sattvic action are Sattvic, Rajasic action Rajasic, etc.... This classification by God defines/underscores the importance of attitude and motive behind action more than the action itself.

TG: Talk about types of renunciation.

HP: Renunciation too is of three types.
- Prescribed duties should not be abandoned. Such deluded renunciation is said to be Tamasic or in the nature of tamas. BG: 18.7
- Giving up prescribed duties due to it being troublesome or causing bodily discomfort is renunciation in the mode of passion. Such renunciation escapism and does not yield desired/beneficial results. BG: 18.8
- Performing prescribed duty because it ought to be done without any, attachment to the duty and its results is said to be in the mode of goodness. He neither hates the unpleasant actions nor loves the pleasant actions, nor is he in doubt as to what is correct and what action is incorrect.BG 18.9 & 18.10.

TG: No one can remain without performing any action even for a moment. Nature compels them to act as per gunas. BG: 3.5. You yourself quoted this verse. How then can anybody renounce actions? Even sustenance of the body is not possible by inaction. BG: 3.8

HP: God has already answered it in subsequent verses. He urges Arjuna to renounce the fruit of actions and not actions by themselves.

TG: Why at all should we renounce fruits of action? There is no motivation for giving up fruits of action. It goes against all management principles.

HP: There are many reasons.
- A person who is not renounced has to bear the effect of the threefold fruits of action, desirable, undesirable, and mixed. But those who are in the renounced order of life have no such result to suffer or enjoy. BG 18.12
- The results of an action are not guaranteed (not in the hands of the performer). There are five causes of action and results. BG 18.13, 18.16 & 18.18.
- Do not lament over the inevitable. BG: 2.27, here three folds fruits accrue if one isn't renounced, results become inevitable. But for one who is in a state of renunciation, is not affected by results.

TG: If we get desirable fruits, why should we renounce?

HP: The results are temporary. After the period of enjoyment in higher planets and after exhaustion of the credit of merits accrued, he is again reborn. BG: 9.21. Thus, he will be caught in the birth-death cycle. To overcome this vicious cycle, we have to renounce fruits of action.

TG: You referred to three types of sacrifice.

HP: They too have three-fold classification. God has spoken about it in BG: 17.11 to 17.13. Sacrifice itself being a parameter, we will postpone this discussion when we take up the subject of sacrifices.

God has informed types of penance and austerity and of what it is constituted. Austerity may be austerity of body, speech or of mind.

- o Bodily austerity comprises of worshipping the Supreme Lord, Spiritual preceptors, elders, etc. It includes cleanliness, simplicity celibacy, and ahimsa. BG: 17.14
- o Speaking truth, in a pleasing and beneficial manner not offensive to others and regular study of scriptures is called austerity of speech. BG: 17.15
- o Self-contentment, simplicity, silent, purity of mind is said to be austerities of the mind. BG: 17.16

About the classification of penances and austerities,

- o The austerities, be it of body, mind or speech, which are performed without expecting benefits but performed for pleasing the Lord is said to be in the mode of Sattva. BG 17.17
- o The same performed out of ego seeking respect and honor is in the mode of Rajas. It is impermanent and unstable. BG 17.18
- o Penance foolishly performed by inflicting self-torture with the aim to destroy or harm others is said to be in the mode of Tamas. BG 17.19

TG: How to identify the type of person?

HP: They may be identified by their food habits, faith, or mode of worship or by symptoms.

- o Persons relishing foods that are healthy, increases life span, juicy and wholesome are said to be Sattvic persons. BG: 17.8 Sattvic persons worship demigods. BG: 17.4. When Knowledge, intelligence shine from the mind and senses, we may know that Sattva is dominant. BG: 14.11
- o Persons enjoying bitter, sour, salty, hot, pungent, foods that are burning and causes thirst and dryness are said to be Rajasic persons. Such foods cause misery discomfort and ill health. BG: 17.9 Tamasic persons worship demons. BG: 17.4. When a person is overcome by greed, restlessness, and activity, we may understand that He is Rajasic. BG: 14.12
- o Persons who eat stale food that is pungent, putrid decomposed with relish are Tamasic persons.BG 17.10 Tamasic persons worship ghosts and spirits. BG: 17.4. When Ignorance, delusion, laziness are the characteristics displayed, we may conclude that he is Tamasic by nature. BG: 14.13.

TG: These are the nature and effects of gunas, the material manifestations of which are visible in the mundane world. What are the spiritual after-effects of these gunas? Surely when God speaks, especially through you, He doesn't speak on the mundane platform.

HP: I am reconciled to the fact that you cannot speak any sentence without taking a dig at me. The effects of acting in any particular guna are already discussed. After-life effects of Gunas are also said by God.

A person dying when Rajas is dominant is born in families attached to activities. IF a person dies when Tamas is dominant, He is born in lower wombs. IF a person dies when Sattva is dominant, he is born in higher regions of believers. BG 14.14 & 14.15.

A person who is thinking of God at the time of death will reach God and will not again be reborn. BG: 8.5.

Sattvic persons are elevated to upper regions, Rajasic persons dwell in the middle regions, and Tamasic persons are thrown in lower regions.BG 14.18

TG: Then, what happens to the theory of Karma? Would they be bypassing fruits of all evil deeds?

HP: Gods' words are divine law and ultimate truth. A person cannot think of God at the time of his death unless he has exhausted all his Karma.

TG: You were telling that even knowledge, faith, etc. are classified?

HP: The threefold classification applies also to Knowledge, faith, and firmness.
- The ability to discriminate between what is to be done and what is to be eschewed, what is to be feared and what is not to be feared and the difference between bondage and liberation is Sattvic. BG 18.30
- The state of confusion arising out of an inability to distinguish between righteousness and unrighteousness, between good acts and prohibited acts is said Rajasic.BG 18.31.
- That understanding which considers unrighteousness to be righteous and untruth to be true under delusion and in ignorance and always pursues the wrong path is Tamasic.BG: 18.32

Now about the classification of Firmness:
- That steadfastness cultivated through the practice of yoga, by which the mind, breath, and senses are controlled is Sattvic. BG: 18.33
- That firmness with which one holds fast to duty, pleasures wealth and fruits of action is Rajasic.BG 18.34
- The firmness with which one adheres to fear, grief, despair, and illusion and refuses to give them up is Tamasic. BG: 18.35

It may be noted that Sattvic firmness pursues positive intangibles like control of self, mind, and senses. Rajasic firmness pursues tangibles or material pleasures and Tamasic firmness pursues negative tangibles and intangibles.

TG: What about the classification of Knowledge?

HP: They too are classified on similar lines.

- The knowledge of People in mode of goodness, i.e., Sattvic sees the same unitary spiritual principle in all beings even though they appear to be divided into different bodies. BG: 18.20
- The knowledge of Rajasic persons see each body as a different type of living being, and unable to see the underlying same unitary spiritual principle in all beings. BG: 18.21
- That knowledge by which a person is engrossed in action in parts, assuming it to be whole, which is not based on reason or truth is Tamasic knowledge. BG 18.22

TG: You mean all beings are the same?

HP: Yes, the underlying life principle or spirit consciousness is the same.

TG: You mean a donkey and a horse is the same?

HP: A learned person sees with equal vision a Brahmin, a cow, an elephant, a dog, and a dog-eater.BG: 5.18. Now, don't say that God refers to dogs and not donkeys.

We see ornaments as chain, necklace, ring, bangle, etc. but a goldsmith sees it as a piece of gold in different forms.

A scientist sees it as atoms made up of electrons, protons, and neutrons, a physicist sees it made up of quarks, antiquarks, leptons, and anti-leptons.

A spiritual scientist sees it as matter particles, anti-matter particles and force particles. Whatever be the substance, the underlying contents are Protons, neutrons, and electrons

Now, about the classification of happiness:

God has said that there are three kinds of happiness. BG: 18.36

- That which appears/tastes like poison in the beginning but tastes like nectar in the end and derived from self-realization and knowledge is Sattvic. BG: 18.37

- That happiness which is experienced due to coming into contact of the senses with their objects and which appears like nectar at first but tastes like poison at the end is Rajasic.BG 18.38

- That happiness which eclipses self-realization with illusion from beginning to end, and is derived from sleep, laziness, and negligence is said to be tamasic.BG 18.39

TG: Please elaborate on scientific exposition, i.e., elements, protons, etc. But before that, about happiness, our experiences do not conform to your statements. Won't you feel happy when sense objects come in touch with senses?

HP: We derive happiness of all three kinds, i.e., Sattvic, Rajasic, and Tamasic. The characteristics of such happiness are explained. Let us see with examples

Supposing, you derive pleasure by drinking coffee or say by eating ice cream, how long does it last? It lasts until you are eating or drinking, i.e., until it is in contact. Even that pleasure depends on your capacity.

After the third or fourth round, the very thing which gave you pleasure will give you distress. It may create stomach disorders or throat discomfort, meaning, pleasant at the beginning but like poison subsequently.

If you have cultivated habit of exercising physically, it appears like poison in beginning but feels like nectar at the end. You will be fit physically and mentally, a better attitude, and better capable of handling work and stress.

Sattvic happiness is of long-lasting and a result of your efforts. Rajasic happiness is a result of your senses coming into contact with sense objects and failing to exercise restraint on senses and Tamasic happiness is a result of your indifference, laziness, and inaction. They are the results of the effort, wrong efforts, and non-efforts.

TG: About Transcendence?

HP: A person who has evolved past Gunas is freed from birth, death, decay, and pain, and attains to God. BG 14.20

The characteristics of a transcendentalist are:
- He is indifferent to light caused by Sattva, activity caused by Rajas and delusion caused by Tamas and does not hanker for the same when absent.BG: 14.22
- He is indifferent and unmoved by the changing Gunas and does not waver.BG 14.23
- He is alike in pleasure and pain, regards a clod of earth and gold alike, responds similarly to the agreeable and disagreeable, same in censure and praise.BG: 14.24
- He is the same when disrespected or respected, same to friend and foe, renouncing all fruitive activities. BG: 14.25

TG: I have been observing, you are just quoting verses from the Gita and passing them off as your own, Smart move, isn't it?

HP: Yes and no. I am quoting God for reference. Besides, it is the subject matter of discussion. I didn't claim it to be mine.

I am presenting the verses in a hitherto unknown perspective or shall we say an alternate perspective? When I present my views, you say that' it is not said by God', and I present what God has said, you say 'you are quoting God'.

TG: Does the principle of perishable and imperishable qualify/pervade sattva, rajas, and tamas also?

HP: Yes and No.

TG: How? Gunas are perishable, i.e., they are changing.

HP: A person is in the grip of gunas, which are changing. He evolves upwards or downwards depending on his propensity. A divine evolves upwards towards Sattva and thereafter to transcendence, a demoniac person evolves downward, and meaning performs Tamasic dominant actions. Gunas are changing, but the innate propensity of divine or demonic is unchanging. A divine person always remains so and a demonic person remains so.

TG: What is divine and demonic?

HP: Simple definition is that God-loving persons are divine and God-hating persons are demonic. Hallmark of divine persons is elaborated in BG: 16.1 to 16.3.

The characteristics of demoniac are delineated in BG: 16.4 to 16.21. How they think, how they act, and the fruits they reap is also mentioned therein.

Just like in Gunas, the divine and demoniac too may be understood by assuming that a person has maximum units of 100.

A person is a combination of some units of divinity and some units of the demoniac.

The topmost are perennial devotees of God and inhabit the regions of God and the more the demoniac qualities, their propensity tends towards the demons and towards lower regions.

Just like there is an interplay of gunas, you add the element of divine/demoniac to the gunas to understand the personality of a person. The Divine or demoniac is the innate nature of a person and doesn't change.

There could be upper mobility or lower mobility within the pre-determined ratio of say from 60:40 to 80:20 and so on, which can be attributed to other factors like, Gods' mercy, Gurus' mercy, or past karma. How does the ratio change?

The innate attribute is covered by good association or bad association and comes to the fore when the association is removed. This explains why a good person behaves in a bad way or a bad person in a good manner. What is divinity? It is the love of God, His activities, His words and all other things connected with Him. What is demonic? The propensity to hate God and like all that is not associated with God and dislike all that is associated with God is demoniac. The description of the divine and demoniac, their attitudes and their destination is delineated in BG: 16.1 to 16.22

TG: Your reply is unconvincing. Facts Bely your reply. Prahalad Maharaj, son of Hiranyakashipu was a demon but had all noble qualities and very dear to God. In fact, he was so dear to God, that God has taken an avatar exclusively for his sake. Bali Maharaj was so full of noble qualities that God volunteered to act as a guard of his kingdom.

HP: TG, my friend, we were discussing divine nature or demoniac nature, not divine birth or demoniac birth. Birth is not a determinant of caste or of divinity or demoniac quality. The threefold gunas of nature too are not determinant of caste etc.

Hiranyakashipu too was of divine nature but had to take birth in the demoniac womb due to curse.

This is being clarified as your next question would be how he went back to the abode of God if he were demoniac.

TG: Can a person of Tamasic nature attain God's abode?

HP: Yes, because gunas are temporary. Today he is Tamasic and tomorrow he may be Sattvic. He may evolve upward in the course of time. Even if he is predominantly Tamasic, if he surrenders/prays/worships God, he can attain Gods' abode.

TG: How is it possible? Can you give a quote or cite an example?

HP: Kaliya the serpent was basically Tamasic, meaning tamas was predominating guna most of the time, yet he was blessed by the Lord. Regarding the quote,

- Even the most sinful man worshipping me must be regarded as holy, for he has rightly resolved. He becomes righteous quickly and obtains everlasting peace.BG: 9.30 & 9.31

TG: Please differentiate between three-fold gunas of nature and two-fold nature of the soul.

HP: Gunas are changing, i.e., perishable, but innate demoniac nature or divine nature doesn't change. The divine ultimately goes back to the abode of God, but the demoniac never goes to the abode of God. Divine evolves from domination of tamas to rajas to sattva and thereafter to transcendence, but a demoniac soul evolves backward. A demoniac person enjoys fruits of action performed during the dominance of Sattva and Rajas which is mistakenly interpreted as 'Bad karma, good results', but after the exhaustion of credit of karma, he falls back and born in wombs of lower species.

So, we have an endless combination of possibilities, like Divine persons under the grip of Rajas and Tamas, Demoniac persons under the dominance of Sattva and rajas and so on.

TG: With the parameters, God has given, may I evaluate your understanding, knowledge, firmness, etc.

HP: Please feel free to do so. May I apply the same yardstick and evaluate you?

TG: I know the end result, but I don't know how you will justify your claims. I am curious. You may go ahead.

HP: Brace yourself, and don't blame me.
- Your firmness may be classified as based on illusion and hence Tamasic keeping in line with:
  o The firmness with which one adheres to fear, grief, despair, and illusion and refuses to give them up is Tamasic. BG: 18.35
- You see each living being as a different type and have gone so far as to draw the analogy of horse and donkey. Hence your knowledge may be considered as Rajasic keeping in line with:
  o The knowledge of Rajasic persons see each body as a different type of living being, and unable to see the underlying same unitary spiritual principle in all beings. BG: 18.21
- Your austerity of speech is devoid of pleasing nature and not inoffensive as mandated by God hence not Sattvic.
  o The austerity of speech consists in speaking that which is the truth, beneficial and inoffensive.BG: 17.15

TG: I anticipated such an analysis and am not surprised. Are you strong enough to hear my assessment about you?

HP: Please go ahead.

TG: Okay, Here I go:
- Anyone who gives up his prescribed duties is in the mode of Rajas. BG: 18.7. Your prescribed duty is the study of scriptures and performs worship and rituals but you barely study anything other than Gita.
- Sacrifices are to be performed as per directions of scripture BG: 17.13, but you tout your mundane activities as a sacrifice and justify it by misquoting God.

- You don't practice worship or rituals and fancy it as renunciation, which is in the nature of Tamas. BG: 18.8. It will not lead towards God or higher destinations.
- Your knowledge of Gita and attachment to it as all-encompassing, to the exclusion of all others, is meager and said to be in the mode of Ignorance. BG: 18.22
- Your actions are bereft of the backing of scriptural injunctions and hence to be considered Tamasic. BG: 18.25

HP: Thanks for your assessment, I will try to improve myself.

Prof: Don't digress from the subject matter and bring in individual personalities, Okay?

TG: You told me that there are many ways to look at these gunas. Would you be kind enough to substantiate?

HP: Some scientists have proposed that Sattva, Rajas, and Tamas are nothing but electron, proton, and neutron.

TG: Is it true, I mean Gita refers to electron, proton, and neutron as Sattva, Rajas, and Tamas?

HP: Maybe, or may not be. IT could be the Sanskrit equivalent of English words. The similarities are too much to ignore. They are ubiquitous and make up all matter. Remember, God, says, all exist because I exist. He also says I am everywhere, there is no place, where I am not present. All things are made up of Positive, negative and neutral energy or forces, corresponding to Sattva, Rajas, and Tamas.

Atoms are the building blocks of matter. They are the small particles of an element that still have the element's properties. Elements, in turn, are pure substances—such as nickel, hydrogen, and helium—that make up all kinds of matter.

Subatomic particles are particles that are smaller than the atom. Protons, neutrons, and electrons are the three main subatomic particles found in an atom. Protons have a positive (+) charge. Electrons have negative charge and neutrons has no charge.

In particle physics, an elementary particle is a particle with no substructure, meaning it is not composed of other particles.

Particles currently thought to be elementary include the fundamental fermions which are made up of quarks, leptons, antiquarks, and antileptons. They are generally "matter particles" and "antimatter particles", as well as the fundamental bosons (gauge bosons and the Higgs boson), which generally are "force particles".

A particle containing two or more elementary particles is a composite particle.

Characteristics of Protons, Neutrons, and Electrons

Protons:	Positive charge.
Neutron:	No charge.
Electron:	Negative charge.
Proton & Neutron	located in nucleus.
Electron:	located outside nucleus.

TG: What other ways to look at Gunas?

HP: There is the holy trinity, viz. Brahma, Vishnu, and Maheshwara, representing the acts of creation, sustenance, and destruction. Creation is in the mode of passion or Rajas, Sustenance is in the mode of goodness or Sattva, and destruction is in the mode of ignorance or Tamasic.

TG: Is it verified and proven or an off the cuff remark?

HP: I am not a scientist, nor do I have aptitude nor deep interest in scientific matters. Just a passing interest more so because it came in the path of spirituality. It is more like an exploration. Take it or leave it.

Prof: Okay, then we shall break for the day and assemble again tomorrow.

They all walked to their rooms. Christina invited Hari to her place. There she questioned Hari about her doubts.

CH: Why God made different gunas and consequent conflicts? Couldn't it have been homogeneous?

HP: God didn't make it. He just identified the existing types of gunas. I will put it in a different context where after you can appreciate it better.

- o Sattva regulates the mind and senses.
- o Rajas regulate bodily and physical and material activities.
- o Tamas doesn't regulate at all. Just goes where it pleases.

It is an absolute necessity for all these to exist in cohesion and not independently. There will be sociological upheavals if balance is not maintained between themselves inter-se.

Only Rajas oriented society will have constant quarrels and conflicts. The only sattva would bring the world to a standstill. Pure sattva, rajas, and tamas don't exist. God, Himself has said that each one tries to and dominates the others at different times.

The three gunas and the four Varna (castes) also becomes a parameter demonstrating that not all instructions are meant for all. They are selectively directed. These should coexist to maintain cosmic harmony. But the Time element of God changes everything that is changeable leaving the unchangeable untouched. When this imbalance reaches intolerable levels, God descends as an Avatar/Incarnation to remedy the imbalances in different ways.

CH: What is it about Atoms, metaphysics, etc.?

HP: I am not a qualified physicist or a meta-physicist. I happen to read about it and found it interesting and also a possibility of it being another dimension of truth. I wanted to share it with all and have done so. The point to be noticed is that there is acceptance of Gita and scriptures amongst scientists, but laymen discount Gita saying that it is unscientific. They swear by science but doubt Gita.

CH: Rajasic and Tamasic gunas cloud wisdom, but how does Sattva cloud judgment? When Sattva is in the mode of goodness, why should we transcend Sattva too?

HP: For maintaining social balance as already told. Inability and refusal to see the need for punitive and preventive measures due to being blinded by sympathy, a Sattvic quality due to which.
   o   Arjuna refused to fight.
   o   Sage Uttanaka attempted cursing Lord Himself for not preventing the Kurukshetra holocaust.

The removal of the veil of Maya by God saw both of them overcoming the clutches of Guna. Christina was happy. They took leave of each other by bidding goodnight.

18. K- 8 – CAUSES OF ACTION AND RESULTS

All the students and the professor had assembled and ready for the discussion to begin. The Professor looked up from his pile of papers and asked if everyone was ready. Ready cried all of them in unison. Start commanded the Professor.

HP: Today, I present slokas numbered 18.13 to 18.16 and 4.14 from the Gita, on the causes of accomplishment of all actions as a parameter
- There are five causes for the accomplishment of all actions.BG: 18.13
- The body, the performer, the senses, the endeavors, and God are the five factors of action. BG: 18.14
- Whatever action a person performs by body, mind, and senses, whether it right or wrong is caused by these five factors. BG: 18.15
- Anyone who thinks himself is the doer, without considering the five factors, is foolish, and ignorant. BG: 18.16
- Actions do not taint (affect) God. BG: 4.14.

Thereafter, I intend presenting sloka 18.38 as a parameter.

Every action has some taint just as fire is covered by smoke. Hence, one should not give up working even if such work is full of faults. BG: 18.48

TG: Have you said anything other than parameters? Carry on.

HP: All five factors are required to perform an action. Persons generally discount the God factor and appropriate all good results to their efforts and discount their role and put blame on God in case of failure.

TG: Theists say that God is the performer of all actions and giver of results of all actions but Atheists say that it is we who put in efforts.

  Not only we, even animals and other lower species put in efforts. A bee extracts honey, a lion hunt and so on. What is the truth?

HP: Can animals put in efforts without body or without sense organs?

TG: Yes, but what about the God factor in animals or in Atheists?

HP: God is a performer of all actions even in lower species, leave alone humans, even atheists. It is the misconception of atheists that there is no God. They are unaware of God as are the lower species, but that doesn't change the fact about God.

TG: When you are doing everything, how can you attribute it to God? Now, both you and I are speaking. Is it we speaking or is it God speaking?

HP: It is both God speaking through the medium of you and me and also us speaking at the will and behest of God.

TG: Please clear the concept.

HP: We are the proximate cause of action and God is the ultimate cause. This can be viewed from many angles.

- o You are given a fellowship. The amount is given to you by an accountant. Is the accountant the giver? He is acting on behalf of the government. Here, the immediate cause is the accountant and the ultimate cause is the Government. The accountant is impelled by the Government to act as per its instructions.

- In the realm of spirituality, all actions are impelled by the Lord, thus making Him the ultimate cause. The immediate cause may be the performer.

- There are times when all the factors are present, but you are unable to put in the effort, maybe due to paucity of time, lack of resources, lack of knowledge, ill health, etc. This is the God factor at play.

- Going further, even the efforts are put, but the results are not forthcoming.
  Even when results are forthcoming, it could be undesirable results. Atheists may call it luck factor, but that isn't so.

- Sometimes, the effort put in is negligible or no effort is put in, but there are astounding results. All this can be accounted for by God factor.

Hasn't God said ....

- o Gunas perform an action. The deluded persons think he is performing an action, but a wise person sees that gunas are performing an action. BG: 3.27
- o The entire world is deluded by three Gunas. BG: 7.13
- o The gunas are very difficult to surmount. Only those taking refuge of me can overcome gunas BG: 7:14
- o He who thinks of himself as the killer and the one who thinks he is killed is ignorant. BG: 2.19   Man is not the doer; he is only the proximate cause. The actual doer is God. God is the ultimate cause/doer of all actions. Beings are a mere instrument.
- o Kill Drona, Bhishma, Jayadratha, Karna and other warriors who are already killed by me. BG: 11.34
  - ▪ All the warriors were killed by Arjuna later. God says that He has killed them even when they were alive and were subsequently killed by Arjuna. Here God is implying that He is the ultimate cause though Arjuna is the proximate cause.

TG: You just said that God is the performer/cause of all actions. Now you say that it is gunas that perform an action. You are confusing me. Tell me with certainty which is correct. Whether it is God or Gunas?

HP: Let us put it this way. Gunas are the performer. Body/self is the medium through action is performed. God is the impeller or the cause.

TG: So far, you have quoted God extensively. Now explain with an example reconciling what God has said with reality.

HP: You are hungry. You go to the canteen, order food, and eat it. Your body is the medium through which the actions of walking up to the canteen, ordering, and eating is performed.

The type of food you order and the way your place order and how you eat is determined by Gunas. IT was God who gave you hunger, the food, the ability to eat and digest, etc.

TG: How?

HP: Action cannot be performed without a body. Hence, the body is the medium. Your request for food is in the mode of Sattva. If you demand food, it is in the mode of Rajas and if you command or forcibly take it is in the Tamasic mode. The type of food you order is also dependent on the gunas. That you have the ability to feel hunger, knowledge as to how to satisfy hunger, eating and digesting the same is God gift. (BG: 15.15) Food is made available to you by God, who permeates the earth and nourishes all living beings and plants with the juice of life. BG: 15.13.

Further, a dead person cannot perform any action.

TG: Who said a dead person performs any action?

HP: The body is present, why can't he perform any action?

TG: The other factors like effort, senses are not there.

HP: Exactly, because God has taken away the soul, mind, and senses, with He, just like the wind carries away the fragrance. BG: 15.7 and 15.8. Hence, God, Senses and mind and effort is missing. So, who is performing an action?

TG: God of course.

HP: Triumphantly, So, you agree?

TG: I agree with God, not with you.

Loud laughter erupted. The professor also joined in the laughter and it took a good three minutes for the environment to return back to sobriety.

HP: Even the results of actions are awarded by God. That is probably why they say that God is the actual doer.

TG: God is the giver of fruits of action?

HP: Yes. Even when prayers are offered to other gods, the fruits so obtained by them is sanctioned by the Supreme Lord. BG: 7.22

TG: Then, why does God say don't work with an eye on fruits of action, but perform the same as a duty, as a sacrifice unto Him?

HP: Because God is the giver of fruits, and we cannot determine the fruits of action.

TG: God gives the fruit of action, why then should we not hanker for fruits of action?

HP: For the simple reason that you will be more focused on the fruits than the actual assignment on hand. Besides, as per the theory of Karma, you should have accumulated sufficient credit of positive karma to enjoy the positive results of your actions. Conversely, even for experiencing distress, you should have sufficient credit of negative karma. Hence, there could be a time lag in experiencing the results. The results could also be immediate. This time lag can be a few minutes to 'n' number of births.

If you notice carefully, you can only act, you have no control over the results. Hence, it is said that do not eye the fruits while performing an action. Suppose you eat food; your act is restricted to putting food in your mouth and chewing and swallowing it.

Whether it digests or not, provides strength or not, whether you evacuate partly or completely is a process, which goes on without you having any say in the matter. You can only initiate the process. When you don't perform any action but the only process, God too only initiates the process. The Gunas does the rest.

This explains, many other things like
- o Why bad things happen to good people and vice versa.
- o Why some people are crowned with success with, little effort and others have to struggle repeatedly for success.
- o Why it appears that some prayers are answered immediately and others appear to have been ignored.

This answers another question asked by some of my friends a few months ago. Whether God's answers to prayers are real-time/run-time or deferred-time/asynchronous?

It is both, depending on the amount of credit you have accumulated. Time is an essential ingredient. The credit of piety is another ingredient.

Instances where prayers have been answered real-time
- o Gajendra, the elephant king, rescued from the crocodile.
- o Draupadi saved from the embarrassment of disrobement by Dushasan
- o Bhīma's' invitation to Krishna for lunch answered before the fall of the mace thrown aloft.

Instances, where prayers are answered deferred-time.
- o Dhruva, Meeting the Lord and obtaining kingship of a separate universe
- o Saints being born as Cowherd lasses (Gopis) after many births of penance.

○ Lord answering prayers of Diti, mother of Indra, king of gods, by taking dwarf incarnation.

There is a gestation period for everything, be it plants, animals or humans. It is known that it takes 9 months from conception until a baby is born. There are different gestation periods for plants from seedling to producing fruits or vegetables. Similarly, for our actions to yield results, there would be time lag or what is termed as the gestation period.

Some actions yield quick results, some take time. The reaction of karma undergone by Dhritarashtra is case in point. Dhritarashtra had the misfortune of feeling the loss of his 100 sons, which was nothing but karma playing its part. In an earlier lifetime, while hunting, a male bird escaped his arrows and flew away. Enraged, he killed one hundred baby birds in the nest, whilst the father bird was helplessly watching the massacre in agony. Why did he have to wait many lifetimes to undergo punishment? It requires an enormous amount of piety to beget one hundred sons, which has taken many lifetimes to accumulate. Both good karma and bad karma fructified during his birth as Dhritarashtra.

To laymen it appears that there is injustice, prayers are unanswered and bad elements have a field day, but karma surely catches up. There is no escape as it is not man-made law but divine law.

TG: But the element of time is not mentioned in the five causes of accomplishment of all action.

HP: When God factor is mentioned, it includes time.

TG: Yes, it includes time and everything else you may want to include and may choose to include subsequently as an afterthought.

HP: Hasn't God said, 'I am the time'? BG: 11.32. Again, hasn't He said that among the reckoners of time I am the time? BG: 10.30

TG: I repeat, Time is not mentioned as a cause of action.

HP: TG, what God has said in 10.30 & 11.32 is a qualifier for what has been said in 18.14 & 18.15.

Actually, it can be understood without the qualifier verses, because, God factor is mentioned, and God includes His potency. You cannot isolate God without His attributes and claim that it is not mentioned. I am sure you too agree with my explanation deep within, but not conceding any ground for the sake of victory.

TG's face broke into a grin. She turned red in embarrassment; she had been caught red-handed.

TG: You said that there are five causes, namely the body, the senses, the endeavors, the performer, and God. You have also given a reference. Am I right?

HP: Yes, of course.

TG: God also has accomplished many feats. He has performed many actions. Isn't it?

HP: True. He performs actions in two ways.
- By himself or by being the direct or proximate cause.
- By impelling others to do it.

TG: Then, the elements of the body, senses, etc. are missing.

HP: NO, He plays both the roles of self (soul) and super soul (God). So, no element is missing.

TG: But you yourself said that the body is required for performing an action. God does not have a body (form) BG: 12.2.

HP: God (in flesh and blood) in two-armed form was standing before Arjuna and delivered the Gita discourse.

- God showed His four-armed form and cosmic form.

- The Entire chapter describes the cosmic form of God right from verses 11.15 to 11.30.

- His hands, feet, heads, eyes, and faces were everywhere. BG: 13.14

Yet you say, the element of the body is missing.

TG: That vision of cosmic form and four-armed form was an illusion.

HP: You are laboring under an illusion.
- God has said that He will show His cosmic form, not illusory form.
- Arjuna was under delusion (illusion) which was overcome after Gita discourse. BG: 11.1. So, God is removing the illusion and not promoting Illusion.
- God has also said that Arjuna cannot see Him with his human eye (whose sight is illusory) and hence awarded him divine sight (which is free from illusion) BG: 11.8
- Arjuna himself said that he is no longer in illusion. BG: 18.73
  - Arjuna's action was restricted to only praying for cosmic vision. It is God who presented the vision.
    - Even thereafter, he couldn't see, when God had to give him divine eyesight to slake the cosmic vision.

TG: I only quoted Gita or at times repeating what you might have said. Then what about the other factor senses? Surely, that is the missing element.

HP: It means that He can perceive everything without senses or sensory organs.

- He perceives all sense-objects although He is devoid of the senses.BG: 13.15.
- We have seen that He has hands, feet, eyes face (Sense organs) everywhere.
- When God was standing before Arjuna, the functioning of all His sense faculties was sound.
- He Himself says, of the senses, I am the Mind. BG: 10.22 and Mind is the best of sense organs.

TG: You have said that whatever action, right or wrong is caused by five factors as per BG: 18.15. Isn't it?

HP: Yes.

TG: You have said that God also performs actions. Do you mean to say that God can also do wrong actions?

HP: God is blemishless. This is a fundamental attribute. We have already seen it.
  - o God is addressed as Achyuta, meaning the infallible one in BG: 11.42
  - o God's birth and actions are divine. BG: 4.9
  - o Actions do not bind God. BG: 9.9
  - o Actions do not taint God. BG: 4.14

TG: God is Himself the cause of action and also a doer of the action. His words say that He can do no wrong. But His actions don't match His words. Even, I can quote God but does it justify His actions? Even I am a believer. God's quote satisfies me, but will it satisfy non-believers or for people of other faith?

HP: What actions are you speaking of?

TG: There are many. I will just name a few.
  - o God breaking His vow of not lifting Arms in the battle.
  - o God resorting to trickery to enable Arjuna to kill Jayadratha
  - o God encouraging Bhīma to use foul means to kill Duryodhana.
  - o Pushing Bali, His devotee to nether worlds after accepting the gift of three steps of land.

HP: Actions are but tools. By itself, they are neither good nor bad. The purpose behind and the end results thereof determines whether an action is good or bad.
  - God descended to our earth planet to re-establish Dharma and to punish the wicked. His actions were in agreement with His objectives for which He took avatar.
  - God is beyond Gunas, so the actions performed too would not be tainted by any Gunas. God does not refrain from performing an

action because it is branded Tamasic nor will he rush to perform an action because it is termed Sattvic.

- See the devastation that resulted from the Sattvic action of being wedded to the vow by Bhishma or the escaping from the war by Balarama.
- There are three types of actions stated by God, namely, Action, Inaction, and prohibited action. BG: 4.17
- A person performing action devoid of desire for sense gratification is called a wise person. BG: 4.19

He is not concerned about the outcomes of His action and always in equanimity. BG: 4.20. Lord's actions come under this classification, i.e., inaction in action.

- A performing action in action is one who acts with an eye on end results in view. This is defined in BG: 4.20
- Non-action is the performance of prohibited action.
- God's action and inaction are as defined in BG: 4.18, i.e., inaction in action. Not attached to results, performing work for work's sake.

TG: Does that justify His dubious deeds? Isn't it prohibited?

HP: God, His words, deed, etc. don't require justification. It requires perspective to view correctly. When you say prohibited, the question arises, prohibited by whom? Prohibited for whom? God is the one who is prohibiting. He is exempt from all laws, which are His even though HE finds Himself to the same, so as to set an example. Let me preempt you from asking the next question by answering it before you ask. In military installations or in any workplace, we find boards, "No Admission".

This restriction is not applicable to the imposer or to the authorized personnel. That is the best analogy, I could come up. It may not be perfect, but it can communicate the essence. An apparent wrong action at the right time, in the larger interest, is no longer wrong. Likewise, an apparent right action at the wrong time which causes greater harm than good is not the right action. For example.......

TG: Give examples or justification of God's dubious actions instead of other examples. It would help clear the air.

HP: When God broke His vow, two important purposes were served.
- o Firstly, He was up keeping the vow of His devotee, Bhishma, who had vowed that He would make God break His promise by lifting arms. He gave precedence to His devotees' vow rather than His own vow.
- o Secondly, it was a lesson to Bhishma that an individual vow is secondary in importance in the larger interests of the community.

In the Jayadratha case too, two purposes were accomplished.
- o God helped Arjuna keep his vow of killing Jayadratha before sunset.

- o The punishment was repayment to Jayadratha's negative karma of abducting Pandavas' spouse.

In the case of Bhima using foul means, the perspective is

- o Same as in the case of Jayadratha, up keeping of vow and Catching up with bad Karma.

TG: Okay, but what about Bali? After having surrendered everything, He was dispossessed of everything and pushed to the nether world.

HP: Inscrutable are God's ways. This secret can only be understood by the devotees.

God played the role of a supplicant before Bali. Imagine the lord of all universes seeking and accepting a favor from a mortal. See the glory of Lord Bali, who had an opportunity of giving alms to the almighty lord, reversing the normal roles, wherein everyone seeks alms from Him. See the magnanimity of the Lord.

- o God promised to make him King of gods (Indra) in another manavantara.
- o He was temporarily made the ruler of the Nether world.
- o God personally stood guard to protect the kingdom of Bali.

The gods in heaven themselves envied Bali Maharaj, who was favored by God. The extent of favor extended to the demon lineage of Bali can be seen by the fact that

- o God has taken Avatara exclusively for the sake of Prahalad Maharaj, Bali's grandfather.
- o God has taken Avatara exclusively for sake of Bali, whilst appearing to favor Indra, king of gods.
- o He is stretching arms from mortals for alms like a commoner, from a family of demon that too not for His own sake but for god, Indra's sake.

TG: You have talked about results of action real-time or deferred-time. In that context, what about the results of Gods' actions?

HP: God is Time incarnate, Time Himself and master of time.

TG: Meaning?

HP: There need not be any gestation period. The results are always forthcoming and positive and of course instantaneous. There is no need for accumulating piety or credits etc., for God's actions to bear fruit.

TG: You mean God has not failed or God's actions yield fruitful results always and also immediately?

HP: I understand what you aver. God hasn't failed. You have the Gods' apparent failure in a peace mission in mind. It was more of setting an example to explore all peace initiatives before war rather than failure. Next, where results require a credit of piety for the beneficiary, there is a wait or no-wait period depending on credit accumulated. Where the beneficiary is GOD Himself, there is no wait or question of credits, etc.

Further, as already said, God's actions have no taint. God is unaffected by actions, unlike us mortals. BG: 4.14. As a corollary, it means, humans are affected by actions and their results thus tainting their actions. Thence the question of success or failure comes into the picture.

TG: Okay, now move on to your next parameter 18.48.

HP: All actions have taint. I present this as a parameter. This is supported by sloka 18.48 of BG.

- Every endeavor is covered by some sort of fault, just as fire is covered by smoke. Therefore, one should not give up working, even if such work is full of fault. BG: 18.48

TG: How can every work have a taint? Good works aren't tainted.

HP: There are three aspects. The work, the results of the work and the purpose behind work. Taint in work means ill executing, incomplete work. Results are not in agents' (our) control. There are many other factors controlling the results. Taint herein implies desirable results, undesirable results, and mixed results.

Taint also may imply good for some and bad for the other. The taint in purpose is described as Tamasic and done with not so good intentions.

Now, in the war, or the work itself, isn't it tainted? Even if fought without breaking rules, wasn't it tainted? Coming to the results of war, it was mixed results for the Pandavas and undesirable results for the Kauravas. For other citizens of Hastinapur, gods and other celestial beings and our folks, the results are a treat. It gave the denizens of heavens and us the Gita, sublime and pristine words of God. As regards the purpose or the motivation behind the drive, It was noble on the part of Pandavas and selfish and jealousy-driven for Kauravas. This is in a broad framework. If we dwell individually, Individual motives had some taint. Karna wanted to display his supremacy, Shalya worked for Pandavas though he was fighting on Kaurava's side, Drona and Bhishma compromised their ethics and values and fought on the side of Kauravas notwithstanding their affinity to Pandavas. There too, they didn't do justice to the side they were fighting for by breaching security/loyalty norms and yielding to the opposite side against the best interests of their side.

Even Karna too bound himself by his own promises against his better judgment. Now, don't tell me that the Kurukshetra war itself is not good work. Saying so tantamounts to saying that Gita itself is tainted.

TG: Any exceptions?

HP: Yes, God Almighty Himself is an exception.

- Activities do not taint God, nor does he act with a desire for fruits of action. Knowing this, a person is not bound by karmic reactions. BG: 4.14

TG: Why is it so?

HP: Because, the doer (God), His actions, His motives, and results thereof are all blemishless. This is despite the fact that it doesn't appear so. The very basis of understanding God or Gita rests on the fact that He is blemishless. But we are missing the main point while pursuing secondary matters.

TG: What is the main point which we have side-stepped?

HP: The connotations of "All actions have taint". It is

- Don't refrain from any action because it has taint.

- When viewing/judging others'actions, look at the positives, not the tainted part.

TG: With a victorious smirk, you said that taint can be because of ill motives, so we can perform ill-motivated actions also?

HP: Firstly, look at the untainted part of what I said, i.e., the positives. Next, each one acts as per his nature, repression cannot help as is borne out by history and quoted by the Lord Himself. Next, it is vikarma or prohibited action as explained by the Lord.

Lastly, all actions yield results, good actions yield good results and bad action yields bad results. You remind me of our country's opposition party.

Both the political arena and this forum have a larger purpose, the sight of which should not be lost. The purpose is an exploration of truth and in a political context, constructive opposition, not opposition for sake of opposition. There is another thing called Yogyate, in Dwaita philosophy.

This means commensurate with capacity, eligibility/deservedness. This capacity is in respect of both efforts and dedication put in and also the capacity to receive and sustain. God has said that He responds to the devotee in proportion to his devotion, (not necessarily in quantity)

Many a time it is observed that the blessings we receive are infinitely more than we deserve, so here it means the capacity of sustenance. Answer to prayers are customized keeping in view what is prayed for, what is desired, what is deserving, what is good and the capacity to receive. The capacity to receive grace is also finite. If we receive more than we are capable, there is misuse or abuse or counterproductive. Due to this awareness of self-limitation, Arjuna asks "If you think I can behold your cosmic vision, please confer on me the sight of the cosmic vision.

Prof: Do you have anything to add or present on the subject?

TG: No sir.

HP: I have concluded for the day, sir.

Prof: We will break now to meet again tomorrow.

Everybody left the hall. HP and Christina walked into the canteen and sat in the lounge. Christina was waiting for an opportunity to speak to HP in private. She found her chance.

CH: HP, why have you left out the most important sloka, the very heart of Gita from today's debate?

HP: Which one?

CH: कर्मण्येवाधिकारस्ते मा फलेषु कदाचन |BG 2.47: You have a right to perform your prescribed duties, not the fruits of your actions.

HP: I have made a brief mention. But that is not the heart of Gita. It is the heart only for Karma Yogi, not for others.

CH: You mean it is not important, or that there are other more important verses?

HP: All verses are important depending on our needs and context. The soul of Gita for Karma yogi is that verse you related. There are different hearts (essence) for different types of Yogi.

CH: Please talk about the others. I am finding it new.

HP: Well, it is like this.

- o For Dhyana Yogi, it is Sloka 6.31
  - The yogi who is established in union with God and worships God as the Supreme Soul residing in all beings dwells only in God though engaged in all kinds of activities. BG: 6.31
  - Because this is the pinnacle of achievement for a Dhyana yogi.
- o For Jnana Yogi, it is 13.8 to 13.12
  - Humility, freedom from hypocrisy, non-violence, forgiveness, simplicity, cleanliness of body and mind, steadfastness, self-control, dispassion, awareness of evils of birth, disease, old age, and death, non-attachment, constant and exclusive devotion toward God all are declared to be knowledge, and what is contrary to it is called ignorance.
  - Because, Jnani pursues knowledge, and the highest knowledge and its identification are declared in this sloka.
- o For Bhakti Yogi, it is 18.66
  - Abandon all varieties of dharma and surrender unto God, He will liberate you from all sinful reactions. BG: 18.66

- Because this is the only instruction a practitioner of Bhakti Yoga needs to follow to attain to God.

There could be other verses, more suitable, but this is what I perceive.

CH: Of course, everyone has his or her opinion and individuality. I will stick with your version. Do you have any other perspectives on the action, which is missed out?

HP: Good you reminded me. All slokas are intertwined. We have seen the perishable and imperishable in the earlier days. That is all-pervasive, meaning it can be applied to actions and results also. Each action may have a material/physical component and a spiritual component. Likewise, the results too may have two components. Their proportion of components inter-se may vary.

CH: How?

HP: Dhruva had the material desire, that of adorning the throne of his father. His penance was partly material and partly spiritual. His physical rigors constitute material efforts, His prayer to God was a spiritual component. God appeared before him and bestowed him the kingship of Pole star. He was crowned king of the kingdom of his father which he earlier coveted. Prahalad Maharaj didn't do any penance. His penance was a complete dependence on the Lord and remembering God. His entire actions were spiritual.

CH: How can physical action have a spiritual component?

HP: The act may be physical, but the spirit behind action could be material or spiritual. You perform philanthropic acts with altruistic spirit, your action is physical but the intent is spiritual and if it is meant to please God, it is beyond both physical and material if your act was performed with desire for publicity, it is completely physical.

CH: How to distinguish spiritual and mundane?

HP: Be it a realm of action, results, intent, or knowledge, spirituality has the following characteristics. It would be
- Permanent or   Imperishable
- No loss of effort (credit system)
- Freedom from fear.
- No adverse results

The above is quoted from BG: 2.40

CH: Yes, I recollect, but couldn't correlate it. Thank you.

HP: Regarding the perspectives you asked, I simplify and repeat what I said earlier, as there are five causes for the results of an action, and we don't have control over all the causes. We may have partial control over the body, with limiting factors being capacity, strength, good health, etc.

The next cause is our very self. Unless we have control over self, we cannot accomplish any action. Similarly, we have to exercise control over senses, which includes mind, failing which your efforts will be deviated in satisfaction of senses rather than in fulfillment of your object. God's will be another factor. So, for the accomplishment of any results, apart from efforts, (action in furtherance of the result), you must also put efforts to be fit and healthy, put in efforts to keep mind and senses under control and pray God to obtain His blessings/favor. With that, they parted their ways.

19. K 9 – TIME AND SPACE AS PARAMETERS

The clock struck six. This was the cue. The professor asked the debate to begin.

HP: Today, I present the concepts of time and space as parameters.

- o They are taken as a parameter because it qualifies most of the slokas so as to shed light on the otherwise hidden wisdom.
- o Taken as a parameter in the sense of time as context.
- o By qualifying most of the verses, and turns irrelevant to relevant, obsolete to contemporary.
- o Time qualifies all our transactions but doesn't qualify God's actions due to His absolute nature and Absolute activities.
- o Explains/removes misconception/misunderstanding due to non-reckoning of the time factor in the interpretation of any verse in the Gita or for that matter in any scripture.
- o Reconciles between what is stated in scriptures and what is actually in existence.

Many definitions have been put forth about time.
Some of the definitions are

- What clocks measure, according to physicists Albert Einstein, Donald Ivey, and others
- A linear continuum of instants, according to philosopher Adolf Grünbaum.
- A continuum that lacks spatial dimensions according to Encyclopedia Britannica. A non-spatial system in which events appear to happen in irreversible succession according to Word Smyth Dictionary.
- The inevitable progression into the future with the passing of present events into the past according to Wiktionary.
- The indefinite continued progress of existence and events in the past, present, and future regarded as a whole as per Google.
- A dimension in which events can be ordered from the past through the present into the future, and also the measure of durations of events and the intervals between them, according to Wikipedia.

Viewed in another sense, Time may be said to compromise of past, present, and future.

It may be noted that neither is time merely a dimension, quantity or concept. Indeed, time has many aspects and appears to represent different things to different peopleindifferentcircumstances. More about that later
....

Both Time and space have been mentioned in the Gita in various contexts. Let us see the concepts of time in the Gita.

Gods' wisdom on time.

- I am the time come to destroy all. BG: 11.32
  - Here, Time is used as a noun, referring to Almighty. Just like the saying 'Handsome is what Handsome does' Time is what time does. As seen earlier, Sanskrit words derive meaning from their attributes, God ascribes Time to Himself. What does time do? It destroys everything. What is meant by destroying? It means changing of form from the existing format to another. God herein is implying that He is the harbinger of change, a catalyst who ushers in change.
  - This is a noticeable phenomenon. We ourselves are changing. Our environment changes, our thoughts change. In fact, everything changes. Change is a property of Time.
- There was never a time when you or I or the kings didn't exist. BG: 2.12
  - Here, Time is used in the sense of 'instant as an object' — one point on the time axis, or simply put a moment, (a kshana, a microsecond or Nanosecond, whichever is the smallest unit by which we can denote it).
    Being an object, it has no value. God is telling that there is not even a fraction of a moment when Arjuna and other warring Kings didn't exist. They always existed and would continue to exist. Here Arjuna and the kings refer to the imperishable souls of Arjuna and the Kings. The bodies may be destroyed but the soul exists.
    Meaning, the form of the soul remains forever into eternity, the body is destroyed and may acquire new body form.
- A gift given to the right person at the right time is Sattvic. BG: 17.20
  - Here, time is used in the sense of appropriateness. The right time is an appropriate time. The wrong time is inappropriate time. In other words, time means context. The deciding factor being appropriateness and context. The giving of gift or any other act, by itself, is immaterial, the appropriateness and the context therein is material for reckoning/judging merits or otherwise of the action. We may extend the analogy for our understanding of the Gita too.
- I know all the past, present, and future. BG: 7.26.
  - Here, time is used in the sense of a particular period considered as distinct from other periods. Google's definition seems appropriate here which states 'The indefinite continued progress of existence and events in the past, present, and future regarded as a whole'. These three periods together is complete and whole. Here, the implication is that there is nothing that is not known by God.
- Among the measures of reckoning, I am time. BG: 10.30.

- o Time is used as a unit of measurement. Here time is a quantity characterizing an interval duration. As a quantity, it has a value, such as a number of day's years, etc.

- Time as Brahma's day and night. BG 8.17:
  - o A day of Brahma (Kalp) lasts a thousand cycles of the four ages (Maha yuga) and his night also extends for the same span of time. The wise who know this understand the reality about day and night. If we read between the lines, we understand that the Time scale is not uniform for all beings or in different planets. Time is relative to all beings with the only exception being God and inhabitants of His abode.
- I am the endless Time BG 10.33
  - o Here, Time is used as a noun, referring to Almighty, being described with one of His many qualities, beginning-less & endless imperishable and ever existing.

Properties of time.

- Time is both absolute and relative. It is relative for us and absolute for God.
- God is both time and beyond time. The time when taken in the sense of "what it does", Time changes everything. This is being carried out under the supervision of God. As God remains unchanged, He is beyond change.
- As a unit of measurement, time scales are different among different planets/Lokas. As God's abode is beyond all planets, Time is absolute and unchanging, vis-à-vis God and inhabitants of His abode.
- Due to the property of changing constantly, time is irreversible, with the exception when you are in God's abode.
- In the human sense, there is favorable time and unfavorable time, in the divine realm there is no distinction.
- In the sense of context, God says I am time, meaning He is the context.
- In the sense of appropriateness.

All the differing meanings of time taken together form the context. This context is a variable and along with other variables should be factored whilst deriving conclusions or judging things or to come to an understanding.

TG: Please substantiate, how time is absolute or relative and how time changes everything etc.

HP: In Vaikuntha, there is no period interval, no death, no rebirth i.e., you remain unchanging. Your body remains the same without undergoing modifications like growth, aging disease, etc. hence, it is said to be absolute.

Scriptures describe Sarupya moksha as one who has similar bodily features as God confirming the unchanging nature of the body in Vaikuntha.

Irreversible property of time is an observable phenomenon. We grow from infant to childhood to youth and progress to old age. Our body keeps changing.

TG: You said time is past, present, and future, isn't it?

HP: Yes.

- The past may be defined as those events which occurred before a given point in time, events that are usually considered to be fixed and immutable. It can be accessed through memory or, since the advent of written language, recorded history. The study of the past, in particular as it relates to humans, is called history.

- The present may be defined as the time associated with the events perceived directly and for the first time, i.e., not as a recollection of the past, or as a speculation of the future.

- It is equivalent to the word "now", and is the period of time located between the past and the future. Just how long a period of time the present incorporates, however, depends on the context, and can vary from an infinitesimal or duration-less moment to a day to a whole era, depending on how it is being used.

- The future is the indefinite time period after the present moment. It is the portion of the projected timeline that is anticipated to occur and may be considered as potentially infinite in its extent, or as circumscribed and finite, depending on the context.

- While some people may see the future as fixed and predetermined, most see it as essentially unknown (and perhaps unknowable), and open to many different possibilities and permutations. The study of postulating possible, probable, and preferable futures and worldviews is called futurology.

TG: You said God knows past, present, and future. How is it related to time? How does He know the past present and future?

HP: God is the creator, sustainer, and destroyer. He performs these activities either by Himself or through His assistants/agents/expansions. Creation is associated with past; sustenance is associated with present and destruction with the future. Since He Himself causes, sustains, and destroys, He knows everything. That is why He is time and said to be beyond time, meaning unaffected by time.

TG: What is the context?

HP: Context is a variable. Context is the state of all things prevalent at a given point/period /interval of time.

TG: What is meant by saying God is context?

HP: When God says He is time, He is time, i.e., all variants of time. He is the sum total of all contexts ever, Plus ...... So, He is a time in the form of context also.

TG: But there could be innumerable contexts?

HP: Doesn't Gods' omnipresence and all-pervasiveness allow Him to be innumerable?

TG: My question is how context becomes God? Is it verifiable?

HP: Gods' words are non- different from God. Regarding verification, whenever the context is also taken into consideration, you understand correctly or perfectly. If you ignore the context, your conclusion or understanding is garbage. Another reason why context is important is that many things are implied or understood.

"Come here" is generally understood as "You come here" "Come tomorrow" holds good only until the subsequent day (Tomorrow). "Kill the enemies" holds good only as long as we are in a state of war. Neither enemy exists nor does the command to kill hold good once the war ends. Absolute belief in His words /scriptures, Saints/Prophets are good, provided you understand the context then prevalent and the spirit behind. Otherwise, you will be a fanatic and cannot assimilate into society. The Rituals, prescriptions, proscriptions, holy war/crusade, proselytism, etc. would result in the very opposite of what was originally envisaged by the prescribers.

Context is a variable which auto-updates and an intelligent person will be conscious of auto-updating concepts whilst viewing, understanding, interpreting, or doing things in perspective. Suppose, you open a word document, and use the "Insert date" option, the dynamic current date is displayed whenever you open the document. Likewise, in software, newer versions have the inbuilt feature of version compatibility which enables them to work with older versions of the software.

Just as these cannot be called incorrect, contextual reading and interpretation of original divine words don't constitute a material alteration of the Divine word.

In fact, reading it as it is without application of mind and ignoring the context and causing upheavals in the society constitutes non-adherence to God's word.

TG: Your imagination is running riot. Your contention may be realistic but does not have the authoritative backing of God. I am time doesn't mean I am context. Nor does it mean that take context into account while interpretation/understanding of scriptures. Substantiate your claim with a quote.

HP: Okay, you tell me the meaning or your comments on the phrase "I am time"

TG: The commentary/interpretation of the sloka 11.32 as told by our Guru is ....

Chorus by other members of the DR group interrupted TG's flow of words. The professor inquired as to what was the matter. The group admonished TG and told that since he represented the group whose beliefs and philosophies are varied and different, it is unfair to put forth the version subscribed by him by shelving other viewpoints.

Prof: TG, your friends do have a point.

TG: Sir, HP gets an opportunity to present her version, I don't get the same. HP has an unfair advantage.

Prof: The objections are by your own group members. Besides, the viewpoint held by you and the differing ones held by other members of the group has already been put forth and debated an innumerable number of times by great scholars/seers for many centuries until now in a better fashion and more authoritative manner than any of you, or rather by any of us. Can anyone of you put across the viewpoints of your Acharya, better than the Acharyas themselves?

SILENCE

TG: It gives HP an unfair advantage, there should be level playing ground, Sir.

Prof: Either don't put the views at all or put brief consolidated views of each of the representatives of your group.

TG: Okay sir, I will consult my friends. Please give a break of 10 minutes.

The session had a break, where TG consulted her friends who were all of the opinions that the diverse views of each of their masters must be put forth. Otherwise, they would be unfaithful to their creed and their masters. TG collected the interpretation/commentary of a few group members who were conversant with the issue and returned and requested the debate to begin.

TG: Great seers and masters have interpreted/commented on the said sloka, the gist of which is

- I am the world-destroying Time grown in stature. Hear the purpose for which I have grown in stature: I am now engaged in annihilating the worlds......... Adwaita Sampradaya.

- Kala (Time) is the calculator that calculates (Kalayati). Calculating the end of the lives of all those under the leadership of Dhritarashtra's sons, I am causing their destruction.

  Fully manifesting Myself with this fierce form, I have begun to destroy the hosts of kings...... Sri Vaishnava sampradaya.

- Supreme Lord Krishna partially revealed His absolute and ultimate position in this verse and the next two in comparison to material existence beginning with the words *kalo'smi loka* declaring that He is the terrible and intrepid time the conqueror of all and is on the battlefield to destroy all these mighty warriors....... Rudra Sampradaya

The supreme lord states *kalo'smi loka-ksaya-krt pravrddho* meaning He is an all-powerful time destroyer of all the worlds. By Lord Krishna's desire, imbued with His power and might, time itself will destroy all these armies arrayed in battle even without Arjuna participating in the fight.......... Kumara sampradaya.

- The word *kalo* means time and includes containing and terminating as well as the embodiment of eternal wisdom and the perennial principles of the resplendent Supreme Lord Krishna. The word kalo has as its root the word *Kala* which is described as a container, a binder, an integrator, as wisdom and as a provider of all desires. The word *pravriddho* meaning great denotes completeness in its entirety since the beginning. *Pra* in *pravriddho* refers to the Supreme Lord and propitiation to Him is eulogizing His holy names. The word *api* is used to convey the message that except for Arjuna's brothers and a few others all the warriors of the Kauravas and the Pandavas will be annihilated by each other.

- The word *pratyanikesu* means the opposing armies on both sides and that is why it is spoken in the plural sense. Reference has been made to Bhagavata Purana, Moksha Dharma and Varaha Purana which describes the time aspect of GOD .... Brahma sampradaya

HP: They are the opinions of Acharyas, what about yours?

TG: Our opinion is the sum total of their opinions.

HP: You agree with other sampradayas?

TG: Caught in a catch 22 situation, whispers 'yes' much against her conviction (for the sole purposes of debate). Shouts Do you know more than them?

HP: How do you reconcile with their conflicting viewpoints?

LONG SILENCE.................. Thereafter

TG: How does your philosophy reconcile conflicting standpoints?

HP: In what I have proposed, there is no conflicting stand at all. So, there is no one-up-manship of my philosophy versus your philosophy. It is another way of viewing things. In God's order, any number of opposing viewpoints can be accommodated. Otherwise, there is no difference between our finite view and His infinite view. Next, you view each of the theories propounded in its proper perspective or correct context. There will not be any conflict.

TG: How is it that your viewpoint isn't reflected in any of the existing theories/commentaries propounded or put forth? How can your viewpoint be taken as authentic, without any precedent or prior mention anywhere?

HP: There has to be a first time always, as it was in case of existing commentaries. Next, my approach has been conceptual and object-oriented rather than focus on the syntactic or semantic approach adopted by all others. A 3600 view differs from a frontal view or side view which also differs from the Arial view.

HP: How are the views put forth by your parameters?

TG: You introduced parameters, not I, we don't believe in your parameters. We believe in wisdom handed over in succession via parampara and not mental concoctions.Can you show another reference in the Gita in support of your claim?

HP: Among the debaters, I am the right type of reasoning. BG: 10.32. Are you satisfied?

TG: That is your reasoning, Not God's reasoning. So, you are God?

Prof: TG, behave yourself.

HP: This is why God said He is Context and mandated people to follow Him and not view/do things independent of the context. The story of emperor Muchukunda brings out the nature and properties of time. He was a brave and valorous king, who was invited to heavens to counter Asuras attacking denizens of heaven. After a long battle, He was offered a boon to which he replied that he wanted to return back to earth to his kingdom and family. The gods informed that the time scale in heaven and earth is different, many generations of Kings have ruled and left after Muchukunda, and that his kingdom too has changed.

The points of observation are
- o   The time scale varies in different planets.
- o   Time affects different persons differently.
- o   The life span too differs inter-se between planets.
- o   Time and space are closely inter-related.
- o   In earth itself, there are different time zones.

TG: I still feel that your logic that time is context and context is God a bit farfetched. Accepting your arguments is an insult to our rational and legal faculties.

Prof: Hari, can you elucidate or simplify your point to make it intelligible to your friends?

HP: Sir, any scripture, any theory or principle makes use of analogous logic. Even the presently widely accepted beliefs propounded by scientists or mathematicians or management experts are established with the help of analogous logic.

The commentaries of great seers on Gita which are accepted by my friends also have relied on analogous logic to drive home their point. God, Himself has used analogous logic to

- Drive home the point.
- Condense complete knowledge.
- Make patterns and identify them.
- Appropriate pattern for the appropriate occasion.

If we see the interpretations sourced by my friend, TG, it can be seen that I have only highlighted the different interpretations of different Acharyas.

Each Acharya has taken the words to mean different things in a different context, all of which are valid with the clinching evidence being it is observable reality and truth can be experienced. My supposition hasn't left out any meaning propounded by any Acharya, and hence more inclusive, more correct with the backing of five Acharyas herein quoted backed by God's own words. Still, my learned friends and her shouting brigade has problems with my version.

TG: God could have used the words, "I am context" Why did He use "Time"

HP: God is a supremely independent person who can use His choice of words without having to consult TG. Another reason being, the use of the word 'Context' would preclude all other meanings of the word Time. In English alone, Time has more than fifty synonyms and by using that word, God seeks to convey the variegated multiplicity of His nature and time.

TG: What of space? How is it related to Gita?

Space has been defined differently as:
  i. A continuous area or expanse which is free or unoccupied.
  ii. The dimensions of height, depth, and width within which all things exist and move.
  iii. The physical universe beyond the earth's atmosphere.
  iv. A mathematical concept generally regarded as a set of points having some specified structure.
  v. Position (two or more items) at a distance from one another.

There are at least two quotes/references to space in the Gita. Gita quotes on space.

- The space between heaven and earth and all directions are pervaded by you alone. BG: 11.20

    o When both time zones and time scales are different in different planets/universes, God is present in all time scales and zones and was visible to Arjuna transcending time and space.

    o The effects of time and space like changing, aging, death, etc. didn't have an effect on the Lord, who is Himself the Lord and Master of space and time. Arjuna was fortunate enough to see that unchanging, non-aging form of God.

- As the mighty wind always rests in space, so do all beings rest in me. BG: 9.6.

    o This clearly shows that the abode of all beings' rests in God in different time zones and time scales and in different spaces, which is beyond both space and time.

The said quotes support all the above definitions of space, meaning, science meets spirituality. Similar to time, space is also taken as a parameter. Both time and space are components of context and are always together.

Prof: Can you explain with examples?

HP: In the earlier quoted story of Muchukunda, If he hadn't left earth for heavens, he would be subjected to the laws of earth and would have aged and died in a normal course like his family members and his subjects/ citizens.

The components of time and space produce effects that should be taken into account whilst studying/concluding about anything. If we ignore them, the conclusions arrived would be off tangent and irrelevant.

The after-effects of ignoring it would give rise to orthodoxy, bigotry, fundamentalism, and radicalism. A true incident would bring home the point.

Onoda Hirō was an Imperial Japanese Army intelligence officer who fought in World War II and was a Japanese officer who didn't surrender.

He was unaware of the end of the war and spent 29 years hiding in jungles out in the Philippines until his former commander traveled from Japan for formally relieving him from duty in 1974.

He held the rank of second lieutenant in the Imperial Japanese Army. Here, Hiro was 29 years behind time and around 3000 KM away from place (Space) Whilst his loyalty and faith is commendable, they were out of context and based on ignorance. Hiro was informed of Japanese surrender 29 years back, but the soldier streak in him wanted orders of surrender only from his commander.

People still have this Hiro syndrome and are caught in time warp 1400+ years ago and beyond extending to 2000+ years or even dating back to 3000 BC. They don't take into account the context, then prevalent. Practices modified based on context are labeled deviation, unfaithful, treason, blasphemy, and many such choice adjectives.

Prof: Your hypothesis is very interesting, especially, the one about analogous logic, but how do you separate chaff from grain?

HP: Pardon?

Prof: Nicely said, but if everyone starts meddling with Gods' words, how do you segregate Gods' words from subsequent human interpolations and extrapolations?

HP: Sir, the introduction of parameters is for deciding this very question. The introduction of the concept-based study and an object-oriented approach is to overcome this difficulty.

Prof: I get the drift now. It all adds up. There are still some bits of a jigsaw puzzle not fitting into the frame. I am sure you would clear it in the days to come.

HP: Yes Sir. I will make an attempt.

Prof: A personal question, are your anti-god/anti-religion or anti-establishment? How do you see views of other denominations?

HP: No. I have no grouse against any establishment. I respect the viewpoints of all previous great personages. I may or may not subscribe to part or whole of their philosophy, nor do I discount their say despite my disagreement. The original seers have communicated what they have experienced, aural or ocular reception comes at a price .... persistence, discipline and intense endeavors. Their words are not off the cuff remarks. With the passage of time, things change ....

Prof: I am relieved Hari, my gut feeling is confirmed, at times, I suspected your debate of being exhibitionist or attention-grabbing act.

TG: If you respect the viewpoints of Gurus, why do you oppose them? Why do you follow something not prescribed?

HP: I follow what God has said/prescribed, of course to the extent possible. How His words are to be understood too is the gift given by Him (BG: 10.10), to which everyone may or may not be privy to. I make it clear; I am not opposed to contrary viewpoints.

TG: This reminds me of a quote by Adlai Stevenson. "It is often easier to fight for your principles than to live up to them".

HP: So true, isn't it?

Laughter erupts. TG red-faced ask HP to continue.

HP: I have concluded unless you want to ask something.

Prof: We will stop for the day. Good evening.

Everyone dispersed. Hari and Christina wandered around the campus for some time and they sat down in the park. Christina had some questions. She wanted more examples and more simplicity in her explanation, after all, she argued, that she comes from a different culture. Priya answered that her point of view had more in common with Christina's culture and thinking than her own people who confined their infinite philosophy to orthodoxy.

She continued explaining....

Time is imperishable. It is all-pervasive. It is inseparable from anything and leaves its' signature.

She put forth an analogy to bring home the point. Any cyber transaction would create a log. It would have a time and date, owner and creator stamp. This would be used by cyber forensic auditors or cyber-security officers. The same concept holds good in reality. Every action, word, or thought would leave a trial. Any judgment should not be made in isolation but in conjunction with the place, time, circumstances then prevailing, etc. Our ancients were aware of the same. Hence, they incorporated all details of time, place, etc. in the ritualistic Sankalpa.

CH: What is Sankalpa?

HP: Sankalpa is a solemn resolve on oath prior to the fulfillment of the actual resolved act.

At the beginning of any ritual, one has to say Sankalpa - a formulaic utterance where you tell the gods where and when in the Universe the ritual is being conducted, the purpose of the ritual, etc.

This is accompanied by ritualistic cleansing of one's hands with water and sipping of water thrice in a prescribed manner and performing appropriate gestures whilst invoking the Almighty.

The Sankalpa, which we say is in all pujas /rituals at the start, consisting of four sections together to announce four important things.
- The time-cycle in which we are presently situated.
- The place where we are performing this ritual
- The day and time, we are doing it.
- What we will be doing in the course of this ritual.

See, both the time and place, purpose, the author is mentioned.

CH: You told that all our actions etc. are recorded like a cyber log?

HP: Yes. We have Chitragupta, god Yama's' assistant keeping track of everyone's deeds. We have a day of judgment in Christianity also. How can there be judgment if there is no record?

Coming back to our present world, Variations of time and space is also used as adjuncts. As we already know, Adjuncts adds to the meaning of a word, although the sentence could do without adjunct and still be correct. It is also called adverbial.

Here are some types of adjuncts with examples.

- Time Adjuncts (Adverbs of Time)
  - The alarm went off again yesterday.
- Manner Adjuncts (Adverbs of Manner)
  - Present your case carefully.
  - Therefore, you fight without attachment.
- Place Adjuncts (Adverbs of Place)
  - Here the situation is completely different.
- Frequency Adjuncts (Adverbs of Frequency)
  - She comes here often.
  - They repeatedly take birth and die.
- Reason Adjuncts (Adverbs of Reason)
  - As it is Friday, you can stay up for another hour.
  - As it is inevitable, don't grieve.
- Degree Adjuncts (Adverbs of Degree)
  - She is as smart as she is brilliant.

A word of caution. These are culled from English grammar, but the original words were all in Sanskrit and I am not sure that Sanskrit grammar supports adjuncts or not. Nevertheless, the concept is conveyed effectively.

CH: Can you give more examples so as to hard code it into my memory?

HP: You are my dear friend. I will never refuse you. Let me make a few statements first and then explain based on the statements.

- India is the eastern neighbor of Pakistan, a Western neighbor of Bangladesh, Southern neighbor of China and northern neighbor of SriLanka. This is from the perspective of residents of India. But residents of our neighboring make exactly the opposite claim.
  They are correct from their perspective. Viewed from space, also the spaceman's vision depends on the point of his location.
- It is daytime in your country now, but it is night here.
- The duration of day and night may be different at different locations say like at poles and in the mid equator. The duration of day and nights in this place itself varies depending on the season, solstice, etc. at the same place

271

- It may be simultaneously raining and not raining in the same place within a few yards difference.

CH Firstly let me acquaint myself with the geography of India. Googling her I-Pad and nodding her head appreciatively, I understood the concept of space as a parameter. Your example requires no further explanation. Each statement necessarily implies at a particular place and particular time. But the time concept as parameter didn't register fully in my mind as yet.

HP: Suppose the first statement is made prior to 1972 or prior to 1947 then?

CH: I didn't understand.

HP: Sorry, you are unaware of Indian history. Bangladesh didn't exist prior to 1972, nor did Pakistan exist before 1947. India itself was a British dominion without independent existence. So, the statements made make sense only thereafter, isn't it?

CH: Oh, I see.

HP: Now, when we have to check reality or verify facts in a different time than when the subjects' existence or nonexistence, we have to take into account that time in history and geography then prevalent. 'It should be realizable or verifiable' is also a parameter. How can you realize or experience, when the subject doesn't exist?

CH: So, time is also understood as a perspective?

HP: Yes, because they are taken into account while judging. Our judgment must be kept in abeyance until time proves the truth, instead of criticizing something as unscientific.

HP: Time and space define context and perspective which in turn decides plausibility and possibility or otherwise of the subject.

CH: I have one more query. See, in BG: 11.32 God says' I am mighty Time come to destroy the worlds. The warriors in the opposing army shall be killed even if you don't do so.

HP: Correct, what is your doubt?

CH: But Kritivarma, Ashwattama, Satyaki, and Kripacharya survived the war, isn't it?

HP: Very nice observation. This is an example of an instance where words should not be taken literally but symbolically. Literal interpretation should be made where exactitude is required.

CH: Yes, I can now better appreciate God's usage of word time in the infinite and universal context. Thank you. With that, they left for their places.

20. K -10   SACRIFICES IN THE GITA

The professor sat at his designated place and greeted all the students.

Prof: Shall we commence?

Yes, chorused the whole lot.

HP: Today, I present verse no 4.31 of BG as a parameter, along with all the slokas which refer to sacrifices.

For one who does not perform sacrifices, there is no joy in this world or in the world's after-life. BG: 4.31 says that the performance of sacrifice is imperative for joy herein and hereafter.

TG: It is said in the Gita, but do you believe it?

HP: Of course, I believe in it, unquestionably.

HP: TO the extent possible and is practical, I practice and follow the teachings of the Gita.

TG: You mean some of the teachings are not practical?

HP: I didn't say so nor imply as such. Whether possible or practical is with reference to my ability and commitment, not Gita. Besides the consequences of practice (Joy in this world and next) or non-practice and the quality of the same is borne by me and has no bearing on this debate.

TG: It has relevance. Traditionally, animal sacrifice is offered on Dasara. This sacrifice is performed by the Royal first family. You refused to attend the same when invited by Puja. Not only did you not attend but also condemned animal sacrifice. You accepted the invitation of Shweta to attend Sudarshana Homa being performed by them in the temple. Your selective attendance smacks of casteist bias.

Einstein states "Ego=1/Knowledge". "More the knowledge lesser the ego, lesser the knowledge more the ego." You have read some books about Gita and have developed an ego that you are master of the Gita and know more than all the great Gurus and saints. With this knowledge, you twist logic and defend your incorrect actions by quoting or rather misquoting the Gita.

HP: Common perceptions and practices need not reflect the truth. What God said about sacrifices is absolute truth.

God Himself has spoken about
- What is a sacrifice?
- Types of sacrifices.
- List of sacrifices.

- Hierarchy or gradation of sacrifices.
- Ingredients /components of Sacrifices.
- Why performs a sacrifice?

TG: Oh! God told you don't attend Dasara sacrifice. Haripriya, oh great devotee! Please attend Sudarshana Homa. I approve of the latter and disapprove of the former. Firstly, please tell me where God has condemned Animal sacrifice and approved of Sudarshana Homa.

HP: God has not mentioned or listed animal sacrifice in the Gita.

TG: Are you alluding that silence is condemnation? Silence can also be taken as acquiescence.

HP: All your questions will be automatically answered when I tell you about what God spoke.

TG: Didn't Lord himself encourage and assist Pandavas in performing horse sacrifice?

HP: I repeat, all your queries would be resolved if you allow me to speak. Besides, Precedence is given to Gods' words over His actions. I am listing the verses wherein Gita refers to Sacrifices.
1. All karma is completely dissolved for one who is detached, liberated, situated in knowledge and performs an action only in sacrifice. BG: 4.23
2. The sacrifice and the act of sacrifice, the ingredients of sacrifice, the performer of sacrifice, the recipient of sacrifice, are all absolute and the outcome thereof is (attains) absolute. BG: 4.24
3. Some offer sacrifice in the form of worship to demigods, while others perform sacrifice by offering the self (dedicating the self to Self) (GOD.) BG: 4.25
4. Others offer as sacrifice their senses of hearing etc., into the fires of self-discipline. Few offer sound and other objects of perception into the fires of the senses. BG: 4.26
5. Some Offer the functions of mind and senses and breathe as oblations into the fire of self-control. BG: 4.27
6. Some make material offerings in sacrifice, others practice austerities, whilst few, practice yoga as a sacrifice and still others observe austere vows. A few opt for sacrifice by way of studying scriptures. BG: 4.28
7. Some regulate their exhalation and some their inhalation and some control both as an act of sacrifice. A few regulate observe diet as a matter of sacrifice. BG:4.29
8. Many forms of sacrifice have been explained in the Vedas. They involve the action of mind, senses, and body. Thus, knowing the truth about them you will be liberated. BG: 4.32
9. Arjuna, sacrifice through Knowledge, is superior to sacrifice performed with material things.
10. All actions without exception culminate in Knowledge. BG: 4.33

11. When you have understood the truth (of knowledge), ignorance will not delude you. With this knowledge, you will see the entire creation first within your own Self, and then in Me. BG: 4.35.

12. Men with good disposition worship gods, those of passionate temperament worship demigods, and the demons, and those in the mode of ignorance worship the spirits of the dead and ghosts. BG: 17.4

13. That sacrifice which is performed as per scriptural injunctions without expectation of any return and performed with a sense of duty is in the mode of goodness or Sattvic.BG: 17.11

14. That sacrifice, which is performed for the sake of show or with an eye on the fruits thereof, is said to be in the mode of passion or Rajasic. BG: 17.12

15. That sacrifice, which is contrary to scriptural injunctions, in which no food is offered, and no fees are paid, is not accompanied by chanting of hymns, or is devoid of faith, is said in the mode of ignorance or Tamasic. BG 17.13

16. Om tat sat-have been used to indicate the Supreme Absolute Truth [Brahman]. They were uttered while chanting Vedic hymns and during sacrifices to satisfy the Supreme. BG:17.23

17. Acts of sacrifice, charity and austerity are always commenced with the recitation of Vedic chants and invocation of the Supreme by chanting OM. BG: 17.24

18. Sacrifices, austerities, and charities performed without faith in the Supreme are termed Asat and are useless both herein and hereinafter. BG: 17.28

19. Acts of sacrifice, charity, and penance are not to be given up but should be performed. Indeed, sacrifice, charity, and penance purify even the great souls. BG:18.5

20. Charity, sacrifice, and penances should be performed without any expectation of fruits thereof. They should be performed as a matter of duty. BG:18.6

21. That understanding by which one can discriminate between what ought to be done and what should not be done, what is to be feared and what is not to be feared, what is binding and what is liberating, that understanding is said to be in the mode of goodness. BG:18.30

22. That happiness which is derived from contact of the senses with their objects and which appears like nectar at first but poison at the end is said to be of the nature of passion. BG: 18.38.

23. Bhakti is bestowed on one who teaches secrets of the Gita to the devotees. He will reach me in the end. BG:18.68

24. The one who explains my teachings in the Gita, is a very dear servant of mine in this world and there is none dearer to me than him, nor will there ever be anyone dearer.BG:18.69

25. Whosoever studies this sacred dialogue of ours in the form of the Gita, by him too shall I be worshipped with Yajna of Knowledge. BG: 18.70

As you can see, all your queries are answered in the listed verses.
The sacrifices listed in the Gita are

- Worship of demigods/Gods as stated in   BG: 4.25.
- Worship of demigods/God present within the self, as stated in   BG: 4.25.
- Control of the sense of hearing by self-restraint as stated in   BG: 4.26.
- Control of the sense of speech by self-restraint as stated in   BG: 4.26.
- Control of all senses by restraining sense organs as stated in   BG: 4.26.
- Control of mind and senses as stated in   BG: 4.27.
- By way of material offerings as stated in   BG: 4.28.
- By way of austerities as stated in   BG: 4.28.
- By a study of scriptures or keeping difficult vows as stated in   BG: 4.28.
- By regulation of inhalation or exhalation or both as stated in   BG: 4.28.
- Those referred by Vedas involving mind, body, and senses in   BG: 4.32.
- By studying and teaching the Gita as stated in   BG:18.68 to 18.70

The types of sacrifices spoken by the Lord are:

- Sattvic, or the sacrifice in the mode of goodness.
- Rajasic or the sacrifice in the mode of passion.
- Tamasic or the sacrifice in the mode of ignorance.
- Transcendental or one without gunas.

Ingredients of Sacrifice as mentioned in the Gita.

- Action of mind, body, and senses.   BG: 4.32.
- Should commence with uttering the Syllable OM.   BG: 17.23
- Performed as a matter of duty without expectation of reward.   BG: 17.11.
- As per scriptural injunctions (not contrary to)   BG: 17.13.
- Should be complemented with offering of food,payment of fee BG: 17.13
- Should be full of faith.   BG: 17.13
- Aim is to please the Lord   BG: 17.23.
- Sacrifice without faith in Almighty is useless.   BG:17.28

Effects/after effects of sacrifice.

- All Karma is dissolved.   BG: 4.23
- Will attain liberation.   BG: 4.32
- Will purify even great souls   BG: 18.5
- Will attain equal or balanced vision.   BG: 4.35

Special effects/Special after-effects of Gita Yajna.

- Blessed with Bhakti/devotion and reach the Lord.   BG: 18.68
- Will endear yourself to God.   BG: 18.69
- Will be treated as Knowledge of Yajna.   BG: 18.70

TG: Why should Yajna be performed?

HP: By performing Yajna,

o   You will be bestowed with all the desired objects.   BG: 3.10

o   Desirable objects could be material or spiritual or both.

o   All actions (Yajna) culminate in knowledge.   BG: 4.33

o   Acts such as Yajna and charity purify great souls   BG: 18.15

o   Acts like Yajna and charity should not be given up   BG: 18.5

o   Giving up such acts tantamounts disregarding Gods' fiat.

TG: But you haven't told what sacrifice is.

HP: Yajna has been defined as a ritual sacrifice with a specific objective. It literally means "sacrifice, devotion, worship, offering", and refers in Hinduism to any ritual done in front of a sacred fire, often with mantras. This is the dictionary and Wiki definition of Yajna.

On the other hand, the dictionary defines sacrifice as an act of slaughtering an animal or person or surrendering a possession as an offering to a deity.

This definition of Sacrifice is widely accepted by skeptics and the western world. What God has said in Gita is more acceptable to us devotees. Hence, Sacrifice means
   o   Those that are listed in the Gita.
   o   Those that have an external reference in the Gita i.e., those referred in the Vedas etc.
   o   Those whose outcome is as per outcomes mentioned in the Gita.
   o   Those acts wherein the ingredients as mentioned in the Gita are present.

TG: But isn't fire an essential ingredient of any sacrifice? How can any sacrifice be complete without fire especially when you follow Vedic traditions? Hasn't God Himself said that "He is a true yogi, who performs an action but gives up fruits of action and not he who **lights no fire** and performs no work. BG: 6.1."?

HP: God has used the word fire in two different senses. In some places, He has used it in a figurative sense and in the verse quoted by you, He has used it in the literal sense. For example, God says" Some Yogis offer the functions of all the senses, as well as the breath as oblations into the fire of the controlled mind." There is no physical fire in the mind.

It means the sense organs are controlled as is the breathing function. In almost all the verses, God has used the word fire figuratively to imply sacrificing of the objects of functions of mind, senses and breathe.

TG: Then is the Navagraha Homa, Sudarshana Homa, etc. not sacrifice?

HP: Who said it is not a sacrifice?

TG: It is not mentioned in the Gita.

HP: TG, please recall our conversation a couple of minutes back. IT is not specifically mentioned in the Gita but stated generally as "Those that are referred in the scriptures or in the Vedas"

TG: How do you say Animal sacrifice is not good?

HP: In material terms, when you sacrifice something, you must be put to some suffering or pain which you willingly bear for the pleasure of Lord or for achieving greater good than the loss incurred. Here, the sacrificial animal, the Goat or the chicken, undergoes pain and loss of life. Is it the performer of sacrifice or the poor animal which is sacrificing?

TG: But the practice of animal sacrifices has been in vogue since time immemorial, even amongst Vedic followers. Mahabharata itself has many instances of animal sacrifice with the active participation of the Lord Himself.

HP: Three things are to be noted here.
- As already stated earlier, Gods' words have precedence over Gods' actions.
- Animal sacrifice is treated as a material sacrifice.
- It (Material sacrifice) is treated as the last in gradation or hierarchy of sacrifices.
- The very meaning of sacrifice is "without any expectation of fruits" whereas in all material sacrifices, including Animal sacrifices, has an expectation of fruits of sacrifice. For example, In Ashwamedha sacrifice, there is an expectation of fruit of Emperorship.

TG: Why is it ranked lowest in the hierarchy of sacrifices?

HP: Each sacrifice is an action. Each action produces results. These results may be good, bad, or mixed. The fruits of action are temporary. Hence, it is ranked lowest.

TG: Why are they temporary?

HP: Anything associated with Gunas is temporary. Be it sacrifice or fruits of sacrifice. Hasn't God Himself said that each of gunas is temporary as it suppresses others and remains dominant until another takes over?

TG: Then, what is permanent? All sacrifices are material in the sense materials are used. Nowhere is the world free from Gunas.

HP: Acts transcending the gunas, without expectations and for the pleasure of the Lord are permanent.

TG: Okay, you have said that Sense control is a sacrifice. How can it be permanent?

HP: I have not said so, God has said so, and I have quoted what My God has said. Breath control, sense control, etc., have to be done without any expectation of any fruits and for the pleasure of the Lord. If there is an expectation, it becomes guna tainted and the result becomes temporary.

TG: How is it experiential or practical? My friend Jyoti practices Pranayama. Her personality has changed drastically for the good. But it isn't permanent.

HP: One who practices yoga with faith but unable to complete his practice due to death, will again continue from that point forward. BG: 6.43. Doesn't it imply that the results are permanent? Now, a person performing say, Dhanvantri Yajna or Sudarshana Homa, will at best get relief from ill health, or will be blessed with wealth for which sake the Yajna was conducted. Likewise, other sacrifices would yield the results like good progeny, good spouse, acquisition of house or position of power and fame as per the Yajna performed.

Will these follow the person after death in his next birth? Regarding the observable reality you were inquiring, don't we see child prodigy endowed with exceptional skill in say sports or in studies? It is the result of past practice in earlier lives. Coming to the case of Jyoti, you have told me that there is a drastic change in personality. Isn't it permanent?

TG: What is the gradation/hierarchy of sacrifices?

HP: IT is nothing but the types of sacrifices graded according to the results that accrue. Tamasic sacrifice ranks lowest in the hierarchy but is better than not performing any sacrifice at all. This is followed by Rajasic sacrifice and the best of all is Sattvic sacrifice. But the super sacrifice overriding all these is the transcendental one.

TG: What is the basis of the gradation or hierarchy?

HP: Purpose of performance of sacrifice, Ingredients of sacrifice, nature of the performer, results thereof are the basis on which it is graded. If the purpose of a sacrifice is to bring harm to another, it is Tamasic and lowest in the order. If the purpose is for obtaining any benefit, say getting wealth or good progeny, it is Rajasic. If the purpose is that it is being performed as it is duty without any expectation, say for general welfare and peace of mankind or rainfall across the country, it is Sattvic. If a sacrifice is performed for the pleasure of the Lord and to please Him, it is transcendental.

If ingredients of sacrifice are material like say an animal, or Gold or wealth, the sacrifice is material. If the performer is in Sattvic mode and is divine, that sacrifice is Sattvic.

TG: We now live in the iron age of the Kaliyuga and the environment is entirely materially contaminated. Our sacrifices would necessarily be material. Is it not useful?

HP: You mean, can material sacrifices yield spiritual results?

TG: Yes, more precisely, does it yield only material results?

HP: God has said that there is a perishable and imperishable part. The act of sacrifice too has a perishable part and an imperishable part. So too, the results thereof. Meaning there are material remains and the spiritual remnants. The material remnants are taken as Prasad and eaten, applied as a Tilak on the forehead, or worn on the body as an adornment.

The spiritual part will be to your credit and takes effect when you have sufficient units to your credit. This accumulation of credit may span many lifetimes. IT is not only credits that are accumulated and spent but also debits. So, any act has a material component and a spiritual component and a material result and a spiritual result. The material part gives material gain and the spiritual part gives spiritual bliss. It is just like when a person dies, each of the elements in the body goes back and merges with that element present in the universe, and the soul either joins the super soul or acquires a new body.

TG: This concept of credit is your own creation and not backed by Gods' words.

HP: It isn't my creation. God has said in BG: 9.21, after exhaustion of credit of all stock of merit, (which enabled him to be transported him to heaven) the person will fall from heaven and start a fresh cycle of birth and death again.

TG: Could you give examples or cite precedents?

HP: Nahusha was not only transported to heaven but also made the king of demigods. His misdemeanors exhausted him of his credit of merits and was cursed to fall back to earth. Not only that, he was cursed to become a python. What a fall from King of gods in heaven to the animal eating python on the earth!

TG: I was asking examples and precedents of permanent and temporary components of sacrifices which you were speaking.

HP: Hiranyakashipu, the Demon King, performed penances. His sacrifice makes a good subject for a case study. The aim was to obtain immortality.

The object was to harm others (Devas). The sacrifice was controlling, regulating, and stoppage of breath. He stopped taking food and water, unmindful of the torture to his body.

His prayers were addressed to Lord Brahma.
- The purpose and object of sacrifice were Tamasic.
    - Penance and austerities performed by way of self-torture, or to destroy or injure others, are said to be in the mode of ignorance. BG: 17.19
- There is an expectation of the fruit of action.
    - Charity, sacrifice, and penances should be performed without any expectation of fruits thereof. They should be performed as a matter of duty. BG:18.6
- Demigod i.e., Brahma is approached.
    - Men with good disposition worship gods, those of passionate temperament worship demigods, and the demons, and those in the mode of ignorance worship the spirits of the dead and ghosts. BG:17.4
- Breath regulation is a valid form of Yajna approved by the Lord.
    - Some regulate their exhalation and some their inhalation and some control both as an act of sacrifice. A few regulate observe diet as a matter of sacrifice. BG:4.29
- Inflicting of torture on self and the resident God inside the body is wrongful.
    - Goaded by desire and attachment, they torment their body also I who dwell within them as the Supreme Soul. Know these senseless people to be of demoniacal resolves. BG: 17.6
- It was for self-aggrandizement and not for the pleasure of the Lord.
    - That sacrifice, which is performed for the sake of show or with an eye on the fruits thereof, is said to be in the mode of passion or Rajasic. BG: 17.12

It can be seen from verse 17.6 that when God doesn't like the torture of one's self, how then can He approve of animal sacrifice, wherein another creature is killed?

Another subject for a case study is Dhruv Maharaj.

His Aim was to incur his father's pleasure and become King. He too gradually abstained from the consumption of food and water. He performed Japa Yajna or the repetition of holy names. He too regulated breathing and slowly gave up breathing. His resolve to attain God was firm. The aim was an audience with God to attain the object.
- The object was to endear himself with his father and become King.
- Approached God directly.
- Performed Japa Yajna, which is approved by God.

- Regulation of breath valid form of Yajna.
- His resolve was firm and unwavering.
  o That firmness which is unshakeable, steadfast by virtue of yoga, controlling the mind, life, and the senses, is in the mode of goodness. BG: 18.33

Analysis of the sacrifices performed by them would clear all doubts and gives deep insights about sacrifices as created by the Lord.

TG: I have some observations.
- The fees and offerings of the food component of Yajna were missing. Hence, it is Tamasic as ordained by the Lord.
  o That sacrifice, in which no food is offered, and no fees are paid nor hymns chanted devoid of faith, is in the mode of ignorance or Tamasic. BG 17.13
- There is no fire so as to constitute a sacrifice. Lighting fire in Yajna Kunda is an essential ingredient.
  o He is the true Yogi, who is not attached to fruits of action, not the one who doesn't light the sacred fire and performs no work. BG: 6.1

HP: So, you mean both penances performed by both Dhruva Maharaj and Hiranyakashipu isn't a Yajna? Then how did the Lord appear before Dhruva Maharaj, or how Lord Brahma appeared before Hiranyakashipu?

TG: I am not telling so. I have just quoted Gods' words from the Gita. How then do you reconcile Gods' words with His own words in the self-same Gita and the actual happenings you quoted? You said analysis would clear the fog. Go ahead and analyze for the benefit of poor souls with a lesser intellect like us.

HP: A sacrifice as approved in the Vedas made with material ingredients requires fire. It also requires a performer called Hotri accompanied by assistants, a Yajmana or for whose benefit it is performed, Brahman who is the superintendent of the entire Homa. There could be numerous ingredients as per prescription. Now, in sacrifices like Pranayama and sense control or Japa as specified in the Gita do not require all these ingredients. There is no priest to pay or receive fees while doing Japa, nor is there anybody to offer or receive food. Of course, it is good to offer food and give charity subsequently. But this does not make it a non-sacrifice.

TG: What does this mean?

HP: Not all ingredients or components are essential in all sacrifices. They differ depending on the different types of sacrifice. Non-material sacrifices do not necessarily require material ingredients.

This can be seen in the Yajna performed by Hiranyakashipu and Dhruva Maharaj. On analyzing the sacrifice performed by Hiranyakashipu, we may notice that the Breath regulation/control form of Yajna is valid and recommended by the Lord Himself. The sacrifice is considered amongst Sattvic type, only if the aims and objects too are Sattvic. All other components were Rajasic or Tamasic. The prayer too was Rajasic as demigod was approached.

The divine laws of God being infallible, His sacrifice yielded desired results, well not exactly desired result, but something very close to the desired result, i.e., next to immortality.

TG: But he got liberation?

HP: That wasn't the result of sacrifice. His invincibility against all odds and most of the things was the fruits of his sacrifice. He went back to the abode of God after being killed by the Lord Himself. We may safely conclude that even if the ingredients of sacrifice are Sattvic but the aim of sacrifice is Tamasic, the results too would be Tamasic, i.e., of lesser quality or impermanent, meaning material. Conversely, if the aim/objective is Sattvic, even if the components are Tamasic, the result is Sattvic. Lord accepting Sabari's half-eaten fruits, or accepting the garland already worn by Andal are some of the examples.

Now, see Dhruva's Yajna. The object was material, but having approached the Lord Himself, he had an audience with the Almighty Himself, was overcome with dispassion to material life and sought the Lord Himself instead of pursuing his original desire of sitting on the throne.

This indicates that God has favored him with knowledge, discrimination and most of all, the devotion which is superior to liberation.

Prof: Nice examples. Any other example or case study to underscore your points?

HP: Thank you, sir, our discussion would be incomplete without touching the sacrifice of Bali Maharaj. Bali was the emperor of three planets. He attained this by his might, both personal and military. At the instance of his Guru, He performed a great sacrifice, for paying homage to the Lord and to perpetuate his reign and ward off threats to his sovereignty. During the sacrifice, a Brahmin dwarf approached the king seeking alms in charity.

The sacrifice stipulates that alms sought should be necessarily given. The Brahmin asked for a land equivalent to three steps as measured by His feet. The King scoffed at the Brahmin for asking for mere three steps of land and that too from an emperor. He further told that being a young boy, he wasn't aware of what is good for him and suggested that he ask for something substantial. The boy reiterated His request. As a gift, the deed is drawn and signed and registered in modern days. In ancient days, the gift was deemed complete after pouring water across the palms of the hand and expressing the intention of the donor to gift a specific thing to the donee. The gods presiding the elements like fire, directions, air were invoked as a witness. In keeping with the customs prevalent then, Bali Maharaj too declared his intention in the prescribed manner. Thereafter he asked the Brahmin to measure his choice of land.

The Brahmin who was none other than the Lord Vishnu, grew huge and covered the entire earth with one foot and the heavens with another foot and asked Bali for space for placing his Third foot.

Bali, who could understand that it was His object of worship, the Almighty Himself, folded his hands and asked God to place His foot on his head and thus fulfilled his promise.

- The Aim of the sacrifice was to retain emperorship, i.e. Rajasic.
- Ingredients employed therein were materials, meaning Rajasic.
- All ingredients/components, viz. fire, priest, chanting of Vedic hymns, payment of fees, charity, food distribution was present.
- Invoked the Lord Himself (Vishnu) as prescribed by Vedas and approved by Lord in the Gita.

The results obtained were
- Audience with the Lord coupled with blessings.
- Immortal fame.
- Acted as a benefactor to the Lord Himself. (A very rare privilege)
- Pleased Lord to such an extent that
  - God guards his new kingdom in the nether world.
  - The promise of reinstatement of emperorship in a future manavantara.
  - Assured ultimate liberation.

From this, we may infer that:
- Seeing God face to Face is the culmination of all endeavors.
- It is the ultimate achievement.
- Pleasing the Lord completes the undertaken sacrifice.
  - Bali's sacrifice was interrupted (and therefore incomplete in an orthodox sense) by the Lord and he was pushed into the netherworld. When the object of invocation is present and is pleased, where is the need for continuing/completing any other form of sacrifice?
- Pleasing the Lord is the ultimate the results have a spiritual trait and best amongst all sacrifices.

TG: How is the Yajna of pranayama and sense-control spiritual or non-material?

HP: It is listed as Yajna by God Himself.

TG: But God has mentioned other forms of Yajna also.

HP: No, Sorry, What I meant was Yajna activities are performed by the mind and senses which are permanent. As their results are permanent, which is a spiritual trait, The Yajna too is spiritual.

TG: How is it so?

HP: In Gita, 15.7, God says that all living beings are my eternal parts. They are struggling hard with their senses.

In the next verse, He says, the lord carries away these as the wind carries away the fragrance of the flower. The Lord doesn't say that the Lord carries away the body. He carries the six senses inclusive of the mind which is one of the types of senses.

The mind has a memory of all past impressions.

That is why any spiritual effort put in stands to our credit and we commence our endeavor in the next life from that point onwards. This means that we have the same mind and senses. We acquire only a new body, depending on our previous activities.

TG: New body? Old senses?

HP: Yes, New Sense Organs, but old senses. Something like a new hard disk or pen drive with old data.   Further,

- God has stated that the mind is very difficult to control   BG: 6.35.
- It can be controlled by constant practice   BG: 6.35 & 6.36
- Among the senses, I am the mind   BG: 10.22
- By exclusive devotion, you can see me as I am standing before you.
  BG: 11.54

- Implying that God puts Himself under the control of His devotees.
  - God acting as a charioteer to Arjuna in the battle.
  - Lord's weapon, Disc pursuing Durvasa for insulting Ambarisha a great devotee Shows why mind and sense related sacrifices are superior to material sacrifice.

TG: What sacrifice is to be performed by us? Please answer the same based on your experience and understanding.

HP: It is individual-based, meaning, the answer depends on whether the person is of Sattvic temperament or Rajasic temperament or Tamasic nature.

Further, I am a novice and not a Pandita or Vidwan, who has undergone the prescribed period of study under strict discipline. Nevertheless, In the light of the say of God in the Gita, and keeping the pragmatic aspect and the environment, Japa may be undertaken.

TG: You said "in the light of the Gita", wherein is it said so?

HP: God says, Among the Yajna, I am the Japa BG: 10.25.

TG: You mean mere chanting of Gods' names constitutes Yajna?

HP: Of course, God Himself has vouchsafed for it.

TG: Do you perform any sacrifice?

HP: Yes, I do Japa.

TG: And that constitutes sacrifice?

HP: Yes, but not in the way as understood by traditionalists, but as underscored in the Gita and as understood by me.

TG: Can you give any precedents or examples?

HP: Narada Muni is an example. He is always occupied in chantingGod's names. Lord Hanuman is another example who has proved God's name is more powerful than God Himself.

TG: Is Japa a Sattvic form of sacrifice?

HP: The act is not determinant of what type of sacrifice it is. It is the spirit behind which mostly determines what type of sacrifice it is. Yes, Japa is a Sattvic form of sacrifice if performed as detailed by God. Even if performed in Tamasic way, i.e., offensively, repeated chanting elevates you to higher planes and purifies both the chanter and her chanting.

TG: What name should be chanted?

HP: Any of the Gods' names can be chanted. Some say that only Maha-mantra must be chanted or the names of particular deities must be chanted.

God has not specified any such restriction. It depends on the individual's personal preferences and affinity towards a particular form.

TG: Can Japa be transcendental?

HP: OF course, if it fulfills all the necessary pre-qualifications.

TG: So Japa is both Sattvic and transcendental?

HP: Yes, depending on the fulfillment of conditions or otherwise.

TG: Which is the supreme form of Japa?

HP: God has said, Among the Japa, I am Gayatri. Even in Gayatri, the first Syllable, OM by itself is complete and transcendental.

TG: Reality check of Gayatri, please?

HP: The child hermit, Rishyashringa, cursed Maharaja Parikshit to die of snake bit in seven days. How did this child hermit acquire so much power?

It is said that Shringi acquired such powers by ascetically being steadfast in doing Gayatri Japa

God has listed three types of austerities, Austerities of body, speech, and mind. He walked His talk. He worshipped Brahmins, teachers and liberated souls.

- He was upright and content and wedded to non-violence as mentioned in BG 17.14
- His speech was pleasing, inoffensive, truthful, and beneficial. BG: 17.15
- Needless to add that His mind was always controlled. BG: 17.16
    o These are found in great souls and seers.

The best example of austerity of speech is the 701 verse Gita itself. Pithy, complete and beneficial and not any single extra or unwanted word.

All waited for some rejoinder or query from TG. When none was forthcoming, the Professor asked the participants if they had any questions. On confirmation that none of them had any queries, he wound up the session, with instructions to meet the next evening.

Christina and HP walked together. Christina invited HP to her room for sharing cookies. Once inside, they commenced discussion across the table sipping tea.

CH: You follow God's words literally?

HP: I believe in His words literally. About the following part, it depends on my capability, level of convenience.

CH: Yajna should be accompanied by payment of fees and charity. Food should be distributed, isn't it?

HP: Yes.

CH: But this is not possible in spiritual sacrifices, like controlling of mind and senses, etc.?

HP: Yes. Let me put it this way. Payment of fees can be done through the denomination of time also.

CH: How? You are confusing me.

HP: You visit professional, say a doctor, technocrat, etc. He charges you per hour. Isn't time a denomination? Again, God says He is time. Isn't that time dedicated and endearing to God valuable?

CH: I see.

HP: I will further clarify. Dhruva Maharaj did not offer fees or offer food or charity nor did he have priests whilst doing penance. God appeared before Him. Isn't the result culmination of acceptance of his sacrifice by God?

God could have bestowed him with kingdom without appearing before Dhruva Maharaj, pleading that the sacrifice did not have requisite ingredients. The end result has conclusively determined what sacrifice is.

HP: Offering to God constitutes a sacrifice. Offering to others complies with God's instructions. The amount contributed constitutes fees and charity. You are eating remnants of what is consumed by the Lord, thus incurring the highest form of blessings. Giving to God is a higher form, as you are routing the fees and charity through God. Only you must perform the act with that perception and faith.

CH: What is eating remnants of sacrifice?

HP: God has mentioned in BG 3.13 that only remnant of food offered in sacrifices is to be consumed. Offering food to God is also a sacrifice. If taken in a broader sense, it may be applied to anything other than food. That personality change in her friend referred by TG is the remnant of Pranayama, a form of approved sacrifice. The consequences thereof too is interesting.

Sage Narada Muni was the son of the maidservant in his previous birth. During the four months of the rainy season, when monks are prohibited from traveling, they stationed in the village where Narada muni was staying as a boy. His mother served them well. The boy was keenly hearing all the discourses. He was consuming the leftovers of the food partaken by the monks with their permission. This resulted in his attaining the exalted birth as a son of Lord Brahma himself in the next birth, without having to traverse 84 lakh species of wombs, unlike other lesser mortals. Imagine eating remnants of food partaken by God Himself.

I will tell you a story which would clinch the issue.
A disciple asked how our offerings are consumed by God when even after the bhog, the food remains as it is with no noticeable decrease in quantity.

The Guru just smiled, which bewildered the disciple and also raised doubts about the knowledge of Guru. The next day, the Guru gave the assignment to memorize a particular adhyaya of Veda. The student did so and repeated the entire adhyaya without any error and with correct intonation and diction.

The Guru asked if the student had memorized what was assigned. The disciple was surprised and told that he had just recited the entire Adhyaya. The Guru asked, then, why has the book/manuscript from which he had memorized still remained the same without any outward change? The disciple had learned his lesson. We may apply that analogy, as regards payment of fees, gifts, etc.

Christina, as per BG: 18.68, You have to explain this supreme secret to devotees to be eligible for guaranteed devotion to the Lord. It is further stated that in the end, he will come back to Me, meaning, after completion of your assignment of teaching the secrets to devotees, you will go back to Him. As per the next verse, you will endear yourself to the Lord, only after qualifying by completing the task of explaining the secret.

The next two verses declare your endeavor thus far as Knowledge sacrifice, meaning the sacrifice is still in progress because your study of the conversation of God is still not complete. Verse no 18.71 assures freedom from sinful reaction, which is the level you have crossed so far.

CH: How?

HP: You have read, listened and studied Gita with faith and without envy, isn't it?

CH: You mean, Study of Gita is itself a spiritual practice?

HP: Yes, but not confined to spiritual practice. Apart from being a spiritual practice, it constitutes a sacrifice. The highest form of sacrifice, because you would be endearing yourself to God, apart from other goodies like the fulfillment of desires, salvation, etc. thrown in together.

CH: Yes, thank you. You are very dear to me my friend.

HP: Likewise, here, my friend. You are repeating verbatim what God told Arjuna. This is another characteristic of a devotee. Always speaking about the Lord, His words and His pastimes. You now have to carry forward and disseminate this knowledge.

CH: Thanks, and Good Night.

21. K- 11 - FAITH AS PARAMETER

All were assembled in the hall. Ten minutes later, he motioned to TG and HP to begin the show.

HP:Today, I wish to introduce faith as a parameter. Faith has been given primacy and importance, next only to "God is supreme". The opposite of faith is doubt. Both faith and doubt find numerous mentions in the Gita. First, we will explore Faith and doubt in a mundane context and then correlate it to the faith as mentioned in the Gita.

- Faith has been defined variedly as
  - o Belief or complete trust or confidence in someone or something.
  - o Strong belief in the doctrines of a religion, based on spiritual conviction rather than proof.
  - o In the context of religion, faith is confidence or trust in a particular system of religious belief, within which faith may equate to confidence based on some perceived degree of justification/authority, in contrast to a definition of faith as being belief without evidence............. Wikipedia.
- Doubt has been defined as
  - o A feeling of uncertainty or lack of conviction.
  - o A feeling of not being certain about something, especially about how good or true it is.
  - o A mental state in which the mind remains suspended between two or more contradictory propositions, unable to assent to any of them. Doubt on an emotional level is indecision between belief and disbelief.......... Wikipedia.

It can be seen that doubt is the opposite of faith.

TG: The second and third definition of faith put forth by you appears realistic. It is just belief or conviction not supported by any evidence.

HP: Even if stated in the Gita?

TG: You haven't mentioned the Gita, besides it should be stated by our Guru, no less.

HP: I am yet to present what Gita says on faith and doubt. Self-experience outweighs evidence.

TG: Self-experience could be deceptive, our sense organs having a finite range of faculties. For example, the Sun appears like a big ball but in reality, its radius is 1.392 million KM and the diameter is 43.67 lakh KM. The vision of a cat is much superior to us human beings, but they cannot be considered superior to us. Self-experience cannot outweigh evidence. Hence, we take the word of Guru.

HP: Yes, let us accept the words of Guru and Guru of Guru, God.

TG: Okay, you win, tell me what is said by the Lord.

HP: Just before the battle, Arjuna was overcome with doubts was in a state between belief and disbelief. He reposed faith in Krishna and the rest is history. Some of the instances where faith is quoted in the Gita are

- Persons abiding by my teachings, with profound faith and free from cavil, are released from the bondage of karma. BG: 3.31
- Persons practicing control of mind and senses with faith, attain divine knowledge. They attain supreme peace.   BG 4.39
- The yogi, those whose mind is always absorbed in me, and who devoted to me with great faith, is considered to be the highest of all. BG 6.47
- Those fixing their minds on Me and engaging in constant devotion with steadfast faith are considered to be the best yogis. BG 12.2:

Effect of having faith coupled with following Gods' teachings, without a carping spirit, practice control of mind and senses.

- You are freed from bondage
- You get divine knowledge and supreme peace
- You will be considered the highest of all and the best of the Yogis.

TG: Faith by itself is not sufficient, but activities should necessarily be with faith, isn't it?

HP: Yes, of course.

TG: Faith in what?

HP: In this context, faith in God and His words. In general sense, it should be faith in one's own self and his ability.

TG: But each person has faith in different persons or things?

HP: God is okay with it. God stabilizes our faith in whatever object or subject it is placed upon.

- Whatever form a devotee seeks to worship with faith, I steady that faith of the devotee. BG 7.21
  - This is a very fluid and malleable parameter. Results are dependent on the subject and object wherein faith is reposed.
  - The form could be any form, that form is steadied, it could be formless, the belief in formless is strengthened. If it is faith, faith is steadied, if it is doubts or lack of faith, your doubt is strengthened.
  - This explanation finds favor with rationalists and psychologists as it is observable in real life.
- Endowed with faith, demigods are worshipped and objects of desire are obtained but in reality, these objects are conferred by Me alone. BG: 7.22
  - This answers your question, people have faith in different persons and things.

- o Those who worship demigods with faith are actually worshipping me but in an incorrect way. BG 9.23.
- o This endorses the fact that God is ONE and you are worshipping that ONE, whomsoever you may worship, in whatever form or name.

TG: Why do you give special importance to faith, over other things, which God has said?

HP: Difficult and hard to achieve things get easier and simpler with faith. That liberation for which people strive for many births can be had by just listening to Gita with FAITH.

- • Those listening to the dialog of God with Arjuna (Gita) with faith will be liberated from sins and reach regions where the pious dwell. BG 18.71
  - o Just like 'Money is what money does' a person is what his faith is. His personality is defined by his faith.
- • The faith of all beings conforms to the nature of their minds. Whatever the nature of their faith that verily he is. BG: 17.3
  - o Any act or sacrifice done without faith is useless. It may or may not yield results. The results may not be what was expected.
- • Acts of sacrifice or penance performed without faith, are termed as "Asat". They are useless in both this world and the next. BG 17.28:
  - o Yoga performed with faith yields imperishable results. Even if our practice remains incomplete due to intervening death, The spiritual credit accrued due to yogic pursuit remains intact, which entitles you to birth in a wealthy family or pious family, wherefrom your spiritual pursuit restarts, from the earlier point where death intervened.

- • The unsuccessful yogis are again reborn into a wealthy family or into a pious family. From they strive for liberation until they succeed. BG: 6.41 & 6.42

TG: You said that God strengthens your resolve in whatever be your faith or absence of faith. So, if a person professes Abrahamic faith, his faith in Abrahamic religion is strengthened. How can Gita, a Hindu scripture advocate Abrahamic religions?

HP: Here, faith does not mean religion professed, but belief professed. Still, it holds good. So, you see, most of the times, a person born in a particular religion has faith in it, and that faith is strengthened to the exclusion of other religions. Gita is not a Hindu scripture; it is a universal scripture. The word Hindu has never been mentioned in any scripture. Gita preaches truism, not a religion, or sects. It does not endorse religion etc. which are a human creation. Faith could be of three types.

TG: Just now, you said that faith doesn't mean religion, now you say that faith is of three kinds?

HP: Three types of faith have been spelled out in the Gita. Faith, as spelt out in the Gita, is innate. The characteristics of each faith, their preferences, their approach, and the method of conducting themselves are different.

- Man is born with innate faith, which can be of three kinds—Sattvic, Rajasic, or Tamasic. BG 17.2
- The object of worship, Food habits, motives, actions, purposes behind actions-sacrifices-charities all differ depending upon the type of faith of the person.

TG: A few days earlier, you had told that sattva, rajas, and tamas keeps changing with each competing with one another for supremacy. Now, you say that it is innate. You had earlier told that Divine/demoniac is an innate quality, but threefold gunas are changing. Your logic is inconsistent.

HP: The modes of nature is acquired, meaning credit outstanding due to past actions. If you recall our earlier discussion, you can see that I have mentioned a scale on which the three gunas slide.

By innate, it is meant that whatever guna or combination of gunas is predominant most of the time.

TG: It is action plus faith. Faith by itself cannot achieve anything in the absence of action, why then do you harp on faith?

HP: Look at it this way, would action without faith produce desired results? Suppose a terminally ill patient has lost his faculties but is kept alive by mechanical means, is he really alive? In War itself, Duryodhana did not have faith in his strength and ability, he feared Bhīma's strength. This is betrayed by his use of adjectives like those that mighty, powerful, skilled, courageous used in describing the Pandavas army. He further betrays his fear, when he says that his soldiers are ready to give up their life. That is the reason he asks Acharya Drona to protect Bhishma from all sides.

TG: Arjuna too didn't have faith, which is borne out by his words "We don't know who will win the war"

HP: For the sake of arguments, let us suppose Arjuna did not have faith in his abilities, but he had something more immensely valuable. He had faith in God, which subsumes all other faiths. Faith in the divine is superior to mundane or human faith. The outcome of the war is the best example of the results of the faith of Duryodhana and Arjuna. God has only made good His words" In whatever way they approach me, I answer their prayers in that way". God made good Duryodhana's words. He also bestowed His famous Narayani Sena upon Duryodhana whilst bestowing himself upon Arjuna as per his request.

TG: You had referred about doubts and its inter-relation with faith. Would you enlighten us?

HP: As already said, doubt is the opposite of faith. Both are inter-related.

- Developing attachment to God and surrender gives knowledge about God without any form of doubt lingering.
  o Listen how, with the mind attached exclusively to Me, and surrendering to me through the devotion, you can know me completely, free from doubt. BG 7.1:
- Persons entertaining doubts and lacking in faith are deprived of happiness both here and hereinafter. They have a downfall.
  o Persons without faith or knowledge, and of a doubting nature, suffer a downfall. For the doubting souls, there is no happiness in neither this world nor the next. BG 4.40:
- Doubts can be overcome with the application of knowledge which acts as a sword in cutting doubts.
  o Sever the doubts arisen with the sword of knowledge. Arise and Act. BG: 4.42
- No one other than God can dispel doubts completely.
  o Krishna, please dispel my doubt completely, for who other than you can do so? BG: 6.39
  o Underscores faith in God superior most and subsuming all other faiths.

TG: Guru can also dispel doubts. See, that statement is made by Arjuna, Krishna didn't say "Only I can dispel doubts completely".

HP: Where did I say they can't? But I cannot resist taking up the challenge.

Didn't Arjuna say, O Krishna, please dispel my doubt completely, for who other than you can do so? BG 6.39:

TG: Krishna was speaking in His capacity as Guru.

HP: How?

TG: Didn't Arjuna say "I am your disciple; I take refuge of thee" BG: 2.7

HP: Nice argument. Thanks. Does it matter if God spoke in His capacity as a Guru or in His capacity of God or His capacity of a friend? In whatever capacity He could have spoken, His words are weighty.

There was an interruption, TG was beckoned by Anushka, and a chit was passed. She opened it, read it and a smile formed on her lips.

TG: You don't take a stand. You are non-committal and seek a via media course instead of confronting.

You agree with whatever everyone says and still don't subscribe to any of our views. You lack the courage of conviction.

HP: I agree, because it is also part truth, not because of appeasement or fear or favor. God has endorsed Gurus many times. It is my agreement with God without any other considerations.

TG: Where has God endorsed Guru? Please give reference excepting the verse I put forth in my support during the earlier days of debate.

HP: You are asking me to prove your contention. Well, so be it, as we are not in disagreement over the crux of the matter, i.e., supremacy of God, but other minor matters.

Here are the verses

- Learn the Truth by approaching a spiritual master. Inquire from him with reverentially by rendering service unto him. That enlightened Saint can impart knowledge unto you because he has seen the Truth. BG 4.34:
- The saintly kings thus received this science of Yoga in a continuous tradition. But with the long passage of time, it was lost to the world BG 4.2:
- I am seated in the hearts of all living beings, and from Me come memory, knowledge, as well as forgetfulness. I alone am to be known by all the Vedas.BG 15.15:
- Out of compassion for them, I, dwelling in their hearts, destroy with the shining lamp of knowledge the darkness born of ignorance BG: 10.11
- Arjun, amongst priests I am Brihaspati, BG 10.24:
- Amongst the thinkers, I am Shukracharya the greatest of the thinkers. BG 10.37:

TG: You have given irrelevant quotes. The first quote is a repeat of what we had adduced on the first day of debate. Regarding the second quote, we cannot approach the saintly kings, we may approach the modern self-styled kings labeled ministers, but it will lead us nowhere.

The third quote is straightforward and advocates self-learning, which argument you yourself had put forth. The fourth quote of God seated in the heart of all beings has already been quoted by you in support of your claim against our claim in favor of the Gurus. It is stated that among priests, I am Brihaspati, and not that among teachers, I am Brihaspati. Similarly, too is your quote about Shukracharya. We have no access to Brihaspati or Shukracharya.

HP: None of the given quotes are irrelevant. You have a myopic view of looking at things. Also, you are guilty of reading verses in isolation and ignoring the larger picture. You are also not connecting the dots. The saintly kings have acquired knowledge via tradition. Extending the same analogy their successors/disciples may be approached. You yourself are following a parampara or a specific tradition, but are questioning just for belittling me. God has made the above point clear because that tradition has been lost, He is reviving the tradition by imparting knowledge to Arjuna. Regarding the third and fourth quote, God is seated in the hearts of all beings and is imparting knowledge.

The knowledge imparted and assimilated is in direct proportion to capacity and receptivity. Knowledge skill sets of different individuals are different. The one who is proficient in a particular branch may impart it to one who may be proficient in some other branch of knowledge.

There could be a mutual exchange of knowledge, each acting part of a teacher and student depending on who is receiving the knowledge and who imparting knowledge is. Don't forget that Brihaspati is the spiritual master of gods, though he is called priest because he belongs to priestly class and performs the duties of the priest for gods and Shukracharya is the preceptor of Asuras, although he is mentioned as a thinker.

TG: Please give me the address of Brihaspati, I want to study under him.

Prof: Sudipta, be warned no sarcasm, and no personal attacks in my court.

HP: Both of them are not names but designations. They change in each manavantara, but functions similarly. Just like the Principal or teacher could be anybody who teaches or heads the school. Qualify yourself to go to heaven so that you may study under the tutelage of Brihaspati in your next birth. Their wisdom has come down in tradition and the very same thing can be learnt from any traditional Gurukula.

TG: Your views keep changing. You take the position both for and against any proposition and debate with the same elan. This makes your motives suspect. I think it is fighting for success at all costs.

HP: You are superimposing my image on your views/beliefs. That is your creed, not that I find fault with it, we have to fight for success. My views are fixed, or rather stable. I am reconciling the same with facts and what is said by seers. As decided upon before the commencement of the debate, this is a truth-finding exercise without victors and vanquished.

The premises with which I commence is simple, great seers cannot be wrong, likewise what God has said cannot be wrong. So begins the exploration of the possibilities. Whereas you begin with the premise that we have to win at all costs and demolish the opponent. there are four types of debate, namely Samvada, Vaada, Jalpa, and Vitanda. Vitanda is the lowest rated type of argument or squabbling descending to the level of quarrel and trickery. The sole aim here is not only to inflict defeat on the opponent but also to demolish and humiliate the opponent. She relentlessly goes on refuting whatever the proponent says, with no thesis of her own. She may or not faith in the truth of his own argument.

TG: And yours is Samavada type as certified by yourself?

Prof: Are you both done with your fight? HP and TG, do you have anything new to present?

Both were embarrassed. They said that they had concluded their presentation for the day.

The professor reminded everyone to assemble the next day and left.

HP and Christina both met again in Hari's room. Christina asked Hari to summarize the day's proceedings. She also pointed out that the entire focus deviated from the main topic and was consumed in interpersonal wrangling. HP too acknowledged her mistake of falling for the bait and deviating from the main point. She opened her book and after glancing her notes began....

See the verses in Gita about faith. There could be more, I could notice this much.

- Those who perform their duties as prescribed by God and follow this teaching faithfully, without envy, become free from the bondage of fruitive actions. BG: 3.31
  - Faith plus action -→ freedom from bondage.
- A faithful person who pursues knowledge and who controls his senses is eligible for such knowledge, and having achieved it he quickly attains the supreme spiritual peace.BG 4.39
  - Faith plus the pursuit of knowledge → Knowledge plus peace

- Of all *yogis*, the one with great faith who always abides in Me, thinks of Me within himself and renders devotional service to God is the most intimately united with God stands highest in the hierarchy.BG: 6.47
  - Faith plus devotion to God, the Highest of a Yogi.
- Those who fix their minds on God are always engaged in worshiping Him with great faith are considered by Me to be most perfect. BG: 12.2
  - Faith plus absorption in God and God worship is considered perfect by Almighty Himself.
- I reside in everyone's heart as the Super soul. As soon as one desires to worship some god, I make his faith steady so that he can devote himself to that particular god. BG: 7.21
  - God reinforces the faith in a form or object as per the desires of the devotee.
    - Faith begets faith with Gods' push.
- Endowed with faith, he endeavors to worship a particular god and obtains fulfillment of his desires. But in actuality, these benefits are bestowed by God. BG: 7.22
  - Using that reinforced faith given by God, man worships and blessed with fulfillment of desire, which is fulfilled by GOD, even though it may be routed through god.

- A person's faith can be of three types depending on the mode of nature, in goodness, in passion or in ignorance. BG: 17.2
  - Three types of faith are identified.

- According to persons' modes of nature, he evolves a particular kind of faith. He is said to be of that particular faith according to the modes he has acquired. BG: 17.3
  - A man is what his faith is.
    - The predominance of a particular nature is his faith by which he is known.
      - This is irrespective of the dominance of other nature at other times.
        - For example, A predominantly lazy person is branded Tamasic even though he may be found active at times.
- Any sacrifice performed contrary to scriptural injunctions, without offerings of food, without chanting of Vedic hymns and payment of fees the priests, and without faith is considered to be in the mode of ignorance.BG: 17.13
  - Negative faith and faith in negative things yield negative results.
- The austerity, performed with faith without expecting material benefits but engaged only for the sake of the Supreme, is called austerity in the mode of goodness.BG 17.17
  - Faith coupled with acts for pleasing the Lord is Sattvic.
- And one who listens with faith and without carping spirit becomes free from sinful reactions and attains to the higher planets where the pious dwell.BG: 18.71
  - Faith plus listening to Gita without carping ensured of higher planets of the pious in the succeeding birth.
- If you observe the slokas you would notice that
  - The word 'Faith' has been used in different senses.
  - Faith by itself is not sufficient. It is always faith plus something. That something without the ingredient of faith is incomplete.
    - Thus, faith is the main qualifier for all slokas, thoughts, and actions.
  - Faith with devotion to God is the highest form of faith and so recognized by God Himself.
  - God has identified three types of faith
  - The prevalence of a nature dominating a person most of the time identifies the faith of the person.
    - This is notwithstanding the fact of the dominance of other nature at other times.

- ○ Lack of faith constitutes or is considered ignorance.
- ○ Mere listening to Gita with FAITH without carping yields the highest results.
  - Such is the potency of faith in the Gita.

Do you have anything else in mind asked HP? Christina replied in negative. They dispersed.

TG and gang were assembled in TG's room. TG was asked if she had faith in God and Gita. She replied in affirmative. Then they asked why she was opposing anything said by HP tooth and nail.

She asked them to venture a guess. Each of them came up with their own repartee.

- It is the job of the opposition to Oppose.
- TG cannot take defeat sportively.
- All is fair in love and war.
- While fighting for our faith, we have to use all resources at our command.

TG smiled and asked is this how well you have understood me? They asked her to clarify.

She replied.

- How will truth see the light of the day except when tested by the fire of opposition?
- I am assigned a role and I intend doing justice to that role.
- I am giving my best and practicing here for the ensuing courtroom real battles once I don the Barrister's coat.

Oh, you are playing the tragic antihero like Karna said SD. Everybody laughed. JS didn't understand the laughter and asked the symbolism behind Karna as the anti-hero.

KA replied that Karna was a truly great personality but was on the wrong side of Dharma due to past Karma.

He was aware of his true relationship with Pandavas. When Krishna met him and asked him to shift to the Pandavas side, he refused. It appears that he spurned the Kingdom offered to him as the eldest Pandava, and also acted in consonance of his loyalty to Duryodhana.

That apart, he was making amends for his adharma by promoting the cause of dharma. How asked JS?

- He was inflicting punishment on himself for one and
- He ensured that Kauravas do not get the throne, for if he defected to the other camp, He would have been crown designate as the eldest of the Pandavas. But due to repay the debt to Duryodhana and for his

- loyalty, he would have handed over the throne on a platter to Duryodhana thus perpetuating Adharma.

TG's gang viewed her in different light thereafter although they were all co-conspirators and part of all scheming. They ended the day on this note.

22. K- 12- BIG PICTURE - EQUITY EQUALITY

Christina was greeted by all the students on her birthday. She thanked everyone profusely. She invited everybody to the canteen. And so it happened that all were assembled in the canteen, and temporarily forgot about the debate. It was the chiming of the clock in the canteen that broke their reverie making them rush to the conference hall. The Professor was already seated. He was calm and wasn't fretting despite the delay. He got wind of the celebrations and was waiting for their return. He greeted Christina with a warm handshake and greeting coupled with blessings. He demanded his share of the cake. Christina had fortunately packed a cake for the Professor. He accepted the same. Next, He was all business and ordered for the commencement of the proceedings.

HP: Today, I present the Slokas, BG: 10.42.

- What is the need for all this detailed knowledge? Suffice it to know that with a fraction of myself I pervade and support this entire universe.BG: 10.42

TG: Why did God give a detailed description in BG: 10.20 to 10.40 and again summarize them in BG: 10.41 saying, 'Know that all beautiful, glorious, and mighty creations spring from but a spark of My splendor.' There wasn't need for detailed knowledge.

HP: God was satisfying the curiosity of Arjuna who expressed a desire for knowing details in BG: 10.18. God summarized the essence in one sloka in BG: 10.42 for the benefit of Arjuna and us.

This is the best example of generalization. If you take it as a generalization, it answers almost any query. Answers would/could imply

- There is no need for you to know or have that knowledge.
  - Because there could be abuse or misuse of knowledge.
    - For example, Ashwattama possessing knowledge of Brahmastra without the competence to withdraw it.
- Knowing this wouldn't serve any useful purpose.
  - Because it does not fit into your scheme of things.
    - For example, Abhimanyu not having knowledge of escaping from Chakravyuh, because he was destined to return to his original parents, the moon-god after 16 years on earth.
- You may not have the ability or competence to comprehend it.
  - This could be due to finite being incapable of holding the infinite.
    - For example, Arjuna not being able to view cosmic vision without Lords bestowing celestial eyes.
- You are not entitled/or eligible, it being confidential or you not possessing the requisite qualifications.
  - For example, Ekalavya was not eligible for earning the science of archery.

- o It is not in your interest to acquire that knowledge.
  - For example, Abichara Homa performed by Sudakshina, son of Kashi Raja, which produced abicharagni, which was directed to destroy Dwarka and its residents. It failed in its mission, due to Dwarka being protected by Krishna's Chakra. It boomeranged and burnt the town of Kashi and its residents. It is the nature of abicharagni that if it cannot hit the enemy, it will hit the very person who has employed it.
- o It is not in the interests of humanity that you possess that knowledge.
  - For example, nuclear technology in the hands of dictatorship countries.

TG: And also avoid answering anything inconvenient or uncomfortable or when ignorant.

HP: Okay, how do you interpret?

TG: Literally, as spoken by God.

HP: You mean literally?

TG: Yes, that would be better as it would be more in tune with God's words.

HP: Then it becomes applicable only to Arjuna.

TG: No, it is applicable to all.

HP: But God has mentioned 'Oh Arjuna', besides even accepting that it has universal applicability in the literal sense, how do you apply it in real-life situations to us? Thereafter how do you make the words meaningful?

TG: You tell me.

HP: I told you. I suggested taking it as a generalization. You wanted it to be specific. As this eliminates all of us from its purview, you then said that make it not Arjuna specific but universal, whilst retaining the literal understanding. You elaborate.

TG: God was telling Arjuna that it is not useful to him and hence no need to give further details.

HP: When it is not found useful to Arjuna, how will it be useful to us?

TG: It is not useful to us either.

HP: Then why is it present in the Gita if it is redundant?

TG: As I told you earlier, God's reply is restricted/applicable only to Arjuna.

HP: Then there is no need for any of us, or any of the mortals to study the Gita. Even this debate is infructuous.

TG: No, I meant it only for this verse.

HP: Going by your analogy, we should be ignoring more than ninety percent of the Gita on the grounds that it is not a generalization or that it is Arjuna specific.

TG: Gita is Arjuna specific, but we learn by Arjun's example. It is a case study of Arjuna.

HP: Pray, tell us why instructions meant for Brahmins, Vaisyas and Sudras are discussed if it is Arjuna specific?

SILENCE

HP: Why is Tamasic guna discussed when Arjuna was Rajasic or Sattvic by nature?

SILENCE

HP: Why the demoniac was discussed, when Arjuna was divine?

SILENCE

HP: Why were other forms of Yoga discussed, when Arjuna was a Karma yogi and Karma yoga yields the same results as that of other Yoga?

SILENCE

HP: Why was renunciation taught to Arjuna, a karma yogi?

TG: Okay, Okay, You Win. I lose. You needn't rub it in.

LAUGHTER

TG: You have mentioned six possible implications of the said sloka. Those aren't implied, if it were so, God would have spelled it out. You are ascribing meanings to Gods' words, other than what is said. Isn't it the commonly held belief that knowledge is power?

HP: Please justify your objections.

TG: Well, it is like this:
- If there is abuse or misuse of knowledge, it is the blemish of the person misusing or abusing knowledge, not knowledge itself per se. How can we know whether a person will misuse it in the future?
- Knowledge always serves a purpose. Otherwise, it isn't knowledge.
- Arjuna isn't incompetent or ineligible for knowledge as is being made out by you.
- A person doesn't seek knowledge if it is not in her interests.

HP: Precisely, hence to prevent misuse, amongst other things, God was telling so. This is reiterated by God in BG: 18.67, wherein Arjuna is asked not to share this knowledge with disbelievers and other undeserving persons. It is like giving a sword to a dacoit. It is not the fault of the sword but the fault of the wielder of the sword and the person providing the sword.

About the purposes served by knowledge, it could serve ulterior purposes like the sword wielder. Regarding your third objection, of course, Arjuna was the most competent person. Though he was not sufficiently capable, he was uplifted up to the mark and enabled to see the cosmic vision. The knowledge being sought by Arjuna was not directly related to his present purpose or assignment of an Archer on the battlefield to fight the enemies. God was reviving the knowledge lost due to the efflux of time. God was also suggesting that going after details rather than the essence, serves no useful purpose. It is as if you need to know how to drive a car, but it isn't necessary to know how to manufacture a car unless you are a manufacturer. God is implying that the same generalization espoused by HIM can be used when a person is deviating from the main purpose.

TG: It was told that all that is glorious is a spark of splendor.

HP: Yes, of course.

TG: Terrorists kill innocents and their followers find it great. They say we acted in the name of God and for the glorification of God.

HP: It is Tamasic. All the acts of understanding, sacrifice, acts, etc. fulfill the conditions ascribed to tamas in the Gita.

TG: You mean it is Tamasic glorious.

HP: It isn't glorious at all. Their acts didn't bring glory either to themselves or to God. Whereas when Arjuna applied measured violence, it brought glory to him and also brought glory to God. There is a flaw in the level of understanding itself rendering all subsequent acts sinful and disgraceful.

Prof: Do you have any counter-arguments or presentation on this subject?

TG: No, sir.

Prof: HP, how about you?

HP: No sir, I have concluded my say.

Prof: Glancing at his watch, there is still time, HP, you may introduce a new parameter, it would help us complete our debate quickly.

HP: Sir, I had prepared for only one topic.

TG: We should continue discussions today. The presentation of HP being her own creation and imagination, and the need to consult other commentaries or teachers don't arise.

HP: Resignedly, Okay.

Prof: That's the spirit. Go ahead.

HP: My next parameter is DO to others what you want to be done to yourself.

TG: HP is conducting moral science classes instead of debating on the Gita.

HP: I base my contention on the following verses of the Gita.
- The purified yogis, see the same super soul (God) all living beings. BG: 5.7
- The perfect yogi sees all living beings equally and responds to their joys and sorrows as if it were his own. BG: 6.32
- The yogis, see with equal eye, all living beings in God and God in all living beings. BG 6.29
- Those who see me everywhere and see all things in me, we are never lost to each other. BG 6.30
- The learned person sees with equal vision a Brahmin, a cow, an elephant, a dog, and a dog-eater. BG 5.18
- That knowledge is in the mode of goodness by which a person sees one undivided imperishable reality within all diverse living beings. BG: 18.20
- One who is equal to friends and enemies, who is equipoised in honor and dishonor, etc. is very dear to Me. BG: 12.18-19
  - The summary of these slokas is
    - They see all creatures as Gods, creation similar to themselves.
    - They see god and godliness in all creatures.
    - Their behavior is molded such that they do to others, only those acts which they feel good if done to them by others.
    - Such an attitude in a person is dear to God.

TG: That is a general truism.

HP: Yes, I am glad you agreed with me for a change.

TG: Isn't this a mundane matter? Why bring mundane matters into the spiritual debate?

HP: When God has uttered some words, it transcends the tag of mundaneness.

TG: How does it transform into spirituality?

HP: This behavior is used to
- Identify the correctness or otherwise of any action.
- Judge the correctness or otherwise of any theory, action, behavior, scripture or conclusions derived.
- Accept or reject the same based on such evaluation, and not decide by blind faith or belief.

TG: I agree with the action part of your statement but extending it to theory, scripture, etc. is beyond my comprehension.

HP: Action need not be individual action. It could be a collective action of a class or group of individuals.

The group's actions are prompted by theory, belief tenets, etc. of the group. This collective conscience is dead.

HP: Supposing there are three ideologies each propagating different approaches and .... Prof: Be specific.

HP: For sake of example, there is a democracy, dictatorship, and socialism. The rules governing them should be the same irrespective of who holds the reins. Similarly, in religion, the ground rules for evaluating religion or practice should be the same. There should be the same thumb rule for all.

If one religion prescribes a particular attire or outfit to be worn during prayers, and another religion prescribes another attire, either both of them are correct or both of them are wrong. IT cannot be said that "A" religion has the prerogative to prescribe dress code whilst in "B" religion it violates freedom of choice of wearing any dress. Similarly, anything which is correct for group "A" should be correct for group "B" and if it is restrictive or regressive, it is so for both the groups. If it is a matter of faith, it is so for both groups.

TG: But it is the prerogative of the group, why interfere?

HP: Now, who prescribed the dress code or included the restrictive practices? Surely, God had better things to do than intervening in day-to-day activities at an individual level.

TG: Where is it leading? You are digressing.

HP: No. Is providing an inducement to vote for a particular candidate or party, correct?

TG: No.

HP: Is employing coercion and threats for voting, correct?

TG: No, that is why there is a watchdog called election commission.

HP: On similar lines, inducement or coercion for conversion – is it correct?

TG: No, that is why there is a law against it.

HP: We are talking about correctness in the spiritual realm. Not legal correctness. When something is wrong at the basic mundane level, can it be correct at Gods' level?

TG: Of course not. Who said so?

HP: Then could the claim that "It has Gods' sanction" be tenable?

TG: No, it has a human misunderstanding or extrapolation. What are you driving at?

HP: To judge the correct interpretation of God's words, we should use this parameter.

TG: How?

HP: Does God discriminate between adherents and non-adherents? If yes, God is partial, a deficiency, which is an ungodly characteristic and hence not God. If no, then the interpretations being made by adherents are wrong.

TG: But God bestows special favors on devotees?

HP: Yes and No. Not at the cost of others. God has formulated rules, do's and don't's, which are not class-specific or individual specific. It is equally applicable to all. ***The rules form the law of cause and effect, which is divine.*** So, when a person finds fault at another's religious practices and calls it irrational or illogical, He should apply a similar yardstick about his own religious beliefs. The results or conclusion arrived at should be the same in both the cases, otherwise, his judgment/understanding is wrong. He is bypassing the All-Correct God and is subordinating Gods' Pure teachings to his impure understanding.

TG: They are conditioned into believing so.

HP: Such conditioning does not make their words that of Gods. Nor can they peddle human words as God's words.

TG: But it is going on, isn't it? How can you be confident that it is human words and not divine?

HP: That is due to ignorance of the proponent and gullibility of the flock. This parameter is meant to check the claims of people to determine if it is true or false. Regarding the latter part, let us see the effect of their actions.

It is consensual that God is one. They may be called by different names, with each thinking that she is correct to the exclusion of others.

But the characteristics of Supreme God is verily the same, like supreme, omnipotent, omnipotence, etc.......... It is also an agreed fact that Other than God; nobody possesses those qualities in full measure. So, all are propitiating the same person/power etc.

So, the persons are only advocating that their means of worship the performance of rituals, etc.are correct. The truth is that their means may be correct but it is not the only correct means. There could be other ways, as told by God Himself.

If there is only one way, it excludes the majority of the worshippers from the grace of God. If this were so, Then God would not be most merciful, impartial, equal, etc. The world is heterogeneous and not homogeneous. The methods of worshiping God too should necessarily be heterogeneous. That way, the superlative characteristics of God would not be brought to question.

But with the claims of single only way, the very foundation of infinite nature and Omni-ness of God becomes questionable. But is it so? The answer is no.

So, if we introspect, we cannot but conclude that these are human additions.

These could be due to overzealousness, innocence, vested interests, etc. which is beside the point. Individual misinterpretation or interpolation itself causes havoc, imagine what would happen if there is an institutional and collective interpolation.

Analyzing further, let us suppose that A persuades B to give up X religion/God and embraces Y religion/God.

TG: What are the effects of the same on A and B?

HP: There is no change or effect on B because he has changed only the mode of worship, rituals followed, etc. Not his belief and faith in God nor can he change his God. He is neither punished by his erstwhile God nor rewarded by his newly professed God (because God is one).

TG: What is its effect on A?

HP: She will reap the results of his action.

TG: What results will she reap?

HP: This depends on her action.

TG: Please elaborate.

HP: If any inducement is given,
   - It tantamounts to bribe, in the mundane sense. In a spiritual sense, that gift given with the expectation of something in return is Rajasic. The results of Rajasic action too would be Rajasic. The results too would not be long-lasting.
   - If there is any compulsion or force, it amounts to coercion in mundane sense and regarded as Tamasic in a spiritual sense. The results of Tamasic actions would necessarily be Tamasic.

TG: And if it is done only by convincing and persuasion without misuse?

HP: How does it affect God if rituals are changed? It doesn't affect God and there aren't any effects on the persuader or the person changing the rituals.

There could be some changes or effects if there is up-gradation in rituals from Tamasic to Rajasic or Rajasic to Sattvic or from Sattvic to transcendental. This change is not due to rituals per-se but the attitude with which rituals are performed.

TG: If an atheist is persuaded?

HP: Now, you are talking. This would endear her to God and help in attaining God.

TG: And if the persuasion is unholy?

HP: It works similarly is in case of coercion or inducement as stated earlier.

TG: But atheists cannot be persuaded.

HP: You yourself said that if they are persuaded, not me. They cannot be persuaded.

TG: Then, how can it endear the person who is attempting so to God?

HP: There are two kinds, the divine, and the demoniac. The divine may have fallen down due to karma or due to the bad association and forgotten his divine nature or earlier divine association. Their divinity could be rekindled by persuasion, which would endear you to God.

Prof: Glancing at the clock, it is getting late Does either of you has anything else to add?

HP & TG together No Sir.

Prof: Good evening. I will be seeing all of you tomorrow.

Everybody dispersed to their rooms.

HP and Christina walked to the terrace. Christina was ill at ease. HP could make out the discomfort and asked what was bothering her.

NK: You have attacked proselytization. I am a Hindu by belief but Christian by birth. I am confused about proselytization. My heart says that it is right but my head says it is wrong.

HP: Christina, I haven't singled out any religion nor have been judgmental about any practices. I am only telling that the same rule of thumb should apply whilst evaluating any religious practices inter-se religions. See, if inducements and coercion are bad in mundane civil affairs like election etc. how much more so in the realm of spirituality.

Besides, it is not Gods' commandment, but man-made, because it doesn't pass the test of equity as defined in the parameter.

NK: Shouldn't we broadcast the glories of God? Hasn't Krishna Himself said that His devotees derive pleasure by speaking to each other of His pastimes? BG: 10.9.

HP: Of course, we should enlighten each other of God's pastimes, but not coerce, nor induce. But that is beside the point. The crux of the issue is not inducement or coercion but something more serious and important, which is being missed by all.

NK: What is it that we have overlooked?

HP: It is already agreed that God is one. So, all are in agreement on that issue. Then what is it they are preaching? It is the practices, modes, and methods of worship. DO they really matter?

NK: What do you say?

HP: They matter only to us, not to God. It is accepted that the objects of action and intention are more important than the action itself. So, whether you hold a Christian symbol or a Hindu symbol or a Jew symbol, or they address God in different ways or call him by different names, how does it matter?

NK: Is it the important thing we all overlook?

HP: Let me put it this way. Supposing five of us believe in God, but profess different faiths. We pray/worship in different ways. Each of us would try to convince that only she is correct. What each is actually telling is that the rituals, methods, and mode of worship are followed by them is correct, to the exclusion of other modes of worship. It is already accepted that externals and mode of worship are incidental and doesn't interfere with the outcomes.

NK: I am unable to understand what you are hinting about. Please spell out the implication.

HP: The externals. Mode of worship and prayers etc. are incidental details not relevant to the main theme of God.

These are prescribed by great humans but not by God. Once it has a human touch, it is liable to change with the place, time people, etc. The followers have misplaced belief that the words of seers are the words of God and ascribe the same rigidity of un-changeability to their words as ascribed to Gods' words. You too have fallen victim, like once I was.

NK: Nice, but my doubt is only partly cleared.

HP: Let me sum it up for you.
- PreachGod's glories and words, not methods or form of worship.
  - Look with the same respect others who do so.
  - Methods and ways are not incorrect but come with limitations of human frailty and restrictions of time, place, nature of the audience, etc.
  - Methods are to be viewed always as a variable and in context.
  - Apply the parameter test and distinguish between god's words and other's words.
  - Give it its due but do not elevate it to the level of God's words.
  - Inducements and coercion is strict taboo.

NK: Oh my God! You mean that ....

HP: Yes, human words are being attributed to God and attempts made to enforce it. Subtle and not so subtle coercive and inducing methods are employed.

If you study the history of Christianity, you will see that the Protestants group broke away from the Catholic group, one of the main reasons being selling of remission of sins for money by the church, which the poor could ill afford. This phenomenon isn't confined to any one religion or sect but prevalent everywhere. As long as humans acquiesce to greed and selfishness, self-styled guardians of God or for that matter any institution make hay at the cost of adherents. They don't hesitate to substitute their words and palm it off as Gods'.

NK: You ....

HP: Yes, I can read you, Hinduism included.

NK: One more query?

HP: GO ahead.

NK: Regarding your take persuading atheists, Hasn't God told not to share this knowledge with non-believers?

HP: Yes, you can never change an atheist by persuasion, if she changes, it means they are devotees temporarily gone astray whom you are bringing back to fold. And, converting a person from one religion to another religion doesn't endear her to god nor the person converted gets any advantage.

This is because, as it is, they already believed in ONE SINGLE God who is omniscient, omnipresent and omnipotent, most merciful, etc. They continue to pray to the same entity, though called by a different name. Only the rituals may change. Changing rituals doesn't change the core results. In fact, there could be an adverse effect, if rituals performed are Rajasic or Tamasic.

The term Hinduism is in reality reference to Sanatana Dharma. Sanatana Dharma is the way of life. What a proselytist does is to change the way of life.

The core belief is not altered, even though this is disputed. This conversion need not necessarily mean from Hinduism to other religions but could be vice versa, or inter-see any religion. This truth was known to ancients. Hence, they concentrated on self-realization and God-realization rather than conversion. Hindus, Jews, Parsis, Jains, Sikhs do not convert, because they know that conversion is only about externals

So, the net result is that time is wasted, more divisions are created. In a lighter vein, lawyers, judges, and politicians are given more employment.

NK: Sorry Hari, I misread your intentions.

HP: It is okay. How does it matter if I am called Priya or Diya? Similarly, does it matter if you are called Georgina or Christina? Isn't Rose sweet by whatever name it is called?

HP: Christina, Shall I speak in my way or in Gods' manner?

NK: Put it in Gods' way.

HP: You are very dear to me ....

NK: And in your way?

HP: I love you, my friend.

With this, they left after promising to meet again the next day.

23. K- 13 — MIND AND ITS MACHINATIONS

Christina went up to the Professor's chair and called for everyone's attention. The professor had informed her to conduct the proceedings and that he would be late. This was not acceptable to many of the students. They preferred to wait, more so as the expected delay was marginal. Many went to the canteen to refresh themselves. Some were discussing the proceedings of the previous days. Haripriya too had garnered supporters over the past ten days, unlike her first day, where she had to confront a hostile atmosphere. But she herself wasn't aware of the inroads made by her. The professor arrived ten minutes later and sent the watchman to bring in the students from the canteen. Thereafter, He asked HP to start.

HP: Today, I present the Mind as a parameter supported by verse BG: 6.5, 6.6, and 6.36. Thereafter I propose to present Brooding on sense objects as a parameter supported by Verses BG: 2.63 and 2.64.
  - The mind is both a friend and an enemy as well. BG: 6.5
  - The mind is the friend of a person who controls it, and an enemy if he is controlled by it. BG: 6.6
  - Yoga is difficult to attain for one whose mind is uncontrolled. For those who have learned to control the mind, and who strive earnestly can attain perfection in Yoga.BG: 6.36

TG: What is Mind?

HP: According to Gita, it
  o It is one of the forms of material energy of God.
    ▪ Earth, water, fire, air, space, mind, intellect, and ego are the eight components of Gods' material energy.
      BG: 7.4
  o Is one of the fields of activities
    ▪ The field of activities is composed of the five great elements, the ego, the intellect, the unmanifest primordial matter, the eleven senses, and the five objects of the senses. BG: 13.6
  o It is a tool to kill the enemy called Lust/passion/desire. BG: 3.43
    ▪ Subdue the self, comprising of senses, mind, and intellect by the self (soul) and kill this enemy called lust.BG: 3.43
  o It is one of the residences of desire, other residences being sense and intellect.
    ▪ The senses, mind, and intellect are the dwellings of desire. Through them, it clouds knowledge and deludes a person.BG: 3.40
  o It is the best of sense organs.
    ▪ Amongst the senses, I am the mind.   BG:10.22
  o It is one of the performers of action other than body and speech.

- Whatever right or wrong action a man performs by body, mind, or speech is caused by these five factors. BG: 18.15
  o It is a sense organ through which sense objects are enjoyed.
    - Using the sense perceptions of the ears, eyes, skin, tongue, and nose, which are grouped around the mind, he enjoys the objects of the senses. BG: 15.9
  o It is a field of activity and interactions of elements, senses, sense-objects and its' results.
    - The field of activities is composed of the five elements, the ego, the intellect, the unmanifest primeval matter, the eleven senses, and the five objects of the senses. BG:13.6
    - Desire and detestation, happiness and sorrowfulness the body, consciousness —all these comprise the field and its modifications. BG: 13.7

In the mundane world, the mind is defined as
- The element of a person that enables him to perceive, think and to feel. It is the faculty of consciousness and thought.

TG: When is the mind an enemy and why

HP: The mind is an enemy of a person when it controls him instead of controlling it. BG: 6.6.

TG: Why?

HP: The mind (with thoughts) will lead us astray, when not controlled. This will cause us to be under an illusion. The illusion is the deluding energy (called Maya) of the lord. But when the mind is controlled, we will be seeing things truly, as it is.
- I am veiled by Maya, my deluding potency. BG: 7.25

TG: Suppose we prefer to be under an illusion, how does it affect us adversely?

HP: It is like this. You go to ruin. You lose your happiness and peace of mind.
- When memory is bewildered, intelligence is lost. Which leads to ruin.
  o Anger clouds judgment resulting in the bewilderment of the memory. Due to this intelligence is destroyed. These spells ruin. 2.63
- A person without control over the mind and senses has no peace. There cannot be happiness without peace.
  o A person who has not controlled the mind and senses, cannot have steady intellect nor does he have peace. How can one who lacks peace be happy? BG: 2.66

TG: You say the mind is a friend if you control it. In real life, let us say you have a friend and you attempt to control her. She will tolerate you twice or thrice and will prefer to break friendship with you. This exercising hegemony is not correct.

HP: Your mind is an intrinsic part of you. It is not external like other beings. Spiritual truisms should not be judged on a material scale. Assuming otherwise also, if you are a real friend, you will control your friends' activities which is detrimental to her interests. Her choice of continuation or non-continuation of friendship doesn't alter the fact that you are her friend.

Don't go by the classic dictionary meaning of friendship alone. Let us understand what a friend is or who is a friend and who is an enemy.

A friend is one who acts in your best interests and conversely an enemy is one who acts against your best interests. God, Himself acts in the best interests of His devotees even though it appears harsh or inimical.

 The classic example is that of Bali Maharaj, who was apparently deprived of all his wealth and kingship but got something more valuable than his wealth or emperorship in return. Other examples where Gods actions appear inimical but were friendly and with the purpose of correcting His devotees are

Giving Narada muni the face of a monkey, allowing the bridge of arrows built by Arjuna to be broken by Hanuman, Allowing the newborn babies of Brahmana to be stolen away by Yama, etc. There are many references to friends and friendship in the Gita and also anecdotes highlighting friends and friendship in Mahabharata and the Bhagavata.

Prof: HP, you are deviating from the stated subject, the mind. First, complete it and then introduce friendship too if you need to do so.

HP: Okay sir, sorry!

TG: How do you cultivate your friendship with the mind?

HP: You guide your mind to austerity. The mind will work for you. The austerity of the mind is explained by God in verse no BG: 17.16

- Serenity, gentleness, gravity, self-control, and purity of thoughts are the austerities of the mind. BG: 17.16
  - o You may also cultivate friendship with the mind by surrendering to the dictates of the mind. Then, it not only leads you astray but also will turn into an enemy.

TG: What is the prescription to overcome Maya?

HP: Apart from mind control, Worshipping God and surrendering unto Him is prescribed to overcome Maya.

- Maya, compromising of three modes of nature, is very difficult to overcome. But those who surrender unto Me overcome Maya. BG: 7.14.

TG: Suppose, a person only wants to control the mind and not surrender unto God?

HP: Theoretically, it may be possible, but it is very difficult to overcome Maya. By worshipping God, it is very easy to overcome Maya. BG: 7.14.

Besides, Arjuna himself says that it is easier to control the tumultuous wind rather than control the mind and senses which is very difficult. BG: 6.34. When Arjuna, a confidante of God himself finds it difficult to control the mind, can we ordinary folks succeed?

TG: But God Himself said that it is possible by dispassion and practice. BG: 6.35

HP: Yes, it is possible but difficult. Hence, God has given an easier option of surrendering unto Him. If you want to do it the hard way, please go ahead. I wish you all the success and best of luck.

The advantage of surrendering to God is that it is easier and we can always fall back on Him to deliver us.

There is a possibility of falling back/reverting back to unbridled ways when we are on our own. Just look back at ourselves.

TG: Suppose, we only surrender and do not practice control of the mind?

HP: Surrender unto Him is complete by itself and you have His guarantee of reaching Him just like a sovereign guarantee of the Government. Surrender is not only a means but also an end. There could be a delay, but the ultimate results are assured. God goes a step further and asks Arjuna, to proclaim boldly on oath, that "My devotees don't perish" BG: 9.31.

TG: Why should I control the mind? Isn't it sufficient that I control my senses?

HP: All the senses are grouped under the category of 'Mind"

- Using the five sense perceptions of the ears, eyes, skin, tongue, and nose, grouped under the mind, beings enjoy the objects of the senses. BG: 15.9

Controlling the senses is dictated by the mind

All activities are dictated by the mind. In the hierarchy of things, the mind is superior to senses. For controlling the senses, a collaboration of the mind is required. Presuming you control the senses; your mind could still wander over sense objects and lead you astray. Restraining sense organs but glossing over sense objects has been branded as hypocritical by the Lord.

The senses are superior to the gross body, superior to the senses is the mind. Intellect is superior to the mind. Even beyond the intellect is the soul. BG: 3.42
- o This means that by controlling the mind, even the senses are controlled, but the reverse may not be true.
- Completely renouncing all desires arising from thoughts of the world, one should restrain the senses from all sides with the mind.BG: 6.24 .... hence mind superior to senses
- Give up all desires of senses which torment the mind. Become self-realized. BG: 2.55
  - o Here, it can be seen that it is the mind that is tormented by senses, Senses are not tormented by the mind.
- Those who restrain the external organs of action, while continuing to dwell on sense objects in the mind, certainly delude themselves and are to be called hypocrites. BG: 3.6

Functions of breath, mind, and senses are inter-related and work in tandem with one another. This is not stated explicitly but is implied.
- Some of them offer as sacrifice their faculty of hearing and senses in the fire of the restrained mind and others offer objects of senses such as sound as a sacrifice. BG: 4.26
- Some, control the functions of mind, breath, and senses and offer the same as oblations in the fire of the controlled mind.BG: 4.27
- Some sacrifice their material possessions, or undertake yoga or undertake Vedic studies as a sacrificial offering.BG: 4.28
- Other forms of sacrifices practiced are Pranayama and frugal and controlled food habits.BG: 4.29

TG: But isn't it said that the strong senses forcibly carry away the mind even of a person practicing self-control. BG: 2.60. How then can you say that the Mind is superior to the senses?

HP: If you allow the weaker senses to control the stronger mind without asserting the mind which is stronger, it may happen. What is being conveyed herein is that the senses cannot go astray unless acquiesced by the mind.

TG: How does the mind act as an enemy? What are the inimical activities of the mind?

HP: The following feelings are generated by Mind as can be seen from the Gita.
- o Confusion can be seen through Arjunas' affliction. BG: 1.30
- o Torment can be overcome by giving up desire. BG: 2.55
- o Bewilderment as caused by others' words or actions as advised by the Lord. BG: 3.26
- o Elevation or degradation by control of mind or lack of it. BG: 6.5

But as can be observed in real life, anything that is felt, experienced, imagined, etc. is due to the functioning of the mind. NO mind means no cognitive faculty.

TG: Please substantiate the effects of non-control of the mind with real-life examples.

HP: Effects of non-control of the mind.
- o It creates obstacles for the person striving for self-realization. BG: 2.60
  - ▪ EG: Sage Vishwamitra, whose penance was broken by Menaka, the celestial nymph.
- o It becomes devoid of intellect and loses the stability of the mind. BG: 2.66
  - ▪ Kamsa was in grip of constant fear of death by Krishna after listening to the celestial prophecy. He lost his intelligence and constantly worked towards hastening his death. This is the result of giving free rein to the mind.
- o Focusing even on one sense is sufficient to lead the practitioner astray. BG: 2.67
  - ▪ EG: Ravana, who was a Vedic Pandita and very learned but was pulled down due to succumbing to one sense i.e., lust.
- o It kindles desire and clouds knowledge and deludes intellect.
  - ▪ Desire resides in the senses, mind, and intellect. Through them, it clouds one's knowledge and deludes him. BG: 3.40

Effects on persons with control over the mind.
- o See the same soul in all beings. Don't get entangled in fruitive actions. BG: 5.7
  - ▪ EG: Nara and Narayana rishis.
- o When coupled with detachment, such persons are purified. BG: 5.26 & 6.12
- o As an adjunct of purification of mind, they are endowed with the ability to perceive the soul and enjoy spiritual bliss. BG: 6.20
- o They are liberated both herein and hereinafter. BG: 5.26.
  - ▪ EG: King Janaka of Mithila.
- o They enjoy supreme peace and proceed to the abode of God. BG: 6.15

TG: Why is it important to control the mind?

HP: The importance lies in the fact that the results of control or non-control of mind are not restricted to this life. We suffer not only now but the afterlife also maybe for eons together.

This is because
- o Our thoughts at the time of death determine our next birth/destination.
  - ▪ A person remembering Me at the time of death attains to me. BG: 8.5
  - ▪ Whatever a person's thoughts at the time of death, he attains to it. BG: 8.6

- o Thoughts are generated and controlled by the mind. The stimuli could be internal or external.
  - o The best of the senses is the mind.
  - ▪ Of the senses, I am the mind. BG: 10.22
- o Fixing the mind on God results in deliverance from the transmigration cycle of birth and death.
  - ▪ For one who has fixed his mind upon Me, for him, I am the swift deliverer from the ocean of birth and death. BG: 12.7

TG: What is the purpose of subduing the mind and senses?

HP: The underlying purposes are
- Self-Purification.
  - o The yogis perform actions unattached, with their body, senses, mind, and intellect, solely for the purpose of self-purification.BG: 5.11
- Liberation.
  - o Those who have conquered anger and lust through constant effort, who have subdued their mind, and are self-realized and liberated both herein and hereafter. BG: 5.26
- TO perceive the invisible soul and experience inner bliss.
  - o When the mind is consciously stilled by exercising restraint the practitioner is able to behold the soul through the purified mind and experiences infinite bliss. BG: 6.20
- Liberation, mental peace, developing dispassion and freedom from sin.
  - o One whose mind is fixed on Me attains the highest happiness. By unifying with Me, he is liberated, his mind is peaceful, and his passions are subdued and are freed from sin. BG: 6.27
  - o A person conquering the mind has already attained tranquility and reached God. Such a person is not affected by dualities like man happiness and distress, heat and cold, honor and dishonor. BG: 6.7

TG: Explain the process of how to control the mind.

HP: Gita has prescribed many ways.
- Practicing meditation and curbing of desires in a secluded place
  - o They should reside in seclusion and engage in meditation with a controlled mind and body, getting rid of desires and possessions for enjoyment.BG: 6.10
- Purify the mind with single-point concentration.
  - o He should practice yoga by controlling the mind and the senses, purifying the heart and single-pointedly fixing the mind.BG: 6.12
- Practice celibacy and meditate having God as the supreme goal

- o Meditate on Me with unwavering mind, and practicing celibacy and having Me alone as the ultimate goal. BG: 6.14
- Renounce all material desires and restrain all the senses.
  - o Renounce all desires arising from thoughts of the world and restrain all the senses with the help of the mind   BG: 6.24

- Fix your mind on God alone in a gradual manner.
  - o Think of Me alone to the exclusion of everything else gradually with conviction and intellect. BG: 6.25
- Recall the wandering mind from other mundane objects and focus on God
  - o Whenever the restless and unsteady mind deviates from God, bring it back and continually focus it on God. BG: 6.26

TG: How do you know that you have mastered the mind and are successful?

HP: A person who is free from desires and situated in transcendence is said to have mastered the control of the mind.
- A person who by dint of disciplining his mind and is devoid of all material desires has attained to Yoga. BG: 6.18
- Just as a lamp in a windless place does not flicker, the mind of a practitioner of yoga remains unwavering in meditation. BG: 6.19

Amongst those that have conquered their minds, the best among them is one whose mind is fixed in God with faith and devotion.
- Those whose minds are fixed on Me always and engaged in my devotion with steadfast faith is considered the best of yogis. BG: 12.2
- Those whose minds are always absorbed in me, and engaged in faithful devotion to me is considered to be the best of them all. BG: 6.47

TG: In a race, everybody cannot come first or be a winner. IF persons controlling the mind waver or discontinue midway, all their exercise would be in futility. They could have engaged in other fruitful pursuits.

HP: Arjuna put forth a similar query before the Lord when God replied that the doer of good does not fail, nor does his effort go in vain. He would continue his spiritual pursuit, from that point where it was interrupted in the next birth, having been born in the family of the pious and wealthy. This means that unlike material pursuits that do not follow us after death, spiritual pursuits stand to our credit.

What is the fate of the unsuccessful yogi who gives up his practice midway due to an unsteady mind? BG: 6.37

- o God answers that unsuccessful practitioners are reborn into pious and wealthy families. Their wisdom is reawakened by a dint of practice in a previous life and strives for perfection more vigorously. They are drawn o towards God even involuntarily and rise above ritualistic activities and practice harder to attain perfection in that life itself. BG: 6.41 to 6.44

TG: We are part of God; then why do we struggle with the mind and senses?

HP: When did I say so?

TG: It is our experience. Also, it is said in Gita that "The souls in this material world are my eternal fragmental parts. Being bound by nature, they are struggling with the mind and senses BG: 15.7"?

HP: Oh! Thanks a lot. Yes. Let us see by way of an example. You are a part of a family. In a similar sense, you are part of God. If you don't conform to family norms and strictures, you suffer. Likewise, we struggle with our mind and senses due to non-adherence of the part (us) to the diktat of the whole.

Prof: I think you have sufficiently covered the subject. You may move on further if you need to add something new, summarize it in brief. Please don't elucidate the matters already covered.

HP: The mind is an important sense organ. Its utilization is a pre-requisite for the performance of any act, be it good or bad (BG: 18.15). No action can be performed without the mind. Mind being a two-edged weapon may be used for our benefit or destruction. Hence, exercising control over the mind becomes imperative.

I summarize my say but am unable to adhere to instruction not to repeat the same things. God, Himself has repeated some matters in response to different questions in different contexts. This becomes evident when you see the Sloka numbers in the summary.

- The mind is restless and difficult to control but is possible by practice and detachment BG: 6.33 to 6.35
- Attachment of mind to God removes doubts and helps you know God as He is. BG: 7.1
- Performing your duty thinking about God and mind surrendered unto Him ensures attainment to Him. BG: 8.7
- Constantly remembering God and thinking about Him reaches God. BG: 8.8
- Always thinking of God in devotion, dedicating mind and body God will take you to Him. BG: 9.34
- Fix your mind on God and surrender to Him exclusively you will live with Him.BG: 12.8
- Always thinking of God, offering obeisance and worship will lead you to God and endear you to Him. This is the pledge of God. BG: 18.65

- Those, who see God equally present in all beings and who do not degrade themselves by their mind reach the supreme destination. BG: 13.29
- Fearlessness, purity of mind, steadfastness in spiritual knowledge, charity, and control of the senses are found in persons of divine nature. BG: 16.1

TG: If God is repeating something, it means that it is redundant and this is a blemish (dosha), you said that Gita and God are blemishless.

HP: Sorry to rob you of your victory, repetition is a literary device employed by God.

Repetition is used in poetry or song to create rhythm and bring focus towards an idea, and Gita is song celestial. Repetition as a rhetorical device is also used in speeches to bring attention to an idea. But in the present case, there is limited repetition, only reference to mind has been made in different contexts several times.

Repetition is a rhetorical strategy for bringing emphasis, clarity, amplification, or emotional effect.

There are many types/forms of repetition, notably

- Repetition of letters, syllables, sounds
- Repetition of words
- Repetition of clauses and phrases
- Repetition of ideas

Each type of repetition has further classification or divisions which is not the subject matter here.

Prof: Good HP, you have summarized all repetitions with just quotes without elucidating repeatedly. You may proceed further.

HP: Uncontrolled mind leads to mental distress. This has physical manifestations as illness or other bodily symptoms.

TG: Where is it mentioned?

HP: It can be experienced. You yourself had a headache when you were ticked off in class, isn't it?

TG: Of course, but just because it is experiential doesn't authenticate it. Quote Gita reference.

HP In Gita, chapter one, Arjunas' physical maladies due to mental distress is described. Arjuna was overwhelmed with compassion BG: 1.27.

- Arjuna explains his physical maladies to Krishna. He mentions quivering of body and limbs, mouth dryness, trembling of body, hair standing,

- hands, and feet unsteady, and mind reeling and skin burning. BG: 1.29 to 1.31
  o This is experienced by everyone at some time or the other though it may have remained unrecognized. Most of the sickness or disease is mind related and has reached unmanageable proportions due to ignoring the basic symptoms and treating bodily afflictions.
  o God is addressing the problem at the quantum level. His solutions are curative and preventive and not symptomatic. God did not give herbs or potions for those physical manifestations, unlike us who try to treat the same with drugs, etc.

TG: What about your next parameter about brooding?

HP: Brooding on sense objects is mentioned in BG: 2.63 and 2.64. Attachment to sense objects Brooding on sense object results in attachment to it. This awakens the desire for the said object. From desire, anger arises.

This results in the clouding of judgment. This leads to the bewilderment of memory, thereby destroying intellect. Loss of intellect spells ruin.

- Contemplating on sense-objects develops an attachment to them. Attachment leads to desire, and from desire arises anger. Anger leads to clouding of judgment, which leads to the bewilderment of the memory. When the memory is bewildered, the intellect is destroyed which spells ruin.BG: 2.62 & 2.63

TG: I think because of attachment we contemplate and also desire leads to attachment and not vice versa.

HP: It appears so but isn't so as God Himself has told otherwise. Let us say that the boy from neighboring college has caught your fancy.

It would be just a passing infatuation unless you keep contemplating on him. By doing so, you become obsessed with him.

This obsession will lead to attachment and desire. No fireworks so far, but if your desire remains unfulfilled or unrequited, you get angry. Anger will shadow your intellect. You will behave against your best judgment. This is the reason for the foolhardy behavior of teenagers. A stimulus or a situation elicits different responses, depending on your attachment or neutrality. Mere contact with sense object does not trigger the chain reaction, but contemplation on the sense object or brooding thereof takes you to ruin. Contemplation can also be due to negative emotions like anger, hate or fear.

TG: Supposing my love is reciprocated and not unrequited as you say?

HP: Congratulations. You will have a happy marital life attended with all material trappings or a happy marital life with joint spiritual pursuits if both of you are so inclined.

TG: But it is most natural, to think of the matter we like, just like we think about unpleasant involuntarily.

HP: Because it is natural, God advises you to control the mind and senses. Don't contemplate on senses or sense objects.

TG: You have already discussed the mind etc. Then why this additional parameter?

HP: This sloka explains
- How we develop an attachment
- How attachment leads to discontentment
- How anger is born
- How memory is bewildered
- How intellect is destroyed
- And how all these lead us to ruin.

BY knowing this cause-effect cycle, we can avoid discontentment, anger, and other negative emotions which have a cascading effect on our life.

TG: But how to overcome this natural phenomenon?

HP: Don't allow senses to come in contact with sense objects. Whenever you perceive drift towards sense objects, withdraw senses form their objects to the extent possible. In BG: 2.58, the example of a tortoise which withdraws itself into a shell when it sees danger is given and asks us to withdraw senses from sense objects in a similar manner.

At another level, as the mind cannot be still and always requiring fodder of contemplation, use this trait of the mind to contemplate on God. This will work in two ways. You will keep away all negative thoughts and the consequent results.

On the other front, instead of contemplating on sense objects, contemplate on God, you will develop an attachment to God. This attachment will lead to a desire for God. As the desire for God doesn't remain unrequited, you will not get angry, nor will your judgment be clouded. Your memory and intellect will remain intact and lead to God rather than ruin. This will, in turn, endear you to Him, awaken your memory of Him during death, and take you to Him.
- Whatever thought is in the mind at the time of death, one attains that state, being always absorbed in such contemplation. BG: 8.6
- Therefore, Arjuna, you should always think of Me and fight. You will doubtless attain Me. BG: 8.7
- He who meditates on ME his mind constantly engaged in remembering Me is sure to reach Me. BG: 8.8
- Always think of Me, become My devotee. Worship Me and pay homage unto Me. You will come to Me without fail. I promise you this because you are My very dear friend. BG: 18.65

- Engage your mind always in thinking of Me, offer me obeisance and worship. Being completely absorbed in Me, surely you will come to Me. BG: 9.34

HP waited for some query or response which wasn't forthcoming. She concluded her say for the day. The Professor thanked everybody and adjourned the debate for the next day.

Christina visited HP. Christina suggested that HP recapitulate the proceedings of the day. Christina briefly summed up the proceedings. Next, she asked HP to give an example for a better understanding.

HP: All emotions are creations of the mind. They could be positive or negative. When the mind is negative, it acts as an enemy with negative perceptions and when the mind is positive, it acts as a friend. It is the quality of mind to
   o Imagine what is not
   o Not accept what is
   o Endangers well-being both mundane and spiritual life of self and others, when uncontrolled.

Now, for the example you wanted.

Supposing you are offered a treat, it could have many connotations.
   o A Sattvic person-offering treat thinks his act as an act of charity or kindness to give pleasure or satisfy the hunger of a needy person.
   o A Rajasic person would be thinking about what she would be getting in return or how she can leverage this act to her advantage in the future.
   o A Tamasic person would think that the person giving treat is scared of her and placating her due to her power and position over her.

   - A transcendental person thinks she is fortunate that God has given an opportunity to feed Him through the guest.

Now, this thought process is clearly noticeable and understandable because each person would have been under the sway of each of the gunas and would have undergone experiencing the said emotions as either a guest or host.

The thought process of demoniac persons has been spelled out by the lord.

The demoniac person thinks that they have so much wealth now, and will gain more in the future. They gloat that so much is theirs and think of more such acquisitions. They perceive certain persons as the enemy and kill them and think of killing other remaining enemies. They think of themselves as the lord of all material world, and powerful not equaled by others. They perform a sacrifice for purposes of aggrandizement and are in the mode of ignorance. BG: 16.13 to BG: 16.15

Now, when outcomes do not match with their thought process, say as if they are unable to kill their enemies, or cannot acquire more wealth, they suffer depression. This depression is not caused by the non-acquisition of wealth or inability to kill the enemy, but by their thought process. If the mind were controlled, it would have been a friend and so much pain could have been avoided.

Again, to get over the thought process is essential. Brooding over the same set of thoughts binds you into the vicious thought cycle, with attendant features like desire, attachment, disappointment, etc.

About the example of imagining that which is not,

Arjuna says, 'How can I kill Bhishma, Drona, etc. who are worshipable? BG: 2.4

The Lord says, 'Kill, Drona, Bhishma, Karna, etc., your enemies. BG: 11.34

Arjuna's mind is laboring under the delusion that his enemies are worshipable and to be respected whereas, in reality, they are his enemies as being pointed out by the Lord. Arjuna's mind is working as an enemy in this case.

Christina was happy with the explanation. They planned for the proceedings of the next day. They bid goodnight and dispersed.

24. K-14 – RITUALS, PURPOSE & PRAGMATISM

The professor walked in along with HP, who was holding a bag. It contained Pocket-sized Gita with commentaries written by the professor himself. He requested HP to distribute it to each of them after the conclusion of the day's proceedings.

He greeted the students and asked them to commence the proceedings.

HP: Today, I propose to introduce two parameters:
- Knowledge or purpose of action (rituals) better than mere knowledge or action itself.
- Any proposition or theory should be practical, relevant appropriate and observable or should have been observed earlier.

Knowledge of purpose behind the action is better than the mere knowledge or mere action. I put forth the following verses in support of my claim

- Sacrifice performed in knowledge is superior to any reflexive or mechanical material actions. Because all actions culminate in knowledge. BG 4.33.
  - o Just performing some rituals because it is being done since time immemorial and handed over from generations is not an intelligent perception. The underlying circumstances for which the ritual was being performed may have changed or could have become irrelevant.
  - o It is like an organized protest, where all the protesters are unaware of the reason why they are raising slogans or protesting.
- Knowledge is better than autogenetic actions (ritualistic actions) better than knowledge is meditation. Better than meditation is the renunciation of the fruits of actions. BG 12.12.
  - o This is because rituals could have outlived their usefulness and may be in need of modifications.
  - o This need for changes or scrapping of rituals cannot be appreciated without knowledge of rituals. Knowledge of ritual includes, why, how and effects of performance and non-performance of rituals.
  - o Meditation is better than knowledge, because, you will overgrow the need for knowledge or rituals.
  - o How? By absorption in self, you obtain that bliss in self wherein the rituals or knowledge thereof becomes redundant.
  - o Renunciation of fruits is the best, because, for a renunciate, it doesn't matter either way.

- They feel drawn toward God involuntarily on the strength of their past spiritual practices. Such practitioners rise above the ritualistic principles of the scriptures. BG 6.44
- Rituals are not an end by itself. It is a means or a path. It matters little whether 'A' ritual is performed or 'B' ritual is performed or not at all performed.
- A yogi is superior to an ascetic, Jnani and also superior to the Karmi (ritualistic performer). Therefore, strive to be a yogi. BG 6.46:
  - Ritualistic Karmi ranks below Jnani, Ascetic and a Yogi. Why not aspire for the highest? Why aim lower?

TG: If knowing the why, how and what of actions is superior to mechanical actions. All actions lead to knowledge. Then why is action recommended, why not just knowledge, when the end result is knowledge?

HP: There are many reasons.
- Because no one can survive without actions.
- Knowledge doesn't yield results. It helps action.
- Actions yield results.it leads to knowledge.

TG: If meditation is better than knowledge, why not meditate or better still, just renounce?

HP: They are the steps in the evolutionary cycle. You just can't become a renouncer overnight.

It is the culmination of a journey from ritualistic action, knowledge, action in knowledge, meditation, and renunciation over a series of births spanning many birth-death cycles. This is borne out verse 6.44. Besides, there is something above rituals and Yogis are exempted from ritualistic practices. This implies that rituals are only a means and not the end. It also means that there are practices apart from rituals that qualify higher in the ranking than rituals yielding the same results.

TG: Yogi being the topmost in the hierarchy, why at all pursue actions or knowledge? Just be a yogi.

HP: I have answered you just now, which I repeat, it is an evolutionary cycle which we all have to pass to reach that stage.

TG: Suppose, I give an example of persons renouncing directly or going to yoga directly?

HP: Please enlighten me.

TG: The four mind-born sons of Brahma, namely Sanaka, Sanandana, Sanatana, and Sanat Kumara became yogis directly at the instance of Narada Muni.

HP: Nice, but as already told, persons feel drawn toward God involuntarily on the strength of their past spiritual practices and such personalities rise above the ritualistic principles of the scriptures. BG 6.44. The Kumara brothers were in that stage, where they were past all mundane designations.

TG: Can you tell us the story of a previous birth or life story of the Kumaras?

HP: I am sorry, I am not aware. I would be happy to know it from you. You please tell us.

TG: You are not aware, because they don't have a history of past births or the evolutionary cycles as you call them.

HP: All those born are sure to die and all those who die are sure to be born, unless, they are residents of Vaikuntha.

Besides, they don't figure in the list of identified and accepted, Chiranjivi (Immortals) as per Hindu folklore.

TG: Can you give examples?

HP: Of course, with pleasure.
- Rituals are okay but not mandatory. Shabari, a great devotee offered fruits she herself had tasted to ensure its sweetness. In a mundane sense, her offering was leftovers and a taboo and devoid of rituals and unacceptable. But God accepted the same. Vidura, in his excitement, offered God plantain skin throwing out the fruit. God ate without complaining. Both Shabari and Vidura didn't offer ritualistic bhog.
- Needless to add that God is exempt from rituals. When Bali completed the conveyance of three steps of land as measured by the Lord to him by way of ritualistic offering, The God just conferred on him the kingship of heavens in a future manavantara. God did not perform elaborate rituals whilst conferring kingdom to Dhruva Maharaj. Nor did He perform any rituals whilst showering His friend Sudama with untold wealth.
- You may also notice that rituals differ from sect to sect, religion to religion and person to person. What is acceptable to some as the highest of the performance may be looked down upon by people of other denominations. This isn't the case with Yogi or Jnani.
- God has unequivocally stated that it is the attitude that defines the action, not the actual act itself or the materials employed therein.

TG: Where is it stated?

HP: Something as inexpensive and ubiquitous like a leaf, a flower, a leaf, a fruit, or water is acceptable to the Lord.
- If one offers to Me with devotion a leaf, a flower, a fruit, or even water, I delightfully partake of that article offered with love by My devotee. BG 9.26
  - God has not prescribed elaborate and fancy rituals.

    o   Gods' acceptance of our offering is the pinnacle of achievement, stamp of approval, of authority.

    o   Here, the only prescriptions are loving devotion and faith.

    o   Rituals are man-made.

TG: Suppose, you are aware of the purpose behind the ritual, is it okay to perform the ritual?

HP: My point is not performing or non-performing of rituals. That is secondary, God has only said that we should not blindly perform rituals, but know the purpose behind. Non-performance of ritual doesn't cause significant loss. Suppose, the rituals are prescribed with a caveat those not performing it would go to hell, then we as rational beings should question and satisfy ourselves if it is true and observable. If it were true, then non-performers would be going to hell. Not all other religionists would be performing the ritual as it is alien to their religion, so half the earth's populace would be going to hell. The other half too would be performing rituals of their religion and ignoring rituals of other religions. So it stands to logic that the entire populace goes to hell. This doesn't stand to reason. Not all can perform all rituals. Nor can we say that only rituals of a particular religion are true and others are concocted. The point is that the ritual has a limited purpose. But people overemphasize it as overall. God has also described who performs rituals.

TG: Where, please quote with reference.

HP: Those with material desires surrender to gods and worship them practicing rituals prescribed to propitiate them. BG: 7.20. Here two things stand out. People with material desires approach gods, and they follow rituals prescribed to propitiate gods.

God doesn't want elaborate rituals. A leaf, fruit, water flower with faith and love is sufficient. BG: 9.26. Faith and devotion are the prescriptions and not rituals as in the case of gods. Other celestial beings (gods) require to be propitiated with rituals, in a prescribed manner for material benedictions.

TG: Proceed to the next parameter.

HP: Anything must pass the test of practicality and reality. I will quote Acharya Vinoba Bhave

    •   "In Bhagavad Gita, there is no long discussion, nothing elaborates. The main reason for this is that everything stated in the Gita is meant to be tested in the life of every person. It is intended to be verified in practice."

        o   Meaning, it should not be just theory, it should be practical and being practicable, it would become observable. Any proposition or theory should be practical, relevant, useful, appropriate, and observable or should have been observed earlier.

- o If it weren't so, it is just plain fiction and serves nothing except having entertainment value.
- o Another dangerous outcome or possibility is that they may take everything literally as gospel truth, even those things which defy rationality and common sense and are not testable. Any attempt to examine the tenets etc. would be opposed and cause societal unrest inter-se various differing groups.
- o It is for this reason that prior to the debate, it was agreed that to accept anything as proved, it should not only be stated in Gita but also be practicable and observable. What Acharya Bhave has told is observable. Actual Gita compromises just 700 verses. The commentaries offered runs into volumes. Commentaries explain both the theory and practical part.

TG: Correct from a scientific point of view. Put forth Gita's view.

HP: This parameter is derived from Sloka 9.2

This knowledge is the king of sciences and the most secret. It purifies those who hear it. It is directly realizable, in accordance with dharma, easy to practice, and everlasting in effect. BG: 9.2.

- ▪ It purifies those who hear it ……. Thus useful.
- ▪ It is directly realizable ………. meaning it is observable and also relevant.
- ▪ It is easy to practice ………. Meaning, it is practicable.
- ▪ Everlasting in effect …. Meaning, the results are enduring.

TG: What knowledge is being referred to here?

HP: The science of overcoming miseries of material existence. The cycle of creation, sustenance, and destruction undertaken by the Lord as His pastime. It (BG: 9.2) may be said to be applicable in respect of all slokas or may be successfully applied to the whole of Gita.

TG: Please substantiate how the quoted science and Universal cycle of creation is practical, relevant useful appropriate, etc.

HP: I have stated it as a parameter. You may apply it practically and verify it.

TG: You do it in this instance. We will apply the same in the future as and when required.

HP: BG: 9.7 – 9.8 mentions the creation, sustenance, and dissolution of the universe.

At the end of one Kalpa, all living beings merge into My primordial material energy. At the beginning of the next creation, I manifest them again. Presiding over My material energy, I generate these myriad forms repeatedly, in accordance with the force of their natures.BG: 9.7 and 9.8

This is borne out by the ever-changing scenario. Scientists fix the age of the earth as 4.54 billion years. During this period, the landscape has changed. Geologists are still baffled by the fossils they come across which reveal earlier existence of ocean in deserts and fossils of aquatic animals.So, it is an observed phenomenon. This is substantiated by sloka 9.10

Working under the Lord's direction, this material energy brings into being all animate and inanimate forms, due to which the material world undergoes the changes. BG: 9.10

TG: But how is it practical or useful?

HP: Please put this question to Charles Darwin or Georges Lemaitre, who put forth the theories of evolution and the theory of big bang.

LAUGHTER

TG: Don't browbeat me if you can't answer.

HP: The contents of Gita could be anything such as:
- Statement of facts.
- Suppositions
- Analysis
- Reference to facts.
- Positive injunctions.
- Negative injunctions.
- Replies to queries
- Benedictions
- Generalizations which could be:
  - Literal
  - Symbolic
  - Analogous.
  - Stated
  - Implied.

Each of them serves different purposes and different persons at different times. Some need to be acted upon, some need to be understood, some need to be accepted and so on. The usefulness or otherwise of creation of universe etc. is of special interest to cosmologists or astrophysicists, and hence it appears as not useful to you. The usefulness per se, need not be material or tangible. It could satisfy curiosity, clarify a doubt, enrich you, provide an experience (Like cosmic vision witnessed by Arjuna), etc. A mere theory by Darwin or any other human is acceptable, but a fact stated by God is found skeptical.

HP thus concluded her presentation.

Prof: TG, do you have something to add.

TG: Nodding her head horizontally indicated her reply in negative.

With that, the session for the day concluded.

After an hour, HP visited Christina. She offered her cakes and veered the topic of discussion to the day's proceedings. She asked, why at all do people perform rituals? Do they serve any purpose? Who prescribed rituals, if it wasn't God? Is God against rituals? She further said that God Himself actively participated in rituals, thereby endorsing rituals. He should have put an end to the same or at least excused Himself from attending ritualistic ceremonies. HP was wonder stuck with the depth of knowledge of Christina about Krishna and His activities, like participating in Yajna, being with Pandavas during Shradh, etc. and her commitment. She was genuinely happy about the international overreach of Krishna.

HP: God did not prescribe most of the rituals. Even where prescribed it serves a limited purpose and aimed at a particular class of persons. People perform rituals as they are conditioned that way. Rituals have a shelf life and become redundant when original circumstances do not exist.

People still continue to perform rituals in the earlier existing form instead of modifying the same suitably so as to keep in tune with times. Rituals are prescribed by influencers or leaders of the community. They subserve specific needs and a specific audience for a finite period of time.

The original purpose of rituals may or may not be served but some ancillary benefits do accrue. Like
- Serves as a get-together and renewal of ties and bonds.
- Charity is always given, which may help the needy.
- It is a better form of engagement than engaging in destructive engagement.
- It serves as a public notification, like the crowning ceremony or Rajasuya Yajna.
- It could be celebratory or sharing of joy or sorrow depending on the occasion.

Each ritual has a specific purpose. Like, say, Ashwamedha Sacrifice and Rajasuya Yajna are held to declare over lording sovereignty over territories. Putra kameshti Yajna is for obtaining progeny, Mrutyunjay Yajna is for obtaining a long life. Just like the outcomes, the rituals too are different.

God is neither in favor nor against rituals. He is more interested in the motivation and purpose behind the ritual. God is most indifferent, Self-sufficient and independent, nor requiring our ritualistic ceremonies or the offerings accompanying it. He joins the party, as a benediction to the ritual performer. Supposing, I had rejected your pastries offered by you, would you have been pleased? It is like expressing friendship and acceptance of the same and not the cake itself which is offered.

God keeps in tune with times and participates in sacrifices and rituals which do not cause harm to others.

God has stated

- o This form of mine that you are seeing is exceedingly difficult to behold. Even gods are eager to see it. By the study neither of the Vedas, nor by penance, charity, or sacrifices, I can be seen as seen by Arjuna. BG: 11.53.
    - What is the use of all ritualistic practices like Vedic chanting, charity, sacrifices, etc. if you cannot see God, which should be the culminating purposes of all our endeavors?

Christina asked to clarify with another example.

HP:I repeat what I said earlier in the debate.

- If one offers to Me with devotion a leaf, a flower, a fruit, or even water, I delightfully partake of that article offered with love by My devotee. BG 9.26
    - o The item offered is not of consequence. The feelings (of devotion) with which offerings or rituals made are of consequence.
    - o Prescribed Items/Rituals insignificant before the pure heart.
    - o God partakes of that offering means the devotee is offering material item/action/sacrifice for consumption by God, and not for self-consumption.
    - o Also, it is definitely not with the expectation of something in return.
    - o You can offer something to a living being, not to an inanimate thing.
    - o Then why offerings before idols/images? Will they eat?

    - o Yes, God has hands, feet, mouth and sense organs everywhere and can eat or function with or without any of the sense organs in any manner as vouchsafed in BG: 13-14 to BG: 13.16

CH: Very nicely explained.

HP: I will analyze it in a different way so as to understand the essence. People perform Shradh for the departed soul.

CH: What is Shradh?

HP: It is the rituals performed for facilitating the departed soul to reach God and also to ensure hassle-free journey enroute.

CH: So?

HP:This gives rise to doubts like,

- IF it is not performed, will our ancestors suffer in hell?
  - If yes, isn't our life and afterlife determined by our actions or is it dependent on our descendants?
- Do their afterlife bodily requirements like food, clothing, etc come solely from descendants?
  - Then doesn't our good actions during our lifetime count?
- What happens if there are no descendants?
  - What if descendants do not believe or don't want to perform rites?
  - If the rituals are performed incorrectly, what about the consequences?
  - Isn't it additional punishment for the departed soul for the fault of the descendant?
- What happens to other religionists and co-religionists of different subcategories who perform different rituals?

  - According to their scriptures, will our departed souls not be punished for not performing their rituals and vice versa?

See, these are doubts in most general terms. This is only an example. Instead of Shradh, the same query could be made for any rituals.

CH: You have increased my doubts instead of clearing them.

HP: Let me clarify. We have to perform our duties. Duties are two types, mundane prescribed by humans and spiritual prescribed by God. Mundane duties could include your duties as a father, mother, son or as a teacher, driver, etc. I also include your daily activities like eating walking providing, interaction, etc. These activities are essential but how you do them is flexible and left to your choice. The attitude that 'This is the only way to perform the ritual, non-performance thereof is attendant with penal consequence' is wrong and false.

Now about the spiritual duties, Lord has prescribed them depending on their temperament for Brahmins, Kshatriyas, etc. These must be performed. There is no escape. Your nature will force you to do it. If you perform duties in accordance with your nature, you will progress. Otherwise, you will not be in equilibrium.

CH: Thanks, I have some queries about the latter parameter put forth by you.

HP: Feel free my friend. Don't nurse inhibitions.

CH: Supposing scriptures are in conflict with perception? Are we to follow our perception or give primacy to scriptures? IF we adhere to scriptures, will we not be branded bigots and irrational? If we compromise scriptures with reality as perceived by us, we will be haunted ever after for being untrue to God's words and compromising on His pristine blemish-less words? Earlier, I was confident, even though ignorant, but now midway in my spiritual journey, I am aware of the limitations of my sense perceptions. That is what prolongs my dilemma and make it worse.

HP: So many questions in one question. Well, one at a time. Differentiate between scriptures and God's words. God's words too may be termed scripture but it is inviolable and without any blemish, imperishable. It is not subject to interpretation. Scriptures of human origin may be interpreted or modified, that too in the rarest of rare cases.

- Any scriptural text could be either
  - o A statement (of fact or otherwise).
    - In the first instance, it doesn't matter what you believe. You may consider it fact even if it contradicts general perception, or you may choose not to believe it. It doesn't matter either way. Your belief or non-belief doesn't affect anyone. If a real fact is disbelieved, you may realize truth later on after your sensory perceptions are perfected with practice. If realization doesn't dawn on you, your efforts are not in vain, as the same is the point wherefrom you begin in the next life.
    - If a falsehood is believed to be true, then that falsehood doesn't belong to the scripture or it isn't the words of God. It could be subsequent interpolations. God's words have inbuilt checks like parameters to confirm if it is fact or otherwise.
  - o A call for action or instruction.
    - Here, we have to tread cautiously. Irrespective of whether you believe or disbelieve, your action or inaction should not adversely affect others. One way of testing is if that instruction is acted upon by some others and you are adversely affected, would you judge the action of the other as bonafide action backed by scripture? Your answer determines whether scripture is correctly interpreted or not.

If Vedas or for that matter any scripture state that fire is cold or non-incandescent It doesn't become true or valid.

Now, in the instant case, we don't place our hand in fire based on our understanding or misunderstanding, that it is in scripture, it is correct as it is stated. We have to use our rational faculties gifted by the Lord to discriminate fact from non-facts.

There could be

- Contexts
- Exceptions
- Misunderstanding or misperception.
- Later interpolation to scriptures.

Now, imagine a text in scripture which states kill the enemies or boycott the non-believers, etc. You should interpret it and act in the same fashion you would act in the earlier example of fire.

- o Don't act on the text, nor be judgmental on the text until such time you acquire the ability to perceive truth as it is meant to be.
- o For sake of argument with TG, then shouldn't Arjuna fight enemies? Yes, Arjuna should fight, and so should any other soldier on the battlefield as was Arjuna. A soldier needn't fight when we are not at war or has been expressly asked not to fight. Christina burst into laughter. She said that HP was bitten by the TG bug.
- o Not all conflict of perceptions needs to be acted upon. Some just need to be known or understood. It must be assumed that what is intended is different from what we have understood. Our spiritual practices enhance our perceptions resolving many conflicts by itself over a period of time.

Christina thanked Hari for her indulgence in replying to all her doubts. They dispersed to their places.

25. K -15 – GOD IS ONE

Please start the proceedings said the Professor.

HP: I wish to take the following principles as a parameter.
- God is one.
- God answers our prayers in the way we seek/approach.

TG: If based on Gita, it is okay, otherwise I object.

HP: Of course, it is based on the Gita.

- In whatever way people approach Me, so do I answer their prayers. People everywhere follow my path. BG 4.11

   o People everywhere follow Gods' path.

   o Gita recognizes people praying other gods.

   o God foresaw this eventuality and is clarifying that they are praying to him only although the forms or the names could be different.

- In whatever form a devotee worships me with faith, I steady the faith of such a devotee in that form. BG 7.21.

   o The choice of form is left to devotee. God strengthens his faith in that form.

   o God is steadying that faith keeping in mind the likes/dislikes and preferences of the devotee.

   o Gods' answers to prayers are both general and specific. Both customized and universal.

TG: What is the eventuality you were referring to?

HP: People would move away from HIM and start worshipping their own creations, or they would refer to HIM by other names, which would in course of time, would be misunderstood as different persons.

Down the line, in ages to pass, they would question His very existence thus creating doubts in the minds of others.

TG: How do these slokas support your contention that God is One?

HP: People everywhere worship God. The possible objections which I foresee are
- God being worshipped are not the same.
- Each of them is worshipping a different person.
- Their names are different.
- Their forms are different.

- Some people do not accept Gods with form because God is formless.
- The Atheists do not accept as factual the existence of God.

Am I right? Do you have any other objections?

TG: Yes, you are right. These are my objections, for now. Without prejudice to my rights, I may come up with other objections subsequently. You have to prove it not only on the strength of the Gita but also as observable reality. Besides, it should satisfy other religionists as also coreligionists. Needless to add that your say should be acceptable to atheists also.

HP: Your first three contentions are reasonable but the last one is not possible.

TG: So, you accept defeat?

HP: Atheists were debarred from participating in this debate, but could only watch the proceedings. There is ideological variance and hence that ruling. It was also made clear that a separate debate could take place wherein the subject matter is the existence or otherwise of God with atheists in the fray. As the subject matter is beyond the purview, it will be excluded.

Prof: I uphold the contention of HP. Please proceed.

HP: Sir, I seek permission to address the audience to evolve consensus amongst diverse religionists as mandated by TG.

Prof. Go ahead.

HP: Friends, these posers are for all of you except atheists. Do you all believe in God?

Chorus: Yes.

HP: God is the greatest, I suppose?

Chorus: Yes.

HP: SO, all are worshipping the greatest person of all times?

Chorus: Yes.

HP: From these universally agreed positions, where consensus has been evolved, we will explore the views/points of disagreement.

All major religions had a beginning, somewhere between 3000 BC and 1700 AD, ignoring the fact that Hinduism is Sanatana Dharma (for purposes of argument). What do you say?

Chorus Yes, but for the Sanatana dharma quote is just for purposes of argument.

HP:Before the advent/realization/descent of God prior to the founding of each religion, God still existed. Yes, or No?

Chorus: Yes.

HP: Whom were our ancients worshipping during the period prior to the discovery of God?

SILENCE

HP: Either they weren't worshipping at all or they were worshipping some God who was earlier known by a different name. Am I right?

Whispers of Yes.

HP: His form too could have been different from what the founders of each religion put forth?

SILENCE

HP: Whether they were worshipping or not worshipping, it remains that God existed prior to revelation by the respective founders of religion?

Whispers of YES

HP: So the names and forms could vary, but the central essence being worshipped was the same?

TG: Not necessarily, they could be worshipping different gods or persons. They could be worshipping non-gods presuming them to be gods. They could be worshipping demons or spirits.

HP: Both possible and probable. They would be worshipping or imagining worshipping the supreme omnipotent.

Chorus: Yes

HP: Wouldn't they would be revering the most generous, most merciful, most knowledgeable, powerful person?

Chorus: Yes.

HP: In short, they would venerate the possessor of all superlative positive qualities?

Chorus: Yes.

HP: Does anyone other than God possess all super most positive qualities?

Chorus: No

HP: Does more than one person possess all super most positive qualities to the fullest extent?

CHORUS:No

HP: Then, there is only one God?

SILENCE& Whispers of Yes and whispers of No

HP: Then, all are venerating/worshipping the same person, the possessor of super most qualities found exclusively only in Him, though called by different names or visualized in different forms?

TG: Some persons worship god without form, what do you have to say?

HP: Okay, but they worship that formless which has superlative qualities?

TG: But there are a few others who worship the attribute-less.

HP: Though attribute-less, say like a mysterious superpower, nevertheless capable of fulfilling your objects. So, persons are worshipping/adoring some qualities/characteristics which they visualize/find in the person called God.

TG was called aside by her group members and apprised of others' sentiments. She nodded her head.

TG: Theoretically, it is okay, but not many would be comfortable with changing the gods or their names or forms. Gita is supposed to have practical answers as you yourself claimed.

HP: There is no need to change names or forms or objects of worship. Just cultivate awareness that the object of worship of different individuals are not different but the same person.

TG: Would changing perceptions be sufficient?

HP: In the sloka quoted above, God says He strengthens that existing belief/faith. So this reluctance to rename or change gods is neither necessary nor correct. The point to be noted is when all adore the supreme, the syndrome that "My God is supreme & your god is less "is wrong.

To answer you specifically, let us explore the effects and non-effects of changing gods' names forms rituals and practices. Supposing a person converts his religion, without coercion or inducements, of his own free will because of the superiority of religion, what are the changes? Only the externals changes. The form changes. The name changes. The rituals change. Practices changes. But the core essence is he continues to pray to the supreme person, supreme imperishable. His god of earlier faith will not punish him, nor will his god of present faith become endeared or bestow special favor, because both the entities are the same. The truth remains the same. Only perceptions have changed. The object of worship or the person being worshipped is the same, only the inconsequentials have changed.

Murmurs from the audience.

TG: This may not be agreeable to other religionists, who hold that those not believing in their Gods are subject to punishment and barred from heavens.

HP: Will truth change with their agreement or disagreement?

SILENCE.

HP: If their contention is true, doesn't it violate the principle of God is Just, Equitable and merciful?

TG: Yes.

HP: Then, you may derive your own conclusions.

TG: And what is that truth?

HP: God is the supreme one. He is omniscient (BG: 7.26), omnipresent (BG: 6.29) and omnipotent (BG: 9.11). He is Imperishable.

TG: But their disagreement?

HP: The truth of the principle that God is Just, equitable and merciful cannot be tinkered with, Can we?

TG: No.

HP: Then, the only alternative is that their perceptions require change.

TG: Shouldn't perceptions change in tune with reality?

HP: Hasn't God said, "What is real cannot cease to exist and what is unreal cannot exist" (BG: 2.16). Perceptions may be unreal. God is real. Contentions of perceptions may not exist. God exists. So, for perception to be real, the contention should be God is one, by whatever name He is called. If this were not so, god would be the monopoly of a few.

TG: What monopoly?

HP: The contentions that only those belonging to a certain faith go to heaven, or only those worshipping a particular form are entitled to blessings or those belonging to a certain country are gods' chosen people for redemption, or those practicing certain rituals or wearing a particular attire are pious and dear to god, is an attempt at monopoly. This goes against the stated principle that "God is Equal and merciful to all ".

TG is interrupted by Harshita, who places a piece of paper in the hands of TG. She read it, thanked JS as a smile lit up her face.

TG: What is your say on monotheism and polytheism?

HP: I think it is obvious after all the discussions made so far.

TG: You have defended monotheism and upheld the concept of a single God so far.

HP: Yes.

TG: How do you reconcile the belief in the existence of other gods, say Ganapati, Shiva or say Brahma or any other gods in the Hindu pantheon, or shall we say, as per Sanatana dharma? Don't they exist? If yes, your theory is blown to smithereens. If they don't exist, you are contradicting the beliefs of Sanatana Dharma.

HP: The contradiction exists only in your imagination. God is different from god. (Note the capitalization). God is one and gods could be many.

TG: How are they different?

HP: God is one, as put forth in my arguments thus far. But gods could be many. They are the functional/regional/departmental heads taking care of their portfolio. We have an Indra who officiates as the king of gods and also controls and withholds rains. Varuna is the god of water bodies, Agni is the god of fire. We have Dik Palaks who are the presiding deities of different directions.

TG: What about Brahma and Shiva?

HP: They are in charge of creation and destruction respectively.

TG: You mentioned regional heads. You have given an example of functional heads only.

HP: Lankini, was the deity guarding the kingdom of Lanka who prevented Hanuman from entering the city and was bested by Hanuman. The concept of Gram Devata, Kula Devata is widely prevalent. Gram Devata is the deity protecting the village. Kula Devata is the deity worshipped by each Kula or clan.

TG: Then, were Rama, Krishna, Narasimha, etc. and other incarnations different as they performed different functions?

HP: I have been consistent in my belief and presentation that God is one. In the instant case, they are the same. God has no functions or duties to perform. His pastimes are mere divine sports. Primarily God was performing the function of sustenance, as Vishnu, a sustainer.

The process of creation and destruction are entrusted to Brahma and Shiva, though not necessarily in all manavantara. He may sometimes take over those functions Himself.

We can view this in another way. It is already agreed that God is one. It is also agreed that God is supreme, omniscient, omnipresent, and omnipotent. The consensus also arrived about the fact that there cannot be two or more than one supreme person. So, when people say that my God is superior to your God or only my God is true, their claims are fallacious. Their agreement and their beliefs are in conflict.

TG: Why is it so?

HP: Their beliefs are conditioned by persons other than Gods' words. If they truly understand and adhere to Gods' words, both their beliefs and reasoning would be in agreement with God's words. Similarly, persons destroying idols, places of worship or holy books are ignorant. They believe that they are destroying the gods of other faith. Nothing is farther from the truth. Firstly, God is imperishable and not subject to destruction.

The very persons attempting desecration of images or books or places of worship believe in the indestructibility of God and His invincibility. His teachings too are not subject to destruction. Then, what are they destroying?

TG: And what does the One GOD do?

HP: He is not bound to do anything. He is the overall cosmic superintendent. At times, He officiates in various capacities.

He is unchanging or imperishable and has no duties to perform nor anything to achieve nor is anything remaining for Him to achieve.

TG: Where are gods mentioned in the Gita? Where is it mentioned that they are perishable, unlike GOD?

HP: Here are the references.
- Working under Gods' direction, this material energy brings into being all animate and inanimate forms. BG 9.10.
  - God presides over the activities of the material nature of both animate and inanimate things.
- There is no duty prescribed for me, nor do I have anything to gain or attain. Yet, I am engaged in performing actions. BG 3.22
  - God is performing actions for the welfare of all beings, not for His own self.
- In all the worlds of this material creation, up to the highest abode of Brahma, you will be subject to rebirth, but on attaining My Abode, there is no further rebirth.BG: 8.16
  - All worlds upward up to and inclusive of Brahmalok(Abode of Brahma) is subject to rebirth, i.e. caught in the cycle of birth and death

TG: You haven't given references to the existence of demigods or shall we say, gods?

HP: Here is the Gita references sought by you.
- Endowed with faith, the devotee worships a particular god and obtains the objects of desire. But in reality, it is I who bestow the boon. BG 7.22
  - Reference to any particular god is made by Krishna.
- Those who worship the gods go to the abode of gods. While my devotees come to me. BG 7.23
  - Here a distinction is spelled out between Krishna (God and His abode) and gods (gods and their abode)
- All the gods are seeking refuge and entering into you. In awe, some are praising you with folded hands. BG: 11.21

- Worshippers of gods take birth amongst gods, worshippers of the ancestors go to the ancestors, worshippers of ghosts take birth amongst ghosts, but My devotees come to Me alone. BG 9.25.

- o The distinction made in earlier quoted sloka is reiterated here, underscoring the existence and distinction between gods and the GOD.

TG: What about the other principle you mentioned as a parameter?

HP: God answers our prayers in the way we seek/approach. BG: 4.11. So the key here is our way of approach and our prayers. This has different connotations, possible ones being
- In whatever form you seek Him.
  - o Any form, Any name, or formless
- In whatever relationship, you seek Him.
  - o God –devotee, Parent-child, Child-Parent, Friend-friend, Lover-beloved- Spouse-spouse, Enemy-Enemy, Served-Servitor, etc.
- For whatever boons we seek.
  - o Knowledge seeker, seeker of relief from distress, wealth seeker and Seeker of God
- In whatever way you worship or pray.
  - o Whether by folding hands, kneeling down, circumambulating, standing, with or without beads, with or without offerings, but WITH FAITH
- In whatever way you seek answers to your prayer.
  - o You may seek seemingly impossible things, but still, be blessed with the fulfillment of your desired object.
    - A boon granted by God is a law that runs its course. It has the power to be true, to fructify. In law, an agreement to perform an impossible task is void. But divine law is different. It makes seemingly impossible words come true
      - Because nothing is impossible to God
      - Because God works in a different plane and in a different dimension beyond human laws or beyond laws of nature.
  - o By giving devotion
  - o By giving salvation

TG: But many times, our prayer remain unanswered, isn't it?

HP: That is already discussed earlier when dealing with causes of action and results. Apart from the causes of action, faith, and sufficient accrual of merit is required.

TG: Could you substantiate that God confers seemingly impossible things?

HP: The acts seem impossible, or rather it is impossible for us humans but not for God. These are lovingly called miracles by devotees. Some miracles are obvious, others are not so obvious, as they are performed through a medium and not directly. Non-devotees have a scientific explanation, but the devotees know the true cause and the person answering their prayers.

Krishna supplying an endless amount of clothes to Draupadi and saving her modesty, Krishna Protecting Parikshit Maharaj in his mother's womb, are some notable examples. There would be many experiences in each one's life which are nothing short of a miracle.

TG: I am forced to agree with you, albeit grudgingly as I have experienced miracles.

HP: But why grudgingly?

TG: Because it is due to a miracle and not necessarily due to your argument.

HP: I conclude my presentation for the day.

TG: I have nothing to add or cross.

Prof: Court adjourned for the day.

All the students moved towards the auditorium. The popular movie, "Bahubali" was being screened. Nobody wanted to miss the movie.

HP and Christina broke away from the group and headed towards the hostel. HP sought help from Christina.

CH: How can I help you?

HP: Our debate is reaching the final stages; I want to finish the climax in the next three sessions.

CH: But how can I help you?

HP: You may help me by giving transcripts of the sessions held so far. You may also go through the same and tell me the layman's perception. Whether my arguments hold water? Whether I have pulled it off or I have messed it up? Places where I may have lost ground so that I can rectify in the following sessions.

CH: HP, I can't give an outsider's perspective, I myself am involved in this neck deep. I may give you an opinion after a day. I will consult my mentor/guide back home and mail him the transcript.

Thereafter I would discuss with him over SKYPE and get back to you. But do you approve sharing this with an outsider?

HP: Of course, it would be bias-free that way.

CH: My mentor is a gentleman and doesn't hold bias.

HP: I didn't mean personal bias against me. I meant the bias in favor of or against a particular version of Gita, which would affect the judgment.

CH: He is cosmopolitan in outlook, with parents coming from different religions and he himself a follower of Sanatana Dharma. He would study the same and evaluate like a layman. Trust me.

CH: Hari, could you simplify today's proceedings for me to better understand the concept?Summarize the concept without justifications. I want the essence, not justification.

HP: 'Prayers are answered in a personalized way' – this can have many connotations. It could mean
- God in whatever form you visualize.
  - The different avatars are a testimony to this fact.
- The form includes visualization as formless also.
- God with Gunas/attributes as per your visualization.
- Includes visualization without Gunas or attributes.
- The end result as an answer to all your prayer expressed or unexpressed.
  - Reviving Parikshit Maharaj, creating the illusion of sunset to facilitate the killing of Jayadratha.
- God in whatever name you wish to call.
- God in whatever relationship you wish to establish with Him.
- God with whatever qualities you empower Him in your visualization.
  - Example, Kind, forgiving, brave, chastiser, judge, impartial, etc.
- In whatever way you wish to offer prayer, say by kneeling, prostrating, standing, saluting, Namaste, etc.
- Praying to an idol or any other representation of God be it Photo, a symbol, nature or an unseen force.
- Prayers offered in church, temple, mosque, synagogue, home, workplace place of pilgrimage or otherwise, in short anywhere else.
- Prayer may be in any language, loud or silent or in a whisper or in mind, alone in groups or in a congregation.
- Prayer need not be expressed meaning it may be communicated or could be just a thought which remains unexpressed.
  - It could be a non-prayer, meaning any latent thought, fear, desire, or assumption.
    - Many warriors have sided with me ready to give up their life. BG:1.9
      - God answered his fears by making it come true.
- Prayers could be prescribed format or it could be your own composition.
  - All these are backed by Sloka 'I reinforce their belief and make it stronger' BG: 7.21.

Christina thanked Hari. They bade each other goodnight and took leave from each other.

26. K-16. --- CAUSE AND EFFECT

All were seated and waited for the proceedings to start. The professor asked if TG and HP were ready, and on their signifying yes, he asked them to proceed.

HP: Today, I present Cause and Effect as a parameter.

TG: It comes under science or more precisely physics and management branch of studies. HP:The study of cause and effect is widely used in scientific research as rightly pointed out by TG. Gita too is super science. Gita too is a subject matter of research. I will show the relevance in the course of my presentment. Cause and Effect have been mentioned many times, sometimes expressly and sometimes ambiguously. In fact, Gita itself is a study of cause and effects.

- The cause-effect analysis is an action, phenomenon or person and its resultant effects.
  o In some instances, the results are given which could be attributed to some cause.
  o Some dos and don'ts (actions and inactions) are given and the results of the same have been explained.

The universal law of cause-and-effect states that for every effect there is a definite cause, likewise for every cause, there is a definite effect. All thoughts, behaviors, and actions create specific effects. In a cause-and-effect study, we identify and establish a relationship between an independent variable (the cause) which has an effect on the dependent variable of interest (the effect) A cause-effect relationship is a relationship in which one event (the cause) makes another event happen (the effect).

- The cause is the specific reason for the occurrence of something the effect is what happened or the result of the cause.
- Cause plus effect explains why things happen.

Except where both are given, it is for us to identify the cause and search for the result or identify the result and search for the cause and establish the relationship between them.

TG: But how do you identify the relationship?

HP: To determine the cause of something, ask why it happened. To determine the effect of a cause, ask what happened. The cause always precedes the effect.

TG: So, you identify both and establish a relationship, then? How does it help?

HP: You may replicate the favorable causes and eliminate the unfavorable ones. You can avoid disastrous results by tweaking the cause at the root itself.

There are many types of causes.

- Necessary cause – one that must be present for the effect to occur.
- Sufficient cause – one that can produce an effect unaided.
- Contributory cause – one that helps to produce an effect but cannot do so by itself.
- The primary cause is the basis for a causal chain of events.
- The secondary cause or effect is usually an ancillary cause that contributed to an effect or an ancillary effect of a cause.
- The short-term cause or effect or the immediate cause or effect is a single, immediately identifiable event.
- The long-term cause or effect or the underlying cause is a contributing cause or effect that may be difficult to identify, but in the end, the long term is more important than the immediate causes or effects.

This study or analysis is aided by putting forth questions like

- Does a cause-and-effect relationship really exist?
- Are there multiple causes or single cause, if multiple causes, have I taken them into account?
- Does a causal relationship exist between two events or it is assumed due to one event immediately following the other?
- Is the effect single or multiple? Have these multiple effects been considered?
- Is there a chain reaction?

Often cause and effect are subtle, confusing, and hard to distinguish. To determine the cause of something question "Why it happened?" and to determine the effect of a cause, question "What happened?" From Gita, perspective,

- o God has expressly mentioned what are the causes and what and are its' effects.
- o We may infer the same from God's words.
  - In real life, or in History (Purana & Mahabharata) only effects may be mentioned. We are to derive cause.
  - Likewise, in history, only the cause may be mentioned, we have to derive effect.

Sattvic acts	→	Sattvic results
Rajasic acts	→	Rajasic results
Tamasic acts	→	Tamasic results
Transcendental acts	→	Transcendental results.

Past karma, the balance of credit of piety or sin, the motive behind actions also contribute to causes and effects.

- Each cause has a material part and a spiritual part.
- Likewise, each effect could have a material component and a spiritual one.

- The material part is identified by the perishable or temporary nature.
- The spiritual part is identified by the permanence or imperishable nature.

Now, coming to cause and effect in the Gita, the slokas alluded to by TG are

- God is the cause /origin of the entire universe and its destruction. BG: 7.6
  - o Self-explanatory.
- Great devotees know Krishna to be origin/cause of all beings, worship him. BG: 9.13
  - o Here Krishna is stated to be the cause of all beings.
- Krishna is the eternal seed of all beings. BG: 7.10
  - o Implied that Krishna being the originator, He is the cause of all causes.

The above is the summum bonum of cause-effect analysis. An entire third chapter titled 'Karma Yoga' is an analytical study of cause and effect.

- Contact of sense with sense objects cause pleasure and pain. BG: 2.14
  - o Contact is the cause, pleasure and pain are the effect.
- Equanimity and not being perturbed by opposites eligible for salvation. BG: 2.15
  - o Equanimity is the cause, eligibility for salvation is the effect.
  - o. They don't incur sin. Mentioned in BG: 2.38
- Death is certain for those born and birth is certain for the dead. BG: 2.27
  - o Both birth and death are a cause and effect of each other.
    - Those who have attained Moksha is an exception.
- It is a blessing for Kshatriyas who get an opportunity to fight in a battle unsought which is a gateway to heaven.BG: 2.32
  - o Kshatriyas dying in battle is the cause and Attainment of heaven is the effect.
- If you do not participate in this righteous battle, you will incur sin and be subject to infamy BG: 2.33
  - o Dereliction of duty causes the incurring of sin and infamy as its effect.
- Practicing of Karma yoga rids you of the bondage of actions, both good and bad. BG: 2.39
  - o Karma Yoga rids good and bad bondage.
- The ignorant are carried away by the flowery language of Vedas, which offers Joy, wealth and heaven as rewards for following its injunctions. BG: 2.43
  - o Following Vedas confer Joy, heaven and wealth.
- Those who are attracted to the flowery language of Vedas do not attain single-pointed concentration towards God BG: 2.44
  - o Veda's cause losing concentration to God.

- What is attained by a pond of water is also attained by an ocean of water BG: 2.46
  - Vedas likened to pond, and God to an ocean. The benefits of Vedasare also got by approaching God plus something that Vedas may not offer.
- Pursuing Yoga, we may get rid of good and evil effects in this life itself. BG: 2.50
  - Yoga, rids us from the bondage of birth and death cycle, in this birth itself.
- When you overcome delusion, you will attain indifference to all that is heard and yet to be heard BG: 2.52
  - Overcoming delusion causes indifference to pleasures both known and unknown. Succumbing to delusion, we are ensnared by senses and fall prey to sense objects.
- Abstinence results in avoiding sense objects but the taste for it remains. When God is realized, even the relish/taste is lost. BG: 2.59
  - Abstinence causes avoidance of sense objects.
  - WithGod-realization, even the relish or taste for sense objects is lost.
- Musing on sense objects gives rise to the attachment. From attachment springs desire, from desire arises anger, Anger results in delusion. From delusion arises loss of memory. This results in the destruction of good sense and understanding due to which he perishes. BG: 2.62 & 2.63
  - Good sloka giving a chain of cause and effects.
    - Brooding on sense objects causes attachment.
    - Attachment causes desire.
    - Desire, when thwarted, produces anger.
    - Anger results in delusion.
    - Delusion causes misunderstanding and loss of good sense.
    - Loss of sense and understanding causes a person to perish.
- He whose senses are controlled and disciplined attain purity of mind and serenity BG: 2.64
  - Disciplined Mind and controlled senses purify the mind and provide peace.
- Remember me and fight at all times with mind body and self, devoted to me and you shall attain me. BG: 8.7
  - Engaging in the performance of our duty by remembering God and with devotion takes us to His abode.
- Those who have attained me have no more birth and death which is the abode of misery. BG: 8.15
  - Attaining God, we are freed from the cycle of birth and death.
- Sattva binds the person to happiness and knowledge; Rajas binds a person to Action and Tamas born of ignorance binds beings to laziness and sleep. BG: 14.6 to 14.8
  - Cause and effect self-evident.

- Body, The God, the performer, the sense organs, and efforts are the five causes of action. BG: 18.13 & 18.14.
  - Five causes of action. Here, the cause is five factors and the effect is Action. The action itself would become a cause and the results it yields will be the effects, depending on the action performed.

What is mentioned here, is just the tip of an iceberg. Many of the Slokas are not mentioned.

The actual analysis, research, the study is not just the statements found in the Gita, but an application of those statements appropriately. This application could be in our daily life, or to interpret a result of an action or for judging a person. At a deeper level, this study brings us to the inescapable conclusion that God exists originally and independent of any cause and is the cause of all existence and happenings in existence.

TG: If you quote all slokas, then you can get to the iceberg, rather than confining yourself to the tip.

HP: Even if all the slokas are mentioned, IT doesn't do justice to the analysis. If that were so, everybody would have memorized all the slokas and become a master.

TG: Please explain.

HP: Each of the sloka of cause and effect is a generalization and capable of being applied to myriad situations, past, existing and future. How will you or I test its application with all situations many of which aren't in our domain of knowledge? Or yet to occur?

TG: How is the inescapable conclusion that God exists arrived at?

HP: There could be a manifold chain of arguments each leading to the conclusion. I will present one from my point of view. As already stated, the universal law of cause-and-effect states that for every effect there is a definite cause, likewise for every cause, there is a definite effect. All existing beings have a cause. They haven't come into existence on their own.

All inanimate creations like buildings, bridges, tools, and utensils, etc. too, have a maker. But God pre-existed all. He has mentioned it in the Gita. He has also mentioned that He is a creator and source of all creation, without Him having any other source. A building could not have existed without a builder, a pot could not have existed without a potter. Thus, the presence of animate and inanimate beings is a testimony of an original creator/designer.

TG: Taking the argument further, just as if we infer the existence of God, who created the universe, and us, what should we infer from the existence of God?

HP: No further inference. The buck stops here.

TG: Then isn't your inference wrong?

HP: You may take the words of God that He is causeless.

TG receives a note from her friends IC and AB. She reads it, smiles and continues.

TG: IT is mentioned in Gita that is okay. Please substantiate from the science point of view. Is it observable, or inferable or derivable from logic?

HP: So, you admit that God doesn't exist?

TG: I don't admit anything. What about His creator? You prove the existence of God and that He is causeless.

HP: It is already proved. We have all beings and non-beings, intelligent and in perfect harmony, following some mysterious laws. This is circumstantial evidence that God exists.

You show such evidence that He is caused by some other being.

TG: What about His existence?

HP: Yes, show evidence that He doesn't exist along with evidence that He is caused by something.

TG: I cannot show you, but scientists can offer you evidence.

HP: We have given circumstantial evidence. Also, there is a history of people having an audience with God as recently as 400 years ago. Saint Tukaram who was sent a spacecraft for travel to God's abode was witnessed by the whole town. The Presentment of the sword to Shivaji Maharaj by Goddess, Tulja Bhavani is another example. They aren't acceptable to you. You prove the nonexistence of God and that He is caused by something.

TG: This can be done by scientists. My friends AB and IC will answer you if you permit.

HP: I don't mind anyone answering. Please put your request to the chair.

Prof: Go ahead, Vinodini and Aparajita

IC & AB Scientists can prove the nonexistence of God.

HP: If at all anyone can prove, something, be it scientist, logician or anybody, it is the existence of something, say, God, air or electricity, etc. Nobody can prove the nonexistence of anything.

IC & AB Why not?

HP: The conditions required for proving nonexistence doesn't exist.

TG: What conditions?

HP: Non-existence cannot be proven. Existence can only be proven through direct scientific measurement which must be consistently reproducible by experiment.

Meaning after the experiment, we must be able to perceive it through our senses. But non-existence cannot be perceived by senses, nor measurable nor reproducible and hence cannot be proven.

Therefore, there is no proof that God doesn't exist or for that matter, any other being doesn't exist. This logic or debate could be extended to life after death, reincarnation, life in other planets, etc. If there were proof, the debate would be over.

A notable exception is the proof of impossibility. If the impossibility of the existence of God were proved, then it would be proof of non-existence. Two preconditions must be fulfilled to be held as proved. 1) There shouldn't be any unknowns and 2) A confined system. In all-natural circumstances, there are always unknowns, and systems are never confined.

AB & IC:But scientists ….

HP: These conditions are simulated by mathematicians and scientists. They aren't real and are temporary. The conclusions drawn too may change with changing times and advancement.

TG: Show that He is not caused by anything.

HP: The Same reply, show that He is caused by something.

TG, IC, and AB exchange hot words and order are called by the professor. IC and AB go back to their respective seats.

HP: Effect cannot happen without cause. Do you agree?

TG: Yes.

HP: But the cause can exist (self-exist without effect) agreed?

TG: Possibly.

HP: So, God exists but other beings may or may not exist, Okay?

TG: I am not sure, yes, it is probable.

HP: Isn't this proof of both the existence of God and His cause-less-ness?

SILENCE

HP: The Sloka 10.39 needs to be understood in this way. That everything exists because He exists, if He doesn't exist, nothing can exist.

TG: You said that there are two components, a material part, and a spiritual part. Do you mean each cause has two parts and each effect has two parts, would you substantiate?

HP: Yes, each cause has two components and each effect may have two components. The material component and a spiritual component.
- o Supreme Lord resides within the body. He is said to be the Witness, the sanctioning authority, the Support, Transcendental Enjoyer, the ultimate Controller, the Supreme Soul. BG: 13.23
  - ▪ It is consensual that God is spiritual. He is the controller, permitter, etc. Delineates that He is the cause. He resides in the body proves His existence. The non-god part is material.
  - ▪ Any action could be material or spiritual depending on the motive behind the action. Acts such as sacrifice as defined in the Gita are spiritual. Any act to please the Lord is spiritual. Any act contrary to this is material, i.e., acts performed with selfish motive and to please self.
  - • These are declared in Sankhya philosophy to be the place of action, the performer, the senses, the endeavor, and ultimately the Super soul. BG: 18.14
    - o Any action or its fruit is dependent on the Lord as stated here.
  - • I am the goal, the sustainer, the master, the witness, the abode, the refuge, and the dearest friend BG: 9.18
    - o Goal, abode, and refuge is an effect. The spiritual effect, because of its' permanence. Other goals like economic abundance, fam, etc. are material.
  - • I am both being and non-being. BG: 9.19
    - o Both being and non-being is a spiritual part.
    - o Being part is the manifested part and non-being is the unmanifest part.
    - o Non-being is latent and being is not latent.

TG: Tell in the context of the Kurukshetra war, was it spiritual or material? Or both? What is the spiritual part and the material part if it is both?

HP: The war being a physical material act, per se by itself is not under cloud of judgment. The participant's actions therein are under judgment, determines whether acts are material or spiritual.

Killing and being killed is an effect. Material effect. Duryodhana fought for selfish reasons and hence his actions are material. Arjuna fought against his wishes to please God.

His action is the sacrifice of the highest order. The material effects of the war are death, injury, sadness, pain, loss, pleasures of the conquest of kingdom, etc. The spiritual effects are re-establishment of Dharmic rule, pleasing the Lord, reaching His abode, etc.

TG: But Duryodhana, Karna, etc. went to heaven.

HP: They performed their Dharma, i.e., duty of Kshatriya by fighting in the battle and hence eligible for heaven. But don't forget, Heaven too is a temporary place wherefrom you fall down after exhaustion of your merits.

TG: As per your universal law of cause and effect, all results are the effect of causes, isn't it?

HP: Yes, of course.

TG: All causes are actions, right?

HP: It could also be non-action, person, situation, etc.

TG: Earlier you had said that it is gunas that perform an action. My question is if Gunas are the causes of action, why at all pray to God?

HP: Remember, He is the cause of all causes. He may cause the cause that gives result in your favor, meaning He may see that you do not come across situations that have ill effects, or He may tweak your gunas or whatever is causing you harm. He may change your mode or alter your path.

TG: How is it a parameter?

HP: It is taken as a parameter because it tells

- Why prayers remain unanswered.
- Why bad things happen to good people.
- Why positive results come when no effort put in and sometimes results are not forthcoming even if a lot of efforts are put in.
- Why results are contrary to expectation.

TG: How?

HP: It is already dealt with in actions and causes of action and results. Prayers act as a catalyst, hastens the process of fructification. IT is an action that yields results.

TG: So, Prayers are redundant?

HP: Remember God is the permitter, so without the catalyst (God) nothing can happen.

TG: We may derive that prayer by itself is useless but prayer plus action gives results, am I correct?

HP: Probably yes, but possibly no. But those who are solely dependent on God and their action is only dependence on God, this rule doesn't hold good.

You may take the example of Prahalad Maharaj, who didn't

put in efforts to save himself from the tyranny of his father. His efforts were restricted to only remembering and praying to God.

TG: Why possibly no?

HP: Because every cause should have an effect and prayer should necessarily have an effect. Again, prayers aren't unanswered or wasted. Either you get results or you get credit which is redeemable in the future.

TG: I can give one exception to Cause and effect theory.

HP: Please go ahead.

TG: Our behavior is influenced by our association. Our association is determined by birth. How can I be held responsible if I am born in a not pious family but in a family of criminals and terrorists? If I were given a good birth, I might not have taken to criminal activities and would have been a good person.

HP: Your observation apparently looks correct but there is a flaw in logic.

There are good persons in bad surroundings/family and vice versa. How did they get such a birth in the first place? There is a cause. What is the cause? I quote the slokas

Attachment to these (material) qualities is the cause of his birth in good and evil wombs. BG: 13.21

- The cruel, hateful vile and vicious persons of the society, are repeatedly hurled into the lower wombs by Me. BG: 16.19
- Nature is said to be the cause of all material causes and effects, whereas the living entity is the cause of the various sufferings and enjoyments in this world.

See, prima facie it appears that a person is a victim of circumstances, when in reality it is the effect of his deeds earlier in this life or earlier lives. The case of Karna is a classic example. He was noble by birth but fallen amongst evil persons. His baser gunas overcame his good ones because of his association. Why was he associated with such persons? Because it was his karma.

TG: How was it his karma?

HP: It is believed that Karna was Sugriva in his earlier life during the Ramayana period and was held accountable for getting his brother Vali, killed from behind. Nemesis caught hold of him eons later when he was killed by his brother Arjuna through machinations of the same Lord who killed Vali at the behest of Sugriva.

TG: In Gujarat folklore, the widely prevalent belief is that Jara the hunter who shot an arrow at the Lord was Vali.

HP: Possibly, it is not an argument of fact but an argument of concept.

SILENCE

Prof: TG, your take on the matter?

TG: No sir, the subject was discussed at length on the 8th day under the guise of the cause of action and results. Today's session is just old wine in a new bottle.

Prof: Good correlation, they have their similarities as also dissimilarities that were covered today. HP Have you anything to add?

HP: No sir, I have completed my presentation.

Prof: So, we will break for the day and assemble here as usual tomorrow.

Everybody left and so did Christina and HP. After dinner, HP visited Christina and inquired about her discussion with her mentor.

Christina informed that the transcript wasn't ready and hence she mailed the voice recording itself to her mentor. She offered to send a copy to HP but was informed by HP that she was more comfortable with the transcript and was willing to wait. Christina received a reply mail from her mentor. The gist of it was:

His (Mentor's) was of the opinion that his opinion may not be worth it, because he himself wasn't schooled in the traditional Vedic (Gurukula) way. His western education would betray his western bias, which would make it anathema and hence untouchable to the traditionalists. He further opined that time is the best judge. It rides over orthodoxy, traditionalists, and other obstructers, but would gradually find acceptance. The minuscule minority who sticks to their guns needs to be ignored. He further found the idea original, logical and in keeping with times by advocating pragmatism. He further made it clear to Christina that this cannot be a basis/substitute for her thesis.

The school board would sit and decide if this line of thinking is acceptable and can be the basis for research and constitute a thesis. It is either very brilliant or a sham. He clarified that it was his personal opinion and worth a gamble. He had a word of advice... She needn't get disheartened, because it could also be an idea or a concept way ahead of its time, meaning her thinking was far ahead of times. The entire matter being subjective, opinions vary vastly. He confessed that she had kindled his interest and curiosity and was looking forward to seeing her back in Florida. He further reiterated that he would stand by her just not because he was her mentor but also because her ideas stuck a chord and liberated his trapped soul.

Besides, he claimed that the success of his protégé would reflect favorably on him. He had a word of praise for her friend, Haripriya.

HP: So, we are back to square one.

CH: Look at the positives. I am guided by my mentor and have faith in his words. Time will overturn your despondency to buoyancy. Hasn't God said that that happiness is Sattvic which is at first like poison but at the end nectar-like?

HP: You know my weakness. I won't disagree or contradict Gita. You Win.

CH: It is you who wins my friend. I win by your winning.

HP thanked her friend and took leave of her and bade her goodnight.

27. K - 17 PARAMETERS....

The professor beckoned HP and TG and asked them to start.

HP: Today, I take up the subject matter of Parameters. How are they present in the Gita, how are they identified as parameters and other related matter?

Parameters are defined variously as:

- A limit or boundary which defines the scope of a particular process or activity.
- A parameter is a limit. In mathematics, a parameter is a constant in an equation.
- A parameter (as per Wiki) is any characteristic that can help in defining or classifying a particular system (meaning an event, project, object, situation, etc. That is, a parameter is an element of a system that is useful, or critical, when identifying the system, or when evaluating its performance, status, condition, etc.
- A set of facts or a fixed limit that establishes or limits how something can or must happen or be done:

HP: Gita consists of
- Statements of facts.
- Interrogative sentences or questions.
- Reference to statement of facts.
- Instructions.
- Parameters.
- Benchmark/conclusion as to the correctness of our perception.
- Descriptions.

These could have been communicated by way of
- Speech, by the Lord or through His devotees.
- Silence.
- Example by way of conduct.
- By enlightenment.

The test of the application of Parameters.
- Is it stated by God in the Gita?
- Is it stated in the Gita by others and God hasn't contradicted it?
- Is it implied in the Gita?
- Is it an observable phenomenon? Can you experience the truth of it even today?
- Is it a qualifier of most of the verses? I.e., is it all-pervasive?
- Is it universal?
  - If yes, is it applicable to all other scriptures?
- Does it nurture/enhance/underscore the glory of the Lord?

A Parameter
1. States a principle or a Tatva.
   a. Enunciates a principle or a Tatva.
2. It is a generalization.
3. It has a universal application.
4. Refers to knowledge or source of knowledge.
5. Qualifies a statement/sloka.
6. Highlights/underscores the inherent property of a statement/sloka.
7. Shows the cause/necessity of that statement or other statements, or justifies other statements
8. It provides insights or shows things from a new perspective.
9. Removes misconceptions.
10. Act as determinants and affords conclusiveness.
11. It provides relevance to the context.

Entire Gita is a benchmark/guide (parameter) for the Sanatana way of living.

But Gita is ambiguous and difficult to comprehend. Even when understood, doubts creep in whether our understanding or interpretation is correct? Why God made it difficult and not unambiguous? Because it is customized in keeping with, the needs and levels of different individuals who need to understand it differently. Now, to remove this ambiguity in understanding and interpretation God has given parameters.

Our understanding or interpretation should conform to the parameters for it to be correct. As the individual level of comprehension ability varies, the inherent Krishnaness/Gitaness present in the understanding or interpretation plays a role. More the Krishnaness/Gitaness, more correct is your understanding. Our understanding or conclusions arrived at should fulfill or satisfy the criteria mentioned in the parameters.

Any interpretation of any scripture or slokas of the Gita should conform to the parameters or rather should not contradict the parameters.

When God says:
○ I am God.
○ I am the greatest.
○ There is no one superior to me.
○ I am all that is glorious.
○ All the glories are but a spark of My splendor.
Is God boasting? Is He asking subservience to cater to His ego?

He is telling it to show you the parameter, benchmark, and authority. How else can you identify non-god from God? As Gita is a collection of words, His glories cannot be restricted and confined to words. Hence, it is said that Mahabharata has three meanings and each word in the Mahabharata refers to God Himself. Hence, we are adopting a conceptual approach to the study of the Gita.

Gita is the sanjeevini of any/all scriptures. What does sanjeevini do? It brings back to life the dead body. So, how does Gita bring life? Over a period of time, scriptures tend to become obsolete.

They lose their relevance. Without relevance, it is just a book kept on the shelf. But Gita breathes life into scriptures.

This is done by parameters of the Gita by providing auto-updater and keeping it insured against obsolesce. It links ancient scriptures with a modern interpretation to bring back relevance and acceptance. The scriptures by themselves are not obsolete. It is the rigid understanding which makes it so.

TG: Parameter is nowhere mentioned in the Gita. There is no reference or mention of parameters in any scripture or told by God or any Acharya. It is overreach on the part of my friend.

HP: Any commentary on the Gita, or for that matter on any scripture or any subject has extrapolations. This practice is in vogue even amongst management consultants. These extrapolations are implied and inferred and found acceptable by all and the commentator is also held in high esteem and quoted as authority and references made to them in future research/discussions sometimes eclipsing the original author/subject/text. The test would be whether it is implied, if yes, does it satisfy the attributes of the original subject and adjuncts.

In the realm of science, Scientists will say water is made up of hydrogen and oxygen in proportion of 2: 1, is in a liquid state and has certain properties. When anything that doesn't match the above criteria is not called water, we cannot take the plea that it is not said by the scientist that other things are not water, and hence unacceptable. Water was known to all and sundry, but it was scientist Henry Cavendish who discovered the composition of water.

TG: Why only some verses are branded as a parameter? Why not all? What are the criteria for taking as a parameter? Who devised the criteria for selection as a parameter?

HP: The criteria for parameters numbering ten are already told by me. Those have some common patterns based on which generalizations can be inferred and principles can be put forth.

TG: If other slokas are not co-opted as parameters, aren't you limiting the glory of the Lord?

SILENCE

TG: Triumphantly, caught on the wrong foot at last.

Prof: Entire Gita is a parameter vis-à-vis all externals. Slokas in Gita act as parameters vis-à-vis other slokas in the Gita. Am I correct Hari?

HP: Yes sir. Thank you, sir.

TG: Hari, you are playing with Parthasarathy on your side. I have no chance of victory.

HP: Laughs as does the Professor.

HP: How to identify the parameter is already seen. We have seen the properties/characteristics of a parameter. Check if they are present and apply.

Parameters in the Gita is the base to understand God and His actions and His teachings. It also is the base to understand ourselves, and our actions against the benchmark of the Gita. Parameters help reconcile different opinions, be it research purposes or getting a proper perspective of any action in history say, Ramayana or Mahabharata or could be an evaluation of any mundane day-to-day act.

- Statements of facts in the Gita.
  - No need for the application of Parameter. What is stated in Gita is taken as fact and not questioned. The parameter doesn't help you find out if the said statement is a fact or otherwise. Nor does it matter if it is a fact or otherwise, unless you have a special interest in the subject matter, or you base your decision on the said statement and need to act.
- Interrogative sentences or questions.
  - Here too parameters do not have any active role and stand on par with and are similar to the statement of facts.
- Reference to statement of facts.
  - Same treatment as with statement of facts.

- Instructions.
  - Parameters are of immense significance here and have a direct bearing on our actions and results thereof which is in turn dependent on our understanding of instructions.
    - The best example is Arjuna refusing to fight under the pretext of incurring sin and also based on the presumption that renunciation is better than action.
    - The original Sikhism was founded on peace and thereafter turned themselves into the martial race as per changing needs and requirements. So, should Sikhs fight or should they make peace? Should they follow the original Guru or their last Guru?
    - When more than one set of instructions is there, each diametrically opposite of the other, parameters help you make the correct choice.
  - Parameters.
    - They should be identified as such and applied to evaluate the propriety of our actions.
- Benchmark/conclusion.

- These slokas are parameters that serve as a benchmark/ or help arrive at the conclusion as to the correctness of our perception.
- Descriptions.
  - Parameters have very little or no role in descriptive statements in Slokas.

I will list the parameters discussed so far along with reasons for their inclusion in parameters.

This is apart from the earlier ten reasons, as to what parameter does.

1. Gita is Self-contained and self-luminous not requiring the crutches of the Guru or any other external resource/scripture.
   - Taken as a parameter as it is a master reference book, underscoring the principle that external reference is not required.
2. Gita has many parameters within which our interpretation/understanding should remain confined.
   - Parameters are the boundaries or the limits within which our understanding /interpretation should remain confined.
3. Besides, semantic and syntactic study and analysis, there is another dimension hitherto ignored, the conceptual and objective analytical study of Gita.
   - Parameter as it enhances the scope and removes limitations of semantic understanding.
4. God is supreme. From this sloka alone, Gita derives its authority and inherits Gods' legacy. From authority flows veracity and authenticity. This alone makes Gita not being subject to interpretation, unchangeable and not subject to tinkering.
   - Taken as a parameter as it derives authority. Prevents contamination and material modifications and sustains the purity of original teachings.
   - Due to its authority, it pervades or qualifies all other slokas.
5. There are two types, perishable, and imperishable beings. This is also loosely termed the temporary and the permanent, the spiritual and the mundane, the variable and the constant. This characteristic is not confined to beings but to all else, non-beings, actions, and non-actions, causes and effects, etc.
   - This sloka too permeates all other slokas and qualifies most of the slokas.
6. Gita is complete knowledge. This is so quoted in Gita itself. Besides, Gita being a manifestation of God inherits Gods' completeness.
   - Being complete knowledge, consulting other scriptures or persons isn't required. This completeness is achieved by generalization thereby compressing knowledge and making it easy to remember.

- o   Gita is summarized as complete knowledge in another sense of it imparting knowledge, a reference to knowledge, and providing a benchmark to evaluate our interpretation of knowledge.
7.   Earth is a prison full of miseries. Our endeavor should be to end miseries permanently and out of the earth. Searching for joy in the joyless world of the earth is futile.
    - o   Explains the root cause of all afflictions, hence taken as a parameter.
8.   Persons commit sins out of their own volition even unwillingly due to passion and would have to reap consequences of cause and effect spanning many lifetimes.
    - o   Explains the predicament of all human beings.
9.   The three Gunas are ubiquitous and found in all planets and beings.
    - o   Explains many a phenomenon
    - o   Not restricted to beings but also actions, thoughts, results
10.   There are five causes of action and results.
    - o   Identifies the cause of action as a function of result.
11.   Everyone is under the influence of time and space except God.
    - o   Time and space have multiple connotations like context, appropriateness, etc.
    - o   These should be taken into account before coming to any judgment/conclusion.
    - o   Pervades all the slokas and qualifies all the slokas.
12.   Sacrifices, as mentioned in the Gita, are real sacrifice approved by God almighty and result yielding. Other sacrifices are secondary compared to sacrifices listed out by God in the Gita.
    - o   Removes common misconceptions about sacrifice.
13.   Faith is an essential ingredient necessary for success in any venture.
    - o   Explains why some endeavors fail.
14.   Behave with others as you would wish them to behave with you.
    - o   A benchmark to evaluate correctness/ appropriateness or otherwise of any action.
15.   There is no need to go into minute details of everything unless specifically required.
    - o   Overview or general knowledge is sufficient in most of the cases.
16.   The mind is a friend as well as an enemy depending on whether you control it or it controls you.
17.   Brooding causes eventual downfall.
    - o   Sets a chain of events culminating in downfall.
    - o   Cause of most of the problems being faced.
    - o   Closely interrelated with the mind as a friend and an enemy.
18.   Knowledge of the purpose of an action is better than knowledge itself.
    - o   Blindly following rituals as all in all not recommended.
    - o   Path (rituals) is being mistaken as a destination.

19. 'That it is mentioned in scriptures' doesn't make it sacrosanct unless backed by relevance, appropriateness observable and practical. 'That it is practical and observable' by itself doesn't make it spiritual.
    o A point missed out by majority who cling to scriptures even in the face of evidence to the contrary.
    o Scriptures are correct, but the commonly held interpretation of scripture is wrong. Time constraint is not factored and blind faith is reposed in scriptures.
20. God is one, by whatever name you may call and in whatever form you visualize and whatever way you pray.
    o The myth of his god, her god my god their god is dispelled.
    o The misconception of the superiority of one's god over others' god is removed
21. Prayers are answered by God in an individually tailored way.
    o It is a generalization not restricted to tangible or mundane answers.
        ▪ Answers to prayer can be
            • Form of God
            • Fulfillment of unexpressed felt or unfelt inner desire.
            • Bestowing what is sought.
            • Non-fulfillment of desire.
            • Strengthening your belief.
22. Gita is a study of cause and effect.
    o Entire Gita is a cause-effect analysis.
    o Karma Yoga is the prime stone of cause-and-effect analysis.

Gita has given parameters that we have to identify and segregate parameters, knowledge, and means to knowledge, benchmark, and conclusion so as to interpret correctly.

This is a bird's eye view about the parameters.

TG: Gita is complete & self-contained is acceptable. For the sake of argument, let us also accept that it is universal. But how is the universality of Gita be acceptable to other religionists?

HP: There are four possible replies.
    • Assume that it is just a quotation, not a religious statement.
    • Facts do not alter based on acceptance or non-acceptance nor is universality affected due to acceptance /non-acceptance.
    • It may be noted that non-acceptance is due to a lack of belief/faith more than it not being fact or universal.
    • Substitute the word 'Gita' with 'Scripture' and the word 'Krishna' with 'God' it will become acceptable to all religionists. 'Gita' can be substituted with the scripture of any religion and it would find acceptability of that religionist.

TG: As suggested by you, supposing the word 'Scripture' is substituted with a specific scripture of any particular religion, it is possible that it may become acceptable but may not pass the test of being in tune with reality, or observable or being practical, etc.

HP: This throws up interesting possibilities.
- It could be that that the scripture is really incomplete.
- IT could be complete and universal but incorrectly interpreted by ignoring the 'Time' and context factor as mentioned in the parameter.

TG: Are you imputing that scriptures of other religions are incomplete?

HP: Scriptures are defined as writings that are considered holy by any religion. So, a scripture may be holy but need not be universal or complete. Whilst the Shrutis are a holy revelation, the Smriti literature is a product of human intellect.

The Agamas comprising of the mechanics of ritual worship cannot be said to be universal or complete by itself. Scripture is not defined as something that is universal or complete.   The scriptures of other religions could be complete and universal just like Gita.

I don't claim it to be so nor claim it to be otherwise. IT is for the proponents of particular scripture to conduct the exercise and expound the hidden gems therein whilst checking it constantly with reality.

TG: The parameter that earth is Dukhalaya (a place of miseries) also is necessarily Hindu belief and doesn't find concurrence with other religionists, thereby disproving your claim of universality.

HP: If earth were to be a place of joy and celebrations, why do scriptures of different religions promise Heaven, Paradise, Jannat, Swarg, salvation, etc. as a reward for pious activities and hell, purgatory, etc. for sinners?

TG: You have said that sacrifices advised by God in the Gita is real and best followed by what is referred by Him, which are secondary. This too is disputable by other religionists.

HP: God has dealt with the subject by covering the list of sacrifices, listing out the types of sacrifices, defining what is a sacrifice? Gradation of sacrifices, reasons for performing sacrifices, components of sacrifices, and references to other literature as to details of sacrifice. If you observe closely, you will notice that God didn't tell the details of how to perform the sacrifice, except, perhaps indirectly by referring to other literature. Gita is full of generalizations, and God's take on Gita is no exception. It is a generalization.

The gradation of sacrifices mentioned by the Lord subsumes all sacrifices in other religious literature. When the sacrifices prescribed by any religion can be pigeonholed in one or the other type, how can it contradict other religions? Its non-acceptance is at best religious chauvinism or fanaticism. The list of sacrifices mentioned by God is all non-material, observable, practicable, result-oriented and enjoyable.

God has just given a template or generalization. Specifics aren't detailed, meaning it is user-defined as per his religious beliefs. You may experience the results.

I will quote one exception before you object. God has told specifics in one instance in Sloka 6.11 & 6.12 where He asks the aspirant to seat in a sanctified place with the seat being neither too high nor low, hold the body erect in a straight line, controlling the thoughts and meditate.

The answer as to why sacrifice, is nearly the same in all religions. It is to please the Lord, to incur His pleasure, for sake of itself or for some benedictions, which again underscores universality.

TG: Mere mention is scripture doesn't make it sacrosanct as a parameter which too is disputed by many religionists.

HP: This disputation is the prime reason for the birth of bigotry and fanaticism. We see many anti-social acts and acts detrimental to the community, being justified by quoting scriptures. God has in His wisdom provided this parameter. God is encouraging independent thinking and asking you to check His words with a reality independent of His say. The mere mention in scripture doesn't make it sacrosanct and mere reality doesn't make it divine. They both go in tandem.

TG: I will quote a few verses which aren't experiential, practical, or verifiable. God has defined Brahma's day and night. The truth cannot be experienced nor can it be verified. Again, God has displayed His cosmic vision to Arjuna. This too is not experiential nor is it verifiable. How can we accept that it is a reality?

HP: Facts must be taken as it is on faith and belief. Parameters don't address facts. Faith is a prerequisite and itself listed as a parameter. God has also said that for a doubting person, there is neither this life nor the next.

TG: If parameters cannot determine facts, or shall we say facts are beyond the scope of parameters, why have you introduced parameters at all? If the concept of parameter suggested by you is correct, why are stated facts beyond the scope of parameters?

HP: In the case of declarative statements, parameters can guide us whether interpretation should be literal or symbolic, specific or general or class-specific or individual specific or universal. Similar is the case in respect of interrogative sentences. Where God has referred to other literature, parameter plays a neutral role. The role of parameters in optative sentences is a vindication of parameters like God is greatest and God answers prayers in the way He is approached.

TG: Where is it stated that parameters depend on the type of statement?

HP: Types of sentences is in the domain of grammar. Earlier, I was criticized for speaking about algebra, mathematics, moral science, etc. you may observe that each type of sentence does occur in the Gita. You may test it by taking each type of sentence and interpreting it in a symbolic way, and in the literal sense and also check it for specifics and generality and draw your own conclusions.

TG: How do you segregate non-facts with your parameter?

HP: Gita doesn't contain non-facts. Any misunderstanding (by Arjuna), which may be termed non-facts has already been clarified by God. About non-facts, in our day-to-day affairs or in other scriptures we determine by applying the parameters and judging by the resultant Krishnaness/Gitaness of our understanding.

SILENCE.

Prof: TG, any questions?

TG: I will take up the matter after HP completes her statement and conclusion tomorrow.

Prof: Okay, HP, wind up your presentation by tomorrow. We will meet again tomorrow. Saying this, he left his seat.

After the conclusion, everybody left for their places. TG and her friends assembled in her room. They seated themselves comfortably, and everybody reminded her that today was the penultimate day, and tomorrow being the last day, all-out efforts should be made for winning the debate. Other group members too joined her, though they had no stake in the debate or its outcome. Vinodini set the discussion rolling.

IC: So far, you have been bested all the times barring a few exceptions. Tomorrow is the concluding day. It is a do or die situation. Come up with something to recover lost ground.

TG: What can I do? She has a flair for presenting her viewpoints analytically and logically.

IC: You argue more from the heart than from the head.

KA: IT is true, but instead finding fault, suggest a strategy.

AB: You have no stake, you are just an observer, and you aren't even a believer and only inciting divisions and sowing dissent.

IC: I want my friend to win, don't doubt my intentions.

SD: Don't allow her to hog the limelight. Let her present the case in her natural way, but in the way you suggest, within the confines specified by you. We should appear to be arguing in pursuit of truth and none must suspect that we are pulling her down. Ask her to prove parameters within your boundaries that way, she will be diverted from her free flow and restrict her display of oratorical skills. You present something in which you are strong and which she has no idea about and can't contradict you. After all, you are Trikala Gyani and Panditji, which title hasn't been acquired unjustly.

TG: Thanks for the good idea. I will do it. But I find her arguments logical and convincing but unable to accept it for reasons not fathomable to me.

IC: You are a disgrace to your group and disloyal. See, Duryodhana, Karna, etc. They fought to the finish, even though they realized the futility of war midway.

KA: You are just an observer. Please don't foment divisions within us and cause trouble.

AB: See, believers even of other denominations are silent, but non-believers infiltrate and cause dissensions amongst us.

IC: As it was decided that it should be practical and universally applicable, ask her to test run her parameters on existing commentaries or on other religious scriptures. The chaff will be separated from the grain.

TG: Thanks, but no thanks IC. I will be guided by the advice of SD.

With this, all of them dispersed.

HP and Christina were in animated discussion. Christina reminded that she had only one day. She advised HP to prepare herself well and review the proceedings of the past three weeks.

She apologized for not providing the transcript, which was not yet ready. They played the audio and heard the discussion very carefully. HP was making notes by pausing the recording at times. HP informed that she would not present anything new. She would just clarify on parameters and answer any questions that may be thrown at her. HP asked Christina about her plans.

She was informed that Christina plans return to Florida, once the academics are over. She further expressed her desire to visit Kolhapur, Dwarka, and Kurukshetra before the delivery of the verdict by the Professor.

She wanted to savor those victorious moments of her friend in person and with her friend by her side and hence they should return back from the pilgrimage before the verdict.

HP realized for the first time, how much her friend loved her. She had stood by her in thick and thin. She promised to make arrangements for travel and stay. Christina was more interested in arrangements for a guide who would explain the spiritual significance and historical perspective of the places. Travel and accommodation were non-problem according to her.

HP was left pondering. She decided to broach the subject with her father who may be able to make arrangements. CH again reminded HP of her desire to interact with her father. HP laughed it off and said that she would be staying in her house at Kolhapur, so where was the need for an appointment with her father or the need to remind her. HP took leave from her friend and walked back to her room. She was pondering about the possibilities of the next day lying on bed and fell asleep.

28. K- 18— IN DEFENSE OF PARAMETERS

Professor asked if all were ready to commence the debate. On their replying in affirmative, he asked that they commence the proceedings.

HP:Today, we will

o   Evaluate parameter with the concept of Neti, Neti by way of the analogy of:
  ▪   If this isn't true?
  ▪   If this isn't a parameter?

Parameter states that Gita is Self-contained and self-luminous without requiring an external reference.

o   Supposing Gita is not self-contained then?
  ▪   Reference to other scriptures becomes necessary.
  ▪   The other scriptures become superlative leaving Gita behind.
  ▪   Gita cannot be accorded secondary status, it being the Word of The God.
  ▪   Other scriptures would be taken up for study and our debate too would have centered on other scriptures, and not on the Gita.
  ▪   Many of the Slokas in Gita would become falsehood or untruth.
  ▪   That Gita is complete would become untruth.
  ▪   Different denominations fight with each other claiming supremacy of their commentary over other denominations.

Supposing, this is not taken as a parameter?
  ▪   The possibility of coming to the wrong conclusion is high. After reading Bhagavata or Mahabharata, people may conclude that Krishna was a mortal, being born of Devaki and Vasudeva, and met His end at the hands of Jara the hunter who shot an arrow at the feet of the Lord.
  ▪   They can find the answer in Gita, wherein the Lord says that His birth, activities, and disappearance are divine.
  ▪   He further elaborates, foolish people, think of Him as a mere mortal. Without this parameter, people tend to search for answers in other Puranas or scriptures, which isn't necessary. This parameter guides the seeker to look inward into the Gita rather than go after other scriptures in search of an answer.
  ▪   Many commentaries by different Gurus would compete with each other claiming that only their denomination is correct to the exclusion of all others.
  ▪   By parameterizing, the viewpoint of all commentaries is accommodated as another facet of the same truth.
  ▪   What this does is that it precludes us from searching for answers in other scriptures.

- This enunciates the principle that Gita being complete, reference to other scriptures is not necessary, making it a principle enunciating parameter.

Gita has many parameters within which our interpretation/ understanding should remain confined.

- ○ Parameters are the boundaries or the limits within which our understanding /interpretation should remain confined.
- ○ Supposing there are no boundaries or borders?
  - This isn't possible. Imagine, there is no boiling point for water, or there is no range of BP which is considered normal, then how can we distinguish the normal and the abnormal?
- ○ Supposing this isn't a parameter?
  - Then, imaginary values/interpretation would invade scriptures and contamination of scripture would set in besides making it impure.
- ○ This is a parameter by implication, as it holds true but isn't mentioned so.

TG: What is Neti, Neti?

HP: It is the Vedantic concept of the process of elimination. Literally speaking, it means not this, not this and so on.

This analogy was used in describing the soul/super-soul, which are humanly indescribable.

TG: Isn't it advocated by Vedantists, mostly the monists?

HP: Yes. Shankaracharya, the leading light of Adwaita advocated this analysis.

TG: Do you subscribe to its view?

HP: The question of subscribing or not doesn't arise. That portion of whatever is in tune with what is said in the Gita is acceptable to me.

TG: Do you endorse the view of Shankaracharya?

HP: Who am I in front of the stalwart and great revivalist? How does it matter to the Acharya or his followers whether I endorse or not? How is it relevant here?

I am tuning and putting forth my views so as to be inclusive and you attempt to make it more divisive. Einstein gave a theory of relativity, we put it to use, and not question whether you subscribe to his views or not. Most of the mathematical theorems are proved, commencing with the presumption that if the statement is not true (Suppose $A \neq B$ (is not equal) to B) which practice is universally accepted but not acceptable to my learned friend.

This reminds me of the first day of disagreement, which forced us to seek formal debate. There were arguments amongst all my friends of the DR group as to which flavor of Gita is the best.

I suggested an amicable solution and was pulled into the vortex of debate. God, Himself has answered them but they are deaf to His words, 'People worship Me by many methods.

Some see Me as undifferentiated one with them, while others see Me as separate from them. Still, others worship Me in My different manifestations of cosmic form.' BG: 9.15. They are called by God as men of knowledge.

This establishes that they see God differently and worship Him differently and their different forms of worship are acceptable. This single sloka alone answers their query conclusively but no, this debate had to take place.

Prof: I agree, with you Hari, but just to satisfy my curiosity and off record, I want to know your views, do you subscribe to the view?

HP: Sir, Neti, Neti concept is not without utility. As discussed earlier, it is proximity to truth. I will give an example which brings forth my view. God describes Himself (Super Soul) as I am the strength of the strong, taste in water, ability in men, etc. from BG: 7.8 to BG: 7.12. Again, His descriptions of Himself occur from BG: 10.20 to BG: 10.41. God's descriptions are positive and in affirmation whereas Neti, Neti is in negation. This is the difference between God and human creation. So, what I like is pretty obvious. It is also obvious that I do find Neti, Neti practical and value it as words of respectable Acharya.

TG: So, you are implying that Acharya's contention is conflicting with what God has spoken and is in variance with the truth.

HP: That is your imagination. I haven't implied any such thing.

TG: If it isn't imaginary, what then is the truth? What God said or what Acharya's opine?

HP: You are asking me to reconcile what is said by Acharya with what is expressed by God in the Gita, In other words, I should defend your stand?

TG: Not exactly. My point is both are opposites and you claim both are right.

HP: In the initial days of debate, you had said that Acharya's teachings are always in tune with Gods' say. Now you are saying they are opposites.

Prof: HP, you have scored your point, but go ahead and reconcile the conflicting viewpoints for not for debate but for benefit of others.

HP: I have earlier introduced the concept of proximity to the truth which answers TG's question in general sense. Specifically, water, sun, Vedas, men, etc. also have features other than what is described in Gita, like taste in water, manliness in men light in the sun, etc. The features mentioned herein are distinct and distinguishing features different from other features. The features specified are superlative and God component and distinct from the other non-God component. This can be viewed in many other ways also like

- o Each being/entity has a higher nature and a lower nature.
- o Each being has a perishable and non-perishable component.
- o Or each being has a divine and a demoniac element.
- o Or this can be seen as a high concentration of Krishnaness/incidence of properties specified, for example, the taste component in water.

In BG chapter 7, when God says, I am the taste in water, it also means whatever is non-taste in water is not His characteristic, in a similar fashion, I am the strength of the strong means, and whatever is non-strength in the strong is not God/Godly.

God is putting this in a positive way, revered Acharyas are approaching it from another direction and cannot be said to be incorrect.

The words of God and Acharya must be in variance or different as they stand at a different level in the hierarchy and both their words cannot be ranked equal, but also need not necessarily be incorrect.

TG: Isn't it impermissible to refer to other matters such as Vedanta etc. which is outside the Gita as Gita is complete? Also, it was so agreed prior to the commencement of the debate.

HP: Gita being complete, whatever is found in Vedanta is definitely in the Gita.

TG: Isn't your reply to sweeping and general which betrays escapist answer?

HP: Read BG: 2.23, 2.24 and 2.25.

TG: They are descriptions of the soul and has no bearing on the subject matter.

HP: Please read it out.

TG: Reading it aloud
- o Weapons cannot shred the soul, nor can fire burn it. Water cannot wet it, nor can the wind dry it.
- o The soul is unbreakable and incombustible; it can neither be dampened nor dried. It is everlasting, in all places, unalterable, immutable, and primordial.
- o The soul is spoken of as invisible, inconceivable, and unchangeable. Knowing this, you should not grieve for the body.

So where is the relevance?

HP: How is the soul described? Isn't it described as not this, not this?

TG: Neti, Neti isn't specified, meaning not specified as negative.

HP: Use analogous analysis also to learn Gita, which Gita supports.

TG: Okay.

HP: Coming to the next point of disagreement, besides, semantic and syntactic study and analysis, there is another dimension hitherto ignored, the conceptual and objective analytical study of Gita.
- o Parameter as it enhances the scope and removes limitations of semantic understanding.
- o Semantics and syntactic reasoning by itself aren't complete.
- o Cannot explain non-verbal communication if the conceptual analysis is ignored
- o The conceptual study is an observable phenomenon

IC walks up and gives a chit to TG. TG, reading it thanks IC.

TG: Nice presentation, but I feel it could be better and more focused and one-pointed.

HP: How?

TG: By use of structured format, so that nothing is left out and all loose ends are covered.

HP: Nice suggestion. So be it. What structure do you propose?

DR group, IC and others of their ilk were in joy and surprised that HP fell into their trap easily as much as without a suspicion.

TG: I propose the following structure.

- • Examine and analyze each parameter as to
  - o What it does.
  - o Why is it a parameter?
  - o Example of application of parameter.
    - ▪ Being a parameter, does it equally hold good for all religious scriptures and equally applicable as such, meaning does that parameter transcend religion and conform to the COSMIC standard of the word of God and hence passes the test of acceptance of all religions?

HP: Addressing the chair, Sir, I seek permission to adopt the format suggested by my learned friend.

Prof: Good suggestion by TG. Positive response too from HP. Please feel free to go ahead.

HP:Here we go.

S L	PARAMETER & ITS' DERIVATIVES	IMPLICATION THEREOF & WHAT IT DOES	WHY PARAMETER & NETI NETI ANALYSIS	TYPE OF PARAMETER & EXAMPLE OF APPLICATION	UNIVERSALITY of PARAMETER
1	God is supreme.	Comprises of six opulences along with supreme independence, free from blemish, Infinite attributes, and qualities, completeness, eternal/imperishable, and controller of all, Himself is not controlled by anybody.

Natural corollary being, His words, actions, decisions, etc. are supreme. | To verify/cross verify the correctness of our understanding/interpretation.

Supposing God is not supreme, the search for supreme whose writ rules begin.

There could be multiple claims of supremacy.

The competent authority will not be known. | This sloka qualifies all other slokas and makes all slokas binding and entire Gita cohesive.

All slokas derive authority from this sloka.

This sloka permeates all other slokas and infuses life into them. As such, it may be termed qualifier parameter | God is supreme and is acceptable to religions of all orders and from all communities.

The derivatives thereof that His words, actions, and the decision are supreme too is not disputed by any religion. |

S L	PARAMETER & ITS' DERIVATIVES	IMPLICATION THEREOF & WHAT IT DOES	WHY PARAMETER & NETI NETI ANALYSIS	TYPE OF PARAMETER & EXAMPLE OF APPLICATION	UNIVERSALITY of PARAMETER
1a	God is supreme. continued	Therefrom is derived from authority, veracity, authenticity, and controlling ability	Social chaos would prevail. Without this parameter, scriptures, incidents, history, instructions, etc. could be misinterpreted or misunderstood. Gita would become infructuous as would other scriptures. The element of conclusiveness or finality would be lacking.	As all slokas owe their existence to this sloka, It can also be termed an Existential parameter. The instance of Krishna running away from the battlefield while fighting with Kalyavan and His apparent failure in peace mission should be seen in the light of the parameter that God is supreme. Otherwise, we tend to misunderstand the Lord as a coward, or a failure.	It cannot be said that God is supreme in Hinduism and not so in Christianity, or Gods words are supreme in holy Quran but not so in Bible, thereby implying that this parameter and its derivatives are universal in implication and application

S L	PARAMETER & ITS' DERIVATIVES	IMPLICATION THEREOF & WHAT IT DOES	WHY PARAMETER & NETI NETI ANALYSIS	TYPE OF PARAMETER & EXAMPLE OF APPLICATION	UNIVERSALITY of PARAMETER
2	There are two types of beings, the perishable, and the imperishable. We may enlarge the scope to non-beings, actions, and non-actions, causes, and effects, etc. including verses in the Gita.	This is an observable phenomenon. Gita comprising of constants and variables, it is imperative that we identify and distinguish between variables and constants. Gita would become static, rigid and not keeping up with changing times and loses relevance. People tend to doubt scriptures and God and tend towards atheism. It is this parameter that separates the chaff from the grain, i.e. truth from untruth, knowledge from ignorance, the changing and unchanging and matter from spirit.	Supposing everything is perishable or everything is imperishable, then this contradicts observable reality. If this weren't a parameter most of the teachings of the Gita or teachings of any scripture become obsolete and irrelevant. People tend to interpret scripture literally, even in the face of evidence to the contrary and figuratively when it should be literally understood	This sloka too permeates all other slokas and qualifies most of the slokas. This may be classified as a qualifier parameter.	Being a statement of the law of nature and observable, it has no religious connotation and is universally applicable. There cannot be different laws of nature depending on religious denomination.

S L	PARAMETER & ITS' DERIVATIVES	IMPLICATION THEREOF & WHAT IT DOES	WHY PARAMETER & NETI NETI ANALYSIS	TYPE OF PARAMETER & EXAMPLE OF APPLICATION	UNIVERSALITY of PARAMETER
2a	This means that there are four entities. The constant, the dependent variable, the independent variable, and independent constant.	A golden mean between scriptural literalism and symbolism with an inherent mechanism to make an intelligent choice between them inter se.	The conclusion thus arrived at makes no sense, but still, bigots stick to their conclusion.	Gita is an address to Arjuna by the Lord, its teachings are not confined or left to Arjuna but inspire generations till date is the best example of Arjuna being a variable in the 'Gita' with each individual substituting himself in place of Arjuna to derive the benefit of understanding the Gita.	The concept of variable and constant breathes relevance and life to any scriptures of any religion and reflects the true spirit and intent of the scripture.

S L	PARAMETER & ITS' DERIVATIVES	IMPLICATION THEREOF & WHAT IT DOES	WHY PARAMETER & NETI NETI ANALYSIS	TYPE OF PARAMETER & EXAMPLE OF APPLICATION	UNIVERSALITY of PARAMETER
3	Gita is complete knowledge. It precludes us from searching answers outside Gita. It underscores the maxim 'Look inward' This is so quoted in Gita itself. Gita is a manifestation of God, inherits Gods' completeness.	Being complete knowledge, consulting other scriptures or persons isn't required. This completeness is achieved by generalization thereby compressing knowledge and making it easy to remember. Gita is summarized as complete knowledge in another sense of it imparting knowledge, a reference to knowledge, and providing a benchmark to evaluate our interpretation of knowledge.	Supposing Gita isn't complete knowledge, Gods' words would become falsehood, which isn't the case. Suppose this isn't a parameter, search for conclusive meaning outside Gita would begin and it would be a never-ending quest. A wild goose chases.	This can be termed a principle-enunciating parameter in view of its articulating non-necessity of referring external scriptures.	This has a universal application. If 'Gita' is substituted with the scripture of any religion, the universality is clearly discernible. That the source of the parameter is Gita should not be forgotten. Pre-requisite is the acceptance of Bhagavad Gita.

S L	PARAMETER & ITS' DERIVATIVES	IMPLICATION THEREOF & WHAT IT DOES	WHY PARAMETER & NETI NETI ANALYSIS	TYPE OF PARAMETER & EXAMPLE OF APPLICATION	UNIVERSALITY of PARAMETER
4	Earth is a prison full of miseries.

Prison, because we have no choice during our stay here.

Miserable because we have to suffer/endure. | Searching for joy in a joyless world is futile. At best, it brings temporary pleasure.

It redirects our focus from earthly adjustments which provide temporary relief to focus on the spirit for permanent relief.

Supposing this weren't a parameter, people would continue hankering after temporary goodies by sacrifices and appeasement to the exclusion of infinite. | Explains the root cause of all afflictions, and a grim reminder to seek a permanent solution, hence taken as a parameter.

Supposing earth is not a prison or is only full of joy, then ..... It belies reality.

Miseries are an experienced reality.

The choice of birth would have been heaven or Gods' abode, not earth. | It is a guiding parameter in view of its guiding nature.

An example is temporary nature of benefit of appeasing gods, spirits, or performance of sacrifices for material gains which would at best provide blessings sought say, wealth, power, progeny, fame, etc. with a shelf life of maximum tenure being your sentence on this earth. | All religions promise heaven, paradise, Shangri-La

Swarg, Jannat or by whatever name it is called.

If earth were to be rosy and joyful, offering those allurements aren't necessarily underscoring the universality of this parameter. |

S L	PARAMETER & ITS' DERIVATIVES	IMPLICATION THEREOF & WHAT IT DOES	WHY PARAMETER & NETI NETI ANALYSIS	TYPE OF PARAMETER & EXAMPLE OF APPLICATION	UNIVERSALITY of PARAMETER
5	Persons commit sins out of their own volition even unwillingly.	This is due to passion. Consequentially, they would have to reap the consequences of cause and effect spanning many lifetimes. The commitment of sin could be voluntary or involuntarily. The voluntary commitment of sin can't be helped as the person is intrinsically sinful. This warning parameter is for potential involuntary sinners	If this weren't true, there wouldn't be a sin. This parameter highlights the consequence of not controlling passion, which makes us do things even if we are unwilling. Also, throws light as to why a person behaving sinfully, even if he is a good person. This parameter flashes a red light to a reluctant potential sinner pinpointing passion as the cause and warns not to be carried away by passion.	This is a guiding principle or a guiding parameter. This is observable in our daily life. A good person makes an occasional mistake which can be attributed to his inability to overcome passion. Emperor Parikshit draping the sage with a dead snake is another example of a good person succumbing to passion.	The voluntary or involuntary nature of the act is not dependent on religion color etc. That passion is the driving force for committing sin is established. This can be seen in books of the statute that distinguish crime caused by passion and those committed in the heat of the moment.

S L	PARAMETER & ITS' DERIVATIVES	IMPLICATION THEREOF & WHAT IT DOES	WHY PARAMETER & NETI NETI ANALYSIS	TYPE OF PARAMETER & EXAMPLE OF APPLICATION	UNIVERSALITY of PARAMETER
6	The three Gunas viz. Sattva, Rajas, and Tamas are ubiquitous and found in all planets and beings.

Not restricted to beings but also actions, thought and results | Most of the slokas are inter-related and acts as a qualifier inter-se between themselves.

The phenomena explained covers a wide gamut of human understanding, encompassing all behavior patterns.

This parameter explains behavioral patterns and reasons therefor.

These slokas explain many phenomena and put facts in perspective thereby removing misunderstandings. | Serves as a key to explain many a phenomenon.

Supposing they aren't threefold gunas, there would also not be any explanation for different behavioral patterns.

The existing psychological paradigm explaining behavior is incomplete and inadequate. | The slokas of three-fold gunas, pervade and qualify all the slokas, making it a qualifier parameter.

Our experience of different persons behaving differently at different times and the same person behaving differently at different times is the best example. | These patterns aren't dependent on religion, race, birth, color, etc.

These values hold good for all times and for all persons and at all places. |

S L	PARAMETER & ITS' DERIVATIVES	IMPLICATION THEREOF & WHAT IT DOES	WHY PARAMETER & NETI NETI ANALYSIS	TYPE OF PARAMETER & EXAMPLE OF APPLICATION	UNIVERSALITY of PARAMETER
7	There are five causes of action accomplishment of results.	Identifies result as a function of the cause of action, and action.

The body, the performer, the senses, the endeavors, and God are the five factors of action.

Some results cannot be attributed to a specific action. | Some of the causes are visible and perceived and some are not. This parameter informs us about those causes and results which are not perceived or not visible.

Suppose this is not taken as a parameter, the imperceptible would have no explanation. | This is a generalization and also a guiding parameter.

Duryodhana had a larger and more capable army but yet lost his life and battle to the smaller army of Pandavas.

The imperceptible is in play, i.e. the divine will, the fifth factor, God. | Every religion believes in miracles. A miracle is an act of God, God being the fifth factor for the accomplishment of actions. |

385

S L	PARAMETER & ITS' DERIVATIVES	IMPLICATION THEREOF & WHAT IT DOES	WHY PARAMETER & NETI NETI ANALYSIS	TYPE OF PARAMETER & EXAMPLE OF APPLICATION	UNIVERSALITY of PARAMETER
8	The concepts of time and space are taken as a parameter. Everyone everywhere is under the influence of time and space except God. The word 'Time' and the word 'Space' has innumerable meanings. Their usage in Gita could mean any of them singly, any combination of them jointly or severally.	The word has been used with each of the different meanings at different times in different slokas thereby defining acceptability of all meanings. Puts things in context or in perspective. Suppose time is understood in one context meaning unit of measurement only, then half the Gita or any of the scriptures wouldn't make any sense.	It is a parameter because of what it does, i.e. puts things in perspective If this is not taken as a parameter, the context, perspective, and other fifty-plus meanings wouldn't be factored and lead erroneous conclusion.	This pervades all slokas and qualifies all other slokas. In view of the same, maybe termed a qualifier parameter. This can also be termed derivative parameter as it derives meaning from the word based on the context used. The story of Onodo Hiro, a World War II veteran of Japan who didn't surrender for 29 years as he was 29 years behind times and 3000 km away in terms of space, is the classic example.	All scriptures have to be interpreted by factoring into account time and space in all its' meanings, irrespective of the religion to which the scripture is ascribed. Failure to do so makes scripture rigid, out of date and out of time and irrelevant. This would lead to people questioning scripture, religion, and God and then drift away from them due to variance with reality solely due to misinterpretation or for not factoring the time and space

S L	PARAMETER & ITS' DERIVATIVES	IMPLICATION THEREOF & WHAT IT DOES	WHY PARAMETER & NETI NETI ANALYSIS	TYPE OF PARAMETER & EXAMPLE OF APPLICATION	UNIVERSALITY of PARAMETER
9	Gita/God attaches much importance to faith. This is taken as a parameter.	Faith implies both faith in self and abilities of self as well as faith in God.	Supposing we don't have faith, then we don't perform that action at all or even if performed, it would be halfhearted.	As it permeates all slokas and qualifies all of the slokas, it is a qualifier parameter.	Faith is prescribed universally by all religions and all communities.
	Opposite of faith is doubt.	Faith in God because, as already seen earlier, God is one of the factors of results of action.		Supposing you don't have faith in Gita, would you read Gita?	Without faith, scripture would be just another form of literature, God would become another charlatan or magician, human being another confused individual.
	Both of them have been dealt with at length in the Gita.		Supposing this isn't a parameter, people won't act or venture at all.		
		Faith makes things considered impossible earlier, possible.	Gita or any scripture would just be a piece of literature with no spiritual consequence.		Religion, commune, or any other body owes its existence to faith verily.

S L	PARAMETER & ITS' DERIVATIVES	IMPLICATION THEREOF & WHAT IT DOES	WHY PARAMETER & NETI NETI ANALYSIS	TYPE OF PARAMETER & EXAMPLE OF APPLICATION	UNIVERSALITY of PARAMETER
1 1	Do unto others as you would have them do unto you. IF we want to do anything to others but are doubtful as to its permissibility, imagine the act is done to you by others. If it is unpalatable to you, It is definitely wrong. On the other hand, if it gives you pleasure or is acceptable, the act is permissible.	This is a benchmark and a sure indicator to judge our actions without bias. It guides us and puts our acts in a proper perspective.	The principle of equity and equality would become wrong if this isn't accepted. If this is not a parameter, people cannot judge for themselves what is permissible and what is not. They will have two sets of values one for themselves and another for others.	This enunciates a principle and also guiding in nature. It is a guiding parameter. The parameter is so fundamental that it doesn't require any example. Examples can be seen in any body's daily life.	The Parameter is a verbatim quote from the Bible, thereby endorsing the universality. It is mentioned in Gita also, albeit in different words. That this is an observable fact underscores the universality of this parameter.

S L	PARAMETER & ITS' DERIVATIVES	IMPLICATION THEREOF & WHAT IT DOES	WHY PARAMETER & NETI NETI ANALYSIS	TYPE OF PARAMETER & EXAMPLE OF APPLICATION	UNIVERSALITY of PARAMETER
1 2	Knowledge of minute details of everything is not necessary unless it is for a specific purpose or required specifically.	Overview or general knowledge is sufficient in most of the cases. In Gods' words, 'What use of knowing all details', meaning it serves no useful purpose. All cannot have all knowledge, God Himself being a source of and giver of knowledge, What has been given by Him to any individual is all that will be ever required for him.	If this isn't a parameter, people would be pursuing the unimportant things deviating from the pursuit of important.	As this is derived from Gods' words, this is a derived parameter. You own a car, knowledge of driving and important functions of parts is necessary, knowledge of manufacturing cars is not required.	Universally applicable and observable but unaware of reference or mention in any other scriptures.

S L	PARAMETER & ITS' DERIVATIVES	IMPLICATION THEREOF & WHAT IT DOES	WHY PARAMETER & NETI NETI ANALYSIS	TYPE OF PARAMETER & EXAMPLE OF APPLICATION	UNIVERSALITY of PARAMETER
1 3	Mind and its evolutes as a parameter. Derived from the Sloka, the Mind is both a friend and an enemy of self.	A mind is a form of material energy. If you put it to positive use, it is a friend, else an enemy. The mind is a field of activity, if the activity is positive, so is the result. The mind is a tool to kill lust. IF unused, lust overcomes you with attendant consequences. The mind is the residence of desire. Controlling desire through mind makes it a friend. The mind is one of the performers of action, results depending on the type of action performed.	It provides an explanation as to many connotations of mind and its properties and usages. The single key to many problems. The importance of mind can be gauged from the fact that that many verses are devoted to how to control the mind.	Maybe termed guiding parameter. The case study of sage Vishwamitra is the best example.	Effects noticeable universally. We have great personages in all religions who controlled their minds and achieved success.

390

S L	PARAMETER & ITS' DERIVATIVES	IMPLICATION THEREOF & WHAT IT DOES	WHY PARAMETER & NETI NETI ANALYSIS	TYPE OF PARAMETER & EXAMPLE OF APPLICATION	UNIVERSALITY of PARAMETER
1 3 A		The mind is a sense organ through which sense objects are enjoyed. All activities or recreation or work should be tempered with moderation.	If the mind is not controlled, a person is ruined.	The results of the exercise of control over mind and his achievements in the end as compared to his earlier lack of control over mind and losing of spiritual merit are an illuminating example	

S L	PARAMETER & ITS' DERIVATIVES	IMPLICATION THEREOF & WHAT IT DOES	WHY PARAMETER & NETI NETI ANALYSIS	TYPE OF PARAMETER & EXAMPLE OF APPLICATION	UNIVERSALITY of PARAMETER
1 4	Brooding causes eventual downfall.	Sets a chain of events culminating in downfall.	Makes imaginary appear real.	This too is a guiding parameter.	Observable and experiential. It doesn't distinguish between rich or poor, Hindu or Muslim, Indian and American.
	Closely interrelated with 'Mind is a friend as well as an enemy'	Cause of most of the problems being faced.	Supposing this isn't a parameter, people would believe what they think, not what is real, or truth.	The loss of the mental balance of King Kansa, the maternal uncle of Lord Krishna is the best example.	
		Closely interrelated with the mind as a friend and an enemy.		He was always ruminating on his impending death and had literal nightmares.	
		De-focus from negative, imaginary and probable and focus on positive, real and present.			

S L	PARAMETER & ITS' DERIVATIVES	IMPLICATION THEREOF & WHAT IT DOES	WHY PARAMETER & NETI NETI ANALYSIS	TYPE OF PARAMETER & EXAMPLE OF APPLICATION	UNIVERSALITY of PARAMETER
1 5	Knowledge of the purpose of the action is better than knowledge itself.	Blindly following rituals as all in all not recommended. Path (rituals) is being mistaken as piety, spirituality, and endearing to God.	Recommends knowing the purpose of action/ritual before performing ritual/action. Rituals may be modified or dispensed with if the purpose is otherwise served. If not a parameter, people will blindly follow rituals even when it has outlived its utility and has become an exploitation tool.	A guiding parameter. If a ritual is mandatory, non-performance of which sin accrues, it doesn't explain the effects of nonperformance of rituals of other religionists or other communities. If it is confined to only one community, then it isn't universal and is not binding on all persons.	The universality can be tested by speaking to a few adherents of any religion and questioning the significance of any ritual being performed.

393

S L	PARAMETER & ITS' DERIVATIVES	IMPLICATION THEREOF & WHAT IT DOES	WHY PARAMETER & NETI NETI ANALYSIS	TYPE OF PARAMETER & EXAMPLE OF APPLICATION	UNIVERSALITY of PARAMETER
16	The mere mention in scriptures doesn't make it sacrosanct unless backed by relevance, appropriateness observable and practical.	Scriptures could be correct, but the commonly held interpretation of scripture is wrong.	So as to remind people who cling to scriptures verbatim even in the face of evidence of its unrealistic nature.	This is a derived parameter. This also gives the stamp of conclusion.	Best verified on a cross-section of society with subjects varying from differing faiths, community, country, and race.
	That an act or ritual is practical and results are observable by itself doesn't make it spiritual.	Constraints of time, place and circumstances are not factored and blind faith is reposed in scriptures.	Supposing this isn't a parameter, people tend to rely on their interpretation of scriptures even in the face of its impracticality.	Human and animal sacrifice, crusades, jihad, etc. all would get legitimacy on the strength of its mention in scripture, overlooking the perspective, context and appropriateness inbuilt in the scripture.	
	This is derived from the previous parameter.				

S L	PARAMETER & ITS' DERIVATIVES	IMPLICATION THEREOF & WHAT IT DOES	WHY PARAMETER & NETI NETI ANALYSIS	TYPE OF PARAMETER & EXAMPLE OF APPLICATION	UNIVERSALITY of PARAMETER
1 7	God is one. This fact remains, irrespective of Him being addressed by any name, visualized in any form, or prayed in any way.	The myth of his god, her god my god their god is dispelled. The misconception of the superiority of one's god over others' god is removed God is identified by His qualities etc. This is universally acceptable in all religions.	When our supposedly different Gods have the same qualities, which must necessarily be the prerogative of just one person, the inescapable conclusion is that God is one.	Guiding parameter and also a conclusive parameter. Everybody irrespective of his denomination accepts God is one but errs in that his god is that one. Hanuman and Jambavan could see their Lord in the form of Rama in Krishna.	His identity is not decided by His name, form, looks, country, race, or other considerations.

S L	PARAMETER & ITS' DERIVATIVES	IMPLICATION THEREOF & WHAT IT DOES	WHY PARAMETER & NETI NETI ANALYSIS	TYPE OF PARAMETER & EXAMPLE OF APPLICATION	UNIVERSALITY of PARAMETER
1 8	God's answers to prayer are both specific and general as also personalized and customized or universal. It is not one size fits all. It is a generalization not restricted to tangible or mundane answers.	Answers to prayer can be Underscoring belief in a particular form or formlessness of God, method of worship, type of prayer, etc. Fulfillment of desires, both expressed and unexpressed. Bestowing what is sought. Non-fulfillment of a desire not necessarily be non-conducive to your welfare. Strengthening your existing belief. The underlying beauty being each thinking that only his contention is Correct.	Supposing this wasn't a parameter, we cannot make out that God is responding to our prayers as His response could be contrary to desires but conducive to our welfare. Without this parameter, there would be no explanation for the existence of multiple beliefs of different devotees, each conflicting with one another yet subsuming it within the absolute with ease and elan.	This is a derived parameter. The best example or analogy is the Lord dancing with all His paramours simultaneously and each laboring under the impression that the Lord is hers, which is the truth but only part truth.	Observable reality.

S L	PARAMETER & ITS' DERIVATIVES	IMPLICATION THEREOF & WHAT IT DOES	WHY PARAMETER & NETI NETI ANALYSIS	TYPE OF PARAMETER & EXAMPLE OF APPLICATION	UNIVERSALITY of PARAMETER
1 9	Gita is a study of cause and effect. Entire Gita is a cause-effect analysis. .	Karma Yoga is the prime stone of cause-and-effect analysis. It delineates what action produces what type of results. So does the other three yoga of Bhakti, Dhyana, and Gyana to a limited extent.	Self-explanatory as to why a parameter.	Guiding parameter. Application in any sphere at both the individual level and collective level.	Other scriptures have cause and effect incorporate within itself in varying degrees.

There could be many other parameters, which I may have overlooked. This is the broad concept of parameters mooted by me.

TG: Today's presentation is just a repetition of daily discussion in summarized form. Nothing new has been added barring a few exceptions.

HP: The individual parameters mentioned here are a summarization which is an essential component of any debate/presentation. But my friend failed to notice the reasons adduced for it being a parameter, identification of type, test of universality, and test with negative supposition all of which is logically presented. I would be failing in my duty and also lacking in courtesy if I don't give credit to my friend, who proposed this structured format.

Scrutinizing this with Neti, Neti if this format weren't proposed by TG, many important aspects would have been bypassed or left out. She brought out the best in me.

TG: My friend has only given examples of each parameter but not examples of application in respect of many parameters.

HP: I apologize for my lapse. I will rectify the same.

Prof: HP, it is a bit late now. We may infer applications without much effort. Today is the final day, your friend too should be given an opportunity to have her say. TG, do you have anything to say?

TG: A few parameters are not universal or even if universal, it is not so proved.

HP: Which of the parameters are you referring to?

TG: Quite a few like
- Gita is complete knowledge.
  - o Gita may be complete knowledge but what about other scriptures?
- Sattva, Rajas, and Tamas.
  - o There is no mention of it in other scriptures.
- Mind and its evolutes.
  - o Not mentioned in other scriptures.
- Knowledge of the purpose of action more important than action.
  - o Other scriptures don't mention it.

HP: The main reason for non-acceptance of scriptures of denominations other than the one to which we belong is inbuilt mental blocks. Adherents of Gita/Sanatana Dharma, too are not exempt from this.

I offer a simple practical check to find out universal applicability.
- o God is the greatest and is accepted in all religions. His words are supreme too holds good for all religions. His words cannot be

modified, altered or superimposed with others words too find acceptance amongst all religions.

o Forget that the parameters are Krishna's words. Forget that it occurs in Gita. Take a parameter on its' own. Does it apply to adherents of Christianity, Jainism, Buddhists, Muslims, and other religionists?

o The answer should be and is always affirmative.

  • Mention or non-mention is not the criteria. It is always mentioned or implied or observable reality or traditional or customized.

IC: I have a suggestion. Let HP defend her parameters by testing them on anyone commentaries of all four Acharyas on any sloka. The parameters would be tested as well as the commentaries. The truth would come out.

Prof: The court dismisses the plea. The parameters are the subject matter of debate and in dispute and not the commentaries. IT is already decided what subjects can be discussed and persons who may participate and who are precluded. You figure in the persons in the precluded list unless you have a stake, which isn't the case presently, hence disallowed. TG, you may proceed with your presentation or defense.

TG: You say that there are five types of sentences found in the Gita. Further, you claim that parameters are mainly applicable to imperative statements. It means that you are ignoring/belittling the other four types of slokas. If other slokas are unimportant, God wouldn't have spoken them. You are highlighting parameter slokas and undermining other slokas. When more than half of what God said is relegated to the background, it means other slokas are useless and discarded by you. We may also infer your ignorance of those slokas because of your omission.

HP: The other slokas are not to be viewed as parameters but viewed differently. My knowledge or ignorance isn't the subject matter of this debate. You may convene another session for determining the same.

Prof: Your inferences are farfetched and not based on logic. Don't bring personalities into the proceedings. HP, Court is not interested in your knowledge or ignorance. The court will not entertain frivolous petitions. Do continue keeping this in mind.

TG: Sir, I have nothing new to present. My arguments/objections were put forth as and when needed daily during the course of the debate. I would be doing the very thing I objected by repeating my objections in the form of a summary. I bring to your notice:The parameter concept is fictional creation not supported by scriptures.

  • ALL concepts put forth are speculations and concoctions not backed by authority.

  • She has taken the literary/poetic license a bit too far.

  • Similarly, the extrapolation tool has been used indiscriminately.

- These acts diminish reverence and make the divine promiscuous/licentious.
- The premise on which all her arguments rest is itself not proved. Hence all her arguments, as well as conclusions, may be dismissed.
- Regarding charges of blasphemy and other charges against her person, we may extend the benefit of the doubt, as her intentions are honorable and integrity unquestionable. Her presentations betray her honesty.

I congratulate her on her spirited arguments. I thank her for the courtesies extended and request her to ignore my entire diatribe against her, which were purely professional and not to be carried beyond the threshold of this hall.

HP: What is the premise which is not proved and on which all arguments rest?

TG: Gita is non-different from God is the premise on which most of your arguments rest.

HP: God and His words are non-different. Hence, Gita is non-different. Gita is the soul of the Lord and Lord is the soul of the Gita. You cannot segregate one from another. I have made a pitch by narrating a story of devotee erasing a few lines from Gita which was reflected on the body of God. I think that parable suffices as proof.

Regarding my friend's justification for her tactics, I bear no ill will. The real-world arena too doesn't have players with kids' gloves and my friend has played her part remarkably well.

I too thank her for her magnanimity in upholding my honesty and integrity. May the best person win!

Before the conclusion, I wish to reply to her arguments.
- Parameters are fiction not supported by scriptures & concepts put forth are speculation.
    - Parameters are all drawn from Gita or derived from Gita, debunking the argument that it is fiction.
    - Her contention could be that it is not stated that it is a parameter. This can be inferred, and also crosschecked.
- She has taken the literary/poetic license a bit too far.
    - The entire proceedings were either judicial or quasi-judicial and not a literary festival with no scope for taking liberties or license more so under the hawk eye of the plaintiff/prosecutor and the learned Honorable judge.The extrapolation tool has been used indiscriminately.
    - It is acceptable in all fields both mundane and spiritual. A tool is a useful implement. How you put to use is your discretion. All the commentaries on Gita, including those referred to by my friends have used extrapolation tools extensively. Without extrapolation,

the entire Gita would be static and confined to repeating of the 700 slokas verbatim and close the door to newer possibilities and also makes it irrelevant.

- These acts diminish reverence and make the divine promiscuous/licentious.
    o The reverence is based on the individual concerned and, in this case, it is myself. I have not, repeat HAVE NOT disrespected or diminished any scripture, preceptor/saints, religion, God, community or their scripture leave alone Gita, which I hold very dear. Will I disrespect my own soul?

I thank the professor and my friends on both sides of the camp and also other onlookers. Special thanks are due to my friend Christina, who mooted and made this debate possible and who stood by me in thick and thin.

Prof: Does anyone else want to voice their opinion, or summarize the proceedings or give concluding remarks? There could be other perspectives waiting to be discovered and disseminated.

KA: If you permit me, I have certain observations. It is not about the perspectives but about the proceedings.

Prof: Go ahead.

KA: Scriptures aren't to be interpreted. This is a consensual opinion. My friend has said that her views are new and different. She has also stated that each Acharya interprets Gita but claims that they don't interpret it but simplify the same and is faithful to the original. But at the end of the day, I find that we have one more interpretation on our hands without any of us getting any wiser. I find her say another method of interpretation. Secondly, I find that HP has been given free rein but TG hasn't been given an opportunity to put forth her say.

Thirdly, I am a staunch believer of my system of faith and would not become a turncoat abandoning my faith in preference to unsubstantiated theories.

Prof: Consults a dictionary and says that interpretation has been defined differently as

- Explain the meaning of
- Understand as having a particular meaning
- To describe the meaning of something
- Examine, in order to explain
- To decide what is the intended meaning of something.

While Anushka takes it to mean the first two mentioned, the general rule that scriptures should not be interpreted is to be understood in the sense as mentioned in the last-mentioned definition. It is a classic case of interpretation. Everybody laughs. Regarding her charge that TG wasn't given equal opportunity to present her case, it is not true.

In fact, the session began with her presenting BG: 4.34. Her say wasn't contested at all, thereby not requiring a further presentation.

She hasn't lost any opportunity to attack HP both fairly and unfairly and cannot claim not to have been given equal chance. She is the complainant/plaintiff. HP, on the other hand, is the defendant and had to fight her way at each step. When TG and friends wanted to present something, they were asked to summarize the same.

The reasons for it are what they presented is already presented by their seers in a far better/effective way than they could ever hope to. Secondly, the say of TG and friends were not in dispute and outside the scope of this court. This court wasn't approached with a complaint against TG and her speak. In fact, an observant person would have noticed that the stacks were against HP and heavily in favor of TG. HP needn't have defended herself. She could have asked TG to prove her guilt as the court goes by maxim "Innocent till proved guilty"

Prof: Any more opinions/dissents?

AB: I seek permission to put forth my view.

Prof: Please go ahead.

AB: We are all students of law. I have some perspectives from the lawyers' point of view. Every denomination claims that they are faithful to the Lord's words and they do not interpret. But this isn't true. Because the viewpoint of each is different.

Each person explains the meaning differently because a word could have many meanings. So far, it is good. But when the intended meaning is put forth, this is in contravention of what the seers said "don't interpret"

In our daily life, interpretation becomes inevitable. Statutory interpretation is the process by which courts interpret and apply legislation. Judges DO NOT make law.

They only interpret, that too when the situation so warrants. Similarly, we do not make laws. Divine law exists. Seers only interpret. Some amount of interpretation becomes essential when a case involves a statute. Sometimes the words of a statute have a plain and straightforward meaning. But in many cases, there is some ambiguity or vagueness in the words of the statute that must be resolved by the judge. Here too, the interpretation cannot be as per the whims and fancies of the judge. It should be as per the rules of interpretation.

To find the meanings of statutes, judges use various tools and methods. The judiciary may apply rules of statutory interpretation.

Literal rule.

Considers what the statute actually says, rather than what it might mean. Here the words in the statute are taken to mean literally what is said, that is, their plain ordinary everyday meaning, even if the effect of this might be considered unjust or undesirable. This is so because it is the duty of parliament to make laws and not in the domain of the court. If court interferes, it is interfering with the will of the people.

Golden rule.

According to this rule, if the literal interpretation produces an absurdity, then the court should look for different meanings which makes sense so as to avoid absurd results. The grammatical and ordinary sense of the words is to be adhered to unless that would lead to some absurdity or some repugnance or inconsistency, in which case the grammatical and ordinary sense of the words may be modified so as to avoid the absurdity and inconsistency, to that extent.

Mischief rule.

This rule gives the court more discretion. Under this rule, the court looks to what the law was before the statute was passed and find what lacunae /mischief the statute intended to address.

The court thereafter interprets the statute in such a way to ensure that such mischief/gap is addressed/covered.

Purposive approach.

This approach is of recent origin. Here the court looks into what the lawmakers meant rather than what is stated. This could be due to resultant absurdity or defeating the very purpose for which the law was enacted.

- In all cases, the court makes statutory constructions. This is made with certain presumptions. These presumptions are
- A statute is presumed to make no changes in the common law.
- A statute is presumed not to remove an individual's liberty, vested rights, or property.
- A statute is presumed not to apply to the Crown.
- A statute is presumed not to apply retrospectively.
- A statute is to be interpreted so as to uphold international treaties.
- It is presumed that a statute will be interpreted such that words are to be construed in sympathy with their immediate context.
- Where legislation and case law is in conflict, there is a presumption that legislation takes precedence over case law.

The entire debate is within the confines of juristic interpretation. Just like legislation is supreme, Gods' words have been accorded supremacy. The interpretations made there too are within the rules of acceptability and do not violate any legal rules.

The interpretations, whenever made is to give effect to God's words or either to remove absurdities as a result of wrong understanding or to make it pragmatic/enforceable.

In fact, the level of legal adherence herein is far more than that of any commentaries I have come across. The interpretations made stand the test of time.

Unlike in jurisprudence, the rules of construction/interpretation which are external to statute, here the parameters are a part of the Gita, thereby giving it authority and authenticity.

I am not qualified to comment on the scriptural /philosophical point of view. From a legal standpoint, I give 100% marks. HP has more than proved her case and established her innocence.

Prof: Nice observations. The last line is expunged from records. Don't usurp judicial powers. Anybody else wants to put forth their views?

HM: I am a Christian. Am I allowed to express my views?

Prof: When were you debarred/prevented? Only non-believers were debarred from debate or voting. Even they can put forth their view, which will not be taken for arriving at concluding judgment. Please proceed.

HM: My friend has given a legal perspective. As a student of inter-religious studies, I wish to share a scriptural perspective. Biblical hermeneutics is the study of the principles of interpretation concerning the books of the Bible. It is part of the broader field of hermeneutics which involves the study of principles of interpretation for all forms of communication, nonverbal and verbal. Verbal communication includes sounds, words, or speaking. The tone of voice, volume, and pitch qualify the sound or word or speech.

Nonverbal communication includes gestures, facial expressions, body movement, timing, touch, and anything else done without speaking. While interpreting scriptures, the following rules of interpretation should be kept in mind.

- Identify the kind of literature your text is to get insight into its meaning. It may take the form of narrative, prophecy, poetry, history, gospel, epistle, etc. In spite of differences, we may recognize the form of narration and how it affects meaning.
- Context is considered the first and foremost principle for accurate interpretation. Carefully consider the context of the passage for a better

understanding of its meaning. Clues in the surrounding verses may shed light on meanings, which we may miss out on.

- Prefer the plain and obvious meaning of the text first before jumping into symbolic or figurative meaning.
- Try to discern the original author's intentions when he wrote/spoke the words.
- God-centered perspective is the best form of interpretation.

Principles of interpretation.

A few Latin expressions summarize the Principles.

- Sola Scriptura, meaning "Scripture alone" Scriptures provide the only infallible information and perfect rules.
- Scriptura Scripturae interpres, meaning "Scripture interprets Scripture". The best way to understand a passage is to see how the rest of Scripture fits with it and clarifies it.
- Omnis intellectus ac expositio Scripturae sit analogia fidei, meaning "all understanding and exposition of Scripture is but an analogy of faith".

John Cassian, a monk of ancient days identified four ways in which the Bible could be understood. The literal, the symbolic, the ethical, and the mystical.

- The literal approach suggests taking texts at face value, without considering the hidden or symbolic meanings. It means that texts should be read in a historical sense because it deals with actual events, actual people, and actual statements.
- The symbolic method suggests studying text as an allegorical or typological way, and not as it appears. This type of interpretation is widely used and popular.
- A third way, the Ethical way of interpreting scriptures is to look for an ethical/moral meaning. It involves reading between the lines and see how it applies to daily life. The essence is found by putting forward the question, what is this verse trying to teach?
- The Mystical method of interpretation unravels mystical meaning within the texts, not so apparent on the face of it. This could be by way of using coded language.
- Another commonly used method is to distinguish between the letter and the spirit of the verses and opt for the one which is felt to be more meaningful.

Although these rules and principles were formulated for studying of the Bible, it holds valid for any scripture. This is an observable fact.

My friend HP has covered most of these points. She has also provided a missing link.

These principles and rules were external to scriptures, meaning they were authored by someone other than God, could be devotees, divine beings, etc.

This would give it a secondary status and rightfully so as the prime status would be to the word of God. This would also tantamount to mortal framing rules for interpreting the immortal. My friend has given the legitimacy and primacy to these rules/principles by attributing these to God. It is obvious by now that these rules and principles transcend all bars of religion, race country, gender, etc.

Another point of observation is the rules and principles are both subject and object of study, meaning Gita is used to reading, understand, and interpret Gita. For example, the study of the Bible requires the study of hermeneutics as a pre-requisite for the grasping spirit of the Bible apart from studying the Bible. Simply stated, the study of the Bible is separate from the study of Bible interpretation. My friend has shown that this is not so in the case of the Gita.

This is my Eureka moment. As God's words are infallible, the Bible could have inbuilt interpretation clauses and methods. My mission is fulfilled.

The purpose of my journey to India is fulfilled in a spiritual context. In the academic context, my research and thesis centered on this aspect and would conclude with the acceptance of my submission. I thank HP for her insights and showing me the path.

Prof: Any other speaker?

QC: I seek permission to give my perspective as a student of Management.

Prof: Go ahead, Sheila.

QC: Gita is a vast subject. A veritable treasure mine. The entire discussions have revolved around interpretation. All other topics like Moksha, Yoga, Duty, and Sacrifice, etc. which form the edifice of Gita is either ignored or dealt with in a very perfunctory manner. Giving due credit where it is due, the approach is both creative and original. Going further, it is pioneering, but that does not remedy the fact of ignoring 95% of the Gita and harping only on the interpretation part.

HP: The points of difference and divergence of approaches were focused to the exclusion of others. Please tell me the broad areas which have been excluded.

QC:
- Discussions on the soul as narrated in the Gita.
- Secrets and confidential matters expounded in the Gita.
- Whether Moksha is a state of mind or an abode?
- Elaborate and compare verses in support of Dwaita, Adwaita, and Visisht Dwaita.
- Yoga as envisaged in the Gita.
- Refuge in Him, a panacea for all ills, mundane or otherwise.
- Gita on the mind.

- Same words used in Gita with differing meanings at different places.
- Different words having the same meaning in the Gita.
- Pursuing research on loose ends.
- Detailing types of statements in the Gita, i.e. Declarative, Interrogative, Optative, etc.

HP: Now my friend has put forth another nine propositions to discuss. Again, the views of all of us on the same would not be consensual. We will take up the same if the professor permits us.

Prof:Nice observation, but the ignored 95% has been propagated, studied, discussed, and commented upon since time immemorial giving it 99% coverage. The non-ignored 5% is taken up here with 95% focus remedying the historical neglect.

- It must be noted that being a pioneering effort as rightly pointed out by QC, this unexplored territory offers infinite possibilities of exploration and discoveries.
- The interpretation being a quantum level phenomenon, it is more effective, long-lasting and all-pervasive.
- This approach is inclusive, unifying and this unifying nature and inclusiveness can be beheld and experienced.

Regarding the new propositions put forth, I am afraid it is not possible now due to academic pre-occupations. In a lighter vein first, create a controversy and then approach the court, what do you say?

Prof: Anybody wants to voice their opinion?

PK: I may be permitted to voice my opinion.

Prof: Go ahead, but it will not be considered whilst arriving at a verdict.

PK: The entire debate rests on the premise that Krishna is God and Gita are His words. When the premise itself is faulty, the conclusions are bound to be faulty.

IF and AB:On the second day, HP had in course of the debate said that she would test and analyze her paradigm with any existing version of commentary or purport of Gita. The professor disallowing this restricts expression of our opinions.

Prof: IF and PK, this isn't the forum to put forth your view, as your views/ideology isn't the subject matter. Hence, I had precluded all of you from the debate. Your point is noted. Please sit down. Nevertheless, I thank PK and IF for her contribution. Any further addition from anybody?

SILENCE

Prof: Good summation by all. Summation of TG bereft of ill will, which is in the proper spirit. I thank all of you. Christina will give me a copy of the proceedings by tomorrow evening. We will meet again on Sunday at 4 PM. The date was so selected so as to coincide with the declaration of academic results and campus selections. Good evening. Saying thus, he strode off.

Everybody left the hall. Christina increased her strides so as to catch up with HP. They walked towards Christina's room. They both sat down to converse.

CH: Your summary was good but not as forceful or compelling as your previous presentation.

HP: Yes, we have limited scope in summary, because we would already have put forth all our points. Besides, we can't hold the Centre stage every day.

CH: TG's changed tactics and display of bonhomie and warmth is a bit puzzling.

HP: I suppose she was under the grip of the attack of sattva.

CH: Or it could be the realization of a battle lost and making best out of the bad bargain.

HP: Could be, couldn't be, also because it is premature to predict the verdict which may go either way.

CH: You harbor doubts even now?

HP: I am clear and without doubts within myself. But the deciding authority may perceive it differently, and not without justification. Truth and my opinion don't alter and is independent of the verdict or anything external.

CH: Why did the professor disallow IC's suggestion?

HP: Vinodini didn't have a genuine doubt or real quest to unravel the truth. She was attempting to foment dissent between believers of a different denomination. The professor saw through her game and hence disallowed debate. The professor is incorruptible.

He neither fears nor favors. Did you notice, not a single believer, meaning GG group sided with IF and PK? GG group is heterogeneous and consists of persons practicing different religions, but believing in their version of God. The non-believers need not have joined the group nor need they have joined the debate.

CH: Nice explanation, but my doubt persists. Why can't we employ the parameter for testing when the very function of a parameter is testing?

HP: The commentators were seers having seen God and experienced the truths first hand. The commentaries are a narration of their experiences during intense communion. Communion can't happen without purity and selflessness. Compare that with me, where do I stand? I am a conditioned soul with material contamination, which would be partly inherited by my works.

Next, there are many basic units of measure. The unit used for measuring mass is KG, unit of measuring time is second, and the unit of measuring distance is meter and so on. We can't use the same unit or the same tool for measuring substances of a different nature. Can the rules of baseball be used for football? It is something like that.

Another reason for disallowing IC is that the existing commentaries and works focus on verbal communications/skills, meaning the words and syntax completely ignoring nonverbal communication. Our Parameter paradigm focuses mainly on nonverbal cognitive skills with emphasis on reasoning and higher reasoning and metacognitive learning.

You cannot pass judgments on conclusions/hypotheses derived from verbal communication with conclusions arrived at from using non-verbal communication skills. You can at best correlate hypothesis/conclusion derived from verbal skills with nonverbal skills and vice versa.

CH: Would you elaborate?

HP: Besides other skill sets, category formation, and pattern recognition form an important part of cognitive skills. The foundation of our paradigm itself rests on these two skills. Here neither categorization nor pattern recognition means just simile or analogy or just what is stated. It also includes patterns in text/verses. **Logic pattern** deals with the characteristics of various objects and sequences of objects and a **pattern** in the attributes of the objects.

Logical reasoning involves identifying and interpreting patterns, sequences, and relationships inter-see themselves.

You may also observe that we have taken into consideration para-language i.e., the tone, pitch, and gestures accompanying the delivery. We have also considered proxemics or the corporeal, spiritual, and psychological proximity of the communicator with the subject.

CH: What is meta-cognitive learning?

HP: Meta-cognition is cognition about cognition, thinking about thinking, knowing about knowing, aware about awareness. Simply stated, it is higher-order thinking skills, where Meta means beyond.

CH: Can you give an example with reference to our debate?

HP: We have at the very commencement advocated learning Gita through Gita, knowing Gita through Gita and unraveling a higher dimension in Gita through Gita. Can you recognize the pattern enumerated in metacognition in our paradigm of Gita through Gita? It already existed in the Gita.

We have merely categorized as verbal and non-verbal and identified patterns mentioned in metacognition present in the Gita and harnessed/leveraged it for the benefit of mankind.

CH: So, what is the conclusion?

HP: Take the wisdom of all best suited to you. View their person as representative of God and their works as the wisdom of God in a proper perspective and leave the rest to God.

On the other side, the DR group and others had assembled in TG's room. The discussion was on the following lines.

KA: So, the debate has concluded.

TG: What do you think?

AB: It was both a learning experience and an entertaining experience.

TG: No, I mean about the verdict.

SD: We have done our job. Leave the rest to Providence.

SD: You too have cornered her number of times when her replies were mere silence.

SA: What do you think of the results?

AG: Going by juristic prudence, HP will win hands down.

TG: And?

QC: Going by scriptural injunctions, we are in an advantageous position. It all depends on the professor's line of thinking. He is a combination of both legal ingenuity and scriptural nuances.

SD: His conscience will not allow him to decide either way.

PH: You are partly correct. His conscience will not allow bias, but it would also not allow him to digress from duty. It was a truth-finding exercise. I still think it is possible that we win.

KA: Either way, we will move forward and leave behind the bitter past.

TG: Why bitter? I enjoyed the proceedings thoroughly.

KD: Yes, we were enriched.

PD: We gathered new insights, learned to untie new legal knots.

TS: Will the Gita group be disbanded?

PH: Yes, I suppose so. The WhatsApp group may continue.

PD: That would keep us all in touch with each other and also HP and CH.

SD & TG:The rivalry existed only within the confines of debate. There is no room for it in life.

KA: You have truly spoken.

TS: What are your plans?

TG: I will pursue a doctorate with a specialization in legislation and interpretation of the statute.

PD: HP bug has bitten you. It is like sage Vishwamitra pursuing spiritual power after seeing its supremacy over military might.

TG: Possibly, but it would combine learning with pleasure.

They all planned a trip to Horsley hills, before the verdict day. KA suggested that they invite HP and CH but was informed by SD that they were unavailable due to their plans to visit Dwarka and Kurukshetra. KA and TG thanked all of them for their unstinted support and pledged lifelong friendship with all of them. With this, they bade each other goodnight and left.

BOOK - III

29. PRE-VERDICT

Christina and HP were having mixed feelings. Was it their victory? They couldn't tell. They couldn't wait for the judgment day. Christina reminded HP of her promise to accompany her on tour to Kolhapur and other places. They decided to proceed next week and accordingly made their bookings.

They all assembled in the canteen and were animatedly discussing the possible outcomes. DR group was reconciled to defeat although KA and TG were still hopeful of salvaging their reputation. The DB group were angry with DR group for frittering away an opportunity on the last day and also nursed a grudge against the professor for disallowing suggestion from IC. The NA group enjoyed the entire proceedings each day. It was like a play in a theatre group. Many of them changed their attitude towards scriptures and rituals and religious practices from one of indifference to a reverent onlooker.

There was a knock and in walked professor.

Prof: May I join you, just as an observer, I will not join the proceedings, will just be a witness.

Everybody chorused, welcome Sir, it is our privilege. Why do you need our permission?

Prof: Smiling mischievously, because Guru is not needed. Self-learning is possible without the Guru, isn't it?

HP started sobbing. Everybody inquired about the reason and tried to console her. After a few minutes, HP composes herself and replies, I respect the professor and put him on a high pedestal next to God and he misunderstood me. She sobs again.

Prof: See, you put me on a high pedestal. It is difficult to play God. Everybody prays, and expect their prayers to be answered positively and instantly irrespective of the fact of their deserving it or not and whether their prayer is sincere or not.

They treat God intimately and with familiarity and when God reciprocates with the same familiarity which comes with certain privileges they misunderstand and blame god and cry.

HP: Sir, you mean you were joking?

Prof: You are wise enough to expound on Gita but stupid enough not to understand your professor.

HP with all smiles apologizes to the professor who brushes away her apologies. The professor treated everybody with Cake and Ice cream.

The professor interacted with all students in an informal atmosphere. He solicited their opinion. Everybody was unanimous that the debate was gripping and thought-provoking. About the victor, they were divided. Many of them gave thumbs up to HP. A very few sided with TG. Their opinions transcended their affiliations. Some of the students expressed their regret for not having actively participated in the debate and wished or another chance. They didn't expect such interesting twists and turns when the subject was Bhagwad Gita.

All the students asked the professor for his take on the Gita. He asked them to wait until he pronounces his verdict. They clarified that they wanted his opinion on the Gita as a message to his students, and not about the debate. He said, well here are some key takeaways.

God shoulders the responsibility of your attaining to Him, no matter what your birth, gender, caste, religion, nationality, race, etc. This is irrespective of your past; you can always start afresh. If you fix your mind on Him exclusively, subordinating your intellect to His words, you may merge into Him. You needn't make separate endeavors or perform special duties or sacrifice if you are surrendered unto Him.

You will be purged of your sins and reside in Him. This is His Divine guarantee. These are found in slokas 5.5, 9.30 to 9.32, 12.8, and 18.66.

He said that the earth is a prison analogy presented although true appears negative and finds favor only amongst the senior citizens.

The analogy of earth as Lab to experiment with the truths of Gita in our daily lives is a better analogy. This way, they would experience the truth of God's words first hand and would be more relishable and enjoyable.

God has reconciled and shown means of reconciling different viewpoints on any common subject and this is contained in Uddhava Gita 16.5 to 16.9. Briefly, the difference of opinion held by philosophers and the claim of superiority of their say over the say of others is a manifestation of the play of God's Maya. This arises due to the interaction of different perspectives emanating from me. Those who have controlled their minds and senses can perceive the unitary nature of my manifestations, thereby eliminating the causes of disagreement. The conclusions of all philosophers are acceptable to Me (God), as they have a convincing and logical explanation.

He had a message for the antagonists too. Recognizing the difficulty in changing ingrained opinions, he suggested that they stop viewing the same from the prism of religion/spirituality/political affiliation and view the same as an academic, logical legal and literary and intellectual exercise. By this one piece of advice, he conquered the hearts of his students with deviant views.

He asked if anybody was willing to summarise the entire philosophy as discussed including the proceedings that took place informally at the hostel campus. Suma volunteered to do the same. She said that she has made contributions to Wiki

Summary by adding summaries of two of her favorite books. The professor nodded approvingly.

The professor noted all their feelings. He made a mental note of the regrets expressed by non-participants. He was inwardly wondering how he could rectify the situation, now that the debate was over. Christina had already delivered the transcript.

The professor had scheduled reading it for next week. He was otherwise busy with the forthcoming seminar necessitating the postponement of reading the transcript.

HP and Christina packed for their journey to Kolhapur. Many students opted to apprentice under established lawyers. HM planned to visit Nagapattinam. She had found her answers and realized her true calling. She wanted to offer thanks there before returning to her home country. Everybody dispersed.

30. WIKI STYLE SUMMARY

Suma--AG (Ask Google) was happy she got an opportunity to do what she enjoyed most. She sat the whole night and completed the summary. A few gaps were there. She wasn't aware of the discussions that took place in the Rival group. She decided to ask Christina and HP who were only too willing to fill in the gaps. She took it to Professor, who read it and appreciated her keen sense of observation and putting forth the matter concisely. He further commented that just like Eka Sloki Bhagavata or Eka Sloki Gita, her summary was one chapter summary of aKsara Gita. Suma was thrilled. Recognition from Parthasarathy in spiritual terms gave her more pleasure than Mundane or academic recognition either at college or in Google or Wiki.

Summary or core substance/Summum bonum of the Book.

Gita is the infallible word of God Supreme.
He disseminated this knowledge to enable understand:

- God
  - His actions,
  - His teachings
- Humans
  - Themselves
  - Their actions and motivation
- Ourselves
  - And the changes we are undergoing within us.
  - Effective monitoring of those changes in a positive direction
  - And our problems and deal with it effectively
- Gita is a base to understand:
  - God and His actions, (as given in Puranas, etc.).
  - God's teachings in the Gita

The Bhagavad Gita serves as a:

- Study of Gita as a subject matter.
- Study Gita a manual for everyday living.
- Study Gita as a reference book.
- Study of slokas as generalizations
- Use Gita as a benchmark to evaluate
  - Our understanding of Gita
  - Our understanding of other scriptures
  - Our understanding of divine actions stated in scriptures
  - Our understanding of our actions/responses and other's actions in light of wisdom contained in the Gita.

It is about how to understand Gita as Gita is not open to interpretation.

Common mistakes committed in understanding Gita or any other scriptures.

- Mistaking temporary for permanent and vice versa.
- Mistaking path for destination and vice versa.
- Confusing their path to be the only Path.
- Mistaking knowledge for ignorance and vice versa.
- Not translating theory into practice and faulting Gita for non-translation.
- Taking literals to be symbolic and vice versa.
- Assuming general instructions to be specific and specific ones to be general.
- Assuming all instructions are applicable to all.
- Mistaking the complete to be a part and part to be a complete whole.
- Mistaking Gita to be incomplete, as it is a part of Mahabharata.
- Superimposing our finiteness on Gods' words.
- Presuming that Gita is not applicable to other than Hindus.
- Pursuing Gita through means like Dwaita, Adwaita, VIsisht Dwaita, Dwaitadwaita verse, etc. instead of by way of Jnana Yoga, Gyana Yoga, Karma Yoga or Bhakti Yoga.
- Surrendering our thinking faculties to human interpreters, even in face of evident fallacies.

To overcome these mistakes, Acharyas have written commentaries to guide the ignorant. There are more than four thousand commentaries on the Gita, which could be pigeonholed into 21 types. This means that all of the said commentaries can be grouped in the 21 groups and is one of the variants of the identified 21 groups. Unfortunately, this became the case of 'Cure becoming worse than the disease'.

Each commentary has adherents who claim that it is the best or the only true one, which represents what God has said to the exclusion of all other commentaries. They buttress their claim and put forth quotes from God/His representatives from Gita or other scriptures as proof of their claim. So, a commentary that was originally meant to clear the doubts and offer better understanding and forming a united rallying point became a debating point causing disharmony. The problem compounded with many more divisions due to beliefs in other religions, non-believers in the form of atheists and the indecisive agnostics. This was because they tend to forget that

Gita is the word of God. It is infallible.
All the commentaries are based on interpretations, which are again based on the utterances of God. It is common knowledge that words have multiple meanings

giving scope for multiple interpretations as there are possibilities of permutation and combination of the meanings of the words.

Words convey innumerable meanings.
- The word could be spoken directly.
- It could be through His various incarnations.
- It could be through a chain of media like disciplic succession or like Uddhava to Maitreya and Vidura.
- It could be in the real sense or in jest.

The time, tone, tenor, diction. Pitch, the speaker, and the hearer and the body language, etc. all qualify the Word.

The words/communication could have been spoken to:
- An Individual.
- Certain classes of Individuals.
- Entire mankind.
- Spoken to an individual/group of individuals but addressed to the entire mankind.

These Words/communication could be:
- Literal for one and figurative for another and both literal and figurative simultaneously for a third person.
- Meant for all but are to be understood and acted differently, i.e., literally or figuratively by different persons.
- In a similar manner, some communications are meant to be acted upon, some are just for information depending on the person and accompanying context.
  - Understanding of Lords' words is person dependent.
  - It is meant to be understood by each person in a different sense.
  - Time, place, nature, capacity, faith, and belief, etc. play a role in understanding God's words.

These words could be:
- Statement of facts.
- Interrogative sentences.
- Parameters.
- Benchmarks/Conclusion
- Description.
- Suppositions
- Analysis
- Reference to statement of facts.
- Positive injunctions.
- Negative injunctions.

- Replies to queries
- Benedictions
- Generalizations which could be:
  - Literal
  - Symbolic
  - Analogous.
  - Stated
  - Implied

Truth is multi-dimensional. The following types qualify to hold truth-values:
  - Statements
  - Sentences
  - Propositions
  - Theories
  - Facts
  - Assertions
  - Beliefs
  - Opinions
  - Doctrines.

Thereby underscoring the Fact that Gita is Truth, Nay it is absolute truth.

Each of them serves different purposes for different persons at different times. Some need to be acted upon, some need to be understood, some need to be accepted and so on. The usefulness per se, need not be material or tangible. It could satisfy curiosity, clarify a doubt, enrich you, provide an experience (Like cosmic vision witnessed by Arjuna), etc.

The spoken word is just one form of communication. Other forms of communication employed by Lord, which we came across but not necessarily exhaustive are:

- Communication through gestures.
  - Example being God hinting to Bhima, means to overcome Jarasandha and Duryodhana.
- Providing ocular experience, clairvoyance, and telepathy.
  - Sanjaya being made privy to Gita and Arjuna being privy to God's Cosmic form.
- Through His local manifestation within beings.
  - What may be termed inspiration or the inner voice.
- Through musical instruments like the case of Brahmaji, wherein knowledge imparted via flute.
- By setting an example by His actions. These actions could appear contrary to His instructions, thereby meaning that there is a hidden message which needs to be uncovered.
- By actions culminating in apparent failure. Here too hidden message is to be unraveled.

- By being silent.
- By end results, both positive or negative, say for example, by failing in peace mission.

Different sentences have different purposes.

- Statements of facts in the Gita.
  - o No need for the application of Parameter. What is stated in Gita is taken as fact and not questioned. The parameter doesn't help you find out if the said statement is a fact or otherwise. Nor does it matter if it is a fact or otherwise, unless you have a special interest in the subject matter, or you base your decision on the said statement and need to act.
- Interrogative sentences or questions.
  - o Here too parameters do not have any active role and stand on par with and are similar to the statement of facts.
- Reference to statement of facts.
  - o Same treatment as with statement of facts.
- Instructions.
  - o Parameters are of immense significance here and have a direct bearing on our actions and results thereof which is in turn dependent on our understanding of instructions.
    - ▪ The best example is Arjuna refusing to fight under the pretext of incurring sin and also based on the presumption that renunciation is better than action.
    - ▪ The original Sikhism was founded on peace and thereafter turned themselves into the martial race as per changing needs and requirements. So, should Sikhs fight or should they make peace? Should they follow the original Guru or their last Guru?
    - ▪ When more than one set of instructions is there, each diametrically opposite of the other, parameters help you make the correct choice.
- Parameters.
  - o They should be identified as such and applied to evaluate the propriety of our actions and understandings.
- Benchmark/conclusion.
  - o These slokas are parameters that serve as a benchmark/ or help arrive at the conclusion as to the correctness of our perception.
- Descriptions.
  - o Parameters have very little or no role in descriptive statements in Slokas.

Any scriptural text could be either

- A statement (of fact or otherwise).
  - In the first instance, it doesn't matter what you believe. You may consider it fact even if it contradicts general perception, or you may choose not to believe it. It doesn't matter either way. Your belief or non-belief doesn't affect anyone. If a real fact is disbelieved, you may realize truth later on after your sensory perceptions are perfected with practice. If realization doesn't dawn on you, your efforts are not in vain, as the same is the point wherefrom you begin in the next life.
  - If a falsehood is believed to be true, it is the analytic deficiency of the person or if the analysis is correct, then that falsehood doesn't belong to the scripture or it isn't the words of God. It could be subsequent interpolations. God's words have inbuilt checks like parameters to confirm if it is fact or otherwise.
- A call for action or instruction.

Here, we have to tread cautiously. Irrespective of whether you believe or disbelieve, your action or inaction should not adversely affect others. One way of testing is if that instruction is acted upon by some others and you are adversely affected, would you judge the action of the other as bonafide action backed by scripture? Your answer determines whether scripture is correctly interpreted or not.

Most of what is stated above being subjective opens floodgates for diverse interpretation/understanding. How to find out which interpretation or understanding is correct is the exercise being undertaken by this book.

The level of comprehension of the readers is varied and diverse, because, each individual's capability and capacity vary as does the level of comprehension. Gitas' teachings are interpreted at different levels of comprehension by each reader/sadhaka/devotee. Now when comprehension levels are different, interpretations too would be different and varied. They may be correct at that particular level only.

Now, to be able to understand in a more comprehensive manner, we should also be conversant with various devices, like literary devices, legal devices, psychological devices, etc. used in the Gita and its' effects. When interpretation is being undertaken, we must be careful to identify the device used, understand the passage and the underlying context and analyze its fallout thereof, whilst being consciously aware of our level of comprehension.

Despite all care being taken, Doubt's creep in if we have understood/interpreted it correctly. This is more so in the case where our understanding or interpretation is deviant and doesn't agree with any of the earlier interpretations preceding ours. A search for an answer amongst existing commentaries yielded a blank. It was also observed that all the great seers had kept silent on some verses or certain aspects of a few verses. Those verses are important on which base for this book is built.

The reasons for its importance are:

- They provide the base.
- They explain certain core principles of the Gita.
- They highlight some very important properties/characteristics of Gita either through words or through implication.
- Not only the slokas, but their position of placement in Gita also conveys certain things.
- Other slokas/verses rest on the essence of these slokas. Hidden mysteries & Incidents in Bhagavata or Mahabharata get unraveled through these slokas.
- We may enunciate certain principles and sub-principles, to navigate into the ocean of Gita based on the above.
- By previously mentioned ways, we may determine the correctness or otherwise of our comprehension.

They formed the very soul of the Gita. Without these, the **Krishnaness** or the **Gitaness** of the Gita would be found wanting. Hence, those verses were opted for model-building. For this purpose, the concept of Parameter is introduced. These are not brought from external sources but identified and picked from Bhagavad Gita. These slokas and/or their derivatives are taken as parameters.

A Parameter
1. States a principle or a Tatva.
   a. Enunciates a principle or a Tatva.
2. It is a generalization.
3. It has a universal application.
4. Refers to knowledge or source of knowledge.
5. Qualifies a statement/sloka.
6. Highlights/underscores the inherent property of a statement/sloka.
7. Shows the cause/necessity of that statement or other statements, or justifies other statements
8. It provides insights or shows things from a new perspective.
9. Removes misconceptions.
10. Act as determinants and affords conclusiveness.
11. It provides relevance to the context.
12. It could be a characteristic of God or Gita.

The test of the application of Parameters.
- Is it stated by God in the Gita?
- Is it stated in the Gita by others and God hasn't contradicted it?
- Is it implied in the Gita?

- Is it an observable phenomenon? Can you experience the truth of it even today?
- Is it a qualifier of most of the verses? I.e., is it all-pervasive?
- Is it universal?
  o If yes, is it applicable to all other scriptures?
- Does it nurture/enhance/underscore the glory of the Lord?

Entire Gita is a benchmark/guide (parameter) for the Sanatana way of living.

These parameters may be classified as

- Existential parameters
  o Because other verses can't exist or derive meaning without these slokas.
- Principle enunciating Parameters.
- Guiding parameters
  o Because these verses act as guides to understanding the intricacies of Gita
- Implication parameters
  o Because they imply some meaning which is not apparent or gauged prima facie

God has certain characteristics, just like all beings and non-beings have certain properties. These characteristics/properties are distinct and form the very core or essence whilst identifying God or any being or non-being. This core property distinguishes the identified being/thing as different from other beings/things. Gita being a manifestation of God necessarily inherits these characteristics or properties of God as a legacy.

Our understanding or interpretation should conform to those characteristics/properties. If it conforms or is not in variance with the parameters, our understanding is correct.

See the genius of the Lord, He is empowering the Gita as under:

- He vested it with Authority, by speaking it Himself.
- He gave it credibility by living His words
- He made it imperishable by immortalizing it.
- He made it universal and concise by generalizing entire knowledge.
- He customized knowledge as per the different needs of different kinds/classes of people based on their temperament.
- He gave parameters to judge and monitor our understanding.
- He made it dynamic and free from future shock by auto-updater in the form of variables, constants, and dependent constants.
- He made His teachings rigid so as to be tamper-proof and flexible so as to be adaptable to future changes.

- His Knowledge blended concepts with semantics so that infinite is easily grasped and His words do not overshadow the spirit of His words.
- He made this knowledge a judicious combination of the subjective and objective.

Around twenty parameters have been identified by this finite mind and listed here. There could be many more which evaded this puny mind. The book attempts to give a detailed description of each of them.

- The Guru and his role vis-à-vis God/Gita
- Semantics and concept.
- God is supreme.
- The perishable and the imperishable.
- Gita as complete knowledge.
- Earth as a place of corrective detention. Why men sin?
- Sattva, Rajas & Tamas.
- Causes of actions and results.
- Time & space as parameters.
- Sacrifices in the Gita.
- Faith as a parameter.
- Big picture, Equity & Equality.
- Brooding-Mind as a friend & enemy.
- Rituals, purposes & pragmatism.
- God is one & prayers answered in a customized way.
- Cause & effect. And its analysis
- Parameters
- Application and nuances of the parameter.

31. KOLHAPUR WITH CHRISTINA

As usual, Priya's mom came to the railway station and picked them up. Christina greeted Priya's' daddy with Dandavat Pranaam. He welcomed her and asked her to feel at home. Christina wanted to speak to him, but he said that first things come first, she should familiarize herself with Kolhapur, visit all the nearby places. The next two days were spent sightseeing in and around Kolhapur. Hari took her to all the places which were discussed with Christina over the telephone. Christina took a keen interest and was full of questions. They decided that Sunday would be kept exclusively for discussion and so they all assembled at her fathers' study. He first got a brief history of Christina, her background, her interests and her passion for the Gita. He was happy.

DD: How was the debate? Were you successful in establishing your viewpoint? Do you have notes or proceedings of the same?

CH: I had the transcript; the lone copy is given to the professor. I will make a copy and send it to you shortly.

DD: Okay, briefly tell me the gist.

Both HP and CH took turns in updating him about the debate in bits and parts. The, of course, left out the acrimonious bits and parts that dwelt with their dealings with TG. He inquired about the verdict and was informed that it would take time. He invited them to ask any questions they may have.

CH: I will be troubling you as I have a number of doubts.

DD: Feel free, it would be my pleasure.

CH: It all began with Guru, so I would like to hear your opinion from you.

DD: There are many types of Gurus. Some of the types are
- Suchaka Guru is a master of any particular subject, like say healing, management, etc.
- Shiksha Guru is one who imparts knowledge about spiritual matters.
- Diksha Guru, a Guru who initiates a person into spirituality by giving Diksha mantra.
- Bodhaka Guru, A guru who teaches about caste, religion, methods of worship, etc.
- Param Guru or Jagat Guru is one who Dispels doubts, removes the fear of birth and death. He is supreme because he teaches and shows the path of moksha.

Now, everything depends on your requirements/needs. You have an academic teacher, you have a fitness instructor, and you have a mentor at an advanced level. You have a spiritual Guru, a yoga guru, etc. each one serves a different need at different times in different stages of our life. We must not confuse a primary school teacher with a professor or a management professor with a spiritual master. In the Gita context, Guru always means spiritual master. There could be many Shiksha Guru, but only one Diksha Guru. The relationship between Diksha Guru and the disciple is eternal. The Diksha Guru takes the responsibility of the spiritual progress of his disciples right up to going back to the abode of God. The Jagat Guru or the Param Guru is the guru of Shiksha Guru also. He is next to God. This relationship too is eternal. His imparting of knowledge or showering of grace need not necessarily be physical or tangible.

CH: Then, what about mentions made in the Bhagavata about inanimate things and lower species of beings as Guru?

DD: They didn't teach you. You learned from them. Or rather, they set an example wherefrom you learn. So, they may be termed, Suchaka Guru. Proceeding further, when a Guru has accepted you, at what stage is your education complete?

From this query, you may distinguish the type of Guru and its shelf life in your life. After your mastering a subject, your education is complete as regards that subject, meaning that Guru is no longer relevant for your studies on that subject. In the realm of spirit, see the case of Suka Maharishi. He was the son of Vyasa Deva. He was sent for further education to Janaka, the king of Mithila, who was a perfect karma Yogi and was ruling the kingdom and performing other mundane tasks only to set an example. Lord Krishna, Himself has mentioned this in BG: 3.20. When Suka Maharishi arrived at Janaka's palace, No one received him he was ignored totally. He sat at the entrance for three days stoically. After three days, the king along with courtiers came and felicitated him with all royal paraphernalia and made him sit on the throne. He was given royal treatment for three days. There was no change in the behavior or demeanor of Suka Maharishi. King Janaka acknowledged that Suka Maharishi was already equanimous, indifferent and oblivious to pleasure and pain and everything external. He informed that there was nothing which he could teach Suka Maharishi. Suka Maharishi was himself a great saint and the speaker of Bhagavata, which by itself can bestow Moksha on the hearer. So, when you evaluate a Guru or decide to follow him, these things are to be considered. Life with Guru makes things easier, provided you are faithful and follow his instructions and the Guru is real or empowered by God.

CH: Can a Guru, grant Moksha?

DD: No and Yes. By himself, No. On behalf of God Yes. God doesn't refuse the Guru anything. See, Saint Tukaram was summoned to the Lord's abode and an Ariel vehicle sent to bring him. Tukaram invited all the onlookers and fellow residents to join him to the abode of God. Such is the power of saints. Tukaram didn't ask God's permission if he could be accompanied by others. He wasn't a Guru.

Yet, he just bade everyone join him. Alas, even his wife didn't join him let alone other onlookers. They cited mundane engagements and commitments. They needn't have given up their bodies in the conventional sense. Still, they were under the clutches of Maya.

There is another instance of Saint Raghavendra Swami sending his disciple to Moksha. A disciple with deep faith would always ask Swamiji to grant him Moksha. On one such occasion, Swamiji asked him if he was serious, on his confirmation, Swamiji performed purificatory rites on his person and lit a fire and asked him to enter the same. Unfazed, and with deep faith and without a second thought the person jumped into the fire. Even as people were criticizing Swamiji, they heard bells and sound of conch shells and saw an airplane carrying the person to God.

CH: See the following instances.
- o Being situated in that state, even at the hour of death, one is liberated from the birth-death cycle and reaches God. BG: 2.72
- o Those who know me as the governing principle of the material and celestial and as the lord of all sacrifices such persons are in full consciousness of me even at the time of death. BG: 7.30.
- o Those remembering me at the time of death comes to me only undoubtedly. BG: 8.5

God holds out this promise, a shortcut, A bypass, that those who die thinking of Him attains Him. Does this supersede the law of Karma? Next, how is this possible?

DD: Yes, apparently, it is so but in reality, this would be rare. A person cannot remember God if He hasn't accumulated sufficient piety and not remembered God during his lifetime. He should have put in sufficient karma to remember God at the time of death.

The value ascribed to different acts of karma varies with different acts. Devotional service to God is the high-value denomination currency, and this one act more than pays for your entrance to Gods' abode. So, if you remember God during your death, you will assuredly be going to God's abode. Remember, God is the source of memory and forgetfulness. Regarding your next question, how is it possible, unlike in the material world, communication is not gross in the realm of spirit.

Think of the communication as electrical impulses/signals or frequencies in the same wavelength between our indwelling soul and God dwelling in us locally as Paramatma and the same dweller in His original form in Vaikuntha. Just imagine a man-made lifeless telescope or a satellite that can see, hear, and communicate things almost infinitely how much more so the living being and especially the super-being.

CH: Why is this opportunity offered? What is so unique about remembering God at the time of death?

DD: Earlier, Hari was inquiring whether Moksha is an abode or a state of mind. I had clarified that it is both. That state of mind is a pre-requisite for entrance into His abode. In His abode, there is bliss infinite, meaning that state of mind where miseries cannot touch you. Jivan Muktas are perpetually liberated souls, (A state of mind) who are liberated even whilst dwelling outside Vaikuntha, for the betterment of the community. One of the prerequisites for reaching God's abode is that the positive and negative karma should balance or in other words, the person should have exhausted his credit of piety and sin by experiencing the fruits of his good and bad deeds.

If he continues living, he would be caught in the revolving cycle of birth and death extending to many eons. God mercifully makes such a person remember Him at the time of his death and offers him Moksha.

CH: The time of death is uncertain and unknown. How does a person remember God at exactly that point in time?

DD: There are two possibilities. One is by the dint of previous practice of remembering God at all times.

Secondly, God, Himself is the giver of memory and forgetfulness. He removes the forgetfulness and makes him remember Him at that time.

CH: From Priya's presentation, I find that you are views are offbeat and unorthodox. I loved the concept. It is different and helps but unable to say how.

DD: Scriptures are losing relevance. Because they are misinterpreted and misunderstood. People are moving away from tradition and customs. Material pursuits have overtaken spiritual pursuits. Non-material yields are not visible and hence materialists find it irrelevant. People tend to equate rituals, customs, and traditions, which are man-made and perishable with God's prescription or writ which is imperishable. When the man-made rituals fail the reality check, they lose faith in God and move away. Rituals have rules and regulations which must be adhered to in strict sense to yield desired results. Firstly, segregate what is said by God and what is not said by Him. Then study the letter and spirit of what God has said and the rationale behind reconcile it with reality. These are my unorthodox beliefs briefly, which I want to propagate.

CH: Is existence real?

DD: Of course, hasn't the Lord Himself said that there was never a time when you, I, or the kings did not exist nor will we cease to exist in the future?

CH: If it is real, why some persons insist that it is unreal?

DD: It is a matter of perspective. A rational approach is the concept of proximity to truth rather than truth. This is always a non-controversial, better-accepted and better form of evaluation. Now, what is your experience?

CH: Obviously, it is real.

DD: Then why entertain doubts?

CH: There are many intellectual and philosophical debates which I couldn't comprehend, nor am I sitting in judgment of great personages but how could such elementary things be misunderstood?

DD: I will explain their perspective in terms of your perspective such that you will not only respect their viewpoint but also embrace their view. Artificial intelligence rules the technology scenario today. Can a robot perform all tasks which we perform?

CH: Yes, or more correctly yes in the very near future excepting for thinking and feeling.

DD: Could it change in a few years?

CH: Yes, it is possible for robots to think and feel. It is just a matter of time.

DD: Supposing, scientists achieve a breakthrough and are able to create a robot which can think and feel, in say 5 years, how much can it think and how much can it feel?

CH: To the extent allowed by its creator.

DD: Supposing it is given this ability on par with its creator except for its ability to come face to face with its creator and knowledge of its source and creator?

CH: Then?

DD: Is the life of robots real or unreal?

CH: It is unreal, but it doesn't know it.

DD: Then who knows it?

CH: Its creator and whosoever creator wishes to know.

DD: Did you find your answer?

CH: Sets about thinking in silence for a few minutes and exclaims, my God, it is that!

DD: Are you satisfied or shall we proceed?

CH: I am satisfied but not satisfied. Please go ahead with your explanations.

DD: Supposing the robot is informed by its creator the truth and it shares it with other robots?

CH: Other robots may or may not believe what is shared by their fellow robots.

DD: Imagine different scenarios, supposing the original robot who was told itself doesn't believe but shares with other robots which may be believed by some and disbelieved by some, supposing there is another creator of a robot whose skills are far below the original creator of robot? Another scenario, the creator teaches AI to others who continue manufacturing robots and creator sidesteps into the background?

CH: I am succumbing to truth or untruth or whatever you are saying. Please definitely tell me and guide me.

DD: Your basic understanding/foundation must be firm. All the talks we had are very convincing, and cannot be held to be an untruth. It could be midway to the truth.

CH: Why it cannot be the truth?

DD: Does it conform to parameters? Is the creator (of the robot), omniscient, omnipresent and omnipotent? Is he blemishless and full of opulences? Can he give you a new life after the expiry of the shelf date? If yes, is it you or some other robot?

CH: So, life is real and God exists?

DD: But isn't it unreal?

HP: Daddy, stop playing games and confusing her.

DD: Okay, the debate wasn't about reality or otherwise of existence. It was about how people understand something so fundamental and basic in different ways. Did you understand how this basic thing is misunderstood?

HP: Daddy, you are training her in misunderstanding instead of in understanding.

DD: You mean Neti Neti, in action?

Everybody laughed

CH: Whether Moksha is an abode or a state of mind?

DD: Gita has verses in support of both contentions. It is a separate topic in itself. I will tell you briefly without going into the specifics.
   o For mortals, death is a pre-requisite for admission into the abode of God. It means not only freedom from death but also freedom from the birth-death cycle, which means the abode of God. Humans visiting immortal land in the mortal body is very rare or near impossible.

- o An example of king Trishanku is the most appropriate. He couldn't reach Indra Loka/heavens the abode of Indra, what to speak of abode of God.
- o The state of mind of equanimity and reconciliation of all good and bad acts having been balanced is another requisite.
- o The thoughts of God exclusively at the time of death is the gateway to His abode without having to traverse the path of rebirths in remaining species, a bye in sports parlance.
- o Advaitins believe in the state of mind concept, as an end in itself. Dvaitins believe in the concept of abode, for which prescribed state of mind is a pre-requisite.
- o Why is the Advaitins concept a part- truth?
  - ▪ Because, the earth is a dukhalaya, a place of miseries. It is also called mrutyaloka, or place predominated by death, which is inescapable.
    The state of mind achieved through great efforts is also temporary which is the property of matter (Earth planet), the mind itself being fickle.
- o This is borne out by facts that celestial beings are cursed to be born on the earth planet.

CH: The practice of Sati in medieval India is reprehensible. How did it get official sanction?

DD: You have studied Gita minutely and read it many times. Has God advised that a widow should burn herself in the pyre of her husband?

CH: What is the relationship between God and Arjuna?

DD: In a material sense, they were maternal cousins. God, Himself says that you are my friend and devotee. BG: 4.3. thereby delineating the Friend-Friend, God devotee relationship. Arjuna says that he surrenders to Him and seeks acceptance as a disciple. BG: 2.7. Thereby creating a relationship of a Guru-Shishya. So, God apart from being cousin, is also Guru, God, and Friend of Arjuna. God calls Arjuna endearingly many times. He goes out of the way and even served as a charioteer for Arjuna. God addresses Arjuna as Anagha, meaning sinless one. Arjuna is a man of action, despite performing actions, he is called sinless by none other than God Himself. The implications thereof and reasons therefor are:

- • He is a true karma yogi, performing actions without motives for others' welfare.
- • He is a fit candidate for salvation.
  - o He visited heaven even in his mortal body.
  - o God calls him a friend.
  - o God reveals celestial and cosmic secrets to him.

CH: Which is the most sacred relationship that can be established with God?

DD: This is a matter of opinion. Two main conflicting schools of thought prevalent. One says that the conjugal relationship is the supreme most relationship that can be established with God. They give examples of Radha Rani and other Gopis in support of their claim.

The other school says that the Master-servant relationship is the superior most relationship and cites the example of Hanuman.

CH: Please explain with reference to the Gita.

DD: It isn't mentioned directly in the Gita. Some relationships are invoked from which we may make inferences, like when Arjuna seeks forgiveness in BG: 11.44

'Please forgive me for my offenses, as a father tolerates his son, a friend forgives his friend, and a lover pardons the beloved, BG: 11.44', three relationships are invoked. All of them have incidents/episodes in God's life serving as precedent. God Himself has extolled the devotees and has expressed His helplessness and lack of independence where His devotees are concerned. The supremacy of devotee is reiterated by God in BG: 9.31 wherein He states "Arjuna, declare boldly that no devotee of Mine is ever defeated." The fundamental requirement is one should be a devotee, in whatever relationship best suited to them. The relationship by itself is not materially consequential but the depth of relationship and the quantum of surrender is a matter of consequence.

CH: God has prescribed duties for Kshatriya, Brahmana, Vaisya, and Sudra. Me being a Christian, what are duties prescribed for me?

DD: The fourfold classification is not decided as per birth but as per nature. Examine your nature and decide for yourself. I remember you telling me that you are a Hindu by belief and Christian by birth. Then, this doubt shouldn't arise. Also, logically any prescription is based on aptitude and not on birth or belonging.

God's laws being universal, duties aren't different for Christians or Sikhs or Jains, etc. Actions and gunas are intertwined and act on one another, not birth, and actions. It is gunas that perform actions and man cannot be without action even for a moment. Birth is not considered for classification because it is not birth/parentage that perform actions, nor do they have gunas.

Even as per cause and effect, the action is the cause and result of the effect. Birth is not a cause. Besides, birth is not absolute until the next transmigration. Unlike gunas, lineage does not yield results of action.

DD: What do you plan to become?

CH: I want to become Haripriya.

DD: What!

HP was embarrassed and looked away.

CH: She is committed, doesn't have doubts, her vision is clear, she is gentle but firm. She has the courage of conviction and is not intimidated or browbeaten either by increased decibel levels or by sheer numbers in the form of the crowd. Her firmness is what is characterized as Sattvic firmness in the Gita. She is a fit candidate to espouse God's cause. Her clarity is matched by her communication skills.

DD: No, I meant as a career proposition. I suppose you will be taking up teaching assignments?

CH: Yes, but I will be teaching, teaching to teachers. In Hari's words, I will be doing Meta-teaching. That way I would have wider coverage.

DD: It makes sense. It brings name, fame and of course greater economic prosperity all the while doing what you enjoy.

CH: No Sir, not in that sense. They could possibly be accompaniments, but the main aim and objective are to disseminate Gita.

DD: Why!

HP: What!

CH: To endear myself to God. What better way to endear me to Him than by spreading His gospel?

Why the surprise/exclamation? Am I not eligible? Is my birth a hindering factor? Or is it because of being an inmate of a country that is across the seas? I can't help these things, but if it is effort or dedication, I will redouble the same. Even if my being an American is an issue, my efforts will not go in vain, because, I will be re-commencing my efforts in my next birth from India, from that point where I had earlier stopped in the USA.

HP: Excommunicating someone who crosses the sea is a man-made practice and not divinely mandated. Have you come across such words or implication in the Gita?

DD: CH, my child, you are as precious to Him as He is to you. Go ahead and continue pursuing your first love. I see great things in you and a great future for mankind. You are already Hari-Priya in many ways.

CH: Which ways?

DD: You are dear to Him as He is dear to you. Haripriya is my daughter both by name and by implication. God bless you.

He got up and went to his room and opened the cupboard and came out with a small jewelry box. It had the name "Tanishq" embossed on it. He placed it in the hands of Christina. She refused at first but accepted on being told that blessings are not to be refused. She inquired what it was, to which he asked her to have a look. She opened the box and found a small pendant/locket in pure

Gold. It didn't make any sense to her as the locket didn't resemble any God or mystic symbol like OM. She asked what it was. He said that the entire Bhagavad Gita was engraved on the pendant using Nano Technology.

He informed that the same can be viewed using the Loupe tool. She was overjoyed. She looked at her friend's neck but found the locket of their Kula Devata, Lord Narasimha Swami. She asked why HP didn't have such a locket. He replied that each had a different form of Hari. He placed his hands on her head conveying his blessings and moved away towards his room.

32. THE PILIGRIMAGE

Christina and Priya sat in the taxi and asked the driver to proceed. They then waved good-bye to her parents and commenced their spiritual journey. The cab dropped them at Mumbai airport. They flew to Jamnagar and thereafter drove to Dwarka. It was evening when they reached Dwarka. They hurriedly had a wash and proceeded to have evening Darshan of Dwarkadish. Both were excited. They got lost and were in raptures. They returned to the hotel. They had a surprise waiting. Munni, Hari's cousin from Ahmedabad was waiting for them. She had learned from her Aunt that Hari was visiting Dwarka and had made it a point to meet them so as to show them around. Both of them welcomed her and were glad to have a local person as a guide. They chatted for a while and dozed off in the midst of chat itself.

They got up early and went to the river Gomati. Both had a holy dip. Hari dipped herself in the river number of times, each time on behalf of one of her family members. On knowing it, Christina followed suit. They lit earthen lamps and made religious offerings and let the lighted lamp across the river. They entered the temple and visited all the shrines within the precincts. They sang songs glorifying the lord and offered many prayers both standard and self-composed. Shouts of 'Jai Ranchor, Makhan Chor' rent the air. They visited all the shrines inside the temple complex.

Munni explained that Dwar means entrance and Dwarka meant gateway to Moksha. In ancient days, Dwarka was called Kushasthali. Dwarka is one of the Char Dhams, others being Jagannath Puri, Badrinath, and Rameshwar, in each of the four directions. It is also one of the sapta Puri others being Ayodhya, Mathura, Kashi, Ujjain, Haridwar, and Kashi. The earlier name of Dwarka was Dwaravati.

Dham translates into English as a place of stay or residence. Puri translates as an important ancient town/city, especially of religious significance. She explained that the main entrance was called Moksha Dwar and the entrance from the riverside was called Swarg Dwar, meaning gateway to heaven. The temple is originally believed to have been constructed by the grandson of Krishna, Vajranabha around 2300 BC. Daily, the flag is hoisted which is made up of fifty-two pieces each representing a Yadava clan.

Munni narrated the story of Kusheshwar Mahadev temple within the precincts of the main temple. Opposite to this temple, we have seen shrine dedicated to Pradyumna and a smaller shrine dedicated to Aniruddha, who is the son and grandson of Lord Krishna respectively.

There is Satya Narayana temple and the Navagraha temple. Next to them is a temple of Goddess Ambaji Family deity of Lord Krishna. Moving ahead, we saw the temple of Shri Purushottama.

A shrine dedicated to Durvasa Rishi; the family priest of Lord Krishna is right behind Shri Dwarkadhish Mandir. Nearby, are the temples dedicated to the principal queens of the Lord, Jambavati, and Satyabhama. Temples dedicated to Radha Rani with Lord Krishna, Shri Lakshmi Narayan and Gopal Krishna, Shri Lakshmi and Saraswathi temples were also seen.

Then there is a shrine housing Lord in the form of Trivikrama. Nearby we find Garuda and Lord Ganesha with his spouses. Opposite to the Lord Dwarkadhish, we prayed to Mother Devaki. In the vicinity, we saw the temple dedicated to Balarama, elder brother of the Lord.

They came to the banks of Gomati Ghat. Hari made a beeline to the temple dedicated to Vasishta and Gomati. Munni explained that is Ganga descended from heaven accompanying Vasishta at the behest of Brahma, and is considered the daughter of Vasishta.

After darshan, they walked further and reached the place of confluence of River Gomati and the ocean. Samudra Narayan temple beckoned them.

They had darshan. Munni explained that the Lord petitioned Samudra (Ocean) for land for purposes of establishing His city and the lord of seas ceded 108 yojanas of land by receding water backward. Dwarka was built on this site. It is believed that the entire city was constructed in two days by the celestial architect, Vishwakarma. A dip in the confluence is believed to confer liberation to the self as well as ancestors. Tempted by the bargain, they all had a holy dip and invoked gods and dedicated their prayers for the benefit of their ancestors.

Christina noticed Shamal Shah Temple. Munni took them inside. They had darshan and came out. Munni told her that there was a great devotee called Narsi Mehta. He gave up all his wealth to the lord and embraced poverty and became entirely dependent on the Lord. The town's people were jealous of him and would always look for ways to trouble him. Once certain merchants on pilgrimage were on the lookout for a person who could write a note of credit payable at Dwarka. People directed them to Narsi Mehta to shame him. Narsi Mehta put faith in the lord and made out a hundi (Letter of credit) payable by Seth Shamal Shah at Dwarka.

The drawee didn't exist, the merchants visited Dwarka and made inquiries with a person who confessed that He was the Shamal Shah they were searching and honored the hundi drawn by Narsi Mehta. It was the Lord Himself who had come in the guise of Shamal Shah and enhanced the prestige of His devotee. This temple is dedicated to them.

They hailed a boat and crossed the river. Munni further explained that The Five Pandava Well or the Panchananda Thirtha is situated across the Gomati River. They offered their prayers. And then returned. After refreshing themselves, they proceeded to Beyt Dwarka.

They halted at Rukmini Mandir and had darshan. Water was offered as Prasad. This surprised Christina and asked Munni the reason. Munni narrated the story behind.

Lord Krishna wished to have dinner in the company of sage Durvasa. Hence, He set out with Rukmini to the ashram of Durvasa to extend an invitation. Sage Durvasa agreed on the condition that they both should pull the chariot in which he would travel. They agreed to this condition. Mid-way Rukmini felt thirsty and asked Lord Krishna for water. The Lord struck the earth with his foot and Ganga gushed forth. Rukmini quenched her thirst.

On seeing this, Durvasa flew into a rage because he was not offered water first as per social etiquette, the guest must be offered anything before the host can consume it. It is well known that Durvasa was a sage with a very short temper who always was ready with a curse for any misdemeanor, real or imagined. In his rage, he cursed Rukmini that the couple would always live apart. Because of this, her temple is not in the main precincts of Dwarka with the Lord but outside the city.

Christina had a perplexed look on her face which was not lost on either Munni or Hari. Hari understood her friend's dilemma and answered....... God and His spouse feel neither tired nor thirsty. These are human traits that they willingly accept during their sojourn on earth so as to enact their human role to perfection. The curse of sage Durvasa has a nil effect on God or His spouse but is a voluntary acceptance in deference to the sage. This can be seen in another earlier incident wherein Sage Durvasa Himself was running helter-skelter trying to escape the attack by Sudarshana Chakra of the Lord because he had cursed Ambarisha, a devotee saintly King for a similar offense. When the curse of Durvasa has no effect on a king, how can it harm the Lord? This highlights another trait of the Lord. He will accept any hurts, insults, etc. and forgives but cannot take it when someone hurts His devotees.

The Lord sportively accepted the curse of Gandhari. He blessed sage Uttanaka who was about to curse the Lord.

He even forgave sage Bhirgu, who kicked the lord on His chest. It is also noteworthy that the temple stands on barren land amid rocks bereft of water.

They visited Nageshwar Temple, Gopi Talav, Beyt Dwarka and other adjoining temples and nearby temples.

Munni narrated the history of Beyt Dwarka. Bet Dwarka is believed to have been the residence of Lord Krishna. It is said the lord resided with His family at Bet Dwarka. The place derived its name from the 'bet' or 'gift' that Lord Krishna received at this place from his friend Sudama. This place was also known as 'Antardvipa' in ancient days. It was also known as Shankhodhar. The reasons underlying the name being it being home of different varieties of Shankh (Conch Shell) and secondly due to the island resembling the shape of a conch. The

Marine Archaeology Centre of the National Institute of Oceanography had carried out series of explorations along the Bet Dwarka shore and intertidal zone. Their findings indicate the existence of a prosperous port city dating back to earlier than 1500 BC.

They returned back to Dwarka. Everyone dozed off except Christina. She was chanting Lords' names even whilst lying down. She was overwhelmed and in ecstasy after seeing the Lord. It was a dream come true. The next day, they again prayed in Dwarkadhish temple and then set forth to Somnath.

They proceeded towards Porbandar, enroute Somnath. They visited the Sudama temple in Porbandar. Before Munni could tell history, Christina chimed "Isn't this the place of, Sudama the childhood friend of Lord Krishna at Rishi Sandipani ashram in Mathura? Everybody laughed. Munni explained this temple is built at the same place where a Sudama temple existed earlier under the patronage of Sri Ramdev Ji Jethwa from the royal family of Porbandar. Sudama hailed from this place and went to Rishi Sandipani Ashram at Mathura, for studies.

Krishna who was studying there befriended Sudama. While Krishna became a King, Sudama remained a poor Brahmin and refused to be drawn into material pursuits. Acute poverty and the nagging of his wife made Sudama visit Dwarka to meet his childhood friend to seek help.

He relished the prospect of meeting his friend and God again but had inwardly decided not to seek help. He was welcomed with open arms by the Lord and was well received and attended by the Lords' consorts. Time flew and it was time for Sudama to return.

The all-knowing Lord was moved by the self-respecting attitude of Sudama who never expressed his need for help, as also his refusal to be ensnared with materialistic hankerings and his utter devotion. When Sudama returned, he couldn't trace his hut which he called his house. It was transformed into a palace with riches. Sudama could see the Gods' hand and his devotion increased manifold.

They continued their journey. They came to Bhalka Thirtha. They entered the temple. There was an idol of Krishna. It depicted the Lord reclining with one foot over another. Christina found a board and read the description therein. It stated that this is the place where Lord Krishna was shot with an arrow whilst reclining against a Pipal tree by Jara, the hunter. The lord was mortally wounded.

Jara mistook the partly visible foot to be a deer shot an arrow. Realizing his mistake, he sought forgiveness of the Lord. The Lord explained that all actions happen with His concurrence.

He further explained that it was as per the law of Karma, Jara was destined to Kill Him because, in Treta Yuga, He had killed Jara the hunter stealthily who was Vali in that birth. Christina took a fistful of sand from the place and also a leaf from the tree across which Krishna had rested His back and placed it carefully in a pouch.

They continued their journey and came to Triveni Sangam. There they visited Dehotsarg, and Balrama Gufa and the sun temple. Munni explained the significance of these places.

Munni said, that the event itself was orchestrated by the lord years earlier when Gandhari, unable to bear the sorrow of the death of all her sons had cursed the Lord that He too would witness the destruction of His clan/race and would have an inglorious death. The Lord accepted the curse cheerfully.

Thirty-six years later the Yadavas in an inebriated condition had a petty quarrel and killed each other in His very presence. The Lord saw His brother Balarama sitting in meditation withdrawing from his body and heading to his original abode in his original form of Shesh Nag. He willed ending His incarnation and was relaxing under the Pipal tree when He was struck by an arrow shot by Jara. After being consoled by Krishna, Jara circumambulated the Lord and left the place. The Lord limped after hurting His feet and reached Dehotsarg on the banks of river Hiranya just above Triveni Sangam and breathed His last in a cave. His mortal remains were taken to the Triveni Sangam and cremated there, by Arjuna, His cousin, friend, and a devotee.

They proceeded to Somnath and offered their prayers. Christina was awe stuck seeing the temple. How much grander could have been the original temple mused Christina. They were all very tired. They made a brief stop and refreshed themselves. Munni inquired if they wanted to visit the Sasan Gir forest? This was a world-famous Lion sanctuary and housed more than 500 lions and 300 leopards apart from other wildlife.

Both Christina and Priya refused, saying that this was a spiritual and educational trip and not for fun and frolic. Christina further said that she had seen the Indian Lion roar in Madison square and not interested in seeing a pride of Asiatic lions. It took a full minute for both Munni and Hari to sink in what Christina was hinting. Welcome to the Namo Club they chorused and high fived.

The next morning, they had an early darshan and left for Ahmedabad. They visited Akshardham and spent the night in Munni's house. The next day she dropped them at the airport.

Priya hugged her cousin and thanked her. Christina had no words to express her gratefulness. Munni was embarrassed by this display of affection and disengaged herself. She too thanked them. Hari picked up her ringing phone. It was Monica, her father's colleague stationed at Kurukshetra.

Her dad had phoned Monica and informed about her trip to Kurukshetra. Monica was very glad to show around places of interest in her home state of Haryana. She asked the time of departure and the name of the flight and asked them to wait at the main entrance of the airport in Delhi. She would take charge of them thereafter.

They flew to Delhi, enroute Kurukshetra. They were received at the airport by Monica. She made preliminary social inquiries and guided them to a waiting car. They rode to Kurukshetra. Monica's parents welcomed them and made them feel at home. They relaxed for a while. Monica suggested that they commence their sightseeing the next day and they go for local shopping, and so it was. The next day they left for sightseeing. Monica briefed them about history. Kurukshetra was earlier known as Thanesar which is derived from the Sanskrit 'Sthaneshwar', which can be translated to 'place of god'. Legend has it that Kurukshetra was named after the King Kuru, who was the ancestor of Pandavas and Kauravas. King Kuru selected this place for incorporating eight virtues, which are Brahmacharya, Yajna, charity, purity, kindness, forgiveness, truth, and austerity.

They reached Sanhit Sarovar. They got down and offered prayers. They had a symbolic head bath by dipping their hands in the river and sprinkling it on their heads. Monica explained, that this place is the abode of Lord Vishnu. It is a popular belief that this is the meeting point of seven Saraswathi on the new moon day. The Hindu genealogy registers are housed here. They visited the shrines dedicated to Lord Vishnu, Dhruva Narayan, Lakshmi Narayan, Dhruva Bhagat, Sri Hanuman, and Goddess Durga. Next, they headed to Brahma Sarovar. They had a cool wash and sprinkled the holy waters over themselves. They offered prayers in the adjoining Shiva temple. Monica explained that 'Brahma' stands for Lord Brahma who created the universe and 'Sarovar' means pond, is dedicated to Lord Brahma who created the universe after a huge Yajna. In ancient times, the tank was known as Ramahard and Samanta Panchaka.

This is the same Samanta Panchaka where Lord Parushararam killed the wicked Kshatriyas and dug up five tanks in the ground to fill the blood of all his enemies. They visited the old Draupadi Koop temple. It was here that Draupadi washed her hair with the blood of Dushasan in fulfillment of her vow. After registering a victory, Maharaja Yudhishtara erected a tower symbolizing his victory. It is also believed that Barbarik, the grandson of Bhima was witnessing the war with his head impaled on a spear from a nearby place. Duryodhana sought the refuge of the cool waters of this lake while hiding himself underwater on the final day of the war. Both Priya and Christina were engrossed with what was told by Monica. They proceeded to the Bhadrakali Temple. Bhadrakali is a form of Shakti. This is considered to be one of the 51 Shakti 'peethas' of India.

The Pandavas along with Lord Krishna worshipped Ma Durga and after the victory in Mahabharata battle. It is the local belief that 'mundan' (hair removing) ceremony of Shri Krishna and Balarama was performed in this temple. They offered their prayers. They spent some time and then left for Jyotisar. Monica explained that this was the place where God spoke Gita. Jyoti translates into light and Sar translates into essence. This was the place where God displayed His

Cosmic vision and empowered Arjuna with celestial eyes fit enough to behold the Divine vision. They saw the Banyan tree. This was the very same Banyan tree which was a witness to the preaching of the Gita. They saw the marble statue depicting Krishna preaching Gita to Arjuna. They visited the old Shiva temple in another part of the complex.

They came back near the banyan tree. Christina opened her bag and removed glass and spoon. She sat down and meditated for well over an hour. She sipped water thrice in a ceremonial gesture. Monica and Hari could meditate for just a few minutes. When Christina came out of her reverie, Hari told her that her thesis would be accepted because of her own compelling presentation and painstaking efforts.

Sankalpa or formal symbolic resolve wasn't necessary. She further asked what the resolution/Sankalpa was made. Christina just smiled enigmatically and diverted the conversation. Christina took some mud from the sacred spot and also a fallen leaf from the Banyan tree and stored it carefully in her bag along with the leaf and sand of Bhalka Thirtha.

They set out for Bhishma Kund, a large reservoir dedicated to Bhishma, grandfather of Kaurava and Pandava brothers. This is the place where Bhishma lay on a bed of arrows and Arjuna quenched his thirst by shooting Parjanya Astra and bringing forth water from the bowels of the earth. It is also known as Banganga. They paid respects to Bhishma, a persona respected even by the Lord and then proceeded to Amin Mound, which was the place where Dronacharya strategized Chakravyuh, in which Abhimanyu, the son of Arjuna was trapped. Amin is also known as 'Abhimanyu Khera' or the mound of Abhimanyu. They visited the adjoining temple.

Next, they made towards Karnal. They visited the Sita temple at Karnal. They offered their prayers. Monica explained that this was the exact spot where mother earth swallowed Sita Mataji after Agni Pariksha. They proceeded to Karna Lake. At the lake, they offered their prayers. Monica explained that this was the place where Karna offered prayers to Sun God and give away in charity whatever anyone may care to ask him.And it was here that he was dispossessed of his Kavach and Kundal, (Armor and Earrings), by Indra, the king of gods. This city is called the city of Karna in local parlance. They returned back to Jyotisar.

The music and light show were a full one hour away. They once again sat in meditation and then trooped into the show. The show was mesmerizing.

The next day, they thanked Monica and returned back to their house. They thanked Monica and her parents profusely and a number of times before proceeding back to Delhi enroute to Mumbai and from there to Kolhapur. It was late night by the time they reached Kolhapur. They refused to have dinner as they were tired and dozed off the moment they lay on the bed.

Three more days were remaining for them to present themselves at Tirupati. They just enjoyed lazing around. They spoke of their plans. They promised to remain friends forever and keep in touch even after Christina returning to the U.S.

On Friday, they had a darshan of Mahalaxmi and left for Tirupati. They were waiting for designated Sunday eagerly.

33. THE VERDICT

Christina and HP were the first to enter the hall. They sat in the front row eagerly and in anticipation of things to come. They were joined by others one by one. There were whisperings amongst themselves. Professor strode in and gestured everyone to sit down after initial greetings.

Prof Parthasarathy had received the report of daily proceedings (Transcription of the daily proceedings) from Christina. He found time to go through the same only after 3 days. He settled comfortably on the chair and started reading slowly. It took just over an hour. He read it again and re-read it again. The presentation was brilliant, pithy and to the point. His logical mind could not help but appreciate it.

His tryst with legal fraternity was 35 years old but his tryst with Krishna and Gita was more than 60 years old. Hailing from an orthodox family of priests, his mind was ingrained with Sri Vaishnava philosophy and an ardent devotee of the founder of that sect. His upbringing and innate nature would not allow him to be partial, speak falsehood, or take sides or to go against his beliefs although he appreciated the viewpoint of others. Now, this report flummoxed him. He had already seen the overshadowing of his traditional beliefs by these upstart children, in course of the debate. His loyalty and his sense of justice were in conflict. Besides, he himself felt the force of truth in the arguments put forth. Recusing himself was against his nature, besides it would disappoint all his students for whom he was an Ideal. He accepted all the individual recommendations, but like expedient Justices/judges, he preferred to reserve his judgment.

He called the attention of everyone by banging the gavel and read out his verdict as under:

Friends, Considering the sensitive nature and sentiments involved and the uncompromising nature of the duty thrust upon us, I reserve my judgment, in perpetuation.

There was a groan amongst all the participants. OH No sighed all together in chorus.

In these testing times, relying on my own individual judgment may or may not serve the purposes of justice, continued Parthasarathy. In furtherance of the cause of justice, I borrow from the American jurisprudence, or shall I say, revive our own earlier practice, hitherto discontinued, the concept, and practice of Jury system. I call upon all the group members to accept the honor of being members of the jury. Interested individuals, who participated in the discussions are barred from joining the board of Jury. Specifically, Christina, Haripriya, BG & TG,

Dharam-Rakshak, and Non-believers' group are barred from deciding on the case.

All of the jury members debate, deliberate, discuss from all angles and view the same through all dimensions. I call upon all of you to be true to your conscience, true to the cause of justice and true to the God in whom you all believe and hold dear. Thank you. We will assemble here again after three days at 4.00 PM. Thanks once again. Saying this He left.

All the students were stunned by the turn of events. Their admiration of Prof Parthasarathy turned from one of admiration to AWE. They placed him on an even higher pedestal than they had done earlier.

The Dharam Rakshak group was left clueless. They had anticipated an adverse verdict, if not a moderate verdict, given the credentials of the Professor, although they had entertained a ray of hope considering the classic, orthodox, and traditional outlook of the professor.

Christina and Haripriya too were surprised. They were conscious of their role in ferreting out the truth, but they couldn't trust their fellow students, notwithstanding the absence of TG & BG gang in the Jury board. The only qualifications of the members of the jury were that they were not aligned to any group and were without any bias. They did not have background knowledge of the Gita, besides their individual temperaments were not fair under trying circumstances. Besides, how could a motley bunch of students with diverse backgrounds **arrive at a unanimous conclusion?**

They resigned themselves to fate after consoling themselves that TRUTH ALWAYS TRIUMPHS and KRISHNA ALWAYS PROTECTS TRUTH.

The group that was assigned the task of jury duty was elated. They had keenly followed the proceedings. They had secretly wished that they too should have involved actively instead of passive participation. Well, it appeared that God had answered their prayers and offered them a role. They were aware also of the enormous responsibility thrust upon them. They decided to dedicate the entire day of Sunday for discussions and deliberations.

Everybody left for their place after deciding to meet at the canteen.

The students met at the canteen and began their discussions in the right earnest. Each of them expressed their views which were divergent, but agreed on a common thread, that they weren't big enough to express verdict in the presence of the professor. Doing so would tantamount to insulting their Guru.

They utilized the remaining part of Sunday and the entire Monday and committed it in writing and placed it in an envelope to be delivered to the Professor.

The D-day arrived and the students handed over the sealed envelope to the professor. The professor opened the envelope and read it out loud.

We the students playing the role of jury understand the solemn responsibility thrust upon us by our beloved Guru, Professor Parthasarathy.

We have dissected and discussed at lengths about the same. As jury verdict needs to be unanimous it called for drawing of innate strength from the deep recesses of our hearts to subordinate our own viewpoint to the collective viewpoint without compromising on our individual opinion.

Most of us have been traditionally brought up with strong Indian values inculcated notwithstanding western education including our dabbling in LAW.

We find that most of the issues have been corroborated with evidence of different orders and met the standards of legal scrutiny applied in the realm of spirit and spiritual scrutiny in the legal sense. About our verdict. We are unanimous in our opinion –

What the learned Professor would not do, his students will definitely not do, more so in his presence. It is unthinkable for us to express our insignificant opinion in front of him. We thank the professor for the opportunity provided and conclude that we have said our SAY.

The professor was stunned. Tears trickled down his eyes. He covered them by wearing goggles. Tears of love, tears of joy, tears for the love of Gita and his students. He took it as a divine command asking him to express his verdict. He adjourned the proceedings, with instructions to be present after two days at 6.00 PM for hearing the verdict.

At home, he pored over all the books and commentaries on Gita. He was searching for an answer, but he himself did not know what he was looking for. He again scanned the report. He was beginning to feel frustrated. He slowly went through the actual daily proceedings. The Nickname of Christina (Na ham Karta) caught his attention. His query was partly answered.

He liked the nickname because it succinctly expressed his philosophy. He decided to adopt the same as the pen name for his future works. Scanning further, he came across the request made by HP to conduct the proceedings in the name of Gita as it was Gita that spoke through her.

The professor mused, *"Wasn't it Gita that delivers judgment and not he Mr. Parthasarathy"* jumping with joy shouting Eureka, Eureka. He moved to his study and sat down to write his verdict. But when he sat down to write, he again couldn't come up with judgment worthy of the debate. He had so many things in mind but had trouble committing it to paper. He postponed writing his judgment.

He retired for the night and was tossing in bed. His thoughts went back to his lawyer days and his days as a judge. He recalled a few instances wherein the court had referred a case to a larger bench. It was a second eureka moment as he jumped up and rushed to his study and started writing the judgment.

I have closely followed the proceedings very carefully and minutely. The debate was a revelation in more than one way. The perspective put forth is unique and worth examining from all directions and exploring all possibilities.

The subject matter i.e. The Gita is not penned by a finite person but authored by the Infinite Lord Himself. The concept too is infinite just like it's' author. All the interpretation that has been put forth so far and is in currency is but another one perspective. Infinite can accommodate any number of perspectives. This basic dictum has been ignored by all paving way for claiming the infallibility of their version and demeaning of the other versions.

Any version or interpretation must satisfy all the basics which have been enumerated as parameters. These have been culled from Gita itself, thus lending it authenticity.

Supposing an interpretation which doesn't satisfy the basic premise that God is supreme, or His teaching is imperishable or His glory is limitless is limiting the infinite characteristics of Gods' teachings. It would be like fire without heat or water which isn't wet. Such an interpretation could at best be a part of the whole truth, if not wholly untruth.

That such a perspective is being put forth for the first time in 5300 plus years of history can only mean that the Infinite has chosen the finite to broadcast this truth, probably revealed at times of intense communion. *More so because this could also be an answer to the desperate need of putting truth in true perspective in these troubled times to quell the fast disintegration of the society.* It cannot be conception or concoction of the human mind, especially so since I know my wards and students fairly well and they haven't displayed any spark of spiritual fervor leave alone flair for spiritual analysis.

In view of the same, it would be wrong on my part to sit on the judgment of these esoteric truths.

The entire exposition is just what God has said being viewed from different alternative perspectives. The perspectives available so far are tried and tested and accepted by different schools of thought and the belief is firmly in place. They too came in for criticism/review or debate when first expounded. This exposition too should be subject to trial by fire, with no easy way out.

I wanted a jury trial for this debate so as to tap the collective wisdom. My students have a much larger perspective than I had ever had or I had imagined. A perspective so large which cannot be handled by a jury. Just as they have introduced new concepts in the realm of spirit, I too wish to apply the concept of referring legal matters to a larger bench, to a jury trial. I mean to refer the matter to a larger jury. No, I don't mean grand jury. Bigger than the grand jury? Yes, an Omni-Jury. A jury, as large as the depth of the subject matter, nothing less. What is the composition of the Jury?

How far would it be binding? I would be laying a rule of thumb covering those matters.

The subject matter is unlimited; hence the number of jurors is not to be limited and should accommodate anybody willing to board the bus. About the composition of the jury, all the participants or stakeholders willing to be juror may be allowed to deliberate on the issue. These include but not limited to the spectators, readers, Gita's lovers, spiritualists, etc.

The deliberations can be solitude or in groups. It may be in private or in public. The findings and verdict of each individual juror may be delivered or reserved, maybe even indefinitely as it binds none except himself. Each individual verdict or finding is truth tailor-made/customized so as to be meaningful for that individual. The universe is God's creation. Unlike the traditional jury, there needn't be unanimity on the findings. Why? The universe is God's creation. It isn't homogeneous. Gita too is authored by God. Its understanding must necessarily be heterogeneous. Because each person's judgment is part truth, a new perspective as long as it is in tune with what God has said or implied or inferred from His sayings and in concord with the spirit of His sayings. This is in the true spirit of the Gita.

He felt a strange sense of peace after his decision. He now had to write letters to the prospective jurors about their appointment, their duties, dos and don'ts.

He rummaged his drawers and found the old letterhead, which mentioned his earlier stint in the judiciary and his present assignment as a professor. He started writing ....

From the desk of Justice (Retired) Parthasarathy
Professor, Sri Venkateshwara Law University

Dear readers/Gita's lovers/Spiritual enthusiasts

Being a Gita lover/Spiritual enthusiast/Reader, you are an ex-officio member of the jury. You have been co-opted as a member of the jury and called upon to decide whether the issues raised hereinafter in the proceedings is proved.

It is my duty to advise you on the rules of law that you must use in deciding this case. After I've completed this advisory, you may begin your deliberations alone, or in group/s.

You must decide whether the Dharam Rakshak group has proved beyond a reasonable doubt that the Defendant is guilty of disrespecting Gurus and the scriptures which is venerable.

You must also decide if the unorthodox issues presented by the defendant are proved or has the plaintiff been successful in countering the presentment of the defendant and thus her presentment is not proved or rendered invalid.

Your decision must be based only on the evidence presented here. You must not be influenced in any way by either sympathy or prejudice for or against the Defendant or the plaintiffs. You must also follow the rules of law explained by me even if you do not agree with me or the rule of the law being put forth...............................

He continued thus and after finishing it, put the letter in an envelope to be delivered as a judgment on the designated day.

BOOK - IV

ILLUSTRATIONS

WHAT IS SAID

Always think of me, be devoted to me, worship me, offer obeisance to me. Doing so, you will certainly come to me. This is my pledge to you, for you are very dear to me.

WHAT IS UNDERSTOOD

सर्वभूतेषु येनैकं भावमव्ययमीक्षते
अविभक्तं विभक्तेषु तज्ज्ञानं विद्धि सात्त्विकम् ।
पृथक्त्वेन तु यज्ज्ञानं नानाभावान्पृथग्विधान्
वेत्ति सर्वेषु भूतेषु तज्ज्ञानं विद्धि राजसम् ॥
यत्तु कृत्स्नवदेकस्मिन्कार्ये सक्तमहैतुकम्
अतत्त्वार्थवदल्पं च तत्तामसमुदाहृतम् ॥

WHAT IS SAID

The knowledge by which one sees undivided imperishable entity in all beings is sattvic, & each being is seen as a seperate entity is Rajasic and where only one kind of action is considered completely & all others as inconsequential is Tamasic.

WHAT IS UNDERSTOOD

WHAT IS SAID
रसोऽहमप्सु कौन्तेय प्रभास्मि शशिसूर्ययोः
प्रणवः सर्ववेदेषु शब्दः खे पौरुषं नृषु ॥
I am the taste in water, O son of Kunti,
and the radiance of the sun &
the moon. I am the sacred
syllable 'om' in the vedic
manthas, I am the sound in ether,
and the ability in humans.

NETI NETI
Not this, Not this ......
WHAT IS UNDERSTOOD

अथवा बहुनैतेन किं ज्ञातेन तवार्जुन
विष्टभ्याहमिदं कृत्स्नमेकांशेन
स्थितो जगत ॥
WHAT IS SAID
what is the need for all this detailed knowledge, O Arjuna? Simply know that by one fraction of my being, I pervade and support this entire creation.

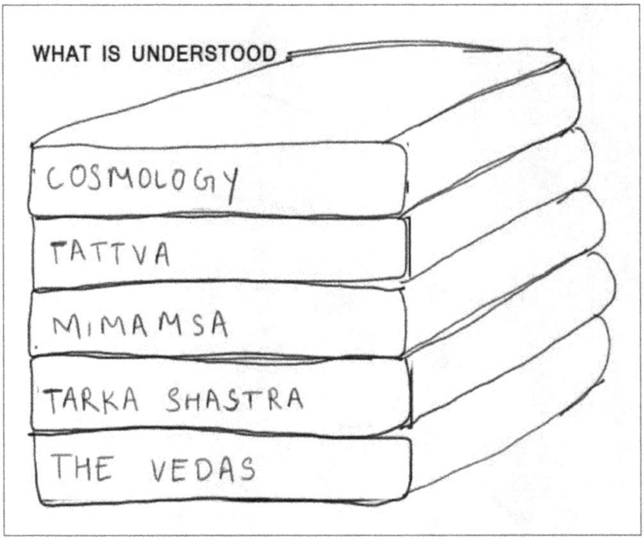
WHAT IS UNDERSTOOD
COSMOLOGY
TATTVA
MIMAMSA
TARKA SHASTRA
THE VEDAS

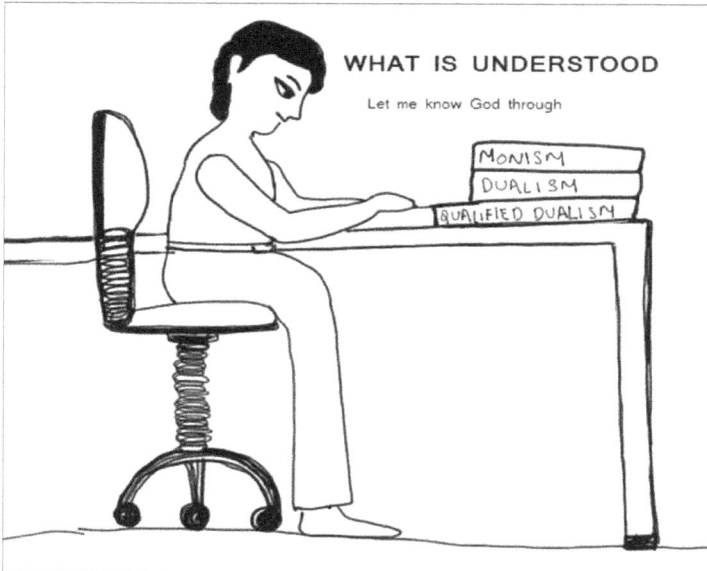

न तु मां शक्यसे द्रष्टुमनेनैव स्वचक्षुषा ।
दिव्यं ददामि ते चक्षुः पश्य मे योगमैश्वरम्॥
BG; 11.18

WHAT IS SAID

you cannot see my cosmic form
with these physical eyes of yours.
Therefore, I grant you divine
vision, Behold my majestic
opulence!

WHAT IS UNDERSTOOD

Let us use scientific tools
to search and see God

454

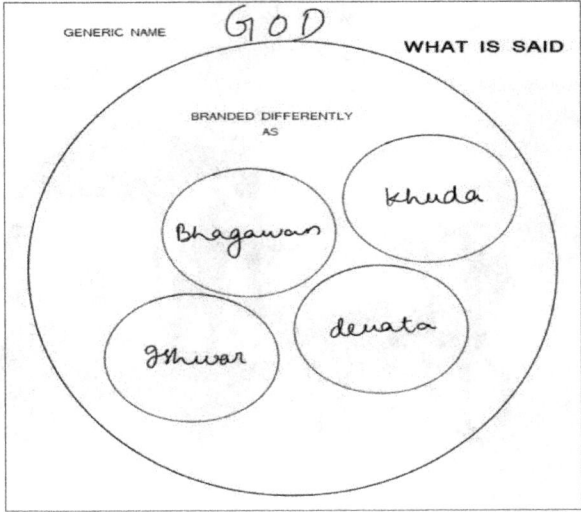

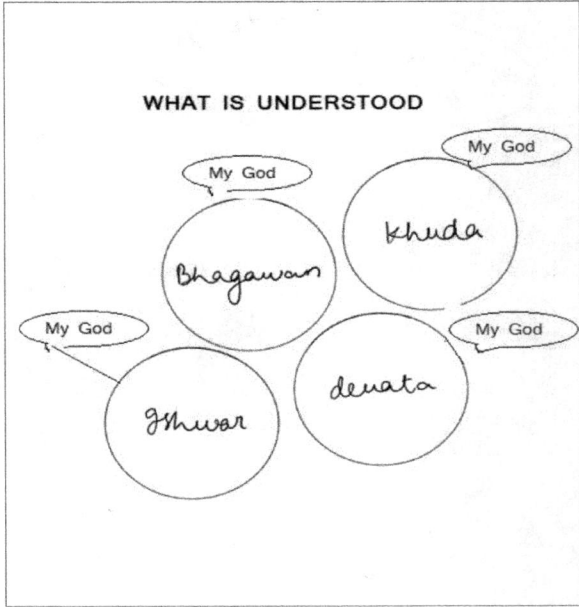

नियतं सङ्गरहितमरागद्वेषतः कृतम् ।
अफलप्रेप्सुना कर्म यत्तत्सात्विकमुच्यते ॥
यत्तुकामेप्सुना कर्म साहङ्कारेण वा पुनः ।
क्रियते बहुलायासं तद्राजसमुदाहृतम् ॥
अनुबन्धं क्षयं हिंसामनपेक्ष्य च पौरुषम्
मोहादरभ्यते कर्म यत्तामसमुच्यते ॥
WHAT IS SAID
Sattvic action yields sattvic results.
Likewise Rajasic and Tamasic actions
yield Rajasic & Tamasic results.

WHAT IS UNDERSTOOD
Bad things are happening to me because God is punishing me!

PROLOGUE AS AN EPILOGUE

Christina was preparing to leave for Florida. When she left Florida for India, she felt a thrill she was going to the Land of Gita. Her University was in the holy town of Tirupati. After the completion of the course, she did not feel a sense of satisfaction or a sense of accomplishment. She felt a sense of incompleteness.

Her mind was in turmoil. She felt that her participation in the classes and debate were more aloof and disinterested. She wished that she could put forth her views like Haripriya. She visited Prof Parthasarathy to take leave of him. There she spoke her mind. The Genial professor said that the **Lord Himself had advocated the path of disinterested action**, besides oratory skills were not the only skill set. He complimented her on her Summation which was brilliant. It revealed her grasp of the subject and deep understanding of the concepts. Her articulation skills via writing would stand in her stead and help her accomplish whatever she may have set to accomplish.

She felt that her role in the cosmic play of things would commence after reaching Florida and that destiny was beckoning her. She was ready to face destiny. Hadn't Parthasarathy Himself told her?

After her pilgrimage to Kolhapur, Dwarka, and Kurukshetra, she knew what she had to do but whether she was capable enough, whether the world was ready for a new order and similar such self-doubts assailed her but with her Professors reassurance, a calm descended over her. Yes, she was willing to take on the world of ignorant. She regained her composure. She was reminded of the saying of the original Parthasarathy – I have already killed all your enemies, be you an instrument and fight. Win fame. She called out Florida, here I come. She lapsed into a slumber only to be awakened by the announcement by flight Captain, we will be landing in Florida in a few minutes. She had literally come.

WITH LOVE FROM THE AUTHOR.

Dear readers, thank you for choosing to read my piece.

HERE IS A MESSAGE FROM THE DESK OF ALMIGHTY HIMSELF.

इति ते ज्ञानमाख्यातं गुह्यादुह्यतरं मया |
विमृश्यैतदशेषेण यथेच्छसि तथा कुरु || 63||

iti te jñānam ākhyātaṁ guhyād guhyataraṁ mayā
vimṛiśhyaitad aśheṣheṇa yathechchhasi tathā kuru

Thus, I have explained to you this confidential knowledge. Ponder on this fully and then do whatever you wish to do. BG 18-63:

www.ingramcontent.com/pod-product-compliance
Lightning Source LLC
Chambersburg PA
CBHW020752300326
41914CB00050B/168